The Social Psychology
of Interaction

The Social Psychology of Interaction

JEROLD HEISS
University of Connecticut

PRENTICE-HALL, INC., *Englewood Cliffs, New Jersey 07632*

Library of Congress Cataloging in Publication Data

Heiss, Jerold.
    The social psychology of interaction.

    Bibliography: p.
    Includes index.
    1. Symbolic interactionism. 2. Social
interaction. I. Title.
HM291.H48   302   80–23102
ISBN 0–13–817718–x

Prentice-Hall Series in Sociology
Neil J. Smelser, Editor

Printed in the United States of America

10 9 8 7 6 5 4 3 2 1

Editorial production supervision and interior design by Fred Bernardi
Cover design by Yudal Kyler
Manufacturing buyer: John Hall

Prentice-Hall International, Inc., *London*
Prentice-Hall of Australia Pty. Limited, *Sydney*
Prentice-Hall of Canada, Ltd., *Toronto*
Prentice-Hall of India Private Limited, *New Delhi*
Prentice-Hall of Japan, Inc., *Tokyo*
Prentice-Hall of Southeast Asia Pte. Ltd., *Singapore*
Whitehall Books Limited, *Wellington, New Zealand*

CONTENTS

PREFACE

This book presents a social psychological theory which is in the symbolic interactionist tradition. As such, it sets as its goal the understanding of the social behavior of human beings, and it owes its greatest intellectual debt to the work of the social philosopher George Herbert Mead.

Those who are aware of the fact that there are already several books about which this might be said are probably already asking themselves, "Why another?", and it is a question that deserves an answer. I won't deny that I am as desirous of fame and fortune as the next person, but I do think that the major impetus to writing this particular book was a feeling of dissatisfaction with the available material and a hope that I could meet a previously unmet need. This is not to suggest that I think that the predecessors of this book are without merit. Quite to the contrary, I think that the authors of several of those books do an excellent job of achieving the goals they set for themselves. My dissatisfaction resides in my view that these books tend to ignore—or at least, to play down—what I consider to be the most important questions and the most fruitful approach. Given this, it would seem that a good way of introducing the reader to the content of this work is to be specific about the causes of my discontent.

As is made clear in the body of the book, there are two major schools of thought within symbolic interactionism, and despite their common heritage they are quite distinct in several ways. All the recently written books are most importantly influenced by the Chicago School of interactionism, and thus they tend to focus on the attributes that all humans have in common and on the general nature of human processes. Although such matters are of crucial importance for the understanding of the human condition, I believe it is an error to stop with them, and most books in the field do not go much beyond them. In my view, the ultimate goal of social psychology is the explanation of the behavior of particular types of people under specified conditions. Behavioral consistencies and variations must be explained, and this book is somewhat different from other interactionist texts in that it focuses on such matters. Certainly, the more general materials are not to be ignored. They are, in fact, the base upon which the other material rests. They are for me, however, the beginning point rather than the end.

Also, partly as a result of their roots in the Chicago tradition, I find a certain parochialism in many of the other interactionist treatises. As is well known, the way in which a scholar practices social psychology is importantly influenced by whether his or her training was in a psychology or sociology department. And it is equally apparent that the members of each group do not pay very much attention to the work of the other group. Chicago School interactionists tend to be sociologists, and they seem to me to be rather extreme in their anti-pyschology stance. I feel that this is a very serious failing. I, too, am a sociologist, but I feel that each group can learn much from the other. Consistent with this view, I have made a concerted effort to draw from the theoretical literature of psychology those ideas which have relevance to the problems with which I am concerned. This search has led me to rediscover ideas which are usually not featured in the work of sociologists, and I feel the book benefits greatly from the inclusion of such "psychological" theories as social learning theory, attitude change theory, cognitive dissonance theory, and so on. I certainly do not believe that I have succeeded in the utopian goal of unifying the discipline, but I do hope I have done something to increase the cosmopolitanism of the sociological wing.

Another objection to the existing works is that they are, in too narrow a sense, "theory books," that is, they present theoretical ideas but make few attempts to test those ideas against the existing empirical data. And when data are considered they are often limited, illustrative, and nonquantitative. This is quite understandable given the nature of the issues Chicagoans study and their methodological stance, but it represents a problem nonetheless. To my mind, theory without data is a perversion of the social psychological enterprise, and although I would not deny the uses of qualitative evidence, I consider quantitative data to be of the utmost value. Therefore, I have made a wide search of the literature for relevant studies and I systematically considered their implications for the theory. Again, I often found myself in unexpected territory. It turned out that many studies in the psychological literature were pertinent even though they were not originally oriented towards interactionist hypotheses, and a number of studies done by sociologists who are not interactionists also proved valuable. I believe this book is much the better for their inclusion.

Finally, I and others have found a certain vagueness and elusiveness in the writings of the Chicago interactionists. This is due to their strong allegiance to the ideas of the fathers of the theory, their denial of the importance of operational definitions, and their suspiciousness of formal theory. The attempt here is to present a work which meets the criteria of theory and to write it in terms which are accessible to the reader with little experience in the field. I do not believe that obscurity and abstractness are signs of profundity.

In attempting to meet all these goals, I have undoubtedly strayed from the interactionist orthodoxy, if there is such a thing. I have in fact striven for originality where originality is needed, and I shall not be bothered in the least by comments to the effect, "That is not what Mead said." This is not an exegesis on the Holy Writ. What I hope I have accomplished is an original synthesis and extension.

In summary, the goal of this book is to present and test an interactionist theory which focuses on the sources of variation in human behavior. It is a synthesis and extension of materials which are widely scattered in the sociological and psychological literatures, and it is based on an appreciation of the fact that the two social psychologies do have mutual relevance (Stryker, 1977).

For me, the writing of a book is a difficult, almost painful task, but in this case I have been fortunate in having excellent assistance. First, I would like to acknowledge my gratitude to my wife Betty and to all the others to whom I am close for their forebearance and understanding during the difficult times. I also owe a considerable debt to the many who gave me assistance in the form of leads, suggestions, criticisms, and a willing ear. Included among these people are: Mark Abrahamson, Robert Broadhead, Gary Brodsky, William Curtin, Edward Dager, Jacqueline Fawcett, Laura Gordon, Michael Gordon, Morris Rosenberg, Jerome Shaffer, and Ronald Taylor. Sandra Golub, Elizabeth Heiss, Marilyn Horton, and Barbara Brand typed the manuscript from almost illegible copy, and their help is gratefully acknowledged. Finally, I would like to thank Edward H. Stanford of Prentice-Hall for his patience and encouragement.

Jerold Heiss

CHAPTER 1

THE INTERACTIONIST APPROACH

Grandiose as it may sound, this book is intended to be about you and everyone you know. If I have done my job at all well, when you penetrate the jargon you should frequently have a shock of recognition. "Yes, I've done that." "Gee, maybe that's why he reacted that way." As a treatise on social psychology, this book presents what is known about certain aspects of human behavior, and thus it has the rather immodest goal of explaining everyone to everyone.

This goal notwithstanding, there are limits to my aspirations. Social psychology is multifaceted, but it is not all-encompassing. It seeks to discover general laws about *selected* aspects of human behavior.

To begin with, the things to be explained are limited to those human activities which occur in interaction with others, that is, the concern is with social behaviors. For example, problem solving is an important human activity, and the general psychologist has an abiding interest in the steps that people typically follow in the solution of a problem. However, a social psychologist would not be interested unless the solution of the problem involved taking others into account.

In addition to this limitation on the things that they attempt to explain, social psychologists also tend to limit their search for causes to certain factors. The emphasis is on the social causes of the social activities. Social psychologists choose to look to people's prior and present social experiences in their search for causes. Furthermore, they limit the scope of their efforts, by using psychological and sociological principles to explain the connections they find.

This does not mean that social psychologists deny the effects of nonsocial

1

experiences. They recognize that a *full* explanation of why actors[1] react as they do would require consideration of a host of factors—physical, chemical, biological, historical, psychological, sociological. Similarly, some social psychologists would accept that sociological and psychological principles may *ultimately* be explained by reducing them to biological, chemical, and physical laws. The essence of the social psychologists' view is the assertion that their approach focuses upon key factors affecting social behavior, and that understanding and control, if it is desired, can be obtained without further reduction.

To take another step back from the opening statement, it should also be noted that no attempt will be made to present all of social psychology in this relatively thin volume. If that were done, it would lead to a very superficial treatment, for there are a number of theoretical schools within the discipline and the approach has been applied to almost all the substantive areas of the social sciences. (There is a social psychology of health and illness, a social psychology of race relations, politics, economic behavior, the family, art—you name it!)

To reduce the task to manageable dimensions, my focus will be limited to a single theoretical approach. Since I am by training and interest a sociologist, it is not surprising that the chosen approach is a variety of symbolic interaction theory. Certainly, not all social psychologists are interactionists, but most of those with socio-logical backgrounds are committed to one or another of the interactionist theories, and there is no other single approach which commands the allegiance of a significant number.

A DEFINITION OF SYMBOLIC INTERACTIONISM

Symbolic interactionism, as I conceive the term, refers to a group of closely related social psychological theories which are descended from the works of a number of important thinkers, chief among whom is George Herbert Mead, a social philosopher.[2]

Herbert Blumer (1969b), the acknowledged heir to Mead's mantle, offers three basic premises to define the symbolic interaction perspective. The first "is that human beings act toward things on the basis of the meanings the things have for them" (Blumer, 1969a: 2).

To understand this statement one must realize that the terms *meaning* and *things* are used in their broadest sense. A thing's meaning includes more than a simple dictionary definition. It includes all the complex images and attitudes that the thing elicits for a person. To say that a particular thing causes fear in a person is to describe part of its meaning. Things, or objects, include *everything* that can have meaning for a person. The term is not limited to inanimate things. Most important, it includes

---

[1] As is common in interactionist writings, I will use the term *actor* to refer to the person who is being focused on. The person with whom actor is interacting will be called *other.*

[2] Other scholars who made important contributions to the early development of symbolic interactionism are Charles Horton Cooley, W. I. Thomas, William James, John Dewey, and James Mark Baldwin.

people—the actor and others. People have images and attitudes about other people and about themselves.

Thus, Blumer is contending that if we are to understand human behavior we must know how the actor defines the situation, for it is from these definitions that behavior emerges. The key data for interactionists are people's perceptions. The fact that an other is, in fact, kindly or cruel may not be very significant. The fact that we *define* him or her as one or the other *is* important, because—regardless of the facts—we will act on that belief.

The second premise states that the meanings of things are derived from, or arise out of, the social interaction that one has with one's fellows (Blumer, 1969a: 2). The definitions that we apply to a situation are based upon our previous interactions and on our experiences in the earlier stages of the present encounter.

The previous paragraph should be read carefully. It says that meanings are developed in social interaction. It does not say that people simply take on the meanings that others hold. Of course we often do that, but we may also modify or reject those meanings. The important thing is that we take others' points of view into account. If we do this, we may be influenced by them even if we totally reject them. When that happens we may be helped in forming our definition by the knowledge that certain others hold differing views.

The third basic premise states that "the actor selects, checks, suspends, regroups, and transforms the meanings in the light of the situation in which he is placed and the direction of his action" (Blumer, 1969a: 5). Definitions guide action, but the process involves more than the application of established meanings. First of all, the actor must decide which of the manifold things in this situation are relevant. For which objects are meanings needed and which others can be ignored? Second, the meanings of things vary with the context and the actor must decide which definition is appropriate to the particular situation. A gun in a display case has a very different meaning from a gun in the hands of a masked man. A rainy day on which we had planned to go fishing is not viewed in the same way as one on which we planned to stay indoors and read a book.

All this suggests that we learn a variety of meanings for the same thing, and at a minimum actor must decide which one to use in a particular situation. Moreover, in many cases, old definitions are inapplicable to new situations, and actor must be flexible enough to learn new meanings. Certain activities which were once evaluated negatively, may become pleasurable if performed with a partner who is a special person. And one's attitude toward a neighbor may change drastically should that neighbor complain about a noisy party!

There is little question that these premises do distinguish symbolic interactionism from other theories. Indeed, there are other approaches that either implicitly or explicitly reject each premise. Following Blumer's argument, I would note that much noninteractionist psychological and sociological thought treats meanings inadequately. Behaviorism focuses on objective stimuli and the reactions to them, but gives little attention to the interpretive activities of the actors. Other theories that do consider meanings downplay their social sources. Some of these view meanings as inherent in the thing, while others see them as projections of individual's needs and minds. Also, meanings are frequently viewed as being relatively fixed once they are established. Finally, the underlying assumption of an *active* actor is missing in many theories, perhaps most notably in those learning theories based on the conditioning model.

In addition to its distinctive premises, symbolic interaction theory has a unique conceptual scheme, which identifies it. All theories have sets of concepts which serve to direct the investigators' attention toward certain things rather than toward others. The assumption is, of course, that the things included in the conceptual scheme are the key things to be explained and the key explanatory variables. Interactionist analyses can be recognized by their focus on such things and processes as: language, role taking, the self-concept, the presented self, social roles, and so on. The meanings of these terms will be discussed later. The point to be made here is simply that an analysis becomes an interactionist analysis when it is based on the premises of symbolic interactionism and when it looks at the factors that are central in the symbolic interactionist conceptual scheme.

BASIC ASSUMPTIONS
OF SYMBOLIC INTERACTIONISM

The three premises I have discussed are usually used to set the boundaries of symbolic interactionism. A theory which rejects them is *not* a symbolic interactionist theory. There are, however, several other implicit assumptions in interactionist thought. They are not actually part of the theory, rather they are the "taken-for-granteds" upon which it is based. They are the untested—and often untestable—axioms which serve as the philosophical underpinnings of the theory. To know them helps one to understand why the theory asks the questions it asks and gives the answers it gives. Also, such knowledge helps a critic to pinpoint the sources of error in the theory.

Some assumptions are common to all scientific theories. All such theories assume, for example, that the subject matter follows orderly rules, that humans can discover those rules, that the evidence of the senses can be trusted, and that this is a world of cause and effect.

These are, however, not the kind of assumptions to be considered here. Our focus will be on those premises which vary among social science theories, (in part because I am still concerned with specifying the unique features of symbolic interactionism). These assumptions relate to such questions as "Are humans unique?"; "What are the basic human motives?"; "To what extent do childhood experiences influence adult behavior?"; "What is the relation between individuals and society?"

Human Language is Unique

Traditionally, one of the key assumptions of interactionists has been that humans are, *in important respects,* basically different from the other animals. In contrast to social biologists who tend to be most impressed by the similarities among the animals, interactionists are most taken by the differences. In their view, a key difference is that human language is basically different from the communication systems of lower animals.

The assertion that humans alone possess true language is, in the eyes of some, somewhat debatable. At least it has been suggested that if we look back we may find that "there's an ape gaining on us," and on the basis of recent research it has been contended that "Man is not unique. . .now the end [of this belief] is in sight as man is forced to concede the last significant attribute that was his and his alone—language" (Fleming, 1974: 31).

In part, the disagreement is a result of differing understandings of the nature of language; therefore, we must first specify what the term means.

The Nature of Language. A language is a system of significant symbols used by organisms for communication. A symbol is anything—a word, a design, a whistle—that has an *arbitrary* meaning attached to it; and a *significant* symbol, in contrast to a personal one, has a meaning which is shared by more than one person.

The nature of symbols is best understood by comparing them with naturally occurring signs. A sign, like a symbol, stands for something else, but a sign serves this function because it is "perceived regularly to precede or be connected with [this] something else. The natural sign and what it indicates occur together in the same space-time framework, and both are thus parts of a concrete situation" (Lindesmith, Strauss, and Denzin, 1977: 117). When an organism perceives the connections, dark clouds become a natural sign of rain, a falling barometer a sign of an impending storm, and smoke a sign of fire. When an organism recognizes a sign, the primary effect is the expectation that the referent is—or will soon be—present.

The meaning of a sign is not arbitrary, and from the nature of the case two organisms can learn the same sign for a thing quite independently of each other. All they need do is perceive the connection between the sign and its referent. This does not happen with a symbol because its meaning "is 'moveable' and arbitrary in the sense that different [symbols] (for example, in different languages) may mean the same thing, and that the [symbol] (for example, a word) may be used in situations in which the object referred to is not present" (Lindesmith, Strauss, and Denzin, 1977: 117). The word "book" conveys to its readers or hearers certain perceptions because they are parties to an agreement that "book" means a certain class of objects which includes such things as the object at which you are now looking. Without that agreement, those four letters would be meaningless. Furthermore, if we would all agree, we could substitute "koob" for "book" and "koob" could mean what "book" now means to people who understand English.

To characterize language in terms of symbol usage is acceptable for many purposes, but annoyingly, the distinction between sign and symbol is not always clear. It sometimes appears that even insects use things which are "symbol-like." For example, in the bee dance, in which one bee "tells" the others the direction and distance of nectar, there seem to be at least protosymbolic aspects. The direction is indicated by the direction the bee takes in the straight portion of the dance. The referent point is the sun, but the dance is typically done on the perpendicular honey-comb inside a darkened hive, so the bee cannot simply signal direction by flying at the proper angle to the sun. If the bee flies straight up it means the nectar is directly toward the sun; straight down means it is opposite to the sun. If the bee heads sixty degrees to the left of the vertical, the nectar will be found sixty degrees to the left of the sun. This is certainly not as arbitrary as English speakers agreeing that "When I say go toward the sun it means. . . ," but there is a good degree of arbitrariness about it. Going straight up could mean to go away from the sun, but it doesn't (von Frisch, 1971).

Thus, on the symbol criterion alone, the communication system of bees seems to be a borderline case; but when a more extended definition is used the ambiguity is removed.

Hockett (1960) suggests that a true language has, in addition to arbitrary symbols, the following design features:[3]

1. *Interchangeability.* Each communicator and each receiver is capable of re-producing the same message. In lower animals it is sometimes the case that some in the species can understand messages they cannot produce (and vice versa). An example is to be found in the courtship dances of the stickle-back fish. The male gives off signals which are understood only by females, but females cannot produce the same signs. Interchangeability would seem to facilitate understanding if anything complex is being communicated, and it would be essential if we are to understand the effect that our communications are having on others.

2. *Total feedback.* Each communicator can receive (and understand) the entire message he is sending. This too would seem necessary if we are to judge the effects of our messages; if we don't know what we are saying, how can we predict other's reaction to it?

3. *Specialization.* Our communications are not a side effect of something else. A dog pants when it is hot, which may signal its presence or even a "keep away" message. But such would only be "coincidental"; a dog pants to reduce body heat. Specialization permits control over communication. If our signals were connected to other activities we could not "refuse" to communicate when we engaged in those activities, and we could not "choose" to communi-cate when we were not engaged in them. Intentionality in communication is facilitated by this feature.

4. *Discreteness.* The communicative units are clear-cut. Even when they are similar in sound or form there are clear dividing lines. "Bit" and "pit", although close, are still clearly distinguishable. In contrast, some of the communications of animals are on a continuous scale. Loud sounds communicate anger, but how loud must they be to signify anger? The discreteness of human language allows for greater clarity of meaning.

---

[3]Hockett speaks of language, but his list includes several design features that are clearly characteristic only of speech. Those features are not included here. Though speech is the primary form in which we use language, it does not seem wise to define language in a way that excludes written communication, the sign language of the deaf, and so on. Many of the communication functions which are of interest to social psychologists are served by nonverbal language.

5. *Displacement.* True language permits communication about things and events that are remote in time and space. The discussion of symbols has touched upon this point, and all that needs to be repeated here is that this feature greatly expands the things about which we can communicate.

6. *Productivity.* Language is creative. The units can be combined in innumerable, albeit finite, ways to say new and meaningful things. In comparison to this open system, there is the closed system of certain apes who can produce a limited number of calls, but cannot combine them to any extent into new, meaningful calls. Because of displacement, we can talk about a lot of things; productivity helps us to say many different things about them. Productivity helps give language its depth.

7. *Traditional transmission.* We inherit the capacity to acquire language, and probably also the drive toward acquisition—but we *learn* our languages. In many other animals, the language itself is transmitted genetically.[4] Because it is based on a learning process, human languages are both greatly variable and expandable. Thus, when we need a new word we create it; we don't have to wait for a mutation. And we can teach it to our children; we don't have to depend on the Mendelian odds that they will carry the mutation.

8. *Dual patterning.* When sounds are combined, they derive their meaning from the pattern of the sounds, not simply from the sounds themselves. "Tack," "cat," and "act" are all composed of the same sounds, but they can be distinguished by the order of the sounds, and therefore, each can be given a distinctive meaning. This gives great flexibility to language. Since the number of permutations is greater than the number of combinations, this feature markedly increases the number of words we can create from our finite vocal abilities and from our limited alphabet. Without dual patterning we could still create all the words we would ever need, but the cost would be many extremely long words.

Human language clearly possesses all eight of these traits, and it is thus distinguishable from bee "language" which lacks some of them. The bee's dance language clearly lacks discreteness, traditional transmission,[5] and dual patterning. The bees seem to lack specialization (returning bees dance even if the other bees have been removed from the hive), and it is not certain if they have interchangeability or total feedback to any degree. (In other words, we don't know if a dancing bee knows what he is talking about!) And, as we noted previously, the arbitrariness of the language is limited. Bee language is an open system; the bees can indeed communicate any distance or direction, but the communication is limited to these features. For example, they can't warn of danger along the path. Finally, we should note that bee

---

[4] As with many of the other features of language, this difference is not an absolute one. There is some evidence that in dogs and monkeys, learning is necessary if the animal is to make effective use of the communication system which is characteristic of the species. In addition, a recent report suggests that older apes have the capacity to teach their young a true language which they themselves have been taught by humans (Keerdoja and Manning, 1979).

[5] Although bee language is transmitted genetically, it does have some of the variety that is usually associated with traditional transmission. The dances vary somewhat by geographical area and this has led investigators to speak of the existence of "racial" dialects (Lindauer, 1971).

language does have displacement since the dance is done back at the hive, out of sight of the nectar, and some time after it was found.

The Linguistic Abilities of the Apes. To show that bees do not have true language does not, however, justify the assertion that humans are the only animals who possess language. After all, bees are rather simple insects. Do our closer relatives also lack language?

In their normal states, the answer seems to be yes. Humans alone have shown the capacity both to *create* and *use* complex systems of significant symbols in their everyday activities. In the "wild," animals frequently communicate by means of signs: one cow can alert others to danger by vocalizing in a particular way which will be recognized by another cow as "what I do when I am afraid." Apes have calls that are quite complex in form and meaning (Goodall, 1971); the calls of the gibbon, for example, have many of the characteristics listed by Hockett. However, they lack the essential last four, that is, displacement, productivity, traditional transmission, and duality of patterning (Hockett, 1960).

Beyond this point, one has to be careful. Not too long ago I would have said unequivocally that lower animals cannot engage in language behavior, and I would not have been in conflict with the facts as then known. Today, however, we know that chimpanzees can be taught the sign languages used by the deaf, which are really manual symbol systems. They can also associate objects and events with pieces of plastic which vary in size and shape, as well as with buttons on a special computer console. By these means, chimps can "talk" to humans and can understand linguistic communications from us. Moreover, these chimps can be taught to put their "words" together in meaningful combinations, and to a degree they can create novel sentences which they have *not* been taught. They also seem to be able to abstract the qualities of a category; all kinds of dogs, and even pictures of dogs, are "labeled" as dogs. And there is some evidence that they can use the proper sign when an object is not physically present (Brown and Herrnstein, 1975; Fleming, 1974). Recent findings are even more impressive. Evidence seems to be accumulating that two chimpanzees who have been taught language can use it to talk to each other (Savage-Rumbaugh et al., 1978). Even more important is the as yet unreplicated finding that a chimpanzee can pass on the language it has learned to a baby chimp (Keerdoja and Manning, 1979).[6]

One must be very careful here. It has proved to be risky to attempt to judge the limits of the ape's abilities. Recent events have already required a rewriting of this section. Nonetheless, there do seem to be basic differences between humans and apes, and I don't believe the gap will ever be closed. It is highly unlikely that a group of apes will develop a language without the help of "renegade" humans since

---

[6]It should be noted that one investigator has recently raised questions concerning the validity of the accepted view of ape's linguistic capacity. It has been suggested that some of the apes' accomplishments, for example, in creating original sentences, are really the result of unintended coaching (Sobel, 1979). Others vigorously deny this.

language does not come naturally to apes. Also, apes' capacities seem to be limited. The chimp with the largest vocabulary knows about 200 words. Although this is no mean accomplishment, it is hardly comparable to the extensive, rich, and varied language that is available to humans.[7]

Finally, chimps probably cannot do much with the language they have learned. They can be taught a simple human-like language, but that hardly puts them in our class. They have been given a tool, they can use it in a fumbling way, but they haven't built anything with it. There's a big difference between the ability to hit a nail on the head and the ability to build a house.

Language Leads to Humanness

Another major assumption of the interactionists is that many of the other unique characteristics of humans are a result of our facility with language. Our general distinctiveness is in large part a result of our linguistic abilities. For example, we communicate much more effectively than other animals because our language is superior to other forms of communication. For one thing, signs are not easily found for many of the things about which we want to communicate. A lot of noise of a particular kind is a sign of an approaching train, but many other forms of danger do not signal their approach so conveniently. The communication of concepts and ideas is difficult enough with the aid of symbols; without them such communication is impossible. What is the sign of a symbol?

Even when signs are available for particular things, they permit only limited statements about those things. Signs say little more than that the thing is present or coming. If you are limited to signs, how do you convey the notion that the thing will come in the distant future? And, finally, when signs are adequate for the desired communication, they are often awkward to use. A barometer is a special sign since it is created rather than naturally occurring. But how inefficiently it conveys its message! How much better it is to be able to say "The weatherman predicted rain." The protosymbols that some animals are able to use are better than signs, but they are still grossly inferior to the true symbols we have available.

The wider significance of this becomes clear when it is realized that effective communication is the key to complex behavior. Thus, the distinctiveness of human behavior ultimately rests on our linguistic ability. Let me briefly note a few examples.

In order to have complex social organization, each person must be taught his or her functions, each must be able to predict the actions of the others, coordinated activity is required, and so on. None of these things would be possible without language. We tend to marvel at the social organization of some insects, but in reality it is never very complex. Such societies have only a few categories—workers, drones,

---

[7]It is also clear that apes lack the vocal equipment required for speech. After much effort, Hayes (1951) was able to teach a chimpanzee to produce a few word-like sounds, but these were rather unintelligible.

queens, for example—and they engage in only a few coordinated activities. Anything beyond this would result in chaos, given their limited means of communication.

Without language there would be no culture. Science, religion, art, and philosophy are all symbolic pursuits. Our economic system is based upon objects whose value is totally symbolic. Without symbols, the agencies of social control would be brutal, for they would not have available any of the symbolic sanctions which keep most of us in line.

The availability of language enormously expands the range of things that can be taught, and has a profound effect on the form of teaching. Without language there could only be trial and error learning and imitation, and that would not get us very far. And without language there would be no thinking. Thinking may not simply be internalized conversation, but it does involve such a process. If we cannot use language, we cannot have a conversation with ourselves, and therefore we cannot think. The truth of this statement is revealed by studies (Luria, 1966) which show that when speech processes are disturbed by brain lesions, certain thought processes are also lost.

Finally, I would note that of the other things which make humans distinctive, the things which are of most interest to interactionists are all dependent upon language for their development and use. Included in these things would be role-taking ability—the capacity to put oneself in the place of the other and to "see" things as he or she does; the ability to develop a self-concept—that is, the ability to have attitudes and beliefs about ourselves, etc.[8] The nature of these connections will be made clearer in subsequent chapters. At this point, it is sufficient to note that without language we would lack the basic traits that make us human.

It should be amply clear by now that an organism which possesses language will be rather special—and humans are the *only* animals that can make a claim to that special status. We are unique.

Humanness Depends on Social Life

A third major assumption underlying symbolic interaction theory is that social life is necessary for the development of the characteristics which are uniquely human. The potential for humanity is largely there from the start, but it takes interaction with others to develop that potential. Biological maturation is not enough.

Learning to Interact. In part, of course, this notion follows from previous assumptions. If language is a prerequisite for the development of human qualities, then social life must also be a prerequisite because in order to learn a language one

---

[8] As was previously noted, we must be careful to give the apes their due. Apes who are not reared in social isolation, *do* show self-awareness even if they are not taught language. They give clear indications that they recognize themselves in a mirror. Though there is a difference between a full blown self-concept and self-recognition, the evidence again suggests that apes are closer to humans than was previously thought (Meddin, 1979; Gallup, 1979).

has to interact with people who already know it. The present point goes beyond this, however. Interaction is necessary for language development, but the ability to interact is not present at birth. It develops only through social experience. It is generally accepted that a child has to be taught how to be human. I would go further, however, and assert that a child has to be taught before he or she can benefit from the lessons which usually lead to humanness. This latter statement would not be accepted by all.

Rheingold (1969: 782) puts it forcefully when she proposes that ". . . the human infant begins life as a social organism, that while still very young he behaves in a social fashion, and that he socializes others more than he is socialized. These statements are contrary to the generally held notions that the infant is asocial at birth, that he is taught to be social, and only gradually and by tuition does he acquire the 'dispositions, skills and knowledge' that enable him to participate as a more or less effective member of groups and the society."

To be fair it should be noted that she also says: "To present a complete account. . .it must also be pointed out that the infant's behavior *is* modified by what social encounters he has; in the process he gains knowledge and perfects his skills, and to this extent he too is socialized" (Rheingold, 1969: 780).

Even with this qualification, Rheingold's position is in serious conflict with the interactionist view. When she adds at the end of the previously cited paragraph "It will be my contention that in the beginning the power to socialize resides more in [the infant] than in other persons," the lines are apparently clearly drawn.

Further reading reveals, as Lauer and Handel (1977) first noted, that the dispute rests in part upon semantic differences. No social psychologist would dispute Rheingold's assertions that the newborn is in contact with other organisms from birth and that he or she requires such contacts for survival. What most of them would not accept, however, is her assertion that it follows from this that the infant is social. A social being *interacts*; being acted upon by other organisms is not sufficient.

But isn't she speaking of interaction when she says "As [others] provide stimuli to which [the infant] responds, so [the infant] provides stimuli to which they respond" (Rheingold, 1969: 781)? The answer is no. Certainly infants influence others; anyone who has seen a parent handle a baby knows this is so. Interaction, however, involves more than this. For one thing, I assume that there is no intentionality on the part of the child. The parents will react to an infant's cry, but we would not call it interaction unless the infant cried *because* he or she wished the parents to react. At the beginning, infants cry because they are distressed. The fact that the parent recognizes this sign of distress does not make the exchange an interaction. Only when the cry is emitted because the infant wants to be picked up is there interaction and that does not happen until a later stage.

In addition, the symbolic element is absent, so that even if it were interaction it would not be the human kind of symbolic interaction. Only when the infant begins to use different cries or sounds for different wants does the interaction resemble that of adults. Of course, this stage comes even later.

A third missing element is that the infant does not appear to take the parent's action into account when it decides what to do next. If the parent doesn't respond to the first cry the child will not cry louder because of this. He may cry louder as his discomfort increases, but until he changes his behavior in *response to* the parent's inaction he is not interacting as true humans do.

Rheingold's assertion that the infant socializes others is acceptable to inter-actionists; they always insist that socialization is a mutual process. The student always teaches the teacher. It is, however, not crucial to the issue at hand. It does not seem that "the [infant] is more than an active partner to the process," and he is by no means the "prime mover" (782). Certainly the baby teaches the parents how to be parents, but much of the infant's success in getting parents to do it "his way" is fortuitous.

As one reads further in Rheingold's work, it becomes increasingly clear that her conflict with the interactionists is in large part due to differences in the definition of the terms social being and social interaction. However, all this is important beyond settling an intellectual dispute. By commenting upon Rheingold's work I hope it has been made clear that normal human interaction involves the use of symbolic communication, intentionality, the reaction to social stimuli after they have been interpreted, and the anticipation of the other's response.

To "prove" that a person is not social at birth does not, however, entirely support the point under discussion. Is it also true that the infant and child need to learn to interact, or will simple maturation prepare them for the specific training that they will get later?

In the abstract, it would not be very difficult to design an experiment which would give us a definite answer to this question. It would not be beyond the ingenuity of most researchers to create an environment in which there was a total lack of human socialization but adequate provision for the physical needs of the child. Such a study would, of course, be impossible to carry out. There are, however, situations that occur "naturally" which approach the conditions of this experiment, and they can provide a partial answer to this question.

In a classic article, Davis (1947) describes the cases of Anna and Isabelle, two children who were "brought up" under conditions of extreme isolation from others. Isabelle, for example, was the illegitimate child of—very importantly for our concern— a deaf-mute mother, and she spent most of her first six years alone with her mother in a darkened room.

Parts of Davis' description of Isabelle gives support to our previous point. "When she communicated with her mother it was by means of gestures. . .Her behavior toward strangers, especially men, was almost that of a wild animal manifesting much fear and hostility. In lieu of speech she made a strong croaking sound. In many ways she acted like an infant" (Davis, 1947: 436).

Davis suggests that after discovery it appeared that it would be impossible to train Isabelle. In our terms, she was simply not capable of benefiting from the lessons which were being provided for her. She had not learned the basics and therefore she could not progress. However, once the first breakthroughs occurred "she went through the usual stages of learning characteristic of the years from one to six not only in proper succession but far more rapidly than normal" (Davis, 1947: 436).

In the case of Anna, who was similarly deprived, progress was slower and at the time of her death at the age of ten she was still far from normal. The reason for this slow advancement is not clear; there is the possibility that she was congenitally retarded. But Davis suggests the problem was that she never received the prolonged and expert attention that Isabelle received. Neither girl was able to learn language when discovered, but Isabelle was brought to that point and progressed rapidly. "Had Anna. . .been given a mastery of speech at an earlier point *by intensive training,* her subsequent development might have been much more rapid" (Davis, 1947: 437, emphasis added).

Though by no means unequivocal, these findings do support the notion that one must be prepared if one is to benefit from the postinfancy experiences which lead to the development of true humanity.

Before turning to other matters, two additional points must be made. It should be noted that though the kind of training we are speaking of normally occurs quite early in life, these cases indicate that early training is not essential. When both girls were discovered they were about six years old, and though this made things much more difficult, it was clearly not an insuperable barrier. Second, not all kinds of interaction will serve to make a child social. The case of Genie (Curtiss, 1977) is instructive in this regard. She too was a child who was confined, isolated, and starved for sensory stimulation, but if you stretch the term somewhat she may be viewed as having had more interaction with others than Anna and Isabelle did. All this "interaction" was, however, of the most brutal kind. She knew only threats, beatings, and frightening behavior from others. The description of her condition when discovered is reminiscent of that of Anna and Isabelle. Contact with people is not enough, and the wrong kind of contact may be worse than none. Despite considerable progress, Genie is still not normal in some respects.

Humans are Purposive and Reasoning Animals

One of the things about interactionist theory most likely to impress the reader is that it contains long lists of factors that people supposedly take into consideration before they act. This is not the place to discuss whether the lists must be that long or, for that matter, whether they are seriously incomplete. The point is they appear in the theory because of basic assumptions about humans. A key underpinning of interactionist theory is the belief that people have particular purposes or goals in mind when they interact, and that they act in ways *they believe* will lead to the achievement of those goals. Behavior is chosen on the basis of an evaluation of probable outcomes. (The length of the lists comes from the wide variety of factors that must be considered in order to make such a judgment.)

This is not to say, of course, that there is any assumption that the chosen behavior will in fact lead to the goals. To act rationally is not, necessarily, to act correctly. We misjudge the outcomes of our acts even when we have the facts straight, and often we don't have them straight. We misperceive, we guess wrong, we overlook, and so on. All I am saying is that symbolic interactionists tend to use a model of humans which assumes the use of reason in the pursuit of goals.

Given this view of human nature, it is legitimate to ask where emotions come into symbolic interaction theory. In fact, one of the major criticisms of the theory is that the emotional component in behavior is so thoroughly ignored that the theory suggests an unacceptable image of a purely rational being (Manis and Meltzer, 1978). A fuller consideration of this point will be presented in a later chapter, but for now I would note that although there may be some validity to this criticism, the interactionist would insist that part of the value of the theory is that it reveals the rational components in some behavior which is usually viewed to be a result of blind emotion. The existence of strong emotions does not necessarily lead to unreasoned behavior. To say "I was so much in love (or hated so strongly) that I couldn't help myself," is often simply a rationalization. Love and hate lead us to make certain choices which we might not have made under other circumstances, but this notwithstanding, the process of decision making is the same. When strong emotion is present our perceptions of the situation may deviate further from those of an objective observer than they usually do, and the reasoning process may be truncated and inadequate. But that is not to say that reasoning is absent.

Humans Seek Rewards

We can go a step further by noting that interactionists tend to assume that in very general terms human purpose can be described as the seeking of reward and the avoidance of punishments (costs). This is, of course, not an idea peculiar to interactionism. It is explicit in social exchange theory (Simpson, 1972), and as Weinstein and Tanur (1978: 43) put it "From Aristotle to Schutz, from Homans to Parsons. . . some form of hedonistic assumption is [used] to render social activity as sensible."

The words "some form of" are important in the preceding quotation. The psychological hedonism which lies below the surface of much interactionist thought does not say that we seek immediate gratification. It recognizes that people are often willing to forego present rewards for long-term gains. Interactionists also assume that there are many kinds of rewards and costs. Rewards are not limited to the "pleasures of the flesh" and costs are not limited to physical punishments. In fact, interactionists believe that much of human activity represents an attempt to obtain very different kinds of rewards—self-respect, social approval, conflict-free interaction, and so on.

Human Beings are Conscious Actors

Implicit in the previous points is the assumption that actors have a high degree of awareness. It is rather difficult to assume purposiveness if one does not assume at the same time that "people know what they want." Some interactionists (Travisano,

1975) have succeeded to a degree in finding a place for the unconscious, but the predominant model in the field assumes that people are aware of their goals or become aware of them as interaction proceeds.

In addition to awareness of goals, there is an assumption that actors are highly aware of their environments. If people react to the meanings of the objects in their environment, they must, of course, first be aware that the objects are there.

Mead (1934), the most important progenitor of interactionism, suggests an exception to this view in his discussion of automatic actions. Certain behaviors, if long practiced, can be routinized, and when a particular stimulus occurs the appropriate reaction will follow without awareness, consciousness, or planning. One cannot deny the existence of such a class of behaviors. We do swat at flies without much thought, and some people do habitually nod approval without quite hearing what is said. And it should be noted that such tendencies are useful in getting the routine activities of life done.

It should be obvious, however, that these must be viewed as very special cases, albeit common ones. The entire Meadian scheme is a reaction to an emphasis on such behaviors. In this instance, he appears to be leaning toward the behaviorist view which emphasizes the direct association of stimulus and response.

Furthermore, admitting automatic behaviors takes one only a little way off the main track. For one thing, such behaviors emerge from the usual kind of experiences of which interactionists talk. They may now be automatic, but they develop by normal processes. In addition, Mead himself suggests that such behaviors tend to be unstable. They remain automatic only as long as they remain unproblematic. If an other takes our unthinking nod to represent true acquiescence, we are likely to return quickly to the more "normal" interaction. Finally, note that even in these so-called automatic actions, there is probably more awareness than meets the eye. An "automatic" swatting of a fly suggests that the fly was identified as such and assigned a meaning. It may simply be that the defining processes occur so rapidly in such circumstances that actors are *less* aware than normally that they are using them.

Actors are Active

Reflections of the assumption that humans are active rather than passive are to be found in much of what has already been stated. However, to make the point more explicit: If actors do not simply accept other people's meanings, but accept, modify, or reject them, then they are active in their own socialization. If actors do not simply apply previously learned meanings, but handle and modify them through an interpretive process, then they are active participants in the interaction process. If social interaction involves intentionality and the rational pursuit of goals, then the actor is active in determining his or her fate.

VARIETIES OF SYMBOLIC INTERACTION

The assumptions that we have considered up to this point would probably be accepted by all those who consider themselves to be symbolic interactionists. But these ideas do not touch on all the relevant issues, and beyond this point there is no way that one can present ideas which will find favor with all. The fact of the matter is that there is no "official" theory. The social psychological landscape is by now almost literally strewn with theories that trace their ancestry to Mead, and the differences are not simply in detail; they extend to the basic assumptions.[9]

The version emphasized in this volume is close in its assumptions to the so-called Iowa School, which is an outgrowth of the work of Manford Kuhn at the State University of Iowa. The alternate view is called the Chicago School and it is associated with the work of Herbert Blumer who was at the University of Chicago for many years. The reader should be warned, however, that these labels can be misleading. The ideas of both schools are widely disseminated and adherence to a particular one does not necessarily suggest any connection with the university which has given the view its name. Conversely, association with one of these universities does not necessarily mean that the scholar represents the school of thought named for that institution (Vaughan and Reynolds, 1968).

In my discussion of the remaining assumptions, the focus will be on those that underlie the theory to be presented in this book; however, in order to give an accurate picture of the diversity of interactionist thought, reference will also be made to opposing views.

Human Behavior is Variable

All varieties of symbolic interaction view human behavior as dynamic and changing. Since behavior reflects the actor's definition of the situation, we would expect that behavior would vary when situations vary. A person cannot simply be described as dominant or submissive, for example, because he or she may be dominant in some situations and submissive in others.

It goes well beyond this, however. Since meanings can change, actor may act differently in two similar encounters which occur at different times. Because two situations are objectively similar does not mean that they are defined in similar ways. And even if two encounters are defined in the same way at the start, the course of events may lead to differential change in the definitions as the interaction proceeds.

The standard interpretation has been that if one goes beyond these general statements one finds great differences between the Iowa and Chicago Schools. The

---

[9] It is a commentary on the state of the field that there are wide discrepancies in the number of varieties recognized. Meltzer and Petras (1970) discuss two major versions and Meltzer, Petras, and Reynolds (1975; 1978) speak of four. Kuhn (1964a) and Warshay (1971) see eight or ten varieties. Since the lists do not completely overlap, more than ten versions have been recognized. I will here limit my attention to the two varieties usually considered to be the main forms.

latter has been seen as postulating much more variability in the behavior of actors over time, a view that is supported by such statements as "Roles are thus made anew each time people assemble and orient their conduct toward one another" (Hewitt, 1976: 55).

This notwithstanding, my reading of important representatives of the Chicago School indicates that they see more stability than most people assume they do (see Heiss, forthcoming). Granted, the emphases are different: the Chicagoans are most impressed by the innovations that occur in each interaction, while the Iowans emphasize the carryover from one situation to similar situations. But leaving aside matters of degree, we could all agree that there is both stability and change. Interaction is guided by a "game plan" which sets the framework for action. Since similar plans tend to be used for encounters defined as similar, there would be some consistency. At the same time, the game plans are not strait jackets. They don't contain specific instructions, they permit ad libbing, and they themselves are subject to modification. Thus, there is also a place for variation.

Human Behavior is Orderly

Despite the recognition of variability in human behavior, no social scientist can assume that action is random and unpredictable. In fact, no one can take such a position. It would be difficult to get through the day if we did not assume that the behavior of the people we meet would be within certain limits.

To assume a certain degree of order, however, does not necessarily imply a belief in complete predictability or an assumption that human behavior is completely determined by previous experience—and the two schools of interactionist thought diverge on this matter. The Chicago school has been described as postulating "soft determinism, a view of human behavior as influenced—but not entirely determined—by antecedent events" (Manis and Meltzer, 1978: 8). The Iowa School is more strictly deterministic.

A full discussion of this issue is not possible here, but a brief and superficial statement may suffice. In the Chicagoan view there is an impulsive part of humans which is spontaneous and basically unpredictable in its operation. Any action is initiated by this impulsive part (the "I") and is reacted to by a more socialized part of the person (the "Me"). Behavior results from the interaction between these two elements and it is never completely predictable.

Though they would admit that we are a long way from achieving it, the Iowans would subscribe to the position that there is no reason, in principle, why the complete prediction of human behavior is impossible. They take, in other words, a completely deterministic stance. The causes of behavior are numerous and complex; they include factors which the actors bring to the situations and others which develop within the particular situation. But if all the factors were known, and they are assumed to be potentially knowable, they would predict behavior. Constant conditions would produce constant results.

But what about the "I" of the Chicagoans? How can it be fitted into a deterministic position? One way would be to accept the notion of a bidimensional person while assuming that both parts act in orderly, predictable ways. This position would differ from the Chicago view only in that it would contend that the original, impulsive, unthinking reaction is also caused by antecedent factors. Some of these factors might not be social. There are indications in Mead's work that he sees the "I" as biological in nature, but even if this is accepted the operation of the "I" is not put beyond the realm of cause and effect. Of course, the explanations would become more complex and they would have to take into account factors not normally considered. Social determinism would have to go in favor of a sociobiological determinism. But a deterministic position could be retained. There "must" be a reason why our "impulses" pushed in one direction rather than in another. I see no basis, in principle, for assuming those reasons are forever beyond discovery.

An alternative approach is to deny the existence of two distinct parts to the person. This approach is followed by Kuhn, and it seems preferable. In this view, actor simply reacts to perceived social stimuli, and the reaction is determined by his present "mental state" which is itself a result of all his previous experience—including experiences in the early parts of the present encounter. Little seems to be lost if one takes this view. It is quite consistent with the other assumptions of the theory and has the advantage of being more parsimonious than the Chicago view.

Reductionism is an "Absurdum"

Reductionism has several meanings in science; here it will be used to refer to the explanation of human behavior by reference to the behavior of lower animals—an approach which is currently enjoying a vogue. Given their stand on the uniqueness of man, it is not surprising to learn that symbolic interactionists view this as inappropriate. They do not believe that studies of lower animals have much relevance for the kind of questions which interest them. The behaviors that interactionists wish to explain are frequently not exhibited by lower animals, and when they are, the processes by which they are developed are often basically different. It is stretching the term somewhat, but it could be said that humans and insects both "play roles." The crucial difference is, however, that humans learn their roles and insects act from instinct. Humans and fish both protect their homes at times, but an interactionist would consider it absurd to suggest, as Ardrey (1966) does, that the forces which lead modern nations to defend themselves when attacked are akin to the genetically based "territorial imperative" in fish.

The present version of interactionism accepts this view, but moderates it to some degree. While arguing that the details are markedly different, I believe that we must be willing, at least tentatively, to consider theories regarding *the process of learning* which derive in part from studies of lower animals. The application of such theories to humans will require major alterations in detail. Humans and rats both learn, but rats don't have a language, and language is the key tool in human learning. Nonetheless, there is enough evidence from studies of humans to suggest that ignoring such theories cuts one off from a fertile source of hypotheses. The Chicagoans would probably take the position that the differences make all the difference, and thus general psychological learning theory is of dubious value for an interactionist.[10]

Methods and Data of Social Psychology: Special or Not-So-Special?

If meanings are the engines of human behavior, it would follow that rather than gathering data on "the facts," investigators should concern themselves with people's perceptions and definitions of those facts. Perceptions would be the relevant variables; human action would be explained in terms of such factors. In addition, perceptions, along with social action, would be the key dependent factors. It would be important to explain why people have the perceptions they do.

On this point there is no major disagreement among interactionists. Both schools would agree, though adherents of both groups have been known to study objective factors as substitutes for, or indicators of, perceptions. There is, however, great disagreement concerning the proper way to obtain and handle perceptual data.

Routes to Knowledge. Herbert Blumer (1969b), the key figure of the Chicago group, argues that if human behavior is as it is described in the basic assumptions of symbolic interaction, a special methodology is required. In contrast, Iowans such as Kuhn insist that the usual methods of science will lead to an understanding of human behavior. Both would agree that we must get at the meanings that things have for people, but their ways of determining those meanings are essentially different, and so are their ways of handling the material they have gathered.

A study done by a true Iowan would show all the conventional trappings of a scientific sociological study. There would be a formal theory and deduced hypotheses. Sampling techniques would be used to choose a large number of subjects who would be given structured interviews and questionnaires. The concepts would have operational definitions attached to them, that is, there would be specific instructions about how to determine into which category each case should be placed. The goal would be to define these categories in numerical terms, and in the service of this goal statistical techniques such as factor analysis would be utilized. After the scoring is done for the relevant variables, correlational techniques would be used to determine if the hypothesized relationships did in fact exist. The key words are large numbers, formal theory and hypotheses, operational definitions, systematic data gathering, quantification, and hypothesis testing by means of statistical analysis.

Blumer, a man of strong opinions who pulls no punches in expressing them,

---

[10] Theories such as Bandura's (1977) social learning theory may serve to put this disagreement to rest. Its roots in traditional psychological theory are clear, but it takes particular note of the special characteristics of humans. It may not go far enough for many, but most would agree that it is a big step in the proper direction.

considers the use of such methods in the social and psychological sciences "inadequate and misguided." He finds them "grossly inadequate" and he "marvels at the supreme confidence with which these preoccupations are advanced as the stuff of methodology" (Blumer, 1969a: 26-27).

Blumer does not contend that there is no value to the scientific method; his objection is simply to the application of the physical science model to social psychology. To understand human behavior, one must understand actor's definitions, and in order to do this the investigator "must get inside the actor's world and must see the world as the actor sees it" (Blumer, 1969a: 57-58). To do this requires special techniques. Actor's definitions, he would contend, cannot be obtained from questionnaires; no quantitative measures can adequately represent meanings; and no statistical analyses can explain them.

What, then, is a person to do? Blumer's answer would be that social psychology requires a special method which tempers the scientific approach with procedures that have a strong humanistic component.

We can get a picture of what Blumer wants by noting what he finds specifically lacking in most studies. He complains that "most research inquiry is not designed to develop a close and reasonably full familiarity with the area of life under study" (Blumer, 1969a: 37). He would argue that we cannot isolate a part of that life and expect to understand it; rather, we must come to grips with the whole of it in all its complexity.

In his view, the standard methods stand in the way of the researcher "[doing] a lot of free exploration in the area, getting close to the people involved in it, seeing it in a variety of situations they meet, noting their problems and observing how they handle them, being a party to their conversations, and watching their life as it flows along" (Blumer, 1969a: 37). According to Blumer, only by doing this can one truly understand empirical social reality and the meanings it has for people. Only when one knows an area intimately will "systematic introspection" operate. Then one can put oneself in the place of the actors and truly understand them.

The obvious method of choice would be participant observation,[11] the vehicle of presentation would be ethnographic description, and the method of analysis would be "inspection"—an intensive focused examination of the material. The prescription is to immerse oneself in the data, to consider the material from a variety of perspectives, and then, through a process of flexible scrutiny, to determine if things which are supposed to be connected are in fact related in the real world.

This is not the place to undertake a lengthy discussion of the relative merits of the two methodological stances, but a few points should be made before we leave these matters.

To begin with, it should be emphasized that the conflict in stance is not simply a matter of who is right and who is wrong. Many of the differences emerge from different goals. The Iowa tradition stresses a *nomethetic* approach, that is, they are

---

[11]Other acceptable methods would include case studies, nondirective interviews, and the analysis of personal documents.

most interested in developing generalizations about classes of (human) objects. Chicagoans do not completely forsake this goal, but their main emphasis has often been *idiographic*—the in-depth understanding of unique cases. The methods that best suit one purpose are not the most appropriate for the other. Second, the approaches are not mutually exclusive. The studies of the Chicagoans are often useful to flesh out the picture provided by traditional, scientific methods.

When it comes down to it, however, I clearly prefer standard analysis. To implement my goals, the methods suggested by Blumer too often suffer from what I consider fatal flaws, that is, inadequate canons of proof, lack of agreement among observers, difficulties in replication, unsharable data, and so forth. This is not to say that I fail to recognize the difficulties of standard methods. But I do feel those difficulties are exaggerated by Blumer and others. Variables can capture people's interpretations, processes are not totally immune to quantitative analysis, and when they are, hypotheses which involve them can be tested indirectly. We have a long way to go, but it would seem to me that improvement in our present techniques is the way to reach our goals.

THE NATURE OF THEORY

Up to this point I have not considered it necessary to define the term "theory." I have assumed that anyone capable of reading this book already has a general notion of what a theory is. However, for a work of this kind it is desirable to have more than just a general notion. As you progress through the book, you should consider, among other things, how good, in a technical sense, the theory is. You try to reach an independent judgment about how well it meets the criteria of adequate scientific theories. The next few pages are intended to equip you for this task.

Of the innumerable definitions of theory, most of which say the same thing in different words, I am partial to the extended one given by George Homans (1964) in an important article entitled "Bringing Men Back In."

He starts by stating:

A theory of a phenomenon consists of a series of propositions, each stating a relationship between properties of nature. But not every kind of sentence qualifies as such a proposition. These propositions do not consist of definitions of the properties: the construction of a conceptual scheme is an indispensible part of theory but it is not itself theory. (Homans, 1964: 811)

This is an important point, because many so-called theories in sociology are merely conceptual schemes. They tell you what to look for (or at) and give you definitions that permit categorization. But they do not help you to go beyond that, for they say little or nothing about the interrelationships among the concepts. They do not contain statements of the form: "When A, then B."

However, not all statements of relationships qualify as adequate propositions:

A proposition [may not] simply say that there is *some* relationship among the properties. Instead, if there is some change in one of the properties it must at least begin to *specify* what the change in the other property will be. (Homans, 1964: 811)

Thus, the propositions must at least be directional. If one increases, will the other decrease or increase? It is preferable if the proposition also states the amount of change that will occur, but this is almost never possible in sociology and it is not required. Similarly, propositions may be probabilistic, and may use such terms as "will tend to," or "is likely to," although it is better if a simple "will" can be used.

Some of the propositions in some "nontheories" fall down on this criterion. They do speak of relationships which are not true by definition, but they do not specify what exactly will change and in what way. Structural-functionalism tells us that there is a strain toward integration, so if one cultural element changes the others will change to mesh. But "change to mesh" is a weasel statement—it doesn't specify *what* change. In this kind of theory you can't lose. If the proposition is vague enough, any outcome can be interpreted as confirming evidence. Thus, the theory cannot be disproved, and any theory which does not admit of disproof is unacceptable.

However, even this is not enough. These characteristics are necessary, but they alone are not sufficient. Statements such as "On the average men are taller than women"; "The average female student has a higher grade average than the average male"; "As height increases, weight increases," are not theoretical statements, whether they are taken separately or as a group. Again, quoting Homans:

To constitute a theory, the propositions must take the form of a deductive system. One of them, usually called the lowest-order proposition, is the proposition to be explained. . .The other propositions are either general propositions or statements of particular given conditions. . .The crucial requirement is that each system shall be deductive. That is, the lowest-order proposition follows as a logical conclusion from the general propositions under the specified given conditions. (Homans, 1964: 811-12)

When the lowest-order proposition does follow logically, it is said to be explained. The explanation of a phenomenon is the theory of the phenomenon. A theory is nothing—it is not a theory—unless it is an explanation. (Homans, 1964: 812)

The two propositions "As height increases, weight increases" and "X's are taller than Y's" form a theory when they are combined to explain why X's weigh more than Y's. The three statements form a deductive system in that the last follows from the first two. If the last statement were not known, it could be predicted from the first two.

Although Homans does not make it explicit, his criticism of functionalism can be read to suggest that he has in mind another criterion. A theory merely has to explain and predict, but a *good* theory has explanatory power, which is evidenced when a competent reader says after reading it, "Aha—now I see." A good theory lays curiosity to rest. If the highest order propositions are not taken by the reader to be self-explanatory, the theorist has not gone far enough. Many would not consider this to be a necessary criterion, but it seems to me to be very useful as a guide to theory construction and as a basis for theory evaluation.

In sum:

> One may define properties and categories and one still has no theory. One may state that there are relations between the properties, and one still has no theory. One may state that change in one property will produce a definite change on another property, and one still has no theory. Not until one has properties (concepts), and propositions stating the relations between them, and the propositions form a deductive system—not until one has all three does one have a theory. (Homans, 1964: 812)

SUMMARY

The theory to be presented in this book is a variety of symbolic interactionism. As such it considers it as given that humans learn the meanings of things through their social interaction, and that their behavior emerges from their reactions to their perceived environments. More specifically, in our interaction with other people we have meanings for things presented to us. Though we do not necessarily accept those meanings in the form in which they are presented, the meanings do serve as the basis for the understandings we develop. These understandings, in turn, serve as a basis for the definitions we develop of specific situations we encounter, and it is from these definitions of situations that we develop our plans of action.

The other basic assumptions of the theory are as follows:

1. Humans are unique in their ability to use language.
2. Several other unique human traits are possible because of our linguistic ability.
3. Social life is a prerequisite to the development of human traits.
4. Humans are purposive and rational animals.
5. Humans seek rewards and avoid punishments.
6. Humans are conscious actors.
7. Humans are active, rather than passive, reactors.

The version of interactionist theory to be presented in this book is closer to the Iowa School of symbolic interaction than it is to the Chicago School. Thus, it is further distinguished by its view that:

8. Though human behavior is quite variable, there is some degree of consistency in similar situations.
9. Human behavior is, in principle, totally predictable.

10. In general, studies of lower animals do not tell us much about human behavior, but hypotheses about learning processes may be obtained from such studies.

11. In studying people, the important data are their perceptions, and standard scientific methods are the best way to obtain and handle such material.

CHAPTER 2

LANGUAGE ACQUISITION AND ROLE TAKING

As was indicated in the discussion of Rheingold's work in Chapter 1, social interaction involves, among many other things, symbolic communication and the anticipation of the interaction partner's responses. Therefore, if we are to explain interaction, we must first explain how people develop the capacity to communicate symbolically and how they learn to predict responses of others before such responses actually occur. Symbolic communication implies that the actor can use language, and the prediction of other's response implies *the ability to take the role of the other*—that is, the ability to put oneself in the place of another and to see things as he or she sees them. Thus, the task becomes the description of the process of language acquisition and the explanation of the development of role-taking ability.

Before I turn to these matters, an apparent paradox should be noted. As stated above, to interact requires the ability to use language and to take the role of the other. But, as will be seen, language and role-taking ability are developed in interaction, and learning language requires role taking, which is learned through the use of language. The problem is clear. How can any of these abilities develop if each requires for its development the prior existence of the other two?

The difficulty is akin to the chicken or the egg problem, and I do not want to get bogged down in an extended attempt at resolution. Perhaps it is sufficient to suggest that each of these abilities requires the others for their *full* development, but primitive forms of them do not. "Real" interaction, for example, requires us to understand the meanings of complex symbols, but even in the absence of this capacity proto-interaction can occur through the use of signs. Similarly, the cues regarding what is on the mind of the other are usually symbolic, but some limited basis is provided for role taking by recognition of signs. Later advances are built upon these early steps. Role taking based on signs can lead to the first learning of some simple symbols, which permits an advance in interaction which in turn allows a step forward in language acquisition. Each small step in one area makes possible a step in the other areas which in turn makes possible advances in the original area. Gradually, there is a spiral movement in the direction of true humanness. In the presentations that follow, each ability will be handled separately, and it will be assumed that the necessary "supporting skills" are available at each step. To do otherwise would create great confusion.

THE ACQUISITION OF LANGUAGE

Despite the recognition of the basic importance of language, there is no uniquely interactionist theory of language acquisition. At most, there are a few ideas with a distinctly interactionist flavor that are emphasized in interactionists' writings on the subject. Included here would be the notion that language acquisition involves role taking and the idea that learning the meaning of a symbol involves more than simply learning to what the symbol refers. According to interactionists, when we learn the referent of a symbol we also learn a set of attitudes toward that thing. Language acquisition involves the learning of meanings, and to learn meanings implies more than the memorization of dictionary definitions. When we are taught the names of the various races, for example, we are not only taught a system of classification; simultaneously, we learn a set of attitudes toward the races.

Such ideas are important, but they hardly constitute a theory. Much of the discussion of language and its acquisition appearing in interactionist treatises is frankly borrowed from noninteractionists. Moreover, it is a selective borrowing. Interactionist interest is focused on the acquisition of meanings. Many of the "hot" topics in linguistics, such as the question "How do people come to speak grammatically in the absence of specific instructions on the rules of grammar?" are given little attention by most interactionists. (For an exception to this assertion see Lindesmith, Strauss, and Denzin [1977].)

None of this is said in condemnation, however. Linguistics is a highly complex and specialized area, and much of it is not particularly relevant to the interests of interactionists.

Learning Meanings

A key to the process by which meanings are learned is to be found in rather simple and well known principles of the general psychology of learning. Following Jenkins (1969), I would suggest that the infant first makes "noises" at random, and in this vocalization he is bound to hit upon some sounds which at least his doting parents are able to recognize as being close to the sounds of words in the language they use.

They reinforce these sounds by the use of rewards that the child has learned to value—coos, smiles, food, and so forth. These rewards increase the likelihood that these sounds will be emitted in the future and that unrewarded sounds will gradually be dropped. Of course, this does not happen all at once. The child does not make the connection immediately, but given time and repetition he or she will finally catch on that a reward follows the utterance of certain sounds.

In the early stages, the primary rewards we have noted must follow the utterances. However, through simple conditioning the noises themselves can become rewarding—even in the absence of primary reinforcement. An infant can feel a pleasurable response to his or her own vocalizations because in the past those sounds were associated with actions of others which led to satisfaction. Of course, ultimately the connection between the conditioned stimulus and response would be broken if the primary reinforcements never occurred, but we may assume that they will be forthcoming at least intermittently.

At this point the infant may make sounds which more or less approximate the words of some language, but in fact he or she does not "know" any words. We may assume that there is an awareness that in some mysterious way sounds are associated with pleasure, but as yet the words are, in the usual sense of the term, meaningless—they do not refer to any specific things. "Mama" is something nice to hear that brings rewards, and that is its meaning to the child. It does not mean female parent, or "that thing that feeds me," or anything else along that line.

The next step, and it is an enormous one, occurs when the child starts to attach sounds to objects and concepts. The exact chronology is not clear, but it seems likely that this begins to occur when the caretakers begin to react to the child's sounds with more than simple approval. When they begin to present the objects which they think the infant is asking for, they have started their child on the road to the learning of their language. When "ba" calls forth both a smile and a ball, the groundwork is being laid for learning the meaning of the word "ba."

Particularly if the parents withhold the ball until he says "ba," the child will soon come to understand that he will get the ball *if* he says "ba." If he does, he will have acquired a shared symbol. Henceforth he will know how to communicate his desire for the ball through a symbol, and his parent will have some idea of what the symbol means. Sophisticated role taking is not necessary. He doesn't need to understand that the parent paired "ba" and the ball because they wanted him to say "ba" when he wanted the ball. If he understood his parents' wishes and intentions, communication and learning would be easier, but that is not necessary at this point. All that is required is that he be able to predict the reaction, and this he is capable of doing. The only requirement is a fairly simple associational learning.

Sharpening Meanings. Even when this connection is made, it is likely that the child's understanding of the word does not parallel that of its parents. In the child's mind, "ba" may include eggs and a variety of other objects which are roughly round in shape, or it might encompass all red things, if that is the aspect of the ball the child focuses on. The "proper" distinctions will be made, the child will begin to realize that an egg is not a "ba," when he tries to get an egg by saying "ba" and gets the ball.

If the reinforcing, selecting, and connecting of randomly emitted sounds were the only ways by which words were learned and their meanings refined, the process of acquiring a vocabulary would be even longer and more difficult than it is. However, the task is simplified by the fact that by the time the child is ready to learn words, the ability to imitate has made its appearance and begun to develop.[1]

The tendency of the child to imitate gives the parents or other caretakers a powerful aid in their efforts to teach words. They do not need to wait until the child emits what they consider to be a recognizable word. They can lead him or her to produce desired sounds by uttering them and by providing reward when sufficiently accurate imitation occurs.

At first this process will be supplementary to that previously discussed, but when it is well established it is likely to take precedence. It is particularly useful in sharpening distinctions. The parent can teach the difference between ball and egg by presenting examples of each along with the proper words. Reward will be made conditional on proper imitation. If the child insists on calling the egg "ba" he will get neither. Proper imitation does not ensure that the child will focus on the same characteristics as the parent, but he will finally get the point.

The importance of imitation is even clearer when we realize that although the infant has a wide range of sounds available, some of those to which "we" have decided to attach meaning are not frequently emitted spontaneously, and most of our important words contain a complex combination of sounds. When would Linda ever learn that her sister's name is Elizabeth Gwen if she had to wait until she spontaneously emitted something approximating that? And if this did happen, what assurance would there be that Elizabeth Gwen would be available to be associated with her name?

Obviously, the first imitations are not going to be very accurate. Just as the meanings are going to be only approximate, so will the pronunciation. At the beginning, the parents will probably accept these approximations and even use them themselves. I've known a number of people who were saddled with ridiculous nicknames because their parents thought their younger siblings' first approximation of their names was so cute that the parents themselves adopted it! In most instances, however, as the child matures somewhat the parents will not be satisfied with baby talk, and they will begin to withhold their approval until the child comes closer to standard pronunciation. Gradually the baby talk will be extinguished and mature speech will develop.

Extending Meanings. It should now be clear how meanings in the narrow sense are learned, but as I suggested at the outset, the meanings of things go beyond simple dictionary definitions. A ball is more than a round object called by a particular name.

[1] It would take us too far afield to discuss the development of the ability to imitate. It should be noted, however, that imitative ability typically begins by the age of two months and is fairly well developed by the time the infant begins to learn a vocabulary at the end of the first year. (For a detailed discussion of the development of imitative behavior see Parton, 1976.)

The meaning of a ball includes the act of throwing, catching, hitting, and so on. A snake is not simply a kind of animal; for many, its meaning includes reactions of disgust and fear. How are these wider meanings learned?

The mechanisms should be familiar to you by now. When socializing agents are attaching words to objects, they are also likely to present certain attitudes. The parent does not merely point out a snake—he or she may recoil from it, and the child is likely to perceive that reaction and adopt it. Parents say ball, throw it, and encourage the child to catch it. Or a child may have gotten the idea that a ball is something that one puts in one's mouth. In many cases, parents will try to discourage such practices, and thus a child learns the proper use of a ball. Whatever the details of the matter, the appropriate responses and attitudes are taught along with the labels. This happens to such an extent that a word brings forth a mental picture of an object *and* images of "proper" use and "proper" attitudes.

Further Advances. Once the process is established and the child gets the idea of what it is all about, he or she is then prepared to make rapid strides. Later vocabulary learning is quite similar to the processes I have described. There are, however, differences in detail. Among the major differences are:

1. The imitative mechanism becomes central and the earlier method falls into disuse. The parents no longer wait until the child utters a particular sound that is used in the language they speak. They name things and the child imitates them.

2. The learning of words soon carries its own reward. The parents may still praise the child for learning, but this is no longer essential. The child is now motivated to learn words, and the very act of getting them right becomes pleasurable.

3. The child begins to take a more active part in the process. He does not wait for the parent to decide to teach a new word; he asks "What is this?"

4. After awhile there is no certainty that the child will accept the meaning offered by the parent. What the parent labels as dirty the child may consider delightful; what the parent considers to be a member of the food category the child may insist is totally unpalatable.

5. The role taking becomes more sophisticated. The child begins to understand what the parents want him to do, and he can predict better what they will do if he complies.

6. New words can be defined in terms of words already known; the referent no longer needs to be presented. This is particularly important for learning abstract concepts and the attitudes which are to be associated with things.

7. Other socializing agents, such as siblings, peers, and ultimately, school teachers, became increasingly important.

ROLE TAKING

The terms "taking the role of the other," "taking the attitude of the other," and "role taking" all refer to the same human capacity—the ability to put oneself in the place of others through the use of imagination, to see things with their eyes, and on the basis of these imaginings to predict how they will react.[2] Often, the "thing" of interest is the actor himself. We want to guess how other is going to react to us, and in order to do that we must look at our own actions from his or her perspective. This form of role taking is called reflexive (Turner, 1956). The subject of role taking may, however, be any object. We are taking the role of the other whenever we ask ourselves how other is going to define "this" and what the reaction to that definition will be. The referent for "this" can be any "thing." If the subject is not actor the role taking is nonreflexive.

Animal "Role Taking"

As far as we can tell, the lower animals do not take the roles of others in the same sense that humans do, although the differences are at least as subtle as those between human and animal "languages." Lower animals can predict the behavior of other organisms, but it is probable that the process by which they do so is basically different from human role taking. Animals know when others are going to attack because they can recognize certain natural signs of attack which they have observed in their own behavior or in that of previous others. In addition, through conditioning by a human agent, additional events can be transformed into recognizable signs of things to come.

Although quite impressive, these abilities lack several of the characteristics which distinguish role taking. For one thing, the range of attitudes that can be guessed is markedly different in humans and animals, and so are the number of cues that can be used. The latter is due to the oft-cited inability of animals to use symbols. Signs are fixed in number and if the organism can take cues only from signs, the information which will be available is, of necessity, limited. Associated with this is the absence of an interpretative stage in the "role taking" of animals. Animals react directly to the stimuli; it may even be inappropriate to say that they are predicting the other's future action for that implies a greater degree of consciousness than animals probably possess. They have learned or know instinctively a series of connections between stimuli and responses, but in a true sense they may be said to act unthinkingly. Humans, on the other hand, think about the symbolic cues they are picking up, and they consider their meanings, connotations, and subtleties. The feints of a dog in a dog fight and those of a boxer may have superficial similarity, but they are based on basically different processes.

We should not, however, permit ourselves to become overly impressed by human ability in this regard. The process of role taking always involves guessing; thus there is always a good chance of error. Even when other tells us exactly what

---

[2] Many, myself included, would consider *empathy* to be another synonym. However, some authors limit that term to cases in which actors put themselves in the place of other *and* feel sympathy for him or her (Shibutani, 1965). Role taking carries no connotation of sympathy, and to prevent confusion I will avoid the use of the term *empathy*.

he or she thinks or plans to do, we can never be sure it is not a lie. As a group we are rather adept at it, but accuracy in role taking is never a foregone conclusion.

Traditional symbolic interactionists have focused on the question "How does the individual develop the ability to take the role of the other?" Brief attention will be devoted to that question and then we will turn to the issue which is more central to the version of interactionism being presented here: "What accounts for individual differences in the accuracy with which actors takes others' roles?"

The Early Development of Role-Taking Ability

It is not difficult to guess the basic sources of a child's motivation to learn to take the role of the other. Without this ability, the social world must seem to be an unpredictable, uncontrollable, and therefore frustrating place. For example, at an early age the child wants to do what the parent desires, but how can he do that if the intentions of the parent cannot be judged? At an equally early age, children want to "tell" their parents and others what they want, but how can that be accomplished if they don't know what impression they are making on the parent; if they don't know what the parents understand by the sounds and motions they are making? That this is frustrating cannot be doubted by anyone who has seen the rages that children can build up when they cannot communicate their wishes.

The child begins to get help in this matter when he starts to note that certain acts precede other acts. He is bound to notice that the mother always puts him in the highchair before she feeds him or always smiles before she cuddles him. Just as in lower animals, these preliminary acts come to be signs which allow the child to know what is coming next. Similarly, the child will note that whenever he cries he gets fed, and after awhile he will be able to predict what effect his cry will have on the parent.

Learning to Deduce Intentions. At this point the child has no appreciation of intentions. All he knows is that certain things follow other things. But that is no small achievement. It may not work as well as role taking based on inferred intentions, but it does provide a basis for predicting others' behavior.

As Shibutani (1961) suggests, the child's early attempts to figure out intentions are probably based on projection. It is not so much that the child is putting himself in the place of the other, but rather that he assumes that their observable behavior represents the same intentions that similar behavior on his part represents for him. Even if the conception of "I want that" is very nebulous—and it would certainly be so at this stage—he may conclude that his parents want an object when he notes them reaching for it, because that is what he does when he wants something.

This, too, represents an advance, although it will not get the child very far. Parents and children are too different in the ways that they express their intentions as well as in the actions they take based on those intentions. In the "projection stage," the child will very often be wrong, and there will be many things that will be totally undecipherable.

Again, as Shibutani notes, when children's facility with language is being established, role taking enters a new realm. They now have a much more efficient way of learning what people will do. Others can state their intentions and be understood. Conversely, children can be more accurate in their guesses about the effect their actions will have on others. Through the use of language the others can forewarn the child what they will do if he does a particular thing. Furthermore, the child's ability to explain what he is doing will decrease the likelihood that he will guess incorrectly because the other misunderstood the child's intentions.

Learning to Deduce Feelings. Inner states and feelings are probably a bit more difficult to grasp than are intentions, but with language the child will learn to handle such abstract concepts and thereby add to his ability to take roles by making inferences. As parents ask "Are you angry?" or say "You're overtired," the child develops an ability to identify the states to which these terms refer because he will be experiencing them—assuming that the parents themselves are adequate role takers. When the child has tied his own feelings to words, he will then be able to understand what others are feeling when they use those same terms to describe themselves. When children become aware of what they do when they feel a particular way, they will be able to predict what others will do when they are told that the others feel that way.

At this point the child can recognize intentions, inner states, and feelings if they are specifically announced by the others. He knows how they feel and what those feelings lead to. But something is still lacking. An adult does not have to be "told" that someone is angry to know that that is the case. He can recognize the signs of anger. This is, of course, very important, for often the other does not "cooperate" by explicitly stating his feelings.

The child's ability to recognize the signs of inner states begins when he notes that particular events are associated with the announcement that a state exists. The child will begin to know that sitting bleary-eyed in front of the TV set is a sign of tiredness when he notes that his father says he is tired when he is doing that. Or, alternatively, he may make the connection between overt behavior and an inner state if he recognizes that an action of an other is the same as his own actions when he is feeling a particular way. Regardless of how the connection is made, once it is made the child will be capable of guessing other's feelings without an explicit statement by other or some third person. Some overt action will serve as a cue.

Roles and Role Taking. The focus until now has been on role taking based upon inferred intentions and feelings. It should be obvious, however, that something has been omitted—role taking based on inferences involving roles. A role is a prescription that says people of type X should do Y in situation Z, and we use our knowledge of the content of roles to predict other's behavior. Just as we guess that certain actions will take place because we believe they are consistent with a particular emotion, we also reason that actions will occur because we believe they are consistent with the role prescriptions people hold.

The process involved here is quite the same as the later stages of the process just described. Others are labeled for the child by terms which refer to their identities, and he is taught that those kinds of people tend to abide by these rules for behavior. He is told, "I am your mother, and mommies love their children." Many behaviors and feelings will be tied to the identity of mother, and in the future the child will "know" that certain behaviors are more likely than others because mothers "act that way." And, as time goes on, the child will not need to have other's identity and role spelled out. He will know the signs that indicate particular identities, and he will know the roles that go with them. Again, at the beginning skill will be low—young children seem to assume, for example, that all females over fifteen years of age are mothers. But time and experience will correct that misconception.

Play. In Mead's (1934) view, play is an important activity in which a child practices taking the role of the other. Play, as it is understood here, refers to a particular kind of recreational activity which may more clearly be called play acting or pretending. The child acts as he or she believes someone else would act. A certain degree of role-taking ability is a prerequisite to pretending. You cannot pretend unless you can put yourself in the place of another and "figure out" what the person would do under particular circumstances.

Two types of play should be recognized: *solitary play*, in which one child plays all the roles, and *group play*, in which several children each remain, more or less, in one role.

Solitary play is in some respects more complex than group play because the child must act out many parts. "The child says something in one character, and responds in another character, and then his responding in another character is a stimulus to himself in the first character, and so the conversation goes on" (Mead, 1934: 151). The child is playing at roles, but beyond this must lie the ability to take the role of the other. How else would he or she "know" what B should say after A has spoken?

Solitary play provides the opportunity for practicing role taking, and it probably increases the likelihood that the child will take roles in real life. Unlike other forms of practice, however, solitary practice does not make perfect. Due to limited experience and incompletely developed intellectual capacity, the child is likely to be pretty far off the mark in his play acting. In solitary play no one is present to correct the mistakes, and thus its utility is limited.

Obviously, the child needs someone to direct his play, and in group play another child can serve this function. We have all seen children arguing over who is "doing it right." The trouble with this, of course, is that none of them may know very much about the "right way." At a minimum, however, the child will learn that various people see things differently, and this realization is of great importance if there is to be accuracy.

Adults are often of greater help in turning play into a valuable learning experience. They do this in part by actually participating with the children, but even when they are not playing *with* their children, parents observe it and correct it.

In fact, parents are often the "court" to which the disputing children bring their disagreements.

In the usual case, of course, parents correct the *overt act* that emerges from inaccurate role taking. They don't react to the role taking itself. However, a child does not have to be extraordinarily bright to soon realize that his or her flawed performance resulted from errors in perceiving the attitudes which are proper for the kind of person he is pretending to be.

Important as play is, its significance should not be exaggerated. Play illustrates the practicing of role taking, but such practice is by no means limited to play situations. "What goes on in the game goes on in the life of the child all the time. He is continually taking the attitudes of those about him, especially the roles of those who in some sense control him and on whom he depends" (Mead, 1934: 160).

In this real-life interaction the child will get the most important lessons. Here there is much at stake and he or she is likely to be more attentive. To role-take poorly in play usually does not have very great consequences, but in real life there are goals to be reached and punishments to be avoided, and some degree of accuracy is required to attain these ends. In addition, play is not crucial because play acting presumes some prior ability at role taking. The original source of the ability is not to be found in play. It is merely an activity that gives opportunity for practice.

Games and the Generalized Other. By the time the child reaches this point, he has learned the *a-b-c*s of role taking. Much of what happens afterwards involves refinement and improvement through processes which are only more complex versions of the basic mechanisms I have been describing. There is, however, one aspect of adult role taking which is rather different from that which the child can perform at an early age.

As far as we have taken him, the child has the capacity to take the role of particular others, but much adult interaction requires more than this. Frequently, actors interact with several others simultaneously, and actor must put himself in the place of these several others to figure out what they, as a group, are thinking and are likely to do. Actors must take the role of the *generalized other*.

But it even goes beyond that. In some cases the generalized other includes people who are not physically present in the interaction situation. "In politics, for example, the individual identifies himself with an entire political party and takes the organized attitudes of that entire party" (Mead, 1934: 156). In the most extreme case the actor will ask, "What will people think?" and here the generalized other is even broader. It includes all people or at least that indefinite group whose opinions matter (Quarantelli and Cooper, 1966).

Mead's famous example of taking the role of the generalized other involves a discussion of the activities of a baseball player. Before a second baseman, for example, can decide what to do when a ground ball is hit to him and there are runners on first and second, he must take the roles of the runners, all the infielders, and—to some degree—the outfielders, both managers, the fans, and the sportswriters. He must know what they, as a group, will do, and what they will expect him to do before he can decide what base to throw to.

This should simply be taken as an illustration that typifies the situation. The ability to take the role of the generalized other does not, of course, come about through participation in organized games. Typically, that ability is there before actors have any experience in such activities, and many people who show no difficulties engaging in this form of role taking have never engaged in organized games. I wonder, in fact, whether games teach us much, since the content of the role taking is so different from real life. I would think that role acting in multiperson groups would be more effective.

In any case, to specify the arena in which the ability is demonstrated neither explains what it involves nor how it develops. I believe that some idea of what goes on can be obtained by considering taking the role of the generalized other as an elaboration, extension, and generalization of taking the role of a particular other. Although the essence of generalized other role taking is that particular individuals are not foremost in the role taker's mind, actor's conception of the generalized other is based ultimately on his beliefs about the attitudes of particular persons or categories of persons. These concrete notions are organized and generalized into a view of the whole.

Teaching, if it is done well, involves a great deal of generalized other role taking. Unless a teacher is "playing to" particular students, he or she must constantly ask, "Do they (the students in general) understand what I am saying?" "Will they be offended by that slightly risque example?" If the class is small and the students are well known, the basic judgment will be of the probable reactions of each of them. More usually, the conception will be based upon knowledge of the categories which are probably represented in the class and prior knowledge of how those categories react: "The good students will understand; the poor ones will not." "The feminists will consider it sexist; the traditionalists will think it funny." These separate guesses will then be organized into a composite, which will permit an answer to questions such as, "Did *they* understand?"

In some cases, other tell us the response tendencies of a category of people, but in the absence of such teaching we abstract and generalize from particular cases. We conceptualize the general characteristics of a category of people from knowledge of particular individuals in that category. When we are trying to develop a view of a group which has several categories in it, we also generalize from knowledge of the components of the group. In this case, however, we use our view of the characteristics of the categories as the units for our inferences.

It must be emphasized that in developing this notion of the generalized other, we look for the common core, but we do not suppress all knowledge of variation. The answer to "What will they think?" is not likely to be, simply, "They will accept." More common would be: "Most will think I did right, but a few, particularly the 'Xs,' will consider me to be immoral." A conception of the generalized other which implies unanimity of attitude among the others would often be inconsistent with reality, and lead to inappropriate actions. Usually we must work from central tendencies, predominant views, and so forth.

As was the case with taking individual roles, there is going to be a great deal of error—particularly at the beginning. But also as before, the events which follow the role taking will tell the actor whether he guessed incorrectly, and they will provide him with some indications of how to correct errors if they were made. If there is a flurry of hands waving to ask questions, I may see that not even the good students understand, and a dead silence would suggest that a joke was neither offensive nor funny. Such evidence will permit role taking to be a little more effective the next time.

Accuracy in Role Taking

The processes I have been describing are experienced by all "normally socialized" people, and the resultant ability to take the role of the other is a universal characteristic of all normal people. Role-taking *accuracy* is, however, clearly variable. Some people are, in general, better at it, and a particular actor's accuracy will vary depending on the situation and the identity of the other. For example, an actor who can role take for an other relatively well when a particular matter is involved may do less well with the same person when the subject is different. What is needed is a theory to account for such variation. What determines the accuracy with which actors take other's role?

The key to the needed theory lies in the realization that role taking is not a semimystical process by which one individual in some way enters the "mind" of another. Role taking is a mundane process of guessing. It must be emphasized, however, that the guessing is informed rather than blind. We all assume a certain degree of consistency in human behavior, and we use our previous experience as a basis for a guess or hypothesis about the probable actions of the present other.

If this is the nature of role taking, two basic propositions would follow. Role taking should be more accurate

1. the greater the amount of relevant information available to actor,[3]
2. and the greater actor's ability to deduce the implications of that information for the present situation.

This being the case, the question then becomes what factors affect the amount of useful information and what affects actor's generalizing abilities. Let's consider each in turn.

Types of Information. As a first step in the discussion of the factors related to the store of relevant information available for role taking, it should be noted that the kinds of information used are quite variable (Turner, 1956). In rare instances we begin with no relevant knowledge of the other and no familiarity with the situation. In such circumstances, our guesses at the start of the interaction are based on hunches. Cases in which we have familiarity with the situation, but no knowledge

[3] The reader should not overlook the qualifier. As Jones and Thibaut (1958) note, not all information is equally useful, and redundant or irrelevant information has been shown to cause confusion and to reduce role-taking accuracy.

of the other are somewhat easier. In these situations, our role taking can be based upon knowledge of how some third person reacted in a comparable situation.[4] Since in most situations different people react differently, role taking based on this kind of information is likely to be rather inaccurate. The lack of familiarity with the other implies actor cannot identify him, and thus there is no basis for deciding which third person to use as a guide. Under these circumstances, actor is likely to be forced to reason from estimates of what "most people" or the "typical person" would do. This kind of role taking will be successful only when most people react to a situation in a similar way.

Luckily, the situations just described are quite rare. In real life we usually have information about the other which at least permits us to categorize him or her. If nothing else, the other's appearance will help, and before the encounter has gone very far we are certain to be provided with additional useful data. When we can identify the other, the possibility of accurate role taking is increased even if he or she is a stranger. If we are familiar with the situation, we can base our guesses on our previous experience in such situations with people who resembled the "target other"–the person whose role actor is taking.[5] Such role taking is, in fact, stereo-typing. We assume that people who share certain characteristics will react similarly. It is, of course, not a very good way to role take because people with the same characteristics show a variety of reactions. Nonetheless, stereotyping as used here should not be given the negative connotations it usually has. It is a legitimate way of taking other's role, and when actor's knowledge of other is very limited stereotyping is the most effective way of doing so. This, of course, assumes that the stereotyping is reasonably adequate—an assumption which is not valid for many of the stereotypes that people hold.[6]

When other is a stranger, the actor bases his or her role taking on knowledge of persons other than the target other. I have referred to these persons as third persons, but it should be noted that the "third person" may in fact be the actor. Actor may use knowledge of his own reactions as a basis for deciding what other will do. If this is done, actor is actually projecting, that is, attributing his own feelings to other people.

Useful as they may be when there is limited information about other, stereotypes and projection are by their very nature of limited value in role taking. Although

[4]There are, of course, several ways that an actor can become familiar with a situation without having actually been in it. One can gain familiarity by observing others in that situation or by having been told about it.

[5]Of course, if actor has had no previous experience with people such as the target other, or no experience with such people in comparable situations, actor's ability to classify other will do little good. Identifying the other does not ensure that one will be able to do more than use vague notions of typical responses and blind guesses. The categorization of other is, however, a prerequisite for adequate role taking.

[6]The more detailed and accurate the information which is the basis for the stereotype and the more specific the definition of the group to which it applies, the more useful it is likely to be.

it is true that people within a particular category will show more uniformity of behavior than a random collection of people, assuming that the classification traits are
relevant, it is still certain that there will be great differences in reaction within any
category system we set up.[7]

A marked improvement in accuracy would occur when we can base our prediction on information about the target other's reaction tendencies. Knowledge of the
other's role definitions or of his reaction in a comparable situation would be of most
value, but neither is essential. If we know enough about his or her reactions in "other"
situations, we can deduce what the probable reaction will be in the situation under
consideration. On the other hand, knowledge of roles or of reactions in similar situations does not free the role taker from the need of making a judgment and corrections.
No two situations are completely comparable and people do change. A reaction to a
request given two minutes previously will not, by itself, permit perfect prediction of
the next reaction to such a request, for the fact that the first request had occurred is
an element in the causal chain of the second reaction. We may be perfectly agreeable
to a first request, but reject a second because "we have already done our part," for
example. Nonetheless, to know the other is a great advantage.

In summary: *All other things being equal, role taking will be most accurate
when it is based upon information about the target other's roles and previous actions
in comparable situations, somewhat less accurate when it is based upon stereotypes
or projection, and least accurate when actor cannot classify the target and/or is unfamiliar with the situation.* The notion is that the more directly applicable the actor's
information, the less the need for extension, inference, generalization, and correction
for changed circumstances, the more accurate the prediction. It seems fairly clear that
the need for these decreases as one goes from the first kind of data to the last.

At least indirectly, the evidence supports this ranking. Cline (1964) reports, for
example, that persons who viewed target others in a filmed interview could predict
their responses to a questionnaire more accurately than could people who were simply
told some of the social characteristics of the other. Further, simply knowing that the
subjects were college students was shown in another study (Cline, 1955) to result in
better than chance accuracy. Although observation of film is hardly the equivalent
of true interaction, it did provide information about the target other, and this proved
to be a better basis for role taking than the use of stereotypes. Stereotypes were,
however, better than "nothing."

Quantity of Information. People who base their judgments on information
about the other will do better than people who use other kinds of information, but

---

[7]Although the use of stereotypes and projection is most common when we are not acquainted with the other whose role we are taking, it is not limited to such situations. The results
of Calonico and Thomas' 1973 study of family groups suggest that we use stereotypes and projection even with intimates. We are likely to resort to these processes whenever we have no basis
for knowing or deducing other's view of the matter at hand. This condition is, of course, most
likely to occur with strangers.

among the former, the more information, the better the predictions. The question then becomes what influences the store of information about the target other?

The first relevant factor is obvious and therefore not particularly interesting. It would seem clear that all other things being equal, the greater the amount of previous interaction between actor and other, the greater the store of information. It is not simply a matter of frequency of interaction; numerous short interactions, such as saying good morning everyday, may give us less information than a single long interaction. Amount should be thought of in terms of total time spent together.

No one has ever actually measured amount of interaction in these terms and related it to accuracy, but there are data which approach the issue indirectly by using variables which may be taken as indices of amount of interaction. It is reasonable to assume, for example, that on the average, married couples will have had the most interaction and "just dating" couples the least. Thus, it is not surprising that role-taking accuracy is greater at higher levels of courtship progress and in marriage. (See Lewis, 1972, for a summary of several studies of this type.) In addition, Vernon and Stewart (1957) used number of dates as an index of amount of interaction and found a direct relation between frequency of dating and accuracy.

It is important to note, however, that this relationship may not be as simple as it appears to be. Some data (Udry et al., 1961) show that accuracy does *not* increase with increasing length of marriage and Kirkpatrick and Hobart (1954) found no relation between length of time in a courtship status and accuracy; that is, people who had gone steady for a long time were not more accurate than those who had gone steady for a shorter time. The data available do not settle the issue, but it is quite possible that the relation between extent of interaction and accuracy requires qualification. There is little doubt that a relation exists, but there are probably limits to it.

Why this is so is not entirely clear, but two explanations have been offered. Foote and Cottrell (1955: 72) seem to suggest that after awhile we "stop listening." "There is a crucial point beyond which closer contact with another person will no longer lead to an increase in (accuracy). . .When others are too constantly present, the organism appears to develop a protective resistance to responding to them." Jones and Thibaut (1958), on the other hand, suggest that the problem is continuing to gather information which turns out to be redundant or irrelevant, and operates to "clog the channels."

This points to a second important factor influencing accuracy, that is, the pertinence of previous interaction. If the interaction is irrelevant to the issue at hand, its utility would be limited. There is perhaps a germ of truth in the oft-stated proposition that you never know beforehand how a soldier will react to combat! Thus, persons who have had extensive interaction with the other in interactions comparable to the present one, will be more accurate than those who have known the other in different kinds of situations; and people who have varied interactions with the other will do better than those who have known the person in less varied settings—assuming, of course, that those few settings were not the same or similar to the present one. Within limits, the greater the sample we have of other's reactions, the greater the possibility that we will have information which will permit an accurate inference to the present case.

These two factors—extent and pertinence of previous interaction—are probably the major determinants of the amount of useful information actors will have available for role-taking activities, but they are not the only relevant factors. With extent and pertinence of interaction held constant, there will still be differences in the store of available information; the amount of information carried away from a particular interaction will vary.

In general, the factors which account for differences in the amount of relevant information gained from an interaction of a particular type fall into these four categories:

1. Characteristics of the actor
2. Characteristics of the other
3. Characteristics of the situation
4. Characteristics of the relation between actor and other

Let us now consider each of these in turn.

Characteristics of the Actor.   All other things being equal, the better the actor's memory, the greater the store of useful information he or she will have. We all forget some of the information we have gathered in our interaction, but we do so at different rates. Clearly, then, a retentive memory will give a person an advantage in role taking. In fact, since in most interactions the information must be retrieved very rapidly to be useful, both a quick *and* a retentive memory are decided assets.

However, in order for something to be remembered it first must be learned, and just because information is there to be gathered does not mean that it will be "picked up." Among the characteristics of an actor that will influence the amount of information gathered from a particular interaction is the level of his or her motivation to learn such material. Some people, because of their personalities, are eager to learn the wishes and expectations of others. Therefore, they should be more attentive to the "data" being provided by the other, and those who are more attentive should learn more (see Bandura, 1977).

This category would include those people who are particularly interested in receiving the approval of others. (We receive approval by doing what others wish or expect, and we can only do that if we know what they want.) Actors also differ in the level of their interest in people and in their concern with "what makes people tick." People with such interests should gather more information solely for the intellectual satisfaction it gives them.[8]

---

[8] Hidden in this is a small deductive system of the kind urged by Homans (see page 22). People with certain personality traits (A) are more likely to be interested in wishes and expectations of others (B); people who are interested in such things (B) are more attentive to the information being given out (C); people who are more attentive (C), learn more (D); and people who learn more (D) are more accurate (E). Therefore, people with certain personality traits (A) will be more accurate (E).

Another factor affecting attentiveness would be the extent to which a person has a need for information from external sources to structure his or her experience and action. The distinction has been conceptualized in a variety of ways; Riesman's (1950) categories of inner-directed and other-directed persons are clearly relevant. He assumes that some people (the inners) are relatively autonomous, while the other-directed do not "know who they are" until someone tells them, and do not know what to do until they get directions. Such people would have a greater need to take the role of others, not particularly because they want to please the others, although that may also be true, but primarily because taking the role of the other will provide the guidelines they need for their own behavior. Of course, it is a basic notion of social psychology that we are all to some extent other-directed, but this does not deny the fact that there are wide variations in the extent to which this is true.

Witkin (1972; Witkin et al., 1962) makes a distinction between field-dependent and field-independent people which seems ultimately to focus on degree of need for direction. The concepts refer in the first instance to differences in cognitive style—specifically, the extent to which perceptions of things are influenced by the overall field in which they are placed. But cognitive styles are "manifestations, in the cognitive sphere, of still broader dimensions of personal functioning. . . .Cognitive styles thus speak on more than cognition" (Witkin, 1967: 234).

It seems to work out that the dependents and independents differ in the degree to which they segregate self and nonself. Those who see themselves as sharply differentiated from others (the field-independent types) are less likely to look to others for guidance. They have a sense of separation from their environment and therefore probably don't feel a great need to fit in or to mesh their action with others. They would not feel it so important to know what others want and expect. The field-dependent feels himself to be part of a system, and has a need to know what others are doing, lest he unknowingly throw a monkey wrench into the system.

There are in fact some data which suggest rather clearly that the field dependent seek to gather more information from others. For example, they spend more time looking at the faces of people with whom they interact (Konstadt and Forman, 1965; Neville, 1974; Ruble and Nakamura, 1972); they prefer to be physically close to others (Justice, 1969; Greene, 1973); and they are more likely to seek out other people and enjoy their company (Loveless, 1972; Sousa-Poza and Rohrberg, 1976).

We would also expect that the field dependent would get more information because they would be more likely to explicitly request directions, but on this the evidence is mixed. One study (Alexander and Gudeman, 1965) shows a strong tendency for the field dependent to ask for help when faced with a difficult task, but an earlier study (Elliott, 1961) found little or no correlation. Several other studies show, however, that when others express an opinion, the field dependents are more likely to make use of it (Birmingham, 1974; Busch and DeRidder, 1973; Paeth, 1973).

Earlier, we noted the possibility that too much information may lead to decreased accuracy rather than to an increase, particularly if much of the information is not very relevant. It would seem, then, that actors who are properly selective in their information gathering—those who focus on the important matters and overlook the irrelevant—will have an advantage, particularly when there is much information available. This tendency would be related to the validity of the actor's "implicit personality theory." Although most people would be hard-pressed to specify what causes human behavior, it seems reasonable to postulate that all of us have certain ideas about what those underlying causes are. Given different "theories," different things are of most interest. Some people seem to be interested only in other people's astrological signs; others are constantly looking for "Freudian slips" as a key to the unconscious processes which they believe are the major causes of behavior. Some are particularly sensitive to physical traits, while others are most concerned with their interaction partners' self-concepts and role definitions. The relative utility of the various approaches need not be debated; my bias in the matter is certainly obvious by now. The point is simply that there are clearly better and worse theories, and one who uses a better theory will collect information that is more useful for role taking.

Characteristics of the Other. As in all interaction processes, to focus only upon the actor and what he or she brings to the situation is inadequate. Among other things, one must take into account the nature of the other.

In role taking, an important characteristic of the other is his or her degree of "openness." No matter how highly motivated actor is to gather information about other, the effort will have only limited success if other attempts to hide true feelings from actor or if attempts are made to mislead. As I will suggest in the following paragraphs, the extent to which others give clues about their beliefs and probable actions largely depends upon the situation and their relation to the actors. However, there is reason to believe that people tend to show some consistency in the degree to which they are open with others and that categories of people can be described as being more or less willing to "expose" themselves. Jourard (1971), for example, found that females disclose more than males and whites disclose more than blacks. This would suggest that, all other things being equal, actors would role take more accurately when the other was female or white, for as Lewis' (1967) study showed, it is true that self-disclosure by other is associated with more accurate role taking.

But, as before, the *availability* of information does not ensure that the information will be picked up. If the other is being open, but actor does not perceive that to be the case, he or she is likely to learn less than would be the case when there is an assumption of openness. And to carry it a step further, Jones' (1961) findings suggest that people who act idiosyncratically are thought to be more open. When people act along conventional lines, others have less confidence in their knowledge of them than when they act "out-of-role." Not all conventional behavior is viewed as a cover-up, but the assumption is that no one who wanted to deceive would act "oddly." This is not to say that people fail to note conventional behavior; it is simply that nonconventional behavior is more likely to be attended to because it is more likely to be considered significant. More information will be gathered when other acts unconventionally.

Closely related to openness, but somewhat different, would be the degree to which the other explains the reasons for his or her actions. This point was made by

Kerckhoff (1969) regarding the factors conducive to the early development of role taking, but its significance is not limited to that situation. Some people are "complainers" and some are "explainers," and both kinds—probably without realizing it—make it easier for people to take their roles. Actor does not need to figure out motivations and intentions—they are *told* to him.

Finally, I would reemphasize that the concern is with relevant information, and the extent to which relevant information will be available to be learned is partly a function of the other's consistency. An other can be totally open about his feelings and still provide actor with little that can be used in role taking because by the time an occasion arises for role taking the other has changed his view and the old data are worse than useless. In some cases, the information can go out of date within the same encounter in which it was gathered. Enormous frustration sometimes lies behind the line, "But you just said. . . ."

Characteristics of the Situation. It is quite apparent that taking the role of the other is more difficult under some circumstances than others, and I would suggest that part of the reason for this is that the information needed for role taking is more easily obtained for some situations than it is for others. Such factors as physical distance and the extent of distraction may be obvious, but they are, nonetheless, important. Since some of the information used in role taking in a particular encounter is gathered in that encounter, it would follow that role taking should be less accurate when it occurs under conditions which make it difficult for actor to "see" the available cues in the situation. Since some of the role taking is based upon information gathered prior to the present interaction, it would also be the case that role taking will be diminished if the present interaction requires the actor to utilize information which was presented earlier under difficult conditions.

Somewhat similar, but sociologically more interesting, is the postulate that role taking based upon information gathered in private interaction, whether in the past or in the present, would be more accurate than that which had to rely on public information. The basis for this idea has already been laid. For one thing, there is likely to be less distance and fewer distractions when an interaction is private, and others are likely to be more open in private. Confidences, which are very important bases for accurate role taking because they reveal inner thoughts, are usually expressed in private situations. What people don't mind one person knowing they often do not want many to know.

Another relevant aspect of the interaction situation is its importance to actor. If the outcome will have significant consequences for actor, he or she is likely to want to control that outcome, and an important factor in control is the ability to take the role of the other. Thus, we end up with another factor related to motivation. When the outcome has implications for actor's rewards and punishments, he or she will be more strongly motivated to gather information about the other. And, I should add, actor probably has had more opportunity to gather information if the relationship is defined as important. When we have frequently interacted with a particular other, we are likely to begin to attribute importance to our relationship with him or her.

The subject matter of the interaction would seem to be another aspect of the situation which would affect role-taking accuracy through its effect on the amount of information gathered. All other things being equal, we are likely to have more information about certain feelings and potential actions than we have about others.

There are several bases for this connection. For one thing, there is differential openness depending upon the topic. Jourard (1971) reported that respondents most fully disclose to their parents and friends their tastes and interests in food, music, clothes, and so on. They are almost as open about their attitudes toward work, political, religious, and sexual matters, but they are reticent about attitudes toward money and feelings about their personalities and bodies.

I don't believe it is possible to present a general list of topics ranked in order of the frequency with which information about them will be disclosed. The ordering probably differs by culture, individual, and the identity of the other. For example, some matters which are supposedly taboo topics (sex, religion, and politics) are high on Jourard's disclosure list, and this is probably because the question he used referred to disclosure to people who were very close to the respondent. The list may have been different if the reference were to people who were less close.

I can, however, suggest a few principles that probably operate here. I would assume that people are most open about matters they feel are easily detected, and which, if known, are not likely to result in embarrassment or dispute, and which are not likely to act as a barrier to achievement of goals. The specific topics that these factors translate into would vary from situation to situation.

It would seem—though again, I cannot specify what they are—that certain topics come up with greater frequency in general, and particular topics are frequent issues in particular relations. For example, work mates are likely to have had many opportunities to gather information on each other's attitudes toward the boss, but fewer chances to learn about each other's religious attitudes. It would follow from the "basic amount rule" that people would be better role takers on frequently discussed issues than they are on less common matters of social interaction and conversation. This is independent of willingness to disclose information. The question is not whether other is willing to give information, but rather, whether an occasion to disclose it is likely to occur.

Nature of the Relationship between Actor and Other.   Not all important relationships are intimate, but for most of us all intimate relationships are important. That is one reason why we would expect people to gather more information per unit of time in a relationship which is characterized by affection for the other and a feeling of identification with him or her.

The effect of intimacy upon information gathering does not result only from the importance of such relationships, however. Intimacy has a complex relation to information gathering. In an intimate relationship, for example, there is likely to be a feeling of security that is not present in all important relationships. With true intimates, one doesn't have to worry too much about rejection, disputes, or embarrassment. Thus, intimacy may permit more openness. But acting to counteract this openness to some extent is the extreme importance we tend to place on intimate relationships. If the information is potentially damaging to the relationship, we may be inclined to disclose it because "she will understand," but at the same time the consequences which may follow if she doesn't understand, that is, the breaking off of the relationship, may be viewed as so horrendous that we don't dare take the chance.

There is another reason why there is a limitation on openness between intimates. Given the assumption of intimacy, many things are not said because it is believed that they do not *have* to be said. "I don't have to be explicit, because he (she) understands me completely." "I don't have to tell her I love her; she knows it." It is assumed that so much information has been shared and the ability to take the role of the other is so great that to verbalize certain things would be superfluous. Unfortunately, the degree of understanding is often exaggerated, and as many lovers can testify, misunderstanding, uncertainty, and confusion are not unknown in extremely close relationships.

All this notwithstanding, it seems that the factors making for openness in intimate relations outweigh those which limit it. When one adds the fact that intimate relations imply long duration and frequent interaction, it is not at all surprising that, as previously noted, the data show that accuracy tends to increase as people move from one stage of intimacy to the next.

For some of the same reasons we have just discussed, I would also postulate that in general one gathers more information from people one likes than from disliked others. If actor and other like each other, frequent interaction is likely to occur (Homans, 1950), and the relevance of that should be clear. Also, if actor likes other, there is a tendency for other to like actor, and other would be more open to those he or she likes. For one thing, if actor and other like each other, they are likely to agree on many things (Byrne, 1969; 1971), and agreement is an invitation to openness. As a final point, it can be noted that we generally attach more importance to relationships in which the other is liked.

Implicit in the discussion of the importance of relationships is the idea that accurate role taking is a means of controlling the actions of the other and thus is a means of affecting the outcome of the interaction. Accurate role taking gives a person the same kind of advantage that good intelligence reports give a nation. Accurate role taking allows the actor to "know" what other is likely to do and allows him or her to control the responses of other by choosing self-actions which are likely to bring forth the desired responses. However, it would seem that the advantages of accurate role taking are most important to the person who has less power. If one is superordinate and can get one's own way almost regardless of what other does, much of the motivation for accurate role taking is removed. Such people have less need to take the other into account, and thus why should they bother to gather information about him or her? The person with less power needs all the help he or she can get, and the ability to "psych out" the other may serve to even the score somewhat. Superordinate others also seem to be more open than subordinates. A subordinate must keep his thoughts to himself, while the superordinate can say what he wants without fear that it will be used against him. Thus we would expect more accurate role taking from people of lower status.

This idea is found in some of our truisms. It is generally assumed that workers know more about the boss than he or she knows about them, and the valet knows the master's mind while the master is barely aware that the valet *has* a mind. Thus, people talk before their servants as though the servants weren't there. Such beliefs are not proof of the point, but some systematic evidence does suggest that role-taking ability is inversely related to power. In most families, the father exercises the greatest power, the mother ranks next, and the children last. Among the children as a group, the older male children tend to have most power and the younger female children the least. Given this and the theoretical points just made, it is not particularly surprising to learn that Thomas, Franks, and Calonico (1972) found that the role-taking accuracy of these categories line up in exactly the opposite order. The fathers were the least accurate, the mothers, next, and so on to the younger girls who were best able to predict. The oft-reported small superiority of women's role taking may also be a function of their lower-level of power in this male-dominated society (Taft, 1955; Cline, 1964).

The Ability to Process Role-Taking Information

It is clear that differences in role-taking accuracy are not solely a reflection of differences in the amount of information possessed. People differ in their role-taking accuracy when they have the same amount of information, which suggests that they differ in their ability to handle information. We need, therefore, a theory of the sources of those differences. Before we turn to that, however, it is necessary to determine whether the ability to handle information is general or specific, stable or unstable, because a theory which deals with a phenomenon which is specific and unstable would be very different from one which deals with a general trait.

The issue involves questions such as: "Is a person who can handle one kind of information well also likely to be adept at handling other kinds of information, or do some people do well under some circumstances and others do well under different circumstances?" "Are the people who are good at handling information about religion, for example, the same people who do well when the subject is family attitudes?" "Are people who get the most from limited information the same as those who can do well when there is a lot of data?"

It must be emphasized that no one expects a particular person to do equally well under all circumstances. We consider a trait to be general and stable if, as compared with other people, an actor who does *relatively* well with information from person A also does relatively well with person B, even if his or her rates of success for A and B are quite different.

The data bearing upon questions such as these are numerous and complex (Cline, 1964; Taft, 1955), and this does not seem to be the place to go into them in detail. Perhaps it will suffice to note that the evidence suggests that each of the questions posed above should be answered in a way that is consistent with the notion of generality. People who do well tend to do relatively well regardless of who the other is and what the topic is. At the same time, it must be noted that there are many exceptions. The correlations are usually not very high.

Allport's conclusion of over forty years ago (1937: 512, cited in Taft, 1955) still seems an accurate summary of our knowledge in this regard. The ability to judge people is analogous to artistic ability in that it is neither entirely general nor entirely specific. "It would be unreasonable, therefore, to expect a judge of people to be uniformly successful in estimating every quality of every person. . . .It seems more of an error, however, to consider the ability entirely specific than to consider it entirely general."[9]

It appears possible, then, to present a single theory which contains postulates to the effect that people with this characteristic will tend to handle role-taking information more adequately than people with different traits. At this point in the development of the theory, it does not appear necessary to have separate postulates for different kinds of information, different others, and so on.

Intelligence and Role-Taking Ability. In considering such a theory, one immediately wonders if role-taking ability is related to general intelligence, for the two seem to have some things in common. "The process of judging people is, like intelligence itself, a matter of discerning the relevance of cues, the relations between past and present activities, between cause and effect" (Allport, 1961; 507-508). Data suggest that, in fact, this similarity does exist. Quoting Allport (1961: 507) again, "Most studies discover that some relationship exists between superior intelligence and the ability to judge others. The positive correlation holds even within the narrow range of intelligence that characterizes the selected judges used in most experiments." There is some contradictory evidence, but studies usually find correlations in the .20 to .50 range (Taft, 1955).

Processing Information. Just as with other abilities, however, achievement in role taking is not simply a result of general intelligence. It seems likely that with general ability and amount of information held constant, there will be orderly variation in the effectiveness with which the information is used.

A key factor is the extent to which actor and other share a universe of discourse. The material which is gathered must be understood before its implications can be deduced, and in this case the use of the same language does not ensure that the actor will fully understand the sometimes subtle meanings that the information contains. However, if actor and other share a common universe of discourse, that is, if their outlook on things is the same, if they use the language in the same way, if the mean-

---

[9] This does not mean that the ability to handle role-taking information is a unitary trait anymore than general intelligence is. Tagiuri (1969), after considering the complex data bearing upon the question of a general role-taking ability, accepts that some people are generally good at role taking, but he cautions, "The achievement of these persons is not likely to be based on a unitary ability or process but, rather, upon the convergence, in their particular case, of a multitude of component processes and abilities relevant to understanding others" (413-14).

ings they associate with things are the same, then the ability of actor to process the information should be increased.

Taking one step backward from this notion, it is possible to suggest some of the factors that would contribute to the development of a shared universe of discourse. Following Stryker (1956), I would postulate that shared meanings will increase with more extensive interaction, with lesser status differences, and with greater similarity of interests and background.

On the basis of these general notions, Stryker developed a series of testable hypotheses concerning variations in role-taking accuracy in a sample of adults and their parents. Thus, for example, he hypothesized that accuracy should be greater when the target is a blood relative rather than an in-law because the former has had more extensive interaction with actor. Accuracy should also be greater when the other is of the same sex rather than of the other sex, because people of the same sex are more likely to have similar interests.

The data bearing upon these hypotheses tend to support them, although not overwhelmingly so. Almost all the differences were in the predicted direction, but many of them were not statistically significant, that is, they could have been due to chance. That this is so is not too surprising since most of the actor-other pairs probably had very similar universes of discourses. All the actors were, after all, taking the roles of people who were related to them by birth or marriage, and thus the differences in universe of discourse among categories were probably small. At the same time, we cannot argue that the differences in accuracy were solely a reflection of differences in the ability to handle information, for the effects of differences in the amount of information were not separated out. The results do suggest, however, that the greater the universe of discourse the greater the accuracy.

There are two other factors that will affect the ease with which actor can understand the meaning of the information he or she has, which are not related to the relationship between actor and other. Actors draw out the implications of the information they have about other, and one way they do this is by using what they know to deduce what other's role definitions are. Most people's view of the world suggests that certain traits go together to form an integrated whole. Bruner, Shapiro and Tagiuri (1958) show, for example, that if you tell someone that another person is intelligent, he or she is likely to guess that the other is active, efficient, independent, modest, cheerful, and so on. The situation is similar for roles. If we know that a father spends a lot of time with his children, we are likely to assume that his definition of the father role also involves being nice to them, encouraging them, sacrificing for them, and so forth.

The point is that what goes together is often not obvious, and our success in drawing out the implications of what we know will in part be a function of the validity of the theory of behavior from which we are working. If we know well what tends to go together, we will be more successful in drawing out the implications of what we have learned.

The point is supplementary to my earlier suggestion that a person who had a "good" implicit theory of human behavior would have more relevant information because he or she would know what to look for and what to ignore. Now we add the notion that a good theory of human behavior will help its possessor to handle his or her information more effectively.

As all social scientists know, however, even good theories do not always "work." Assuming the role taker is in fact working from a reasonably adequate theory, his or her success in applying that theory to the other will depend on certain characteristics of the other. If the theory is largely a theory of people in general, its applicability to this other will depend upon the extent to which he or she is a typical person. The theory would also tend to work better when the role is relatively institutionalized, that is, when it is well-established and deviation from the standard is relatively uncommon. If the theory is one which is specific to the particular other, actor's accuracy will be a reflection of the degree of stability of other's behavior. A theory which was adequate when developed might become rather useless if the other is unusually changeable.

This talk of theories of human behavior would seem to suggest that a person's ability to process information might be improved by training in role taking. The evidence, however, does not give one confidence in this idea. The results of various experiments are quite diverse, and they do not show with any consistency that students who have had psychology courses are better at role taking than students without such courses, and professional psychologists do not necessarily do better then professionals in other fields nor better than graduate students in psychology. In fact, as often as not, the less well-trained do better (Taft, 1955; Cline, 1964). In one study, in fact, (Crow, 1957) taking a course in "how to be a good role taker" was associated with lower accuracy. Whether the reason for these results is to be found in the inadequacy of the training, in the selection of psychologists, in the theory now being presented, or in a variety of statistical "excuses" which have been offered, is not clear (Crow, 1957). At a minimum, however, we must admit to some doubt regarding the utility of the theories of human personality which are currently being taught.

We may end this discussion of the factors that influence the processing of the information available for role taking by noting that motivation is important here just as it is in information gathering. No matter how great the ability to do any task, it will not be done unless the person is motivated to utilize his or her abilities. The factors which lead to motivation to do one's best at handling this information should be the same as those related to gathering it, that is, a general interest in human behavior, and a dependence upon the other for rewards or direction.

A METHODOLOGICAL APPENDIX

The observant reader will have noted that only a few of the references to empirical studies carry dates more recent than the late 1950s and early 1960s. This is because beginning in the early 1950s, a number of articles appeared which severely criticized the measures of role-taking accuracy which had been utilized up to that point (Cronbach, 1955; 1958; Hastorf et al., 1956; Hastorf and Bender, 1952; Cline, 1964; Bronfenbrenner et al., 1958; Gage and Cronbach, 1955). More than this, the alternative measures considered by the critics seemed to be impractical and/or failed to meet all the objections. I suspect that most researchers felt that they had only two alternatives—either to use the old measures and leave themselves open to being labeled "naïve empiricists," or to give up research in role-taking accuracy. Unfortunately, many seem to have chosen the latter path.

The fact that I have cited results which are based upon the standard methods does not suggest that I believe that those methods are in fact without fault. Some of the points made by the critics are clearly relevant, but others—and the main ones are included in this group—represent problems only if one's view of role taking is of a particular kind. Since that view is not the one presented here, it seemed justifiable to quote the best available information to give some indication of the empirical standing of the theory. Let me attempt to present the high points of what is a rather technical critique, and after that suggest why I feel its relevance to the present case is rather limited.

On the surface, there would seem to be nothing easier to measure than role-taking accuracy. All one has to do is compare the role-takers' predictions with the others' actual responses. The critics suggest, however, a number of difficulties. They fall into four categories: (1) The accuracy scores are influenced by response sets so that a person may obtain a high score because his or her approach to the task leads him or her to respond in a particular way which limits the range of error; (2) The accuracy scores are multidimensional. Accuracy scores can be analyzed mathematically into several components, and people with the same score may have obtained that score by very different routes. That is, their component scores may be very different although they "add up" to the same total. Furthermore, one may obtain a high score largely from one of the components which does not reflect the ability to distinguish the responses of the target other from that of other people; (3) In some studies, the independent variable is not mathematically distinct from the measure of accuracy. Some of the information used in the construction of one of the measures is also used in calculating the other. Any correlation between such measures is, in part at least, a reflection of the "common-term" and a mathematical necessity rather than a result of cause and effect; (4) In addition to these measurement problems, the literature in this field has been severely criticized on other grounds. Chief among these is the claim that the various studies lack comparability. In different studies the amount and kind of information available for role taking varies widely, the criteria of accuracy vary, the nature of the judging tasks are quite different, and so on.

Problems of Variation in Procedure

This last criticism is the easiest to understand, therefore let us address it first. The studies do, in fact, utilize widely different procedures. In some cases the judge has only still photographs of the other's face. Other studies use tape recordings or motion pictures of the target other, and in some cases actor and other have actually interacted in a real-life situation or in a laboratory. In some instances, the interaction has been life-long, as in the case when actors are taking the roles of relatives. The nature of the predictions vary as much—from the recognition of emotions being expressed, through attempts to predict responses to a questionnaire or personality interview. The subject matter of the predictions can vary from political and religious attitudes, to reactions in cases involving morality, to personality descriptions. In this last matter, the problem is worsened because the measures are often "global measures," containing a heterogeneous collection of items. The heterogeneity of the items makes it difficult to state what, in fact, the judges are being asked to predict, and "effects which operate differently on the several factors may be masked" (Cronbach, 1955: 178).

The general validity of these points cannot be denied. In fact, one could make similar statements about almost any area in sociology and psychology. They represent a problem largely because there is good reason to believe that role taking is not a completely general ability. As previously noted (see pages 46–47), people who do well in one kind of role-taking task only *tend* to do well on other kinds of activities. However, the critics seem to exaggerate the problem by implicitly assuming a greater degree of specificity than actually exists. I would contend that the studies do not have to be identical to be comparable. For example, it seems reasonable to compare studies which are similar except in that one requires the prediction of attitudes toward the family and the other uses items about religion, politics, or general values.

Until we have more information, the best possible solution seems to be the one adopted in my summary of the data. Whenever possible, I focused on studies which approach the real-life situations in which we are interested. Thus, with a few exceptions, I have tended to ignore studies in which the judges are given very limited information; for example, those which require judgments based on pictures of faces. In addition, when evaluating the evidence bearing on a particular hypothesis, an attempt was made to limit consideration to studies which seemed to be similar in relevant respects.

Statistical Problems

The common factor problem is not limited to studies of role-taking accuracy, and it is one which has proven very resistant to solution. It need not detain us here, however, because it did not arise in our discussion. However, if we had needed to correlate real similarity between actor and other with accuracy, the common factor would have been a problem. Real similarity is the difference between actor and other's actual responses; accuracy is the difference between actor's prediction of other's response and other's actual response. The common term, other's actual response, would produce some correlation between the two indices even if they were unrelated in any meaningful way.

Critics have contended that a potentially more troublesome set of statistical problems exist; those which arise simply from the way that the actor approaches the task. Two typical examples will be considered.

I would call one of these the "middle response" problem. It is noted that an actor who predicts that others will be at the extreme, say at one or five on a five-point scale, can err by as much as four points if accuracy is the difference between predicted and actual response. However, an actor who consistently chooses the mid-point can "miss" by only two points. Critics argue that a tendency to choose the extremes or the middle is a personal trait—a response set. Thus, a person who has a midpoint response set, all other things being equal, will score higher—not due to a better ability to role take but because of the way that he or she takes tests.

There is evidence that the people who use a particular part of the range on role-taking tests show the same tendency on other tests (Hastorf, Bender, and Weintraub, 1956), and that suggests that people do have patterns of response. But let us assume that the pattern holds in real life as well. Perhaps there are people who assume that "everyone" tends to be average. A person with that view of the world would predict other's behavior more accurately in real life since extreme behaviors are, in fact, relatively rare. This tendency to avoid the extremes might simply reflect accurate knowledge of the best approach in the absence of a better basis for predicting. There is no reason to assume, as some writers on respone sets seem to, that the behavior demonstrated is unrelated to knowledge of the facts of life or that the pattern is shown only on tests. Any person who gives the same response throughout the test will not do very well, but the person who favors the middle ground will get a higher score than one who favors the extremes. And he or she should score higher, since the actor who did that in real life would in fact be predicting others more accurately. There would be a worrisome problem only if it seemed likely that the approach to the paper and pencil test differed from the approach that the person would take when dealing with the prediction problem in real life.

Another statistical problem is more specific to the study of role taking. I would call it the assumed similarity problem (Sherohman, 1977; Cline, 1964). It has been argued that if all judges assume that the others are similar to them, and therefore predict that the others will respond as they would, the accuracy scores will reflect the extent to which the others are in fact like them, and the latter is simply a function of the sample used. In other words, if actors project, those who seem accurate will be those who were "lucky enough" to have people like them included in the sample of others. It is not their superior insight that produces their high scores, but rather the "luck of the draw."

I also doubt that this should necessarily be interpreted as a failing. There is something of a tendency to assume similarity, but is that wrong? If most people are typical—and they are—in the absence of other information it seems appropriate to assume that the other is typical, and so are you. Furthermore, the tendency to assume similarity is greater when we like the other, and that suggests acuity rather than a mind set. Anyone who has studied introductory sociology should know that people who are similar tend to like each other.

Even critics such as Cline seem to accept this view when they object to simply subtracting an assumed similarity factor from raw accuracy scores to give a refined score. As he puts it, the main problem with that "is that they lose important data because some of the subtracted AS [assumed similarity] data represent true accuracy of judgment" (Cline, 1964: 233).

The problem exists only if one postulates that people assume similarity unthinkingly, and I don't believe they do. When they project, it is because they think they have reason to believe that other is like them or because they feel they don't know anything useful about other and under those circumstances their best guess is to assume similarity. The projector has an "inappropriate" advantage only when the other is fortuitously like him or her and different from the other judges. In such a case, the person who projects gets a high score by chance.

The final criticism is that the accuracy score is multidimensional; that there are actually four main components to a score (Cronbach, 1955). One can get a high score, for example, because one has an accurate stereotype of the group. It is what Bronfenbrenner et al. (1958) called "sensitivity to the generalized other." If a person actually judges the average for all the others being predicted, he or she will tend to have a high accuracy score. This is often compared, unfavorably, to a high accuracy score which arises from differential accuracy or sensitivity to individual differences. Differential accuracy is the extent to which actor accurately predicts the degree to which each other will deviate from the mean of all others for each item. The general argument is that only the differential accuracy score comes close to being an adequate index of judging ability, and even that is flawed (Cline, 1964).

As Sherohman (1977) notes, these assertions overlook the fact that the accuracy score does in fact tell how close the actor came to predicting other's response. The problem arises only if one assumes that there is only one legitimate way to make such predictions. He suggests that such contentions may be valid if you are trying to study some basic role-taking *ability*, but that they do not hold when your theory recognizes several ways to arrive at an accurate judgment of others. The components are present in the role-taking accuracy scores—"but they cannot be classified as 'impurities' or statistical artifacts. Instead, they constitute different sources of role-taking accuracy (Sherohman, 1977:128).

In fact, given our view, to use only a differential accuracy score would be to measure the "wrong thing." A person can have differential accuracy but low role-taking accuracy if he or she can accurately predict that A will be above the group mean and B below it, but is far off in his or her estimate of where the mean is. In order to be accurate, one must have both stereotype accuracy and differential accuracy. Again, the components cause a problem primarily when one conceptualizes role taking as having only one legitimate source.

These are not the only criticisms of accuracy scores, although they are the major ones.[10] I would hope it is understood that I do not believe that all the criticisms of the accuracy measures used in role taking are without merit. In this area, as in

---

[10] Other criticisms include: (1) The scores assume that the differences among the categories of the items are equal, that is, that a person who gives the response numbered "1" differs as much from the person who gives the second response as the person who answers "3" differs from the person who answers "4." (2) The numerical differences between actor and other's responses are usually squared. Therefore the difference scores are not sensitive to the direction of the errors. (3) Studies which use the correlation between actor and other's responses fail to "catch" constant errors such as a tendency to judge that everyone scored higher than they really did (see Cline, 1964; Cronbach, 1958).

every other area of the social sciences, there is need for improvement of measurement and this is particularly so for dyadic measures, scores which are based upon comparisons of the responses of two people.

My argument is not that these measures are free of problems. I believe, only, that much of what some consider problematic and "accidental" can plausibly be considered to be "real." Similarly, I do not deny that a particular score may be arrived at in different ways. Here the contention is that the theory "permits" that.

I would hasten to add, however, that it would be beneficial to be able to know exactly how a particular accuracy score was achieved. It is important, for example, to know whether A did better than B because he or she had a better stereotype, or was more likely to project, or knew more about the specific other. It is not essential, however, to have that information. If the theory says that A will do better than B because of C, and A *does* do better, then we may *tentatively* assume that C is the reason.

The approach is similar to that used when we deal with unmeasured intervening variables. If a theory says X affects Y and Y affects Z, we will often simply relate X and Z, and if they correlate, assert that it is *likely* that Y is the intervening variable and the theory is correct. It is obviously better to be able to measure Y and to do the statistical tests which permit us to determine if Y does indeed intervene. However, in the absence of that ability, we should not refuse to go as far as we can.

We certainly must be careful in interpreting findings, and sometimes we will be wrong. A predicted high accuracy score might be achieved by a high score on the "wrong" component or an obtained relationship may not reflect a causal connection. However, as Allport (1961) suggests, we would be acting nihilistically if these problems led us to throw out years of research and to give up the study of a problem as important as the determinants of role-taking accuracy.

SUMMARY

In order to interact socially, actor must be able to communicate through symbols and anticipate the response of the other. In order to do this, he or she must be able to use language and take the role of the other. The focus of this chapter has been on the acquisition of language, the development of role-taking ability, and the sources of differences in role-taking accuracy.

In their discussions of language acquisition, interactionists are most concerned with the process by which persons learn the meanings of symbols. The first step involves the selecting out of certain sounds from the many that babies emit. Parents do this by rewarding sounds which approximate the words used in their language. The next step involves the association of meanings with particular sounds. When the sound is emitted, the object which goes with it is presented, and then the presentation of the object and the provision of the other rewards is made dependent upon the child's making the desired sound. By similar processes of association and reward, meanings are sharpened and pronunciation perfected. Later steps merely represent refinements of these basic processes. For example, the child's tendency to imitate permits the socializer to attach meaning to sounds without waiting for the child to emit them spontaneously. The socializer says the sounds, and the child attempts to reproduce them. In addition, the child begins to understand what is expected of him and he becomes motivated to learn for the sake of learning. Also, the child begins to initiate the lessons by asking the names of things. The process is further simplified when the definitions of new words can be stated in terms of words already known.

From an early period, the child is strongly motivated to take the role of the other, for this ability allows him to comply with his parents' wishes and to know what consequences his own acts will have. When the child begins to notice that certain events regularly precede others, he is on his way to being able to role take. He can predict reactions from the signs of those reactions.

The more difficult task of understanding other's intentions and feelings is mastered by projection, direct instruction, and observation. The child knows how he acts when he feels a certain way and if he sees other people acting in these ways, he assumes they have the same feelings as he. When he has a better command of language, he can be told directly, "I am doing this because. . ." Later, when the same action occurs, the child will remember that it was done "because. . ." In this way the child also learns that certain kinds of people act in certain ways and have certain feelings. Role taking is practiced and improved in play and organized games as well as in normal interaction. After the ability to take the role of a single other develops, actor then learns to take the role of multiple others—a process called taking the role of the generalized other.

All normally socialized persons can take the role of others but their accuracy in doing so varies greatly. It is postulated that, in general, variations in role-taking ability are a function of (1) the amount of information that actors have for use in making their guesses, and (2) differences among actors in ability to utilize the available information.

When other cannot be identified as belonging to a particular category, actor has to base his judgments on his view of what most people do in this situation. When actor can classify other, he can use his knowledge of how such persons react. Most useful, however, is direct information concerning this particular other's reactions in comparable situations, and the greater the store of such information the greater the accuracy of actor's role taking. Factors affecting actor's store of information concerning other include: the extent of previous interaction between actor and other, the pertinence of the previous interaction, the retentiveness of actor's memory, and the extent to which actor has paid attention in the previous interactions.

Attentiveness is, in turn, related to the extent of actor's need for external approval, the extent to which actor is interested in people in general, and the extent to which actor needs guidance from others. The extent to which actor notices the important aspects of other's behavior is also related to the amount of useful information he will have, and this is related to the adequacy of his implicit theory of human behavior.

In addition, certain characteristics of other, of the situation, and of the relationship between actor and other have an effect. Included in these would be: other's openness, the extent to which other acts idiosyncratically, the extent to which other explains his or her action, and the stability of other's behavior over time. Interaction which takes place under conditions of close proximity, which occur in private, and which are important to actor, will also provide more information. In addition, when certain topics are involved more information will be obtained. Finally, when actor and other are intimate and/or when they like each other, a lot of information is going to be gathered, and subordinate actors gather more information than superordinates do.

The ability to process role-taking information is related to a general ability factor which is correlated with general intelligence, to the extent of the universe of discourse between actor and other, and to the extent of actor's motivation. The adequacy of actor's theory of human behavior will also affect actor's ability to handle information.

The chapter concludes with a discussion of some of the methodological problems involved in testing hypotheses concerning role-taking accuracy. It is concluded that although the problems are real, critics have made a number of assumptions that make the difficulties seem more formidable than they actually are. Although care must be taken, the available techniques do permit us to obtain relevant and valid data on this topic.

CHAPTER 3

THE CENTRAL CONCEPTS

The basic paradigm of this interactionist theory says that through the interaction process—utilizing language and role taking—a set of mental structures develops which have a major influence on the behavior of actor in his or her future interaction. These structures, which consist of the self-concept, role definitions, the presented self, and the role of the presented self, represent the central concepts of the theory. They are central in two senses: they are the key concepts, and they stand in the middle of the theory. In one part of the theory, their content and structure is the thing to be explained, that is, they are the *dependent* variables. In the other part, they are the *antecedent* variables, that is, they are used to explain the course of interaction. In the following two chapters we will consider the nature of these mental structures and the processes by which they develop.

THE SELF-CONCEPT

As I have already noted, one of the major assumptions of interactionist theory is that human beings invest things with meaning and thereby convert them into social objects. One of the things we invest with meaning is ourselves. We become objects to ourselves. Just as I have opinions of other people, I have opinions about myself. Just as I have beliefs about physical objects, I have beliefs about myself. In general, I believe that if something can go wrong with a mechanical object, the chances are rather good that it will. That's a result of my view of the nature of mechanical things. I also believe that if the mechanical things are in my hands, they are almost certain to go wrong. That belief is based upon my view of myself.

This set of beliefs about oneself is called the self-concept. In Rosenberg's (1979: 2) words: "The self-concept is the totality of the individual's thoughts and feelings with reference to himself as an object."[1]

Simple as this definition may be, it says a great deal, for the term "thoughts and feelings" includes many things within its boundaries. Building upon Rosenberg's (1979) and Gordon's (1968) work, I would suggest that the self-concept has four "content areas": an identity set, a set of qualities, a set of evaluations, and a set of self-confidence levels.

The Content of the Self

The *identity set* consists of positional labels which refer to the social categories to which we feel we belong. When I think of myself as a male sociologist, I am representing to myself my view of where I fit in the social world. As Gordon (1968) points out, identities are usually stated in noun or noun-like terms.

When we attempt to define ourselves, we also tend to use adjectives which refer to our *qualities*—tall, thin, introverted, interested in music, and so on. In many ways, these qualities are similar to the elements of the identity set, but the practice has been to limit the term "identities" to *socially recognized* categories. However, the descriptive part of the self-definition is not limited to such labels. Thus, we must recognize this second content area.

Interactionist theory also asserts that people tend to think of themselves in terms which have evaluative connotations; the self-concept also includes a set of *self-evaluations*. The most easily recognized self-evaluations are those which are stated in adjectival form and attached to the identities and qualities in the self-conception. These elements of the evaluative self constitute our view of how good we are at what we are. Thus, people think of themselves as good fathers or poor scholars.

An aspect of the evaluative self that is not so obvious is the actor's view of

---

[1] The distinction between the self-concept and the self should be kept clearly in mind. The latter is a key concept of the Chicago School and it is quite clearly not a structure (Blumer, 1966). In some places, the Chicagoans seem to suggest that the term refers to a human capacity. "It means merely that a human being *can* be an object of his own action" (Blumer, 1969: 12, emphasis added). Just as we can interact with others, we can interact with ourselves. We can talk to ourselves, we develop attitudes toward ourselves, predict what we are likely to do, and so on.

Elsewhere the self seems to be the process of interacting with oneself. Blumer (1966: 535) tells us that "Mead saw the self as a process," and Lindesmith, Strauss, and Denzin (1977) speak of it as a "process of intraindividual communication" (322), and "as a set of more or less consistent and stable responses at a conceptual level" (324).

I would agree with Blumer that it makes no sense to view the self as a structure, but there *is* a mental structure that can be called the self-concept—the organized set of self-attitudes. Much confusion and misdirected criticism has been caused by the tendency of some authors to use the terms interchangeably. In this book that will not be done.

how good it is to be what he or she is. For example, if someone says he is a man, it may simply be a statement of fact and descriptive only of his identity. However, if he believes to be a man means that he is better or worse than other people, this self-definition is also part of his evaluative self. Similarly, to think of oneself as thin may simply describe an attribute or it may also include a self-evaluation. This causes measurement problems, but it should cause no difficulties of conceptualization. A description of self with value connotations for an actor is part of that actor's evaluative self, even if it seems to be a statement of objective fact to the audience.

The last aspect of the self-conception is the person's *levels of self-confidence* (Rosenberg, 1979). They refer to the person's estimate of the extent to which he or she can master challenges and overcome obstacles, that is, the extent to which things can be made to turn out as wanted. (The use of the plural should be noted. Within a particular individual, level of confidence will vary depending on the task involved.)

Many authors do not include self-confidence levels in their descriptions of the content of the self-conception. There is some tendency to include it as part of the evaluative self or to ignore it entirely. Both these approaches seem ill-advised. I have no doubt that we do have estimates of our abilities to control our fates (Rotter, 1966), and although the distinction is somewhat subtle, this is not the same as an evaluation of self. There is probably a correlation between level of self-evaluation and level of self-confidence, but the two are not identical. Obviously, if I think I am pretty good, if I have respect for myself, I am more likely to think that I can control outcomes than if I have the opposite view of myself. Nonetheless, some people with high self-evaluation may have a view of the world which suggests that even the best of people are unable to control their fates because the individual is at the mercy of external forces which are stronger than any of us—the bosses, the Commies, God, and others. Self-confidence may be considered a function of self-evaluation measured against one's view of what is needed to control one's world.

The question now becomes whether these assertions are true. Do people, in fact, carry around in their heads descriptions of themselves which involve the elements I have described? If these four categories are represented in people's self-views, what, in more specific terms, are the typical elements in those conceptions?

The contents of a person's thoughts are obviously not directly accessible to the researcher, but the matter can be investigated given humans' ability to talk and their self-awareness. Unlike other animals, humans can report on the content of their thoughts. These notions led to the development of the "Twenty-Statements" or "Who-Am-I" test, one of the Iowa School's major contributions to symbolic interactionism.

In this test, the subject is instructed: "Ask yourself the question, "Who Am I?" and answer it as if you were giving the answers to yourself, not to anyone else." The resulting list of responses is generally taken to be a representation of the person's self-concept.[2]

---

[2] Simple as it is, there isn't universal agreement that the test is valid, that is, that it really measures what it is supposed to measure. Tucker (1966) discusses a number of implicit assumptions that underlie the test, and he casts some doubt on their tenability. One of the major problems is the assumption that the instrument gets at a general self-conception rather than at one which is

The fact that almost everyone can accomplish this task without difficulty suggests the "reality" of the self-concept. People do have such ideas about themselves and are conscious of them.

Limited data show, furthermore, that the lists have a fair degree of test-retest reliability, that is, responses provided at two different times are not exactly the same, but they *are* similar (Heiss, 1968; Kuhn and McPartland, 1954; Spitzer et al., n.d.). Thus, as the conceptualization implies, there is a certain degree of stability in people's self-views.

More than this, most of the responses to the "Who-Am-I" tests can be classified into one or more of the categories I suggested make up the individual's self-conception. People do think of themselves in these terms. Studies by Gordon (1968) showed that almost everyone made reference to their group memberships and personal qualities. Clearly positive or negative statements about self are also quite common, accounting for about 40 percent of all the responses obtained from several samples.[3] This would suggest that most people gave one or more such responses. References to level of self-confidence are not as common, but are by no means rare. In one of the samples, 23 percent of the respondents made one or more statements which fit into this category. (We are not told what proportion of *all* responses were of this kind, but undoubtedly it was not very large.)

This evidence cannot be considered conclusive, but it does appear that my view of the content areas of the self-concept is consistent with empirical fact. Before we go on to other matters, let us look at the evidence a little more closely to determine the *specific* items included in people's self-views.

Judging by a sample of Iowa residents, family and occupational positions seem to be major elements in the identity sets of most adults, and gender appears to be of moderate importance. Notable by their infrequency were references to race, social class, ethnic group, and membership in a specific religious denomination (Mulford and Salisbury, 1964).

The young people studied by Gordon (1968) showed, as might be expected, a somewhat different pattern. They resemble the Iowa adults in their emphasis on occupation; about 80 percent of the high school sample referred to themselves as

---

specific to the testing situation. Interactionists assume that the situation influences which aspects of the self-concept are most salient, and this suggests that the problem is a real one which is at best partially resolved by attempts to make the context neutral.

Another issue relates to the significance of the order in which concepts are listed. Kuhn and McPartland (1954) consider the elements which are listed first to be most important, but others suggest that the things which come to mind first are the more superficial aspects of the self-concept. The latter believe the more significant elements are mentioned only after the superficial ones are out of the way. Gordon's data (1968) suggest that for some groups the former assumption is more valid and for others it is less valid. Given the lack of a clear answer, it seems wise to ignore the order of mention.

[3]This is, of course, a minimum figure since some labels which have evaluative implications to the actor were likely to be missed because they were stated in a way that made them appear to be simply descriptive.

students. They also resembled the adults by their neglect of race, religious membership, and social class. The big differences between the groups are to be found in the frequent use of gender identifications by the students, and their relative neglect of family status.

Much of this makes intuitive sense. The general emphasis in America upon occupation is indicated in the very phrases we use. When we want to learn about somebody our first question is usually, "What does he (she) do?" and that is always taken to refer to occupation, even though the question is really ambiguous. The lack of emphasis upon class and ethnicity would also be expected in a society such as this one, and it is hardly surprising that students tend to play down the family ties they are probably trying to break or that they focus upon their identities as males and females, given the importance of dating and courtship in this age group.

When we turn to qualities and attributes, we find that beliefs have a large place in self-descriptions—especially for the adults. For example, few of them, as we noted, describe themselves as members of a specific religious group, but one in four say something about the extent of their religious belief. In the student sample, activities (hiker), physical attributes (body build, age), tastes and interests (jazz fan), membership in abstract categories (a person), and personal characteristics (friendly, happy) are quite frequent.

The evaluative references tend to fall into two major subcategories—feelings of moral worth (good-bad, honest-dishonest, reliable-unreliable), and feelings of competence (talented-untalented, creative-uncreative), and so on.[4]

In general, the picture that emerges is one of variation within a framework of consistency. The details of the content of self-conceptions differ from individual to individual and group to group, but certain specific references tend to be much more common than others, and in most instances the major categories of self-reference are represented in each person's self-conception.

The Structure of the Self-Concept

In order to describe the self-conception, it is necessary to do more than simply list the descriptive terms that people use to refer to themselves. An automobile is more than the catalog which lists all its parts, and a person's self-concept is more than a list of specific labels, attitudes, feelings, and beliefs. An adequate description requires a consideration of the way in which the content elements are organized. The identity set, for example, has a structure, and if we are to understand the self-concept, we must inquire into the nature of that structure (see also Rosenberg, 1979).

The Hierarchy of Prominence. A simple but important aspect of the structure of the self-concept relates to the relative importance of the elements. For example, in describing the self-concept it is common to view both identities and qualities as

---

[4]The analysis did not separate out references to self-confidence levels.

being ranked along a hierarchy of prominence. All the identities and attributes in our self-concepts are not of equal importance to us, and two people who describe themselves in the same terms would not have the same self-concept unless they ranked the various elements in the same way. The differential importance that people assign to their various identities and qualities is also recognized in our everyday speech. We often characterize people in terms of the identities which are most important to them. Thus, the "patriot" is one for whom the national identity is central; a "family man" is one who stresses his husband and father identities.

The evaluative component of the self-concept can be viewed similarly. As noted before, there are several criteria by which we can evaluate ourselves, and people will differ in their views regarding which ones it is most important to score high on. The "saint" wants, above all, to be good, the scholar is concerned with being learned, the "do-gooder" with being useful.

Self-Esteem. Level of self-esteem is an aspect of the self-concept's structure which relates only to the evaluative self. Up to this point, my treatment of the evaluative component of the self-concept has focused upon self-evaluations—estimates of worth and competence which are tied to specific identities and qualities, such as good father, well-educated person, and so on. Interactionists also speak of self-esteem. This is the actor's general opinion of self; a global estimate which is not specific to particular activities and positions. In addition to thinking of himself as a good husband and a plumber, a man may also think of himself as being, in general, a pretty good person.

A basic assumption is that this general view of self is derived from the separate self-evaluations. But at the same time self-esteem is not a simple average of the self-evaluations. All self-evaluations influence the level of self-esteem, but they do not all have the same degree of influence. Self-esteem may be viewed as a weighted average of a person's self-evaluations. In effect, each evaluation is "multiplied" by a weighting factor before it is entered into the "equation" used to determine the level of self-esteem. And, as is probably quite obvious, the assumption is that greater weight is given to self-evaluations which are tied to identities and qualities high on the hierarchy of prominence, and to self-evaluations which involve the criteria which we consider to be important.

The implications of this should be made explicit. For example, if a particular person considers trait A to be more important than trait B, the evaluation associated with trait A will have more effect on general self-esteem than the evaluation associated with trait B. If a person considers himself to be a good father but a poor husband, his self-esteem would tend to be low if his father status were not as important to him as his husband status. His self-esteem would tend to be high if his priorities were reversed. Similarly, when one role is evaluated on several criteria of self-evaluation, evaluations associated with the criterion which is considered more important will have the greater effect. If a person considers himself or herself to be a competent but somewhat dishonest merchant, the effect of the merchant identity on self-esteem will depend on actor's view about the relative importance of honesty and competence. Also, it would follow that two people who rate themselves equally on a particular set of traits may have different levels of self-esteem if they differ in their views about the importance of the traits. Some traits are going to have very little effect on self-esteem because the person just doesn't care about them. As William James (1952: 200) put it: "yonder puny fellow. . .whom every one can beat, suffers no chagrin about it, for he has long ago abandoned the attempt to 'carry that line,' as the merchants say, of self at all."

Data reported by Rosenberg (1968) indicate that this view of self-esteem is consistent with reality. He found for a variety of traits that knowledge of how a person rated himself gave some indication of his general rating of himself (his global self-esteem). For example, people who believed they were likeable tended to have high global self-esteem and those who thought they were not likeable tended toward lower self-esteem. Thus there is a relation between evaluation of likeability and global self-esteem. But for this trait, and for all but one of the others, the strength of the relationship depends upon the importance attributed to the trait. For those who care about being likeable, being liked is strongly related to global self-esteem; for those to whom this quality is unimportant, there is little tie between evaluation and global self-esteem. This strongly suggests that a specific self-evaluation will have more effect on general self-esteem when the trait involved is one which actor considers important.

Dimensions of the Self-Concept

In addition to differing in content and structure, self-concepts vary regarding their standing on a series of qualitative dimensions. Let us now consider some of those dimensions.

Stability. It is a basic assumption of this theory that there is some degree of stability to the self-concept. At the same time, there is clear recognition that the self-concept is not a rigid and unchanging construction. Changing events alter one's view of oneself just as they change other opinions.

Although all self-concepts show both stability and change, they do vary in the degree to which they are amenable to change. This variability in the changeability of self-concepts provides a basis for describing the self-concepts of specific persons and groups. For example, one of the differences among adolescent males and females is that the self-concepts of females show greater change over time (Rosenberg, 1976).

It is also true that within a particular self-concept there are likely to be differences regarding which elements are most changeable and which are most stable. Thus, for one person the self-evaluation associated with the family status may be relatively fixed and the athletic evaluation quite changeable. For another person the reverse may be true. This kind of variation provides an additional basis for describing the self-concept. One may note which elements are most stable and which are most changeable.

Consistency. The degree of consistency in a person's various self-evaluations and levels of confidence also show variation. People recognize differences in their abilities in different areas, but the extent of such variation is not the same for all, and people can be distinguished from one another in these terms. We all know of people who think they are great, or awful, period. Such people would be considered to have consistent self-concepts as compared with those who insist, "I'm good at football but not baseball. I'm a good second baseman but a terrible shortstop."

Certainty. In addition to everything else, people's self-concepts differ in the degree of certainty with which they are held. If a researcher insisted, I would be willing to answer all questions put to me in an attempt to learn what my self-concept contains, but I must admit that I would prefer that there was a place for "don't know" responses. I don't think I know myself very well. Others, of course, do not suffer from this lack of certainty.

People may be categorized, then, in regard to their general level of self-certainty. However, just as with stability, for different elements within the self-concept there can be differences in level of certainty. A person who has worked at a job for twenty years will probably have a firm conception of his or her ability, while newcomers might not be very sure of their estimates of their own competence. Regarding other aspects of the self-concept, the newcomers may be the ones who are certain. A full description of the self-concepts of these people should note what they are most certain about and what they are unsure of.

Self-Acceptance and Self-Satisfaction. These two dimensions of the self-concept both involve the reaction of actor to his self-definition, but there is a subtle difference between them. A person who is totally self-satisfied believes that what he or she is, is good. There might be negative self-evaluations in the self-concept of such a person, but he or she would believe that to be bad at those things is unimportant, or even good. People who consider themselves to be poor liars would illustrate this type. The self-satisfied person would give a negative answer to the question, "Would you change anything about yourself if you could?"

To be self-accepting does not require a negative answer to the question. The self-accepting person might very well prefer to be different from what he or she is, but there is no railing against the fates: "I am what I am, and I can live with my faults and my virtues." "It might be nice to be better than I am or different from what I am, but I endure what I am without protest." Self-acceptance without self-satisfaction probably rests on a view that changes are not really possible, and therefore it is futile to fight it. Self-acceptance might have an element of resignation to it; self-satisfaction would not.

Again, these dimensions may be used at either a general or specific level. They may be used to describe the self-concept as a whole or they may refer to specific aspects of it. And, as with self-esteem, the general level is probably a weighted average of the specific feelings of satisfaction and acceptance.

The Tenses of Self

Although I haven't specified it, the entire discussion thusfar has clearly focused upon the self-in-the-present. What does the person think he or she is like at this moment in time? This is an appropriate focus because our ultimate interest is in the effect the self has on human behavior, and our view of what we are like now will usually have the most important effect on what we do.

As Gordon (1968) points out, however, we generally also have a conception of what we have been in the past and a view of what we may be in the future. This ability to look backward and forward is, in fact, an important part of what it means to be human. The key point is that these past- and future-tense selves, under some circumstances, have an important effect on behavior. What we do is affected by what we think we were and what we think we will be. Just as we are inclined to act in ways which are consistent with our present self-image, we also try to act consistently with our past and future self-concepts—particularly when they are favorable. The exiled prince who is now waiting on tables must engage in nonprincely activities, but as the movies of the thirties kept telling us, he is likely to try to avoid certain things if he can possibly do so for they are too far beneath what he was. Similarly, a person with a general desire for upward mobility or for a particular position will avoid certain actions because they are not "right" for a person who will someday be a priest, an opera singer, or a member of the elite. It is not simply that these activities may represent a barrier to the achievement of the goal. Even if there is no such danger, they are avoided because they are considered inappropriate.

With this noted, the point may be dropped for now. All that has been said about the self-in-the-present applies to the self in other tenses. The specifics, of course, differ, but the self-concept in all its tenses can be analyzed in pretty much the same terms.

Lengthy as this discussion has been, I have by no means covered all aspects of the self-concept (see Rosenberg, 1979; Gordon, 1968; Wylie, 1974). These examples must suffice, however, for I am quite sure that I have reached or exceeded the limits of your tolerance. I would note, however, that I have not been engaging in an exercise in hair-splitting. Self-concepts do differ in these regards and the differences do lead to differences in behavior.

ROLES

As with most interactionist concepts, the term "role" is used in rather different ways by different authors. In fact, a rough classification of the various schools of interactionism could be based upon how this term is defined. Perhaps needless to say, the conceptualization to be used here differs rather markedly from that used by Mead and his more orthodox followers.

Simply stated, I view roles as prescriptions for behavior which are associated with particular actor-other combinations. They are the ways we think people of a particular kind ought to act toward various categories of others—the way, for example, a father should act toward his children.

This general definition is acceptable as a starting point, but it does not give much of a feel for the nature of roles. Let me highlight some of the elements in the definition and specify in some detail what the term is intended to connote.

First, it should be noted that in this usage, as compared to that of most orthodox interactionists, roles do not refer to actual behavior. A role is a set of prescriptions for behavior; the behavior itself will be called role performance, role behavior, or role playing. Since it is assumed that people tend to act consistently with their role definitions, roles and role behavior will often be the same. But, it must be emphasized, this is not always true. It is not at all uncommon for people to act in ways which are inconsistent with their role prescriptions and thus the distinction between roles and role behaviors must be made.[5]

It should also be noted that the expectations on which we are focusing are those of the actor, not those of the society or of the other. When the concern is not with actor's definitions, we will use terms such as societal norms, the expectations of others, other's definition of actor's role, or institutionalized roles.

As I am using the term, a role is tied to a specific actor-other pattern. To name a role two labels must be used, one referring to the relevant characteristic of the actor and one referring to the other. In this usage there is no such thing as a father role, there is a father-son role or a father-daughter role. When we mean to refer to all the roles associated with a particular category, we will speak of a role set—the complement of roles that are associated with a particular characteristic (Merton, 1957). There may not be *a* father role, but there is a role set associated with the status of father.

A further complication arises because most roles are multifaceted. Each role is composed of several subroles which may be distinguished along functional lines. The father-son role includes the subroles of teacher, disciplinarian, companion, and so forth. We must not overlook the fact that for each role there are really several sets of expectations. What I consider to be proper behavior when I am teaching my daughters to drive is not what I consider to be appropriate when we are on a fishing trip.

Two other useful terms in the discussion of roles are role repertoire and role norm; these are the largest and smallest units usually recognized. A person's role repertoire is all the roles that he or she knows. It contains all the role sets associated with actor's social traits. Role norms are the specific prescriptions which combine to make up a subrole. They are, in a manner of speaking, the elements of social compounds.

Thus, to summarize, a role repertoire contains all the person's role sets. A role set contains all the roles associated with a given characteristic of the person. A role consists of all the expectations that apply when a particular characteristic of actor is relevant and he is interacting with a specific kind of role partner, and a subrole consists of the expectations considered appropriate for a specific type of actor when he or she engages in a particular kind of activity with a particular kind of other. Norms are the specific rules which when combined constitute a subrole.

All these definitions are commonly used in the literature, although other schema

---

[5] Of course, those who equate roles with actual behavior are not unaware of the distinction between prescriptions and behavior. They typically use terms such as role expectations or role prescriptions when they mean what I mean by the term *role*.

are used with equal frequency. In one matter, however, it seems helpful to depart from common usage. In most cases, authors speak of roles as the behaviors considered appropriate for people in particular social positions, that is, roles are tied to identities. This seems to be an unnecessary and constricting limitation. I would prefer to speak of roles as being associated with *all* the definable social characteristics of the actor and other. I would suggest that the term be extended to the behaviors considered appropriate for categories based on qualities, evaluations, and confidence levels. We all have ideas about what an intelligent person, a good person, and a self-confident person should do when they are interacting with others. Why should those behavioral prescriptions be put in a different category from those associated with socially recognized positions? If the meaning of roles is extended in this way, the parallelism between the self-concept and roles becomes clear. Each aspect of the self-conception has a set of roles associated with it.

The Nature of Roles

With matters of definition out of the way, we may now consider the nature of roles in somewhat more depth. The first question relates to the stability of role expectations.

Discussions of this matter often suggest that there are two markedly different views to be found in the field, but a close reading of the literature suggests that extreme positions are often qualified so that the gaps between authors are not very large (Merton, 1975; Heiss, forthcoming). This notwithstanding, for purposes of exposition it seems useful to briefly describe what the extreme positions would be.

On the one hand, it could be that roles are highly stable over time. If this were so, we would carry around with us general conceptions of what is proper behavior in a particular situation and those conceptions would act as guides for our actions in all interactions of a given kind. According to this view, my conception of how a teacher should act vis-à-vis students will direct my behavior in all my encounters with students.

The opposing extreme would say that there is very little carry over from one of my teacher-student encounters to the next. According to this view, roles are "made anew each time people assemble and orient their conduct toward one another" (Hewitt, 1976: 55). The idea is that every time one enters an interaction setting, one must develop a new notion of what behavior is appropriate for that situation, taking into account the many things that make it unique.

The "moderate" view, which is adopted here, suggests that except when we find ourselves in new and unfamiliar situations, roles learned in previous interactions provide us with general guides to proper behavior. We do not start over again each time. Students know that they should raise their hands before they speak in class; it is not necessary to work that out at every class meeting. This is not to say, however, that interaction is simply the mechanical playing out of prelearned roles. We see how specific others react; we take their roles and learn what they expect us to do; we are aware that things are going well or poorly. In many cases, this kind of information will lead us to modify our role conceptions or will cause us to act in a way inconsistent with them. Students quickly learn that in a particular class they are not expected to raise their hands and wait for recognition.

The relationship between role conceptions and behavior is a complex one which will be discussed in detail in Chapter 7. For now it is sufficient to understand that previous experience is codified into views regarding proper behavior and these are taken into account in working out a course of action. Roles, however, merely provide a game plan. They do not put actors into a straitjacket.

The Content of Roles

As I see it, the specificity and completeness of role prescriptions vary markedly from person to person and from one role to another. Some roles contain rather specific instructions about what one should do for most eventualities. This is not to say, of course, that roles contain the exact wording of the responses we should make. They are not scripts. Interaction is too varied and complex for roles to be that explicit. Nonetheless, some roles do contain rather specific instructions for most of the contingencies that occur. Such roles might include the injunction that one "should meet any reasonable request" and also define what a reasonable request would be. Or a role definition of this kind might say that a husband should help with the housework but not take the major responsibility for it.

In most cases, however, roles are more sketchy than that. Most often, roles are like plot outlines or the instructions given to acting students when they engage in improvisations. Banton (1965), for example, describes roles as statements of appropriate activities and associated rights and obligations. However, the actor must work out for himself what specific actions should be taken to carry on the activities, claim the rights, and meet the obligations. A role of this type would suggest that a husband owes it to his wife to be considerate of her wishes, but would leave it to him to decide if that required him to do the dishes.

It seems obvious that in a particular society some roles will be more complete and specific than others. In this society, for example, occupational roles tend to be more detailed than are roles relating to interaction with in-laws. Such variation is, however, not the only kind that can be seen. For a given role, one person may have a specific and detailed role definition and someone else's may be very sketchy. For example, beginners at any activity are likely to have rather vague role definitions. Finally, it should be noted that for any individual there will be variation in this regard from role to role. Within the role repertoires of each person, we can expect to find some roles which are vague and incomplete and others which are specific and detailed.

The Dimensions of Roles

Just as a self-concept is not adequately described by its content, so too a description of a role requires attention to more than its content. I will now consider some of the other dimensions along which roles may vary. Here we are faced with an embarrassment of riches; the number of classification schemes which have been put forth for role analysis is truly overwhelming (see Biddle and Thomas, 1966). I will focus on a few dimensions which seem particularly relevant for the course of interaction.

Role Commitment. One dimension which fits this criterion is the extent of the individual's commitment to the role, that is, the extent of his or her motivation to live by its dictates (Goode, 1960b).

That commitment is variable seems quite clear. In regard to some roles, there is at best a lukewarm allegiance. We know what we "should" do, and, in fact, if it is not too difficult we will follow the dictates of the role. But when the going gets a little rough we are quick to abandon it without much regret. However, simply failing to abide by role prescriptions does not necessarily indicate low commitment to the role nor does observance of them necessarily indicate high commitment. Role conformity can occur without commitment, and deviance occurs despite commitment. Other factors also influence the actor. Nonetheless, frequent deviation from prescriptions under circumstances which would permit conformity with little trouble, and no real effort to change his or her behavior, would suggest that actor's commitment to the role is low.

Cases of extremely high commitment to the dictates of a role are especially interesting. There are people for whom the observance of a role prescription is so important that they are willing to follow them even when they prescribe suicide. Such behavior is fairly common in military roles, but an even more striking example is the practice of suttee which was a part of the East Indian woman's definition of the wife role. It required that she commit suicide by throwing herself on her husband's funeral pyre. Women's commitment to this norm was so strong that they attempted to obey it even when the British made strong efforts to stamp it out.

Role Strain. Implicit in this discussion of role commitment is the idea that it is not uncommon for there to be some degree of difficulty involved in living up to role norms. When there is such difficulty we speak of the existence of role strain. If, for any one of a number of reasons, actor feels he cannot abide by the role norms he accepts, he or she is experiencing role strain. Since the amount of role strain associated with particular roles varies, we have another basis for differentiating among them.

Institutionalization of Roles. Although our major interest is the individual's definition of his or her role, it is relevant to inquire about the extent to which a role definition is shared by the members of a society. When the norms of a role are generally accepted, they are referred to as institutionalized roles.

These distinctions seem sufficient for our purposes. Let us now turn to the third and fourth central variables.

THE PRESENTED SELF

In social psychology, the idea that people "set the stage" so that others develop a particular view of them goes back at least as far as 1890 to the work of William James (1952). It was Erving Goffman (1959), however, who named and developed the notion of the presented self. In recent years the concept has proven to be a valuable aid in making sense of what goes on in human interaction.

The basic idea is simple enough. It is assumed "that when an individual appears before others he will have many motives for trying to control the impression that they receive of the situation" (Goffman, 1959: 15). It is further assumed that actor is particularly eager to control other's view of him or her. In order to do this, actors engage in "impression management"; they say and do certain things and avoid doing other things so that other's definition of them will be the one they desire. Impression management is the act of presenting a self. We attempt to control other's view of us by "governing, guiding and controlling our own actions, acting in accordance with the type of person we wish to appear" (Rosenberg, 1979: 45).

Perhaps a few examples will convey the flavor of what goes on. Waller (1937: 730) noted that, "It has been reported by many observers that a girl who is called to the telephone in the dormitories will often allow herself to be called several times in order to give all the girls ample opportunity to hear her paged." Perhaps female students in this enlightened age do not do this anymore, but it is clear that Waller is describing a ploy used by the students of his day to present an image of popularity to their dorm-mates. If one is paged several times, the likelihood of others knowing you were called is increased, and if you are lucky, some might even assume that the several pages were associated with more than one call. Such tactics, we might also add, were intended to make an impression on the caller. They suggested that the woman was not the kind who sat around waiting for the phone to ring.

Goffman (1959) presents a passage from a novel by William Sansom (1956: 231) which reveals to the world the mechanisms used by Preedy, an Englishman vacationing at a Spanish beach resort:

> By devious handlings he gave anyone who wanted to look a chance to see the title of his book—a Spanish translation of Homer, classic thus, but not daring, cosmopolitan too—and then gathered together his beach-wrap and bag into a neat sand resistant pile (Methodical and Sensible Preedy), rolled slowly to stretch at ease his huge frame (Big-Cat Preedy), and tossed aside his sandals (Carefree Preedy, after all).

Most examples of presentation of selves focus on the presentation of false selves; that is, they illustrate attempts to get the other to see actor in a way which is not consistent with actor's own view of himself. It must be emphasized, however, that *impression management is also used in the service of presenting a true self-image.* It is one of life's small tragedies that unless we are careful, people will not get the view of us that we consider to be an accurate one. It may not be as difficult to get across a true impression as it is to present a false one, but both require *creating* an impression. If we do not do that we are likely to be "misunderstood." How are people to know that you are a "nice guy" unless you mention events that indicate this is so or do things which lead them to that conclusion?

One final point in this regard. The criterion of labeling a presented self as true or false is not what the person "really" is, but what he thinks he is. The touchstone is the self-conception, not what some objective and all-knowing observer would decide the actor is.

Let me now elaborate on the presented self idea. Most readers have understood Goffman's point to be that actors *consciously, intentionally,* and *frequently* attempt to control other people's view of them. In fact, readers often object to Goffman's work on the grounds that it suggests that humans are more devious than they really are.

Messinger et al. (1962) suggest that this interpretation of Goffman's position is wrong, but let us not get involved in a discussion of what Goffman really means. The important question is to what extent do actors consciously attempt to present a particular image of themselves?

No one denies that deliberate impression management sometimes occurs, but some see it as relatively rare and atypical. The argument is that attempts to consciously set the stage have an alienating effect upon actors—that such efforts have psychological costs. We don't like ourselves when we are not being ourselves or when we are working at being ourselves. Such behaviors are viewed by us as inauthentic. Therefore, it is suggested, people usually do not consciously try to manage impressions.

I would contend, however, that everyday observation clearly indicates that people frequently engage in active attempts to control other's impressions of them. I cannot be specific about the frequency of such efforts, and the only "proof" I have is my unsystematic observation, but I think there can be little doubt that impression management is a common feature of human behavior.

This is not to say, however, that there are no costs involved in the presentation of selves. Admittedly, it is an extreme case, but a statement by Jan Morris, a British writer who underwent a sex change operation, strikes a responsive chord. Our self presentations are different, but our response to them may differ only in degree. In speaking of her life when she was physically a man, but felt herself to be a woman, she says:

> I realize now that the chief cause of my disquiet was the fact that I had [no identity]. I was not to others what I was to myself. . . .The older I grew, the more abjectly I realized, when I allowed myself the melancholy thought, that I would rather die young than live a long life of falsehood. A falsehood to whom, you may ask, since I was to all appearances unequivocally a man? A falsehood to myself. (Morris, 1975: 43, 49)

But if there are costs associated with self-presentations there is also the possibility of rewards, and the latter frequently outweigh the former. When they do, we manage impressions even though the consequences for us are not totally favorable.

To say that people present selves is not to say, however, that we live in a world filled with people out to deceive. Impressions are formed in all interactions, but not all interaction involves the *management* of impressions. Furthermore, not all impression management involves deception, and some of the deception which does occur is unintended. In many instances, the impression management behaviors become habitual and we are barely aware of what we are doing, much less what the effect will be. To recognize that selves are presented does not require us to consider deceptions ubiquitous.

Variations in Self-Presentations

As with other human traits, presentations of self show both variability and stability. We have a repertoire of presented selves, and some of them are specific to particular situations and others are utilized on a variety of occasions. The latter are the qualities that we want "everyone" to see in us, and they are frequently at the core of what we believe ourselves to be or wish that we were. For some, that might be kindly; for others, honest, sophisticated, or hardheaded. The favored images would clearly differ from actor to actor.

Many, if not most, of the images in our presented self repertoire are, however, more situation specific. They are used only with certain audiences. James (1952: 190) captures the essence of this process when he says:

> Many a youth who is demure enough before his parents and teacher, swears and swaggers like a pirate among his "tough" young friends. We do not show ourselves to our children as to our club-companions, to our customers as to the laborers we employ, to our own masters and employers as to our intimate friends.

To go much further than this in discussing the nature of presented selves would lead me into a great deal of repetitiveness, for much that could be said about the presented self has already been noted in regard to the self-concept. The parallels between the two are numerous. For example, the presented self covers the same content areas as the self-concept. There are certain identities, qualities, self-evaluations, and confidence levels that we desire to present to others. Furthermore, the parts are organized in the same way. The various identities, qualities, and so on are arranged in a hierarchy of prominence. We prefer that people see us in some ways rather than others, and the preferred presented selves are more likely to be used. Also, some of the dimensions of presented selves are directly comparable to those of the self-concept. Presented selves of different individuals vary in regard to their stability, consistency, and so on.

The most important similarity, however, is that self-concepts and presented selves function in similar ways. Just as there are roles attached to the elements of the self-concept, so too there are roles attached to the parts of the presented self. At one step removed, both the self-concept and the presented self affect actor's behavior. A given act may reflect actor's attempt to be consistent with his self-definition, it may be an attempt to convey a particular image, or it may be an attempt to meet both goals simultaneously.

THE ROLE ASSOCIATED WITH THE PRESENTED SELF

When we speak of the role associated with the presented self, we refer to the behaviors that actor believes will convey the desired image. Obviously the term "role" as used in this phrase has a different meaning from the one it had when we were speaking of roles per se. However, just as the presented self and self-concept are similar in several ways, so are role and presented-self roles. Both the latter concepts refer to prescribed behavior, in both cases the prescribed behaviors are tied to identities, qualities, evaluations, and confidence levels. Role definitions tell us how people in certain categories ought to behave; presented-self roles tell us how we ought to behave if we want to be defined as having certain characteristics. Perhaps the major difference is that the "ought to" has some implication of obligation in reference to roles. If one disobeys a role definition, there is, more or less, some implication of a personal failing. A failure to follow a role associated with a presented self may lead people to question actor's intelligence, but it is not a matter of character. (In fact, in some cases to follow a presented-self role may be viewed as an indication of low moral worth.)

The parallelism between the two types of roles is seen further in the fact that both vary along many of the same dimensions. Again, to avoid repetition, I will simply list some of the dimensions that are relevant here as they were earlier. As with regular roles, the roles associated with the presented self vary in specificity and detail; different presented-self roles vary in the degree to which they provide clear-cut instructions for the performance. They also differ in regard to the actor's commitment to them, in the degree to which they are fixed or emergent in the specific situation, in the extent to which following them involves strain for the actor, and in the degree to which they are institutionalized, that is, in the degree to which they are similar to the actions that someone else would take in presenting the same self.

One dimension which is often not meaningful when discussing roles, but which is useful in the present case, relates to the question of *utility*. For many roles it does not make sense to ask whether a particular definition is better or worse than another. One may be more acceptable to others, one may be more common than others, but it would be difficult to argue that one role definition of, for example, the son-father role is better than another. When we say someone is a good son, all we usually mean is that his role definition is consistent with our own. Only when there is a specific task which has a measurable outcome does it make any sense to contend that one role definition is better than another. In regard to roles associated with the presented self, however, it is always relevant to inquire into the adequacy of the role, for there is always a task present—to get the other to "buy" a particular view of actor. Presented roles can always be evaluated in terms of the degree to which they succeed in accomplishing this primary goal.

In a later chapter, I will discuss the ways that presented-self roles are learned, and the factors which determine which actions will be chosen to present a particular self when actor knows several which could be used. For now, let us consider some of the general tactics that people use.

The Mechanics of Presenting Selves

At the most general level, I would note, following Goffman (1959), that people convey particular images by controlling the information available to the "audience." Only a very crude actor would explicitly announce what he or she "is." One is much more likely to be successful if he or she lets the others make up their own minds, while at the same time providing information which will "allow" only the desired definition.

Much of other's definition of actor is drawn from the setting of the interaction and from the actor's social front—his or her appearance and manner. These are, therefore, major aspects of the situation which actors desire to control. Let us consider in some detail how they typically go about it.

Controlling the Setting. The setting is that part of the environment which serves as a backdrop for the interaction. It is somewhat separate from the actor and might be likened to the set and props in a play. To a certain degree at least, the setting can be constructed by actors and they are often careful to design it in such a way that it helps convey the desired image or, at least, does not run counter to it. Examples abound. The person who wishes to convey an image of sophistication had better make sure the plastic covers are off the furniture before company arrives. Uncovered furniture doesn't imply sophistication, but covered furniture puts the lie to any such claim. The professor who wishes to appear erudite will be helped considerably if he or she obtains and prominently displays certain books while keeping others out of sight. The next time you are in a teacher's office, look around and see what it is meant to tell you about its occupant. Displaying autographed pictures of prominent people may or may not be an effective way of conveying an image of power, but apparently many people believe it is.

Settings which convey no relevant information may still be important in the presentation of self because they aid the actor in his or her performance. A door between the kitchen and living room does not in itself tell us anything about the person who lives there, but it may be a necessary part of the set if actor is going to successfully come across as an organized and efficient host. In general, the availability of back areas, that is, places where actors can be outside the view of the audience, facilitates the carrying out of an adequate performance. Also important is the availability of the necessary props. One cannot get across an image of hospitality and generosity without a well-stocked larder, for example.

Controlling the Personal Front. If the setting is analogous to the props and sets, the personal front is roughly akin to costume and makeup. Included here would be "insignia of office or rank; clothing; sex, age and racial characteristics; size and looks; posture; speech patterns; facial expressions and the like" (Goffman, 1959: 24). Appearance is the part of personal front which serves to inform the other of actor's social status; manner refers to those aspects which give hints about the way in which actor will play his social role.

It is clear that some aspects of the personal front convey more information than others, it is more acceptable to manipulate some parts than others, and it is easier to do so for some than for others (Stone, 1970, 1962). But they are all to some degree under the control of the actor. Such relatively fixed characteristics as sex, race, and age usually cannot be hidden or altered, but actor is often able to affect the degree to which these traits make an impression upon others by emphasizing or deemphasizing them. Full control may make things easier, but partial control is often sufficient.

Playing the Part. Creating a setting and a personal front is not, however, all there is to impression management. An interaction is not a photograph; it is a movie. It involves movement and action. After the scene is set, actor must act in a way that conveys the desired impression. Actor must play the part correctly or it will soon become clear that the definition suggested by setting and personal front is not valid. How do people convey the desired image?

At a very general level the answer is quite simple. To get others to see you in a particular light, you act in ways which will appear to be consistent with the *other's* definition of the appropriate role, and you make certain he is aware of your behavior but not its motivation. Thus the first part of self-presentation involves accurate role taking. However, even if one knows what actions will produce the desired result, it is not always easy in the rush of an interaction to stay in character. This will be especially true when the actor is presenting a false self, but it is not absent when an attempt is being made to get across a true self-image.

Let us now consider how actor goes about the task. What are the methods and acting techniques employed in playing a part?

1. Dramatic Realization. Actor is engaging in dramatic realization when he or she emphasizes those parts of the activity that convey the desired information. Thus, an umpire gives his call quickly and with exaggerated motions to indicate that he is certain of its correctness, the violinist bows more feverishly than necessary so everyone will know how difficult the piece is, and the trapeze artist asks for silence.

When a true self is being presented, dramatic realization often involves making "invisible costs visible." Actor makes certain that other is aware of the activities that are required to produce the performance, so that he or she is sure of getting the deserved credit. It takes an expert to realize how much work goes into the presentation of a good classroom lecture, and since the audience is not composed of experts, the lecturer will have to do things whose sole purpose is to make clear to them what has gone before. The teacher might even carry notes which are no longer needed to make sure the class knows that he or she has prepared for the session.

In presenting false selves, the problem is frequently the opposite one—the creation of apparent costs which in fact do not exist. The goal is usually to make the audience think that actor worked harder than he or she really did or that the task is more difficult than it is. This is what the violinist is doing by his exaggerated bowing. At other times, we do the opposite. We focus attention on the ease with which we do something, but at the same time convey the idea that others would not be able to do it so easily. Teachers have been known to memorize their lectures to convey the notion that they are speaking spontaneously and that they have a greater command of their subject matter than they do.

Dramatization of an activity is often risky. For one thing, many activities provide few good opportunities for self-dramatization. Any attempt to make a routine activity appear to be something else by dramatic flourishes will only make the actor seem foolish. The waiter who literally spent ten minutes going through a ritual in opening my bottle of wine appeared silly in my eyes—I was not impressed by his "skill."

The risk is compounded by the fact that the effort which goes into dramatization may distract the actor from the technical aspects of the performance and this may lead to blundering. This is particularly so, as Goffman (1959) notes, because the activities which dramatize may be very different from those which lead to successful performance. The quick response of the umpire may lead to a bad call which would not have occurred if some thought had been given beforehand. And, as many teachers have reason to know, too much desire to impress may lead one into confusion and even the presentation of incorrect information.

This notwithstanding, the drive to dramatize activities is exceedingly strong in many people, and they do it despite the difficulties and risks involved. One has only to look at others with this idea in mind to see many examples in everyday life.

2. Underplaying. The opposite of dramatization is *underplaying*. When actor underplays, the goal is to deemphasize some activities which go counter to the desired impression. The prompter at an opera is hidden from the audience, people try to keep others at a distance to hide the shabbiness of their clothes, lecturers sneak looks at their notes so the students will not notice that they don't know what comes next. We are not actually hiding anything; we do what has to be done, but we do it as unobtrusively as possible in the hope that it may be overlooked.

3. Idealization. Goffman (1959) tells us that an actor is idealizing when he "plays it to the hilt" in front of others to put to rest any doubts that he merits the status he seeks. A person who is presenting an idealized performance will not take any shortcuts, even if they are permissible. The person who wishes to appear religious will ensure that he is seen in that light by refusing to accept any of the "easy ways out" even when they become acceptable to religious authorities. He enacts the ideal version of the role. Similarly, people will parade their poverty by not buying things they can afford if they want to be sure that they will be seen as lower class. This is a pattern which was quite common among sociology graduate students when I was in school. (To get as far as graduate school was much more of an accomplishment in our eyes if one came from a deprived background than if one had "all the advantages." It also permitted one to speak knowingly of the culture of the poor in seminars.)

In itself, the notion of idealization is not difficult to grasp. It is simply going to extremes to prove one's merit. To this reader, at least, the difficulty is that it is not clear what Goffman sees as the relationship between idealization and dramatic realization. Without contending that Goffman would agree, I would suggest that they are related. Idealization is *one* way to achieve dramatic realization. People dramatize in order to direct other's attention. To do something in an extreme way usually serves to draw attention to the activity. The umpire with his quick call is trying to direct attention to his certainty *by* acting the role of the umpire in an idealized way. At the same time, idealization is not the only way of dramatizing. We can dramatize by simply mentioning the activities we wish to highlight, for example.

4. Prevarication. Lies are also often used as a means of accomplishing a presentation of self—a point that might seem redundant after the preceding discussion. I don't think it is, however. Dramatization and underplaying involve misrepresentation, but they don't necessarily involve lying—an explicit statement of something known to be untrue.

It seems to me important to make a distinction between lies and misleading impressions achieved by nondisclosure, ambiguous statement, misleading literal truth, and so on. This distinction allows us to see the risks that people are willing to run in order to carry out a presentation of self. Most people distinguish between a lie and other forms of misrepresentation; they consider lies to be much more heinous. Thus the consequences of being caught in a lie are much more serious. At a minimum, there is likely to be strong embarrassment and loss of the respect of the other. In addition, other sanctions may be applied, up to and including ostracism. As Goffman notes, to be caught in a lie leads many audiences to assume that the actor ought never again be fully trusted, and people tend to avoid people they feel they cannot trust. Of course, most people who try to deceive, normally use lies as a last resort rather than a first. In part this is because it is usually possible for actors to create the desired impression without running the risks involved in lying. "Communication techniques such as innuendo, strategic ambiguity, and crucial omissions allow the misinformer to profit from lies without putting himself in the indefensible position of having told a clear-cut lie" (Goffman, 1959: 62). The point is, however, that when all else fails most people will, when the issue is important enough, take their chances and use the technique of lying. Perhaps it is only the "saint" who will never lie on principle, but even they seem to feel that some lies are justified.

To say that presenting a self is so important to many people that they are willing to run risks to accomplish it, is not to say that people are unconcerned about the risks. In fact, it is clear that people go to considerable lengths to minimize risks by taking actions intended to reduce the possibility of discovery. Let us now consider what some of these actions are.

Audience Management. The general category of audience management includes several specific techniques of manipulating the audience so that they are less likely to "see through" the performance. In themselves, they are not ways of communicating an impression. They are things we "do to" the audience in order to get them to accept the impression we are trying to communicate. Two of those techniques are discussed in the following paragraphs.

1. Segregation of audiences. One of the difficulties involved in misrepresenting is that the others often have access to additional sources of information against which they can check the impression fostered by the performance. They can find out if the view they have received is true by asking others who know actor or by observing actor in more private situations or before other audiences.

The obvious solution for actor is to be consistent in all his or her performances so that no audience can be made suspicious by apparently conflicting actions.[6] For most actors, however, that is not a very good solution. Consistent posing is not easy to achieve and sometimes it is a barrier to the achievement of other goals. For example, even the most confirmed poseur would like to relax and be himself on occasion. Also, to be consistent means that one cannot present different impressions to different people, and we have many reasons to want to do that. Our goals in different interaction situations will be different; it is unlikely that a single presented self would serve in all cases. Even the person who is most interested in having other people respect him would want to be thought of as a "fun guy" by some.

The problem can be eliminated if we can arrange it so that we limit the access that our audience has to us. This may be done by physical segregation; the nouveau riche snob never invites the folks from back home to visit, or invites them only to the vacation house, or doesn't invite friends when the family is present. The panic experienced by social climbing parents when their child's wedding approaches and they realize that this kind of segregation will not be possible has been the subject of several comedies.

The physical segregation of audiences is facilitated by the existence in real life of areas which are the equivalent of the theatre's dressing room and "green room." (The latter is a room found in most theatres which is used as a place for relaxing by members of the company. Outsiders are usually not admitted.) A person's home, den, or office may be, depending on circumstances, analogous to the dressing room. Here one can be free from all prying eyes. Admission is by invitation only, and there is usually time to "get oneself together" before one must face others. Equivalents to

---

[6]This does not mean, of course, that all variations in behavior will cause suspicion. Everyone knows that people act differently under different circumstances. The thing to be avoided is variability which does not seem to be due to differences in the situation and those which contradict a previously presented impression.

the "green room" abound—the locker room, the powder room, or the club are some of these. In such areas, people may be themselves, or at least different selves than they are in public, without threatening their public images.

If actual segregation is not possible, the actor can perhaps control the situation by arranging it so that a neutral role may be played when in the presence of several audiences. If family and friends have different views of actor and they must be brought together, the actor may try to do it at the vacation house or some other unusual setting. Due to the special location, the actor may be able to act in a way which will do nothing to cast doubt on the image either group holds of him. The trick, of course, is to arrange it so the situation does not involve interaction which will require actor to engage in activities which can be viewed as disconfirming previous impressions.

2. Suspending Disbelief. In a theatre, an audience enters with a willingness to suspend their disbelief. In order to enjoy a play, we avoid seeing things which are clearly impossible because if we allowed such things to intrude upon our consciousness it would be impossible to take the play seriously. So we fail to note that time passes much too quickly on the stage, that sets use painted backdrops, or that the star is twenty years older than the character he or she is playing.

In real life, however, most audiences are not prepared to suspend disbelief. To the contrary, they approach many encounters with the assumption that there is a chance that actor will try to fool them, and unlike a theatre audience they do not want to allow this. This suspiciousness puts them on guard, and that decreases the chance of a successful performance. The actor is well-advised to reduce this "natural" suspicion—to create an atmosphere which will reduce other's motivation to look too closely.

There are several ways to accomplish this. Goffman (1959) notes that "the maintenance of social distance, provide(s) a way in which awe can be generated and sustained in the audience—a way, as Kenneth Burke has said, in which the audience can be held in a state of mystification in regard to the performer" (Goffman, 1959: 67). Formality of manner, impressive titles, a somewhat condescending air, may so cower the audience that they are in a sense afraid to look too closely. (In addition, pomp, ceremony, and ritual can, paradoxically, be means of underplaying; they can serve to direct attention away from the fact that the monarch is really rather paunchy and not at all prepossessing.)

Under some circumstances, the average person can use these techniques of mystification, although not very frequently. Most of us do not have the necessary props, and if we did, they wouldn't look right in our hands. Most of our attempts to mystify *create* suspicion. We do have available to us, however, techniques which will do at least part of the job. By creating a "special relationship" with the audience, we can convince them that they do not have to worry about being deceived, because under the circumstances attempts at deception are unlikely. You don't try to fool your special friends. In addition, the audience will refuse to see evidence of deception. To do so might lead to breaking the special relationship, and we usually don't want that.

Auto salesmen and politicians are the acknowledged masters of creating special relationships. They immediately go to a first name basis to create a feeling of informality, acceptance, and identification. A good memory for names is the basis for some political careers, but even that is not necessary. If a politician forgets a name, it is easy to make it appear to be a momentary block which usually gets the other to give his name. This is always reacted to in a way which suggests, "Of course, now I remember." A prominent Connecticut politician I know (what technique of impression management am I using by saying that?) seems to follow the practice of acting as though he has previously encountered everyone he meets. If the encounter turns out to be a first one, nothing is lost. No one is insulted by an important other thinking there has been a previous meeting. However, if the politician has met the other, "remembering" him or her suggests that the other is important to the politician; the other is "worth remembering."

In addition, a person can create the desired appearance of a special relation by sharing confidences and by doing favors for the others, or at least by making it seem that he or she is doing that. A car salesman does it by giving a "lower price," because "the customer was so nice," and a politician has the same goal when he promises to make an extra effort to meet a constituent's request and when he reveals the "inside story."

Maintaining Expressive Control.   No matter how good an actor is at manipulating the audience to make his or her presentation of self easier, great care must still be exercised. Others define the actor in large part by taking note of the major aspects of the performance and these are reasonably easy to control just because they are major and likely to be in the forefront of the actor's mind. But small cues do register with the audience and unless the audience is totally befuddled, actor must be sure that minor actions do not negate the central elements. In large part, this involves avoiding certain slips. They would include the following:

1. The actor must avoid unmeant gestures which conflict with the intended impression. Often one must hide signs of annoyance, for example, and mistakes must also be avoided. If he has limited knowledge of French, a smart actor who wants to be seen as a man of the world would do well to go to a French restaurant which prints its menu in English as well as French. And when he orders wine, he would be wise to point or order by bin number. That may appear a little tacky, but it is better than a clear-cut wrong pronunciation.

2. In a sense, all failures of expressive control could be called blunders, but I will reserve the term for intentional behaviors which have unintended consequences. To ask a recently divorced person about his or her wonderful spouse represents a blunder. Even if the actor had no way of knowing of the divorce, such a question may make it almost impossible to convey an image of intimacy with the other. The difficulty is worsened by the fact that blunders often throw people "off their timing." They cause the actor embarrassment, he or she gets flustered, and rather than playing the blunder down, actor apologizes effusively and ends up making it more important than it would have been. Unintended dramatization can ruin a performance.

Given the difficulty of presenting selves, actor often requires help to give a convincing performance. Let us consider some of the aids that are available. (For more details see Goffman, 1959.)

Rehearsal and Tryout. Performances improve with practice, so if the actor can run through the action without an audience, or, even better, in front of an audience which doesn't matter, his or her chances of being "a hit at the opening" are much improved. This is done most systematically and overtly for formal occasions. When people are going to give a speech, they often practice before a mirror or before their spouse to make sure they "have it right," which means more than simply knowing the content. "Right" includes knowing the proper gestures and expressions. If the speech is to have the desired effect, the speechmaker must be careful that the subtle parts of the presentation do not put the lie to the words.

For less formal occasions, the rehearsal may take place in the mind. It is not necessary to actually go through the steps of an encounter in order to practice it. We can think about what is likely to happen and prepare our responses. One would feel silly and perhaps a little guilty if one literally rehearsed for a "date." Just thinking about what might happen is, however, quite acceptable, and perhaps more effective because it is less likely to reduce actor's flexibility when "on stage."

In some instances, it is very difficult to practice the self-presenting elements of a performance until one is actually performing. Even in such cases, however, rehearsal can be very useful. If actor rehearses the other aspects of the performance and gets them down pat, his mind will be left free to work on the self-presenting elements when before the audience. Thus, a wedding rehearsal does not have the atmosphere which would permit the parents to practice how to convey happiness without at the same time showing signs of relief, but it does allow them to know what is going to happen at the wedding. Thus, during the actual ceremony, their minds can be free to work on the expressive elements.

Supporting Casts. In many instances, the actor need not depend solely upon his or her own actions to present a self-image. In fact, all other things being equal, it is better to have a supporting cast, or, as Goffman calls it, a team. Among other things, a supporting cast can serve to reduce suspicion. As noted before, most audiences are at least somewhat suspicious of actors, but they are less suspicious of supporting casts, particularly if the latter are thought to be part of the audience. The others in an interaction often think, quite rightly, that the actor is attempting to manipulate their view of him or her in order to gain some kind of advantage. They are less likely to think that others in the situation have any desire to manipulate the participants' view of actor. This is particularly so if the others are viewed as "one of us." Thus it is to actor's advantage to have others make his claims for him or, at least, to have them validate his claims.

A good supporting cast can be useful, but a poor one can be a disaster. Might not the reluctance of some parents to take their young children into public places be associated with the fact that the immature have a penchant for destroying the images that their parents work so hard to create? It is difficult to get across the image of a good parent when a child who is obviously yours is throwing a tantrum on the floor.

This example suggests that the members of a good cast must know their parts; they must know what the goal of the actor is and they must know what actions by them will help the goal to be achieved. This substantive knowledge is not enough, however. When children get somewhat older, they frequently are quite aware that certain behaviors are inappropriate in public and that others are expected. And it wouldn't be giving them too much credit to suggest that they have at least an elementary understanding of why their parents want them to behave in the accepted way. But, of course, it is not at all certain they will do so. The supporting cast must be committed to its task.

Commitment to such an activity often requires a willingness to submerge one's own short-term interests to those of the "star." If you are helping another person get across a particular self view, it is often difficult to control the impression of yourself which is conveyed. Such sacrifice usually occurs only when the supporting actor is in debt to the lead actor or when the cast member expects a payoff in the future. In some cases, however, the cast benefits directly from the support they give. Thus, the lover is more than willing to sing the praises of the loved one to all who will listen because if others are convinced of the loved one's perfection, it reflects favorably upon the lover.

A good supporting cast must be prepared and loyal, but even this does not ensure that the presentation will be successful. Something akin to acting talent is necessary; that is, the ability to stay "in character" and to give a convincing performance. This is made easier for the average person when there is "type casting," that is, when the role the supporting actor must play is in fact his or her true role. Thus, if you want to convey the image of being much admired, you are well advised to employ a cast composed of persons who in fact do admire you.

A final factor which is conducive to an effective ensemble presentation is the opportunity to rehearse. In fact, rehearsal time is probably more important here than it is in a solo performance. Most of us are reasonably good at playing our parts and ad-libbing when necessary. However, an effective group performance requires the various parts to mesh, and that is much more difficult. Role-taking ability will help, but in a situation in which a single slip can cause confusion and give the show away, a considerable degree of experience is often almost a necessity.

Although this discussion barely scratches the surface of the topic, it will suffice. (For additional details see Goffman, 1959; Brissett and Edgley, 1975.) I don't wish to present a manual on how to win at "the games people play." The major point has been made—people are motivated to create in others a particular impression of themselves, and they use elaborate stratagems to achieve that end.

SUMMARY

The theory postulates that certain mental structures—the self-concept, roles, the presented self, and the roles associated with the presented self—are developed in interaction and influence what actor does in his future interaction.

The self-concept is the individual's thoughts and feelings about himself. It consists of (1) identities—the self-defining elements which refer to the social categories to which actor thinks he belongs; (2) a set of qualities which refer to our beliefs concerning our personal traits—our interests, our physical characteristics, our abilities, and so on; (3) a set of self-evaluations which are attached to our identities and qualities and refer to our view of how good we are at what we think we are; (4) our levels of self-confidence—our estimates of how capable we are of achieving our goals. Data are cited which indicate that most people's self-concepts do contain elements classifiable into these categories.

The self-concept is more than a collection of items; it has a structure. Identities and qualities are, for example, organized into a hierarchy of prominence and self-evaluations are combined into a general estimate of worth—the person's self-esteem. Self-concepts can also be differentiated in terms of their degree of stability, consistency, certainty, acceptance, and satisfaction.

Roles are prescriptions for behavior which are associated with particular actor-other combinations. A person's view of how a father should act toward his son, for example, would represent that individual's definition of the father-son role. Roles, are, however, not limited to recognized identities such as father and son. There are roles for each component of the self-concept.

The view adopted here states that we enter most situations with a view of what is acceptable and that view will provide a general plan of action. This plan is, however, subject to revision if actor's experiences in this situation suggest that change is appropriate. In addition, roles are, to a greater or lesser degree, incomplete, and therefore actor will have to take a creative part in the interaction. Role performance is not akin to the reading of a script.

In addition to variation in specificity, there is variation in the degree of actor's allegiance to the role (role commitment), differences in the degree of difficulty associated with meeting the role prescriptions (role strain), and differences in the degree to which a particular role definition is generally accepted (degree of institutionalization).

The term "presented self" refers to the images that actor wishes other to have of him. When actor behaves in a particular way so that other will see him in the way he desires we say that actor is engaging in "impression management," that is, he is presenting a self. Such activities are used when actor is attempting to get other to see him as he believes he really is and when actor is attempting to convey an image of himself which he does not believe to be accurate. Impression management is considered to be a common occurrence in human interaction, and the selves presented vary depending on the circumstances of the interaction.

The roles associated with the presented self are those behaviors which actor believes will convey the desired image. Such roles vary on many of the same dimensions as roles in general do. These are described—and the chapter ends with a discussion of the various mechanisms which are utilized in the process of impression management. These tactics represent the general content of presented-self roles.

CHAPTER 4

THE PERCEIVED SOCIAL DEFINITION AND SELF-EVALUATIONS

Now that the central concepts have been defined and discussed, we may proceed to a consideration of how the entities they refer to develop. The task is twofold. We must first consider the general processes which lead to the development of each structure, and then we can turn our attention to the factors which account for variations in their content and organization.

The job is made considerably easier by the fact that though there are differences in details, the general process of development is quite similar for each central variable, as are the factors which affect variations. Thus, it will not be necessary to present four or five separate theories. I will present a single theory, focusing on self-evaluation, and then it will be a rather simple matter to indicate the relatively small alterations necessary to make the theory applicable to the other central variables. A large part of the "beauty" of interactionist theory lies in the fact that a relatively concise and simple theory can be utilized to explain several mental structures which apparently are quite different.

THE DEVELOPMENT OF SELF-EVALUATIONS

In the interactionist view, a major basis for a person's self-evaluations is his perception of how others evaluate him—his *perceived social definition*. Our view of ourselves is largely a reflection of what we think others think of us. "Just as the sound 'ba' took on meaning through the responses of others, so too the organism as an object takes on meaning through the behavior of those who respond to that organism. We come to know what we are through others' responses to us" (Stryker, 1959: 116).

Clearly, the interactionist emphasizes the social component in the self-concept, but this is not to say that actor is seen as a sponge that soaks up the opinions of others. The details will be considered later, but here it should be noted that the interactionist position is that actors take an active part in the development of their own self-views. For example, they count some received evaluations more heavily than others, they structure the situation in order to receive a particular kind of evaluation, and so forth.

Furthermore, it is explicitly recognized that the opinions of others are *not* the only source of actor's self-evaluations. Again, the details will be given later, but for now it should be sufficient to say that it is assumed that people also evaluate their own behavior in terms of their personal standards and by comparing their actions with those of others. As I see it, self-evaluations have two sources. The actor gathers information on others' opinions and from this emerges the perceived social definition. Actor also develops a *tentative personal definition* by rating his or her own actions. The self-evaluation which becomes part of the self-conception is a product of these two ingredients.

The first task is, then, to determine if the theory is correct in postulating that others' views are, in fact, major determinants of actors' self-evaluations, for this is not a contention that everyone will accept as obviously true. Many are actually somewhat insulted by the suggestion that it applies to them. They see it as a denial of their individualism and autonomy.

Those who are of this opinion will find little comfort in the empirical literature. The matter has been studied exhaustively and there is now little room for doubt that the interactionist position is valid. Let us briefly consider some of the data.

Research on this subject established rather quickly that there was a correlation between respondents' self-evaluations or self-esteem and their perceptions of how others rate them. Miyamoto and Dornbusch (1956) found, for example, that students gave themselves high ratings on such value-laden traits as intelligence, self-confidence, physical attractiveness, and likeability when they believed that the other members of their group rated them high on these traits, and Quarantelli and Cooper (1966) found this same pattern in regard to the self-evaluations of dental students. Other studies got comparable results for a variety of actor-other combinations: Students who get good grades and those who think their teachers think well of them are more likely to give themselves a high rating as students (Davidson and Lang, 1960; Brookover et al., 1963–64; Coombs and Davies, 1966; Fitts, 1971); enlisted military personnel's self-ratings on leadership and work efficiency correlated with their estimates of their workmates' ratings of them (Reeder et al., 1960); college students who rate themselves positively are more likely to report that their parents think well of them (Jourard and Remy, 1955).

Another series of studies approaches this problem somewhat indirectly. Rather than asking actor what he thinks others think of him, actor describes other in regard to certain traits which permit a deduction concerning actor's perception of other's evaluation of him. Thus, if an actor says his parents are loving, we may assume that he is more likely to feel they evaluate him positively than is the case when the respondent sees the parents as not loving. Studies of this type are consistent in their results. People who view themselves in favorable terms are more likely than those with low self-evaluations to say their parents are: loving and not neglectful (Medinnus, 1965); warm and respectful (Coopersmith, 1967); supportive (Gecas, 1971; Gecas et al., 1970); accepting (Thomas, 1967); and interested in them (Rosenberg, 1965).

To prove that there is a clear relationship between actors' evaluations of self and their perception of others' view of them does not, however, prove that actors take on others' view of them. These findings are consistent with the interactionist view, but they do not prove it, because there are alternative explanations.

The problem is that cause and effect are not clear in these studies. It could be, for example, that those who have high self-evaluations behave in ways which cause others to view them favorably. Thus, high self-evaluation could be the cause of other's approval, rather than the other way around, as interactionist theory suggests. Furthermore, if people who like themselves simply assume that other people must also think highly of them, this would produce some of the associations reported even if other's opinion had no effect on actor. Finally, it could be that people who rate themselves positively convince others to have the same view.[1]

Fortunately, data are available which are free from these ambiguities. Several studies (for example, Israel, 1956; Harvey et al., 1956–57; Videbeck, 1960; Bergin, 1962; Maehr et al., 1962; Gergen, 1965; Haas and Maehr, 1965; Jones, 1966; Tippett and Silber, 1966; Ludwig and Maehr, 1967; Jones and Pines, 1968; Kinch, 1968) all use some variant of the before-after design. The self-concept is measured, one group is given different evaluations from those given the other, and then the self-concept is measured again. If changes occur and they are in the direction of the evaluations given, the only possible explanation is that the persons who were evaluated did accept the evaluations of others and made them part of their self-evaluations. In all the studies cited, the predicted changes were observed.

It would seem, then, rather indisputable that people do, in fact, tend to take the attitudes of others into their self-concepts. Not everyone does it all the time, and there are other ingredients that go to make up a self-concept, but it is clear that our perceptions of others' views are an important source of self-views.

The Adoption of Others' Views

With the empirical question settled, we can return to the theoretical issues. It seems clear that we do incorporate other's views into our self-concepts. How and why does it happen? How do we come to know others' opinions and why do we base our self-views

---

[1]Undoubtedly, this is not an either/or situation. The operation of all these processes would be entirely consistent with the interactionist view. The only concern is whether the correlations are at least partly due to the effects of other's attitudes upon actor.

on them? The answer to the first part has already been suggested by earlier material, but let us review that briefly before we go on.

Knowing Others' Views. In the process of social interaction, the actors are quite interested in knowing what the others have "on their minds." For reasons that will be discussed in detail in Chapter 6, actor wishes to know how the others define the situation and what course of action they are likely to follow. Furthermore, we all know that others' actions are importantly influenced by their evaluation of our behavior. Others' reactions to an act of which they approve are likely to be very different from the reactions to disapproved behavior. Thus, we are particularly interested in knowing others' evaluation of our behavior. This is the source of the basic motivation to know the opinion of other. Actor needs that information to anticipate others' reactions.

The process by which the desired information is obtained has already been described. By means of his role-taking ability, actor puts himself in the place of the others, and guesses how they evaluate him. Of course, this guess may or may not be accurate, but at this point the accuracy of the role taking is not an important issue. The postulate does not say that actor's view of self will be the same as others' view of him. The contention is that the self-view will reflect actor's *perception* of the opinions of others. Frequently, actor will perceive accurately, but this is not essential for the argument being presented here.[2]

What has been said thus far is a beginning, but it does not account for the tendency to *adopt* other's view as our own. It may be clear why we want to know other's opinions and how we know them, but that says nothing about why we tend to integrate them into our own self-view.

Given the importance of the issue, it is quite surprising that it has received little consideration from interactionists. The tendency to take on others' views is often asserted as though it were a self-evident proposition. But when one thinks a moment, it becomes clear that this tendency requires explanation. It is by no means obvious why a person should accept other peoples' evaluations of him or her. Aren't we the best judges of our own behavior? The postulated incorporation of other people's views is particularly problematic when they are negative, since, as will be seen later, we also postulate that people generally have a desire to think well of themselves.

---

[2] The reader will recall from the discussions of role taking and the presentation of self, that this judgment is never easy. Even when other "tells" actor what the evaluation is—through direct verbal statements or through subtle nonverbal gestures such as a smile, a frown, or an approving nod of the head—interpretation is necessary. Is other being sarcastic or should he be taken literally? What do the words really mean? Is the tone of voice such that "pretty good" should be taken to mean "damn good?" What kind of scale is being used? Is praise from other difficult or easy to get? And, is other telling the truth? Especially when praise is involved, the possibility exists that other is attempting to convey a false impression, and actor must decide whether this is so or not.

The basic notions upon which this theory is built suggest why people accept others' definition of them. They do it because they get gain (reward) from doing it. But what, specifically, are the natures of these rewards? McGuire (1969), writing about attitudes and beliefs in general, notes four functions that may be served by accepting the views of others. These functions are the utilitarian (adaptive), the knowledge, the expressive (self-realizing), and the ego-defensive. The first three seem relevant here. Let us first consider their general nature, and then show how they apply in this case.

The Utilitarian Function. To adopt an attitude that has utilitarian value allows the actor to reach an *external* goal; it permits him or her to possess some physical object that is desired, to have a particular kind of reaction from other, to occupy a position that is sought. Such goals may be viewed as somewhat more external than those involved in the functions discussed below. In what follows, the goal is solely to achieve a particular state of mind. The achievement of utilitarian goals may also lead to a desired psychological state, but that is a side effect.

The Knowledge Function. The knowledge function is served when an attitude provides the actor with a feeling that now he or she "understands." Attitudes can fill in the gaps in our knowledge, giving us a basis for making sense out of the world. Ultimately such knowledge may be put to utilitarian purposes, but even in the absence of that it serves a personal function for us—the reduction of our feelings of ignorance. Of course, it is not necessary that our ignorance actually be reduced. To believe that a minority group is genetically inferior may provide us with explanations which are satisfying even if they are incorrect. An attitude or belief serves the knowledge function whenever it gives the actor a *feeling* of knowledge.

The Expressive Function. A third function which may be served by the adoption of others' view is the satisfaction of personal needs other than the need for knowledge. In general attitude theory, the needs referred to under this rubric include the need for release of inner tensions, the need for self-assertion, the need for justification of behavior, and the need for consistency among beliefs. In the case of self-referring attitudes, the goal is to have a positive view of self. An evaluation which will help the person think well of himself or herself is likely to be accepted by virtue of that fact alone. In addition, most people prefer a relatively consistent and stable view of self to one which is constantly changing and complex, and they would tend to adopt a view which would help in these regards.

Now that the functions have been described in general terms, let us apply them to the acceptance of others' view of self by children and adults.

The Adoption of Other's View of Self by Children

For children, the acceptance of others' view of them is likely to lead to the utilitarian goal of interpersonal peace. A child avoids conflict and negative criticism when he adopts other people's evaluations of his behavior. Most parents will not brook contradiction on such matters. A child who insists that he is being good when his parents tell him he is being bad is likely to experience undesirable outcomes.

In addition, to accept the parents' definition of his behavior makes it easier for the child to behave as they think he should—which is a second means of avoiding conflict. When a child accepts the parents' view of him he also accepts their standards for proper behavior. Later, when he acts as he wishes he is at the same time gaining their approval by acting as they wish. Of course, the child could act as they wish without accepting their definition, but that is more difficult and may produce *intra*personal conflict.

The education function is perhaps even more important. We may assume that the child has a desire to know who he is. But how can he arrive at such knowledge independently of other people? He has little basis for making a personal judgment, for he lacks personal standards which will permit him to judge himself. He has only two options—either to accept the view of others or to leave the question unanswered. Even for a child this latter choice is likely to be unpalatable.

Moreover, as has been noted elsewhere (Piaget, 1948; Rosenberg, 1979), the child is likely to assume, with good reason, that older people know better than he, and he has a lot of practice in accepting their views in regard to many things. He is likely to assume that they know better than he what is right just as they know better what is dangerous and what is safe. Accepting their view of him is likely to seem entirely natural.

Finally, the child is likely to accept others' view of him because he feels good when he does so. He feels he is doing what they want of him and that in itself is satisfying. In addition, we may assume that most parents are reasonably accepting of their children. Children in such a situation would be inclined to adopt others' view of them because to do so contributes to their own sense of self-worth.

In summary, children learn to accept the definition of them provided by others because it is to their advantage to do so. It is a means of avoiding conflict, a path to knowledge, and a way of satisfying other needs such as the need for self-approval.

The Adoption of Other's View by Adults

Although the details are somewhat different, similar answers hold when we ask why adults tend to take on other's views. Comparable advantages accrue to adults when they act in this way.[3]

[3]Of course, by the time a person reaches adulthood he or she is likely to have the habit of adopting other's views. However, adult behavior cannot be explained in terms of habits developed in childhood. The habit would quickly be extinguished if it were no longer productive of reward.

For one thing, accepting other's view and acting consistently with it is, for adults also, a way of achieving peaceful interaction. Others make the same demands on adults that they do on children.

In the case of adults, however, there is a complication. The utilitarian function could be served by *appearing* to accept other's view. Adults can give the impression that they are accepting other's view without actually doing so, and they can act consistently with it without accepting it.[4] And, of course, this is what we do sometimes. But more often than not, we actually do take an other's view, and the question is why. Why don't we settle for an apparent acceptance?

The answer lies, I believe, in the costs associated with the presentation of a false self. It will be remembered that it is not easy to present a false self in a convincing manner. If actor does not believe in what he or she is doing, other is likely to see through the charade, and this would intensify rather than reduce the conflict. If one allows oneself to be convinced, the performance is more likely to be accepted. In addition, there are intrapsychic costs involved in performing false selves. Most of us are conflicted when what we are doing and saying does not represent our true beliefs. This conflict can be reduced in a variety of ways but one way of doing it is to change our beliefs, that is, to truly accept other's view. This is not always a conscious process, and when it is conscious, it is likely to be associated with a lot of rationalization, but it does lead to the conversion of actor to other's view.

There is probably at least one other process at work to bring the actor from apparent acceptance to "true" acceptance. The actions which actor undertakes to further the impression of acceptance may lead him to actual acceptance. For example, let us assume that actor does a task in a particular way which other defines unfavorably. Actor does not accept that definition but acts consistently with it, at least part of the time, to "keep peace." In the process of so doing, actor may find that other's way is preferable and come to define himself unfavorably because of his continued allegiance to his original way.

In this case, of course, it can be argued that actor is not, in fact, accepting other's view. He is changing his own view of his behavior which happens to bring him into concordance with other. If there is a distinction here at all, it seems to me that it is very fine and of doubtful significance. To accept another's opinion does not require that the acceptance be based solely on the authority of the other. In this case, the opinion of the other started off a chain of events which led actor to have a view of self consistent with other's view and different from actor's original view. That seems to be enough to warrant the assertion that actor is accepting other's view.

In my discussion of the process of self-formation in children, I suggested that in addition to bringing direct rewards from other, the adoption of other's view serves a knowledge function. It allows children to know themselves in the absence of any

---

[4]This ability is not totally lacking in children, of course. They appear to acquiesce even when they do not really agree. Their capacity to do this is, however, quite limited, and the chances that they would get desired utilitarian rewards is, in the average case, very low. It is too easy to see through them.

basis for reaching an independent judgment. Adults may not be so bereft of personal standards, but there are frequent occasions when they cannot judge themselves any better than children can. These would be most frequent when they are in new and unfamiliar situations, but it is not limited to those times.

In some instances, for example, the only "proper" judge of a performance is the other. I cannot convince myself that I am the one who can best judge how good I am as an author. The criterion is the extent to which I am communicating my ideas, and I cannot know that without knowing the reactions of my readers. If those reactions are unfavorable, telling myself "it makes sense to me" will do my self-evaluation as an author no good. I might say that my opinion of the value of the ideas is worth more than yours, given my greater familiarity with the materials already available in the field, but when it comes to communication I must bow to other's opinions. Matters of this type are not all that uncommon; the same would be true in regard to kindliness, attractiveness, value as a friend, and so on. This is not to say, of course, that we accept all others as competent judges of these qualities. The point is that if people are to know themselves in these regards, the only way to do so is to accept the views of some other or group of others.

The tendency to accept other's evaluation is, however, not limited to these topics. We accept others' views even in matters in which it is "possible" for us to have independent judgments. The general reason for this is that most of us emerge from our early socialization experiences with a greater or lesser lack of confidence in our abilities to judge people. In many matters, we simply recognize that others may know better even if we would not admit total inability. We wonder if our standards are the proper ones, and in the face of authorities who disagree, we accept other's opinion.

Even when we have no doubts about our ability to judge others in a particular regard, our confidence may leave us when it comes to judging ourselves in that regard. The problem is that many of us are never sure that we are being unbiased when it comes to ourselves. Are we being too hard on ourselves or are we too willing to give ourselves the benefit even when there is little doubt? So we look to others and accept their views, not because they know better, but because they are viewed as being more objective.

As a beginning teacher, I was constantly amazed by the small number of complaints I got about grades on term papers. I assumed that most students would not hand in a paper which was not good by their standards and that they would consider their standards to be at least as valid as those of an instructor who was obviously very young, very inexperienced, and very insecure. For every poor grade, I expected an argument. Now I know that both parts of my assumption were wrong. But the important point here is that students apparently did accept my view of their work. Frequently their response was, "I thought it was better than a C paper, but I guess I was wrong." They had little confidence in their ability to judge themselves.

There is direct, systematic evidence that children and adolescents have greater confidence in the opinions of others about them than they have in their independent judgments. Rosenberg (1973) asked a sample of students in grades 3 through 12, "If I asked you and your mother how smart you were, and you said one thing and she said another, who would be right? You or your mother?" Fifty-eight percent said they would be more likely to trust their mother's judgment than their own. When the trait involved was "how good you are," fully two-thirds said, "mother knows best." Even when they are asked, "who knows best what kind of a person you really are? Your mother, your father, yourself, or your best friend?", almost half said someone other than themselves. For adults the proportions are undoubtedly lower; even in Rosenberg's sample the older respondents were much less likely to opt for other's opinions when it conflicted with their own view. But even for the 16 to 18 year olds, the proportions bowing to other's views were between 30 and 47 percent, depending on the question. This is hardly consistent with the view of adolescents as "know-it-alls."

One final point before we proceed to the next issue. The statement that we tend to adopt other's view is based on the assumption that the acceptance of other's view will usually serve a function for actor. I think the examples given suggest that this is plausible. It must be emphasized, however, that it could be that the actor will get no gain from the acceptance of a particular view offered by an other. If that is the case, the logic of my position suggests that the view will be rejected. In other words, the strong tendency to accept other's view is in a sense an "empirical accident." It is by no means a necessity. It occurs because it is *usually* profitable for actor to accept other's view.

Developing a Perceived Social Definition

If actor is receiving evaluations which are consistent with each other, the material presented so far would represent an adequate theory of the *social* sources of self-evaluations. We have explained how actors know the views of others and why they tend to adopt them. All that would remain would be to complete the picture by discussing actor's tendency to make the independent judgments which are also incorporated into the self-image.

Sometimes, of course, all the evaluations received by actor are consistent, but it is more often the case that actor receives conflicting definitions from others. When this is so, the theory presented so far becomes clearly inadequate. The question becomes not will other's views be adopted, but which other's views will be adopted and how will the inconsistencies be resolved? Is each new evaluation taken into the self as a replacement for all the previous evaluations in that area? Is the most commonly received evaluation the influential one? Are all evaluations simply averaged?

I would suggest that none of these is correct. The view of others that actors incorporate into their self-concepts is an amalgam of all the evaluations received. From all the definitions received, actor develops a *general perceived social definition,* that is, a general view of how "people see him," and it is that perceived social definition that will be incorporated into the self-concept.

Certainly, if actor has received many evaluations in a specific area, his view of how he is seen will not reflect only the last evaluation received. Previous evaluations will have left their residue and any new ones will be added into the mix. The addition of a new ingredient may change the "batter," but it won't simply replace what was there before. Adding a little milk to a mixture which was largely flour may make the mixture less "doughy," but it won't change it to milk.

This analogy also suggests that the perceived social definition is not merely a reflection of the most common evaluation. General perceived social definitions do not come in simple positive and negative forms; there are degrees of both. Adding more and more milk may bring the mixture to a point that we stop calling it dough and put it in the milk category. But it will not be simply milk when it crosses over the line; it will be milk with a lot of flour in it, and it will never become pure milk unless we do something to remove the flour. So with the perceived social definition. An evaluation which was originally negative can be changed to a positive one by adding more positive ones and at some point it will cross over the imaginary line and be considered a positive view. But at that time it is not simply a positive evaluation. It is a very weakly positive one, a positive one which can easily be changed. The previous negative evaluations do not disappear, and the person who has had the experience I just described would have a perceived definition which is different from one who has received only positive evaluations from others.

The matter is complicated further by the fact that not all evaluations of a particular kind are given the same weight. Two evaluations which, for example, are very favorable will not necessarily contribute equally to actor's perception of other's views. What we take into the self-concept is a *weighted* average of the evaluations received. Before the evaluations are added up, each evaluation is multiplied by a weighting factor. Then they are averaged. Thus two evaluations which, figuratively, have the value of +10 may have differential impact on the perceived social definition if one is weighted heavily and the other less heavily.[5]

Of course, I do not mean to suggest that the actor sits down and, in effect, uses a calculator to set up a balance sheet. The actual process is certainly more informal and less exact than this. Nonetheless, it is clear that some received evaluations make a deeper impression on actor than others do. We have all seen how a kind word from a particular person can balance out a multitude of harsh criticisms received from previous others, while the same words from a different person have very little influence on the actor's perceptions. The only way to explain such a phenomenon is to postulate something equivalent to the weights used in mathematical calculations.

The next question seems fairly obvious. What are the factors which determine the weight given to a particular evaluation? Let us turn to that now.

The general basis for the answer has already been given. If actors tend, in general, to incorporate other's views into their self-concepts as a mean of obtaining various rewards and avoiding costs, it is only a short step to the proposition that the weighting process used to determine the social definition is intended to serve the same functions. The weight assigned to a particular evaluation will be chosen with a view to

---

[5] Sobieszek and Webster (1973) present evidence that evaluations are averaged, and Anderson (1968) shows that they are weighted before being averaged. Rosenberg (1979) presents indirect evidence to the same effect.

maximizing profits, that is, to increasing rewards and decreasing costs. The more reward associated with the adoption of an evaluation, the greater the weight assigned to it.

The application of this idea to specific cases is, unfortunately, not very simple. Numerous factors influence the reward associated with accepting particular evaluations and it would be rare that the acceptance of any evaluation would bring with it only reward or only cost. For example, we may give some weight to another's evaluation even if it leads to a self-view we do not wish to have (a cost), if to do so will relieve uncertainty (a reward).

In the discussion which follows, I will avoid this problem by considering each factor separately and by assuming in each section that all other things are equal. This is acceptable and necessary in the presentation of the theory, but it must be recognized that I am simplifying reality.

With this matter out of the way, we may now consider the details. Four categories of factors affect the weight given to a received evaluation—characteristics of the participants, aspects of the evaluations themselves, features of the situation in which the evaluation is made, and the nature of the behavior which leads to the evaluation. We will consider each in turn (see Table 4.1, pp. 118-19.)[6]

Characteristics of the Participants

One of the major determinants of the weight given to a perceived evaluation is the identity of the person giving it. In interactionist parlance. we give greater weight to the opinions of *significant others.* As soon as that is said, the question becomes what makes an other significant for us?

The basic postulate that actors weight others' evaluations heavily when to do so would result in reward for them, would lead to the hypothesis that significant others would be those who can control actor's fate—those who can influence rewards and costs. We cannot "afford" to give little attention to evaluations received from some people because to do so has important consequences for us. And who are those who can control our rewards and costs?

Utilitarian Rewards. All other things being equal, it would appear that people of higher social status would be more likely to control utilitarian rewards than those who are lower on the social scale and, similarly, others whose status exceeds actor's are more likely to have such control. Frequently, the utilitarian rewards we seek in inter-

[6]There are many similarities between the ideas presented here and those considered in the general literature on attitude formation. Of course, that material is not directly applicable to the present case. Most attitude studies deal with the simpler situation of a single attitude being presented which can be accepted or rejected. In the case of self-evaluations the problem is which of several attitudes will contribute more to a resulting amalgam. The difference becomes insignificant if we assume, as I believe we should, that a factor which inclines toward the acceptance of a single attitude will also incline toward a greater weighting of an attitude in the formation of a composite.

action are approval and continuing association, and when these are granted to us by people of high status they have more value than when they come from those of low status. Insofar as the goal is to receive other forms of utilitarian rewards, people of high status would also be in a better position to influence what we receive. Those of high status are likely to have greater access to valued things.

It is, however, not simply a matter of the stock of rewarding things which is held by the other. Even if the resources of those who have high status were no greater than those held by other people, they would have greater control over our fates because they would have greater control over the distribution of the rewards available to them. When the desired reward is held by a person of low status, there are many ways that actor may obtain it. He may be able to use coercion or bribery, for example. When the other is of high status, he or she will decide whether to give actor the reward desired, and the "price" will be set by other. High-status people can "demand" that actor accept their view of him, because they can withhold rewards. Lower-status people are less likely to have this power.

Other's control over actor's utilitarian rewards and costs is affected by a number of other factors in addition to other's status and power. If actor expects, and hopes, to interact with other in the future, other will control actor's fate, for actor will be dependent on other's willingness to interact with him or her at a later time. If they are not going to meet again anyway, one of other's major weapons is neutralized. Thus, the weight given to an other's evaluation should be related to actor's perception of the likelihood that the relationship will be resumed into the future. For similar reasons, the longer the present encounter is expected to last, the greater the weight given to other's views.

Our feelings toward the other will also influence the extent to which he or she can control our fate. Among the things we hope to gain by accepting the other's view is approval and continuing interaction, and the value of these rewards would depend upon our attitudes toward other. We want to interact with those we like and it is their approval we seek. There is little gain associated with acceptance by people we dislike.

That approval of the other leads us to see him or her as significant is indicated by Manis' (1955) finding that when students changed their self-evaluations over a six-week period they were likely to move in the direction of their friends' view of them.[7] The gap between them and people they did not consider to be friends did not narrow very much. Sherwood (1965) found essentially the same thing regarding the changes in self-concept that occurred during human relations training.

The focus thus far has been on those factors which influence the extent of other's potential power. It should be noted, however, that to have power does not necessarily mean that it will be exercised. If other does not intend to use his power, and if actor is aware of this, other is not likely to be seen as a significant other. Thus,

---

[7]In this study, as in almost all the available literature, the dependent variable is change in self-evaluation rather than change in perceived social definition. The theory, of course, speaks of change in the latter. It seems acceptable, however, to use changes in self-evaluation as an indication that changes have occurred in the perceived social definition, for in these studies the only plausible source of self-concept change is change in perceived social definition.

for example, if other is disinterested in what is going on in the encounter, he or she may be unwilling to go to the "trouble" involved in rewarding or punishing actor, and thus the ability to control actor's view of himself may be as low or lower than a less powerful person's. It would seem, then, that other's degree of involvement with actor is important, just as actor's degree of involvement with other is.

Knowledge Functions. In addition to varying in the extent to which they can control actor's utilitarian rewards and punishments, others also differ in their ability to influence actor's outcomes in regard to the other functions McGuire (1968) tells us may be served by accepting other's views. For example, the source of an evaluation will influence the degree to which it gives actor a feeling that his self-knowledge has been increased. The general principle is the more accurate actor believes the evaluation to be, the more useful it is. Let us consider how this works out.

At the outset, it appears clear that actor's view of other's competence will be relevant. If actor does not feel that other "knows what he is talking about" there will be little gain in self-knowledge associated with accepting that view. But if the other is an apparent expert in the matter, the gain may be considerable. Thus actor will evaluate the evaluator, and on the basis of that evaluation decide how much weight to give to other's opinion.[8]

The general literature on attitude formation shows, beyond much doubt, the importance of "source credibility." On many issues, when others are described as being competent, their views are more likely to be accepted. But it goes beyond this. People who are thought to have characteristics which are usually taken to be indications of general competence have more effect on attitudes. Thus when an attitude is championed by a person who is viewed as educated, older, higher in social status, a specialist, or intelligent, the opinion is more likely to be accepted than when its proponent does not possess these traits. Putting on a white coat and stethoscope can apparently do wonders for people's ability to convince others of the "rightness" of their attitudes. (See Haiman, 1949; Hovland and Weiss, 1952; Kelman and Hovland, 1953; Rosenbaum and Tucker, 1962. Also see Insko, 1967 for a summary of several other studies.)

The effects of perceived competence are also clear when the opinion offered is about the actor as a person. The most pertinent of the studies bearing upon this issue is the one by Rosenberg (1973). He actually measured the degree of competence that particular others were thought to possess, and discovered there was a close connection between his young subjects' self-evaluations and their perceptions of the others' opinion *only* when the subject thought the other was usually correct in his evaluations. This suggests strongly that we weight the opinion of others heavily only when we believe they are competent to make the judgments, that is, when we think we deserve the evaluations we get from them. (See also Jones, 1966; Harvey et al., 1956-57; Kinch, 1968; Webster and Sobieszek, 1974.)

---

[8]In this case, as in many others, more than one function is served. Approval is a more valuable utilitarian reward when it comes from a competent person.

Before we go any further, it should be made clear that competence is a bi-dimensional trait. A person is competent to make a judgment when he or she has both knowledge of the relevant "facts" and the ability to reach the conclusion the facts call for. In the available studies, these two factors are not separated; the credible sources are assumed to be both informed and capable. In real life, however, these are not always found together, and unless they are, the other is not likely to be significant. Thus some people may not be afforded the status of significant other, though we respect their judgment, because we believe their opinion of us is based upon insufficient evidence. Others are barred from this status, even if they know us quite intimately, because we do not believe they are able to draw the proper conclusions from the information they have.

Our judgment that the other is incapable of handling the information may be based upon a variety of assumptions. We may doubt other's intelligence, or we may believe that his or her biases are getting in the way. If the other is believed to be biased, either for *or* against us, we would not consider the evaluation to be accurate or deserved, and therefore we would not put much stock in it. This is perhaps the reason why recent data suggest that members of minority groups do not have particularly low self-evaluations even though they have almost certainly received more negative evaluations than members of the majority. Many of those negative evaluations come from the majority and are discounted as biased and uninformed (Jacques and Chason, 1977; see Rosenberg and Simmons, n.d., and Baughman, 1971 for summaries of many studies.) And, of course, it works the other way. It is one of life's small tragedies that words of praise from a loved one are unlikely to be given as much weight as they "deserve" because of the belief that their judgment is probably clouded by their willingness to give us the benefit of every doubt.

Even if actor has assurance on all these grounds, he may not feel that he has been given an accurate evaluation. Other may be entirely competent to give an accurate judgment and still not give one because he or she is not "paying attention" to the task of evaluation. Some people seem to make off-hand judgments; they don't seem to be very involved or concerned about what they are doing. They are not sufficiently motivated to use the information they have to their best ability. On the other hand, there is the person Gergen (1971) calls the personalistic communicator—the one "who appears to take into account our every action, who attends to the subtleties in our behavior and modifies his appraisal accordingly" (Gergen, 1971: 44). Because they take the matter seriously, we should take their evaluations more seriously. And the data (Gergen, 1965) suggest we do. The greater the personalism the subject perceived in the evaluator, the greater the change in her self-evaluation. (Pearson r = .45 and .58 for the two groups in the study.)

Going a step backward from this postulate, I would suggest that others are more likely to be personalistic in this sense when they are interested in the issue involved, when they like actor, when the outcome of the interaction is important to them, when they are likely to have further interaction with actor, and so forth. These, of course, are factors which have been mentioned previously. They were said to have an effect upon the effective power that other has over actor. Now we see that they work in a second way also. They incline others to act in a personalistic way which increases actor's feeling that he is being judged accurately, which increases the weight actor gives to the judgment.

Actor may also conclude the other's evaluation is inappropriate, if not exactly inaccurate, if other's standards appear improper. The evaluation must be considered fair or we will not allow ourselves to be strongly affected by it. The scale against which we are being measured must be, by our lights, neither too easy nor too difficult. Most of us get little feeling of accomplishment from receiving an "A" from a teacher who gives almost all A's, and an "F" from a teacher who is "impossibly hard" will not appreciably lower our estimates of ourselves as students. Such grades may have important practical consequences, but they should have little effect upon our self-evaluations.

If other passes all these "tests," actor will be convinced that other can be accurate, but he may not be sure that the judgments made are the same as the ones expressed. If we doubt other's veracity, we will once again decide that he or she is not really informing us about our nature. The other must be able to reach an accurate judgment and then be willing to share it. Thus the positive opinion of a sycophant who will tell us only what we want to hear, or the negative opinion of a person who never has a good word for anyone, is not going to be weighted very heavily.

Finally, if the opinions of other are going to have much effect, actor must feel that he or she fully understands other's meaning. Thus, if other tends to give ambiguous or inconsistent opinions, they are not likely to count for much, for actor will not feel that these views contribute much to self-knowledge.

Expressive Functions. It was suggested earlier that the major expressive function that may be served by the acceptance of an other's evaluation is the satisfaction of the actor's need for a positive self-view. Interactionists and others writing on this subject usually assume that most people have such a need, but it should be noted that this view does not have universal acceptance (Webster and Sobieszek, 1974). Let us assume for the moment that it is correct. Much of the data to be presented in this section will bear upon it indirectly, and when we come to the section on the nature of the evaluations it will be considered again.

If actors do have a desire for a positive view of themselves, they would prefer to receive positive evaluations from others, for this is the means to a positive self-view. And, to go a step further, they would tend to accord significant other status to people who are expected to give them positive evaluations.

It should be noted carefully that this suggests that we will weight heavily the opinions of others who are *expected* to give us positive evaluations even when those evaluations turn out to be negative. Of course, the weight assigned to a negative evaluation from such a person would not be as great as that assigned to a positive reaction from him or her, but it would have a greater effect than a negative one received from a person who was not a significant other. Previous experience leads us to invest an other with a certain degree of importance, and if he or she "does not come through" for us at a particular time, we do not simply withdraw our investment. A series of such experiences with that other may lead us to decide that his or her opinion is not that important, but this would not occur immediately.

From this view, it clearly follows that actor is likely to choose significant others from among those people he or she thinks like him or her, for to say that someone likes you is almost the same as saying that the person has approved of your actions in the past and is expected to do so in the future. Rosenberg (1973) describes the matter as follows:

> We would. . .expect [actor] to conclude that the people whose opinions really matter to him are those who, in his view, think highly of him; conversely, he will be relatively unconcerned with the views of his detractors. (838)

> We thus see rather strikingly how the individual tends to establish his structure of interpersonal valuation in a fashion conducive to self-esteem protection. When we speak of the individual "deciding" that he does or does not care what specific others think of him, of course, we do not mean to imply that this is a conscious, rational decision. The adjustment is probably a more gradual and unconscious one in which a shift in the affect invested in particular others may occur in scarcely perceptible degree. In the long run, however, the individual is more likely to end up caring about the opinions of those who are believed to think well of him than of those who are not. (840)

The point is not simply hypothetical. Rosenberg's (1973) data are quite what one would expect from these considerations. When actors believe that others view them in favorable terms, they are more likely to say that they care very much what the others think of them, and actors' self-views resemble their perceptions of others' opinions primarily when they care very much about those opinions. When actors say that they do not care very much about others' opinions, the correlation between self-view and perception of other's view is usually less than when others' opinions are something that the actors care about. Goslin's (1962) findings are also consistent with this view. People who are rejected by a group tend to have self-views which differ greatly from their peers' view of them.

The tendency to care about the other's view when the other likes you is, however, "limited by reality. . . .Even children who believe their mothers think ill of them rarely deny that their mothers' opinions are important to them; the mother-child relationship is so powerful that it is not easily overcome by selective valuation" (Rosenberg, 1973: 839). Two-thirds of the respondents who said their mothers view them unfavorably said they cared very much about her opinion. When they thought she viewed them favorably, 91 percent cared very much. For fathers, teachers, and the "kids in the class" acceptance by other had a stronger impact upon the assignment of significance, but even for those others a feeling that one was rated poorly did not absolutely prohibit the assignment of significance to an other (Rosenberg, 1973).

Actor should also give greater significance to others who contribute to his or her need for consistency. Almost inevitably, different others give varying evaluations and most of us can put up with this fact of life. But we would hope that a given other would not contribute to this complexity. We would prefer that he or she would be consistent in his or her evaluations—at least for similar actions on our part. Little is more infuriating than being praised by an other for a particular behavior at one time and being disapproved for the same thing at another time. Such people's opinions are likely to be given little weight when we attempt to develop a perceived social definition. They cause a feeling of dissonance, and I might also add, we don't know when to believe them. Therefore, we are also likely to view them as not adding anything to our self-knowledge.

Before concluding my consideration of the factors associated with the significance of others, I should make explicit a point which is only implicit in the material presented thusfar. Although some people may represent significant others for actor in a variety of evaluation areas, the extent to which any given other is significant is likely to vary. The general reason for this is that an other's standing on the factors associated with significance will differ depending on the topic involved. For example, we may consider some people to be competent to judge us in all areas, but it is more likely that we will recognize that most people know more about some things than they do about others. Similarly, the power that a person has over us will vary depending upon the activity in which we are engaged and the goals that we seek.

This view is supported by data from a study of the relation between parental support and adolescents' self-view. As previously mentioned, Gecas (1971; Gecas et al., 1970) found the subjects had higher self-evaluations when they believed their parents were supportive of them, but in his 1972 paper he reports that the correlation holds only when the evaluation was in regard to behavior: "with my family," "with adults," "in the classroom." When the subjects were asked to evaluate themselves in other situations, for example, with a member of the opposite sex, parental support was generally irrelevant. The clear implications is that parents are used as significant others, but not in all contexts.

Heiss and Owens' (1972) data also make sense in terms of this idea. They found that the self-evaluations of blacks were lower than those of whites only in characteristics related to work and intellectuality. In regard to performance in the statuses of spouse, offspring, parent, and so forth, blacks did not rate themselves lower. Part of the explanation seems to be that members of the majority are accepted as significant others for the first group of traits since they often have power over blacks in these areas. If nonblacks are the significant others, blacks will have low self-evaluation for they tend to be downgraded by the larger society. In regard to family performance and such traits, other blacks are the significant others; for one thing, they are considered to be the only ones competent to judge. Black significant others did not give the black respondents an excess of negative evaluations, and therefore the self-evaluations of blacks are as high as those of whites in these matters.

In summary, the degree to which actors weight the evaluations received from particular others will depend upon the extent to which the other's actions are relevant to the three functions which may be served by adopting the view of another. If other has power over actor—if he can influence whether or not actor obtains utilitarian rewards—actor is likely to accept his view as a means to acquisition of those rewards. We also accept others' views because they satisfy our need for self-knowledge, and thus the more confidence we have that the view of other is accurate, the more heavily we are inclined to weight it. Finally, the views of others may be heavily weighted because they are expected to serve an expressive function for us, they are expected to help us achieve the goal of having a favorable self-view, or because they help us to have a simple and coherent view of how we are seen. Thus, our significant others are likely to like us and give us evaluations which are consistent with our existing opinions.

Characteristics of the Evaluations Received

The source of an evaluation is obviously not the only factor that affects the weight it is given. The nature of the evaluation itself is another relevant factor. Let us now consider the aspects of evaluations which influence the weight they are given.

As before, reward value and functionality are the keys. The basic assumption is still that we accept others' opinions if their adoption increases our profits. Evaluations which serve utilitarian, knowledge, or expressive functions will be viewed by us as rewarding. The question then becomes what kind of evaluations will serve these functions.

Three relevant characteristics of evaluations have already been implied in the discussion of significant others. It will be recalled that I postulated that others who are thought to give accurate or deserved evaluations will be considered significant others. That postulate can be rephrased to make it pertinent here. With identity of the other held constant, actors will weight an evaluation they consider to be deserved more heavily than one they consider to be undeserved. The reason for this is simply that an undeserved evaluation does not lead to self-knowledge, while a deserved one does.

The judgment regarding whether an evaluation is deserved or not is based upon our view of other's competence to make such a judgment, and our estimate of other's competence is usually based on information about his characteristics. However, other criteria may also be used. Actor may, for example, decide that an other is not competent because his opinion differs from actor's own view, or because it conflicts with the definition that previous others have given of the same or similar behavior. Thus, other's competence is judged by what he or she says as well as by who he or she is.

Direction of the Evaluation. I also suggested that people who give positive evaluations are more likely to be considered significant others. In this context, that may be rephrased to say that favorable evaluations are weighted more heavily than negative ones. This is because favorable evaluations serve the expressive function of aiding actor to develop and retain a favorable view of self.

Although this postulate is widely accepted, there is, as I noted earlier, some controversy surrounding it. The data bearing upon it are not totally consistent, and it seems important to consider the evidence in some detail.

The data from direct comparisons of the effects of positive and negative evaluations are somewhat mixed. Six studies show, with varying degrees of clarity, that positive evaluations are weighted more heavily; two investigations obtain opposite results.[9]

On the basis of these findings alone, I would not be inclined to postulate a need for positive evaluation, or at least I would do so very tentatively until the inconsistencies were cleared up and more confirming evidence built up. However, the decision need not rest on these materials alone. A number of other studies provide indirect support by showing that processes which serve to protect the self-evaluation are used when actors have been given negative evaluations.

Harvey et al. (1956–57) and Harvey (1962), for example, present direct evidence to show that actors who are evaluated negatively tend to devalue the source, distort the content, and even deny that the source gave the evaluation—particularly when it is strongly negative and comes from a person who knows them well. The subjects in this study were affected by the negative ratings, but these machinations are clearly designed to permit them to reduce the effects.

Similar mechanisms were used by the subjects in a study by Pilisuk (1962) when they were told that an anonymous critic had rated them very poorly. When the critic was revealed as a close friend, the tendency was to believe the critic was not very serious about the task or that the apparent differences between actor's and other's evaluations were not as great as they seemed. It is also worth noting that they seemed to resist hints that the critic was a close friend. We should also note Steiner's (1968) data which show that negative ratings which were inconsistent with the self-view were likely to lead to rejection of the source and errors in recall. Evaluations which were higher than the existing self-evaluation were less likely to have these effects. (See also Graf, 1971.)

Also relevant are studies such as Shrauger and Jones (1968) and Jones et al. (1962) which found that subjects liked people who gave them favorable evaluations more than they did those who gave negative evaluations. Similarly, Backman and Secord (1959) show that people choose to associate with those they believe like them. And, if the postulate is correct, one can make sense of Goslin's (1962) discovery that the discrepancy between self-estimate and the rating given by an "accepting" other is smaller than the difference between self-rating and the rating given by a "rejecting" other. These data would suggest that the rejected subjects were protecting themselves by rejecting the rejection.

In addition to this, the postulate of a need for positive self-evaluation helps to make sense of many data which would be inexplicable without it. This has already been seen in the discussion of the relation between liking another and choice of that person as a significant other. Further examples will be given when I discuss the effects of self-evaluations. The idea also explains why people place the most value on those characteristics they believe themselves to rate well on (Rosenberg, 1968).

[9]Studies by Ludwig and Maehr (1967), Manis (1955), French, Sherwood, and Bradford (1966), Moore (1964), Reeder et al. (1960), and Howard and Berkowitz (1958) support the postulate; studies by Haas and Maehr (1965) and Maehr, Mensing, and Nafzger (1962) obtain opposite results.

All this evidence, of course, says nothing explicitly about a person's desire for a positive view of self. It does suggest very strongly, however, that people prefer to receive positive evaluations from others. To go from this to the postulate under consideration, one must simply accept that the reason people desire positive evaluations is that such evaluations produce positive self-evaluations. It seems to me that this final step is easily taken. All in all, then, despite the existence of some contrary data, I feel it is appropriate to conclude that people do tend to desire a positive view of self. This is not to say, however, that this need is an overpowering one. It certainly varies in its intensity from person to person, and there are other needs which in certain circumstances act to oppose it and overcome it.

Webster and Sobieszek (1974) would not accept this view. They clearly and unequivocally deny that there is a drive to maximize self-esteem. In fact, they label their chapter on the matter "The Maximization Myth," suggesting that the idea is intuitively appealing, widely accepted, but lacking in any empirical support. A full evaluation of their position is beyond the scope of this book, but a few points should be made to indicate why their work does not shake my belief in the existence of a need for positive self-evaluations.

One thing may already be clear to the reader. Webster and Sobieszek and I are not talking about quite the same thing. There is a difference between a drive for self-evaluation maximization and a need for a favorable self-evaluation. The former, for one thing, suggests that actor will never be satisfied; the latter does not. The postulate being urged here is much less sweeping than the one that is Webster and Sobieszek's primary target. It could be, then, that we are all correct.

Unfortunately, the matter is not so easily disposed of. On the basis of their data, Webster and Sobieszek also deny the moderate version of the idea. They are not convinced that people distort the meanings of negative evaluations, that they explain them away, that they tend to overlook them, that they play them down, and that they act in ways designed to produce positive evaluations. I am suggesting, of course, that these things do occur.

Even if Webster and Sobieszek's own materials were unequivocal in their support of their position, I do not feel that they would be sufficient to balance the evidence just presented. But I remain unconvinced that their data are entirely favorable to their view. The issue sometimes revolves around the question of how small a difference must be before it should be considered to be "no difference." And their evidence is always indirect. They do not measure self-evaluation, but rather rejection of another's suggestion in cases of disagreement. Certainly people with higher self-evaluations will be more likely than people with lower self-evaluations to act on their own judgments, (See pp. 197–198) but to use this as a variable is not the same as to directly measure the self-concept or perceived social definitions. Clearly, their assumption is that given their design, the only possible source of differences in the tendency to reject influence are differences in self-evaluation, and this may be valid. I would, however, be more confident if the measure was more direct. Finally, in some of their tests Webster and Sobieszek require that the subjects *ignore* negative evaluations. This seems too stringent.

All that one should expect is that such evaluations should be weighted less heavily than positive ones.

All in all, I would suggest that the postulate, as stated, is supported by the bulk of evidence. Webster and Sobieszek's arguments and data do not shake this opinion.

Consistency of Evaluations. The postulate that we tend to give significant other status to those who give us consistent evaluations can be changed to make it pertinent at this point. In its revised form, it would say that an evaluation which is consistent with the existing self-evaluation will be given greater weight than one which contradicts actor's self-view.

The basis for this postulate is similar to one given before. A consistent evaluation serves the knowledge function better than an inconsistent one does. When new information is the same as old information, actor gets the feeling that he knows "what is up." In addition, inconsistent information causes doubt, confusion, and the effort required to determine which information is correct. When people are confronted with contradictory information, they experience *cognitive dissonance,* and it seems clear that this is defined by most as an unpleasant state. (See Abelson et al., 1968; Festinger, 1954, 1957; Brehm and Cohen, 1962.) People much prefer to have their belief systems uncluttered with contradictions which press for resolution. If we give greater weight to profitable evaluations, it would seem clear that consistent evaluations would be weighted more heavily. Such evaluations increase our self-knowledge without causing us cognitive dissonance.

It is difficult to test this idea, however, because it is difficult to determine directly how much weight is being given to a consistent evaluation. The amount of change in the self-evaluation, which is the usual index of the weight applied to a received evaluation, will not work in this case because a truly consistent evaluation does not suggest that the self-evaluation be changed. A consistent evaluation may increase one's confidence in a previously developed image, but that is more difficult to measure than change in the self-view. At least, it has not as yet been done.

There are, however, indirect indications that the idea is sound. Shrauger and Rosenberg (1970) and Harvey and Clapp (1965) found, for example, that markedly inconsistent evaluations resulted in *less* change in the existing self-image than mildly inconsistent ones did, despite the fact that a markedly divergent view suggests that actor make a larger change.[10] The finding makes sense only if we assume a tendency to reject inconsistent views when the inconsistency is large enough to appear significant.

It is also possible to determine the actor's reactions to consistent and inconsistent evaluations and thereby to get insights into how heavily they are being weighted. The following findings cited by Shrauger (1975) suggest differential weighting of the two kinds of evaluation:

---

[10] If the subjects were affected equally by all the raters, we would expect a larger change for the more divergent ratings. Such a rating says, in effect: if you accept my evaluation, change your self-evaluation a lot.

1. The more discrepant the ratings are from the subject's own ratings, the more inaccurate the recall of the ratings.

2. People who performed at a level consistent with their previous self-evaluation remembered more of the correct answers after they were told what they were.

3. Outcomes which confirmed one's initial expectancies were more likely than inconsistent ones to be attributed to ability rather than luck.

Although there is much evidence for a general consistency effect, the data are frequently quite mixed. A major reason for the difficulty is apparent. The consistency-inconsistency factor interacts with other variables so strongly that it is not particularly useful to deal with it separately. Under condition "A" the reaction to an inconsistent evaluation will be very different from the one which follows from an inconsistent view received under condition "B."

The reason for this is that there are a variety of ways to resolve cognitive dissonance caused by inconsistent evaluations, and the preferred solution will depend upon the situation. For example, we can handle dissonance by convincing ourselves that the new evaluation is wrong or by changing our existing self-view. If the inconsistent evaluation is favorable, the "smart" actor will take the latter tack which is the equivalent of saying he or she will weight the new opinion heavily. Doing this provides the double reward of resolving the dissonance and improving one's self-view simultaneously. Thus when people with low self-evaluations receive inconsistent new evaluations from others—that is, favorable evaluations—the general postulate given earlier would *not* be expected to hold. Only when the self-estimate is high does it make sense for actor to give a low weight to an inconsistent evaluation. This, in fact, is what Ludwig and Maehr (1967) found to be the case. When their subjects had high self-evaluations, inconsistent (negative) evaluations lowered the self-concept only a little. When they had low self-evaluations, inconsistent (positive) information markedly raised the self-concept.

The matter is, however, even more complicated than this. If the new evaluation is markedly divergent it may not be given much weight, even if it is favorable. For, as Gergen (1971: 45) notes, "as the other's appraisal becomes increasingly discrepant from your own [and from previously received evaluations,] it may appear less and less accurate." It is difficult to believe something which is in marked conflict with what you already know. This is probably the reason why people who have not been particularly successful with members of the other sex find it so difficult to believe, when it does happen, "that she's (he's) in love with me." If the other is especially attractive, the difficulty is even greater.

On the other hand, however, a markedly divergent view may lead us to question the accuracy of our previous evaluators, and particularly if the new evaluation is favorable, we may decide that the previous others were inaccurate. If that were the case, the new evaluation would be given a heavy weight. Thus, markedly divergent evaluations may have a variety of consequences.

The matter is not hopeless, however, for we have some idea concerning the factors that will influence which consequence will be forthcoming. For example, if the person who communicates the new view is seen as an expert in the matter, disbelief in the evaluation is difficult to maintain and previous evaluations would become suspect. In this case, the discrepant view would importantly influence the perceived social definition. If the average person is told he or she is an extraordinary lover, the reaction may be "you don't know what you are talking about." But if the person making the statement is very experienced and thus has a good basis for comparison, we may believe it. I would generalize, then, that widely discrepant evaluations are unlikely to be accepted, whether they are positive or negative, *unless* they come from persons who are viewed as very knowledgeable.

This tendency has been investigated in regard to masculinity-femininity, an aspect of the self-concept which has evaluative connotations. Bergin (1962) found that when students were rated by the "project director" in a well-equipped room in the medical school, they tended to accept the director's opinion that they were less typical of their sex than they had said they were. When the same was said by a high-school student, the subjects tended to reject the suggestion and to retain their original self-view.

There is, however, another complication in the matter. Sometimes an extreme rating that is very different from his own may lead actor to question whether the supposed "expert" is giving an expert opinion. Such doubts may take various forms. For example, actor may begin to believe that other couldn't be taking the task seriously if other is so far off base, or actor may believe that other might be giving a biased opinion despite his expertise. And in some instances actor may even begin to doubt the competence of the supposed expert.

It becomes clear how difficult it is to make a meaningful generalization concerning the weight given to evaluations which are consistent or inconsistent with the existing self-concept. There does seem to be a basic tendency to give heavier weight to consistent evaluations, but this trend will not be observed under many conditions. For example, if the existing self-evaluation is low, a new opinion which is inconsistent with it may have a major effect. However, if the evaluation is very divergent it may be given little weight even when it is favorable because actor cannot believe it is true. On the other hand, if the expertise of other is beyond question, an inconsistent view from him may be accepted regardless of its direction or the magnitude of the discrepancy. Thus, the effect of an inconsistent evaluation depends upon its direction, the magnitude of the discrepancy, and the identity of the evaluator.

Conditions under which the Evaluation is Made

What is said and who says it are not the only factors that influence the weight given to a received evaluation. With these factors held constant, the conditions under which the evaluation is given would also tend to have some influence on its effect on the perceived social definition. A person may say something at one time with little impact, and at another time the same words can make a deep impression. Let us consider some of the relevant factors.

Multiple Evaluations. When actor receives evaluations from several others at the same time which are not in agreement, he or she is in a situation which is somewhat analogous to that of the person who has received an evaluation which is inconsistent with an existing self-view. And we would expect a similarly complex set of consequences.

In general, I would predict that the minority opinion would be given somewhat less weight than it would have been given if it were the only evaluation received, and there is some evidence that shows this to be so. Howard and Berkowitz (1958) report that when subjects received three moderate evaluations and one high one, they rated themselves higher (Mean Score = 10.2) than those who received four moderate evaluations (9.1), but lower than those who were rated highly by the one person who evaluated them (13.2). These scores suggest that the deviant high evaluation was not given as much weight as it would have been in the absence of the moderate ones. We may assume that the subjects could not, in the face of three moderate evaluations, simply conclude that the high evaluator was correct.

When the subjects received three moderate and one low evaluation, their self-rating was 9.8, almost as high as the three moderates and one high (10.2), and higher than for the four moderates. The meaning of these findings is not totally clear. The relatively high rating for three moderate and one low evaluation is consistent with expectations. The low rating had very little effect because it was unfavorable and discrepant. What remains unclear is why this group should have rated itself higher than those who received only moderate ratings.

Inconsistency among one's evaluators has been shown to have another interesting effect. When a group of people do not agree about actor he or she tends to downplay all of their opinions, not only those of the person whose view is clearly deviant. Thus, for example, Sherwood (1967) reports that when the evaluations given to actor by a group of others show considerable difference among them, the self-evaluation of actor seems to be affected less than when the others show more agreement. Although it dealt with actor's perceptions of his or her personality rather than with his or her self-evaluations, the findings of Backman et al. (1963) suggest a similar conclusion. They found it easier to change actor's self-concept when he perceived that only some of his friends believed he had a particular trait. If he thought that all his best friends saw him as possessing a characteristic, he was more resistant to accepting new evidence that he did not have it.

In addition to the self-knowledge function implied above, there are utilitarian consequences involved. If there are dissenting opinions, the power of the majority is blunted. If their evaluation is negative and they are unwilling to give actor the rewards associated with adequate performance, actor need not go entirely without. He may still be able to get something from the dissenter. Similarly, if the majority opinion is favorable, their rewards can be diluted to some degree by the actions of the person who disagrees. There is more to be gained and lost when there is agreement among raters. But of course, if there is disagreement, the wise actor will weight the opinion of the majority more heavily because he has more to gain by doing that, all other things being equal.

Evaluations in Groups. Thus far, I have been implicitly assuming that only one actor is being evaluated. Although that situation is frequent, there are other possibilities. For example, quite commonly when an actor is evaluated, the performances of other actors are also evaluated by the same other. The most obvious example of this occurs in the classroom when all the students receive grades on a test. Analogous cases occur when parents interact with several children at the same time, when salary increases are distributed on a merit basis, when a dive or gymnastic routine is judged, and so forth. In such cases, each person is evaluated as an individual, but several are judged at the same time. Also, each person's rating is independent of the other's; we are assuming that there is no "curve," that is, *everyone* could have received an "A," *everyone* who was thought to deserve it got a raise. There is no direct comparison of the individuals or competition between them in the sense that if one is rated well the other cannot be.

Two postulates may be offered about the evaluations given in such a situation:

1. Group members will give little weight to their ratings if all, or most of them, are rated equally.
2. Those who receive an evaluation which was frequent in the group give it less weight than those who receive an evaluation which was uncommon.

Earlier I noted that people are likely to be strongly affected by a rating only when they believe it was done by a competent person using appropriate criteria. This idea provides a base for the first postulate because many people would conclude that a homogeneous set of ratings must be invalid. Uniform ratings conflict with their belief that there is variation in most significant human traits. Rather than give up that assumption they tend to discount the value of the ratings.

Here, too, there are utilitarian consequences involved. If all or most of the group members receive the same rating, in many cases the rater is limited in the extent to which he or she can distribute rewards and punishments. If everyone ends in a tie, who is to get the prize or the booby prize? If, however, there is variation, it is possible to allocate the "goodies" on the basis of performance.

The justification for the second postulate is largely an extension of what has just been said. The person who is singled out is likely to assume that some care was used in making the rating—why else would he or she have been singled out? And the person who receives an "A" when "everyone else" receives an "F" is unlikely to think that the grading was unfair anymore than the person who receives an "F" when everyone else gets an "A" is going to be able to convince himself that the standards were too high. The success of the others will not permit that. The only way to discount the low grade is to claim incompetence or bias, and such a claim would require evidence that is not to be found in the distribution of scores.

Collective Evaluations. Another common variant on the one rater-one actor model is the situation in which the actor receives an evaluation as part of a collectivity. The actor is not being rated as an individual but partakes of the rating given to a group of which he or she is a member. We are among the members of a class which is being "bawled out" by a teacher for poor work or inattention, we are awarded a bonus because our section was most productive, an editorial in a newspaper applauds the members of our profession for their public spirit, and so on.

Such group evaluations probably affect our self-concepts in most cases, but they would receive lower weight than those which were directed specifically to us as individuals. Group evaluations do not contribute that much to self-knowledge. Actors realize that their contribution to the performance of a group is, by the nature of the case, limited. Thus, the amount of credit an actor can claim or the blame he must accept is small. In some cases, in fact, we are aware, or convince ourselves, that it was the others who brought about the evaluation, and that we are not at all responsible. This, of course, is more likely to happen when blame is to be distributed, and it is a way of giving a negative group evaluation a weight of zero in the formation of our perceived social definition.

Deutsch and Solomon (1959) conducted a study which shows that when people receive both individual performance ratings and rating of the performance of their team they put more stock in the individual rating. This shows clearly that individual evaluations are weighted more heavily when both kinds are available. However, this is not the same thing as saying that when one kind of evaluation is given, those who receive the collective evaluation will weight it less heavily than those given an individual evaluation. It could be that when nothing else is available, a collective evaluation is given a great weight. The theoretical considerations mentioned above suggest that this is not so, but we must await further study before we can be sure.

The Timing of the Evaluation. When social scientists speak of the timing of an experience, they are usually interested in primacy and recency effects. If *primacy* operates, the first information about a particular matter has a major influence; if *recency* effects are produced, the last or most recent experience is very influential.

The evidence of general learning theory suggests strongly the existence of both recency and primacy effects, as do studies in social psychology (Brown, 1965). The attempt to determine which one predominates seems a fruitless task, however, for there does not seem to be a *universal* law of either primacy or recency (Insko, 1967; Brown, 1965). The specific conditions of the situation determine which tendency is stronger and, in fact, whether there will be an order effect at all.

For example, Luchins (1957a) did an experiment on how we form impressions of *others* and obtained a strong primacy effect. Then the study was repeated with a warning to the subjects that they not form an opinion "until all the data were in." This was sufficient to almost entirely cancel the primacy effect. When in addition, a short break was introduced in the middle of the presentation, a recency effect was observed (Luchins, 1957b). It gets even more complex. In another study, for subjects who had high interest in the topic, reading the communication to them resulted in a primacy effect and listening to a tape led to a weak recency effect. For those with less interest, the opposite results were obtained (Lana, 1963).

Even if a clear-cut pattern was found which was not so influenced by small changes in conditions, the relevance of many of these studies to our concerns would be limited because they do not deal with received evaluations of ability. When it comes to recency and primacy, judgments of ability may be different from other kinds of judgments, and evaluations of self may differ from evaluations of other. A study by Jones and Welsh (1971) showed, for example, that in a game of strategy the person who did poorly at the beginning and then began to do well at the end was viewed as a better player than his opponent. Unfortunately for those of us who like simplicity, a primacy effect also seemed involved, and a previous similar experiment (Jones et al., 1968) which used puzzle solving as a task showed the primacy effect very strongly, *but only when someone else was being judged.* When the subject judged his own behavior, recency was found to predominate.

Furthermore, the experimental situations are highly artificial. In the studies it is rare for there to be the kind of interruption that Luchins introduced into his third experiment, and as Brown (1965: 620) notes, "life is filled with unrelated interpolated tasks." Also, in most of the studies the time period covered is very short, perhaps a few minutes. Therefore, the material which has primacy is almost as recent as the material given last. Several studies suggest that the time interval between the early and later material and the time between the later material and the test of the effect have an influence on recency and primacy effects. Primacy is strongest when there is no gap in the communication and immediate measurement. When there is a long gap between the two parts of the communication and the effects are measured immediately after the second, recency reaches its peak. As the measurement is delayed, the recency effect decreases. But even these findings are suspect, for the time gaps are no more than two weeks, not the years we find in real life.

Given this great variation, let me simply offer a few general postulates regarding the probable situation in the case of received self-evaluations in real life.

1. If *two* characteristics of actor are evaluated, and if one of the traits has not been judged before, and the other trait has previously been evaluated, all other things being equal, the evaluation which is associated with the previously *unevaluated* trait will be weighted more strongly and its effect will decrease less rapidly. (*Primacy effect*)

2. Any evaluation received has its greatest effect at the time it is received; its effect will then decrease. Thus, a recent evaluation has greater effect than a less recent one. This "decay" in influence will be hastened by the introduction of additional evaluations in that area. (*Recency effect*)

3. If the first evaluation of a trait was received a long time ago (for example, in childhood) and the last one rather recently, the recent one will have a greater effect than the first one. (*Recency greater than Primacy*) As time goes on the "advantage" of the most recent one will decline.

4. I leave unspecified what will occur in more complex cases, for example, when the first evaluation was received at age 10, the second—and only other—at age 20, and the actor is now at age 40. It is unclear whether the effect of the recent one would still be greater, the same, or less than the first one after all those years. It could be, in fact, that both would have been entirely forgotten. Here the specific conditions involved—the importance of the matter, the original

weight given to the evaluations, etc.—would seem to hold the key. (See Jones and Goethals, 1972.)

The effects of recency and primacy are not easily explained in terms of the three functions on which I have been focusing. It would appear that they are more a result of basic elements of human psychology associated with forgetting, the development of learning sets, perception, and loss of attention. However, one of the basic ideas appears relevant. The tendency of evaluations to lose "power" over time regardless of recency and primacy may be partly due to the fact that the older an evaluation, the less it tells us about what we are in the present. Old evaluations tell us what we were, and since we all believe that people change, at least to some degree, an old evaluation serves the knowledge function less adequately.

Public and Private Evaluations. In regard to the conditions under which the evaluation is made, it seems intuitively that evaluations received in public would receive a different weight from those given in private, but when one delves into the matter it appears that there are so many relevant factors operating at cross purposes that one loses hope of ever coming up with a postulate which is not hemmed in by so many qualifications that it is useless. Let us consider the matter for a moment, for it shows the problems which sometimes emerge in applying the principles I have been discussing.

Studies of audience effects tell us that when the interaction of actor and other is observed by third parties, the behavior of the interactants is changed to a considerable degree. Let us first consider the nature of these *general* effects and then I will discuss their implications for the special case of the weighting of evaluations received from others.

One of the effects produced by the presence of an audience is an increase in the goal orientation of the interactants. In an experiment by Blumstein (1974-75), for example, male subjects were put into a situation in which they were required to convince a woman to go on a date or to "go steady." A number, but not all, of the differences in behaviors in the private and public setting suggests that "winning" the woman became more important to the man when he was operating under peer scrutiny.

Avoiding embarrassment appears to be one of the major sources of this increased desire to win. Utilitarian goals become more salient because actors seem to believe that the audience will see the interaction with other as a contest and they wish to avoid the embarrassment they expect to feel if they lose. Thus they become more dominating (Zajonc, 1965) or, if it is thought to be a better strategy, more defensive and deferential (Wilson and Benner, 1971; Blumstein, 1973). In fact, they may combine several approaches. When in the public situation, the men in Blumstein's (1974-75) study asked for more help but they were also more likely to be autonomous, that is, to convey the impression that plenty of other women would be happy to have them.

One experiment suggests rather strongly that with the increased salience of the utilitarian function, there is a concomitant decrease in the importance of the desire for self-knowledge, especially among women (Wilson and Benner, 1971). A similar decline in the need to achieve the expressive goal of consistency between behavior and self-conception has also been seen (Blumstein, 1974–75).

If people receive negative evaluations, they are more likely to say they felt embarrassment if the failure is, or may become, "public knowledge." Importantly, this tendency is clear-cut only when the negative evaluation is thought to be deserved, that is, when the subjects believe that they in fact did fail the task (Archibald and Cohen, 1971). It is also strongest when the audience is composed of friends and when future interaction is anticipated with an audience of acquaintances or strangers (Brown and Garland, 1971).

This is not to say, however, that the negatively evaluated subjects in a public situation simply "take their medicine." In contrast to subjects who had the same experiences in private, they engage in a number of familiar face-saving mechanisms designed to reduce or eliminate the embarrassment. Thus, for example, they are more likely to claim that luck was involved in the task, and they tend to derogate the person who gave them the negative evaluation. In other cases they seem to inflate the difficulty of achieving the goal, apparently as an excuse for their failure. When the interaction is private, people seem to feel less need for such excuses. Thus in Blumstein's (1974–75) study, the men who wooed the woman in public rated her as being more attractive than the other men did. Also, when interaction is public there is a tendency to pick an easier "foe"–another transparent attempt to avoid failure (Wilson and Benner, 1971). A study by Brown (1968) showed that humiliated persons will retaliate against their "tormentors" even when it means giving up utilitarian rewards–in this case, money. In another experiment, Brown (1970) discovered that people try to reduce discomfort by attempting to avoid appearing before an audience to "admit" an embarrassing action, again, even if it costs them money.

One additional point should be made of a rather different order. Zajonc (1965), summarizing a number of early studies on the effects of audiences, some of which used nonhuman subjects, suggests that in the presence of an audience the acquisition of new responses is impaired but the performance of previously learned behaviors is improved. What seems to happen is that the presence of an audience distracts the subject from attending to the cues being presented and in order to diminish this distraction he or she turns inward and focuses attention on the self and what is already present in memory.

What does this suggest about the weighting of received evaluations? The first point is that the effect of an audience will vary depending on the people involved and the specific conditions of the situation. A major consideration is whether the evaluation is positive or negative. We will present our speculations separately for each of these cases.

The situation seems a little simpler when the evaluation is positive. Most of the considerations would suggest that actor would be more likely to give a heavy weight to a public positive evaluation than to a private one. Perhaps the most important reason for downplaying a positive evaluation is the belief that it is undeserved or inconsistent with our previous knowledge of ourselves. However, in public situations we are less concerned with self-knowledge and expressive functions. We want to achieve the utilitarian goals and to avoid embarrassment. There is less point to rejecting a favorable evaluation even if it is undeserved or inconsistent, if third parties are present. In addition, to accept the favorable evaluation will contribute to receiving similar evaluations from the third parties—a possibility that actor is likely to look on with favor.

There are, however, two considerations which would work against a heavier weight for a public sign of approval. In comparison with private approval, it is more likely to be viewed as untruthful and is less likely to be perceived. We all know that most people are somewhat loathe to embarrass others in public, so we may question whether other is just being nice, especially if we think he or she likes us. Although relevant, I suspect that this is not too important. Remember, we reject positive untruthful evaluations because they do not contribute to self-knowledge and in this case the desire for self-knowledge is not that strong.

Of course, it is possible that we will fail to register a favorable evaluation given in public because of the distractions caused by the audience, but that doesn't seem to happen all that often when the evaluation is favorable. Most of us seem to be able to "hear" words of praise no matter how "noisy" the surroundings. Of course, we can all imagine a scene of pandemonium when we will miss "what we want to hear," but in the normal case this tendency does not seem strong enough to begin to overcome the tendencies which favor the heavy weighting of public positive evaluations.

When we consider negative evaluations, however, the matter becomes much more complex. The increase in goal orientation noted for actor also occurs for other. This will lead other to feel shame if his evaluation is rejected by actor. He or she is, therefore, more likely to insist on actor's acquiescence as a condition for giving reward. At the same time, actor is likely to be motivated more strongly than normally to accept a negative evaluation in order to obtain the utilitarian rewards controlled by other. On the basis of these considerations, public negative evaluations should receive heavy weight.

The complications enter because the costs of adopting a negative evaluation are also increased. From what we have said, it is clear that the acceptance of the evaluation is likely to cause embarrassment, and that involves considerable cost. In addition, rewards that actor may have hoped to receive from the third parties may be put in jeopardy by the acceptance of other's unfavorable view. If other sees actor in an unfavorable light, this is likely to influence the audience to see him in a similar way, and if actor acquiesces it is almost certainly going to do that. This would push actor toward giving other's opinion a low weight, for to do otherwise would also lead him or her to receive unfavorable evaluations from the audience.

In the case of negative evaluations, the distractions presented by the presence of third persons might have a significant influence upon attention, unlike the case when the evaluation is positive. In public, the actor is more likely not to perceive the negative evaluation and to have more difficulty "learning" it, as Zajonc's (1965) article indicates.

Thus, in the case of public negative evaluations there are opposing tendencies. It does not seem possible to reach a general conclusion about which will predominate. It would seem to depend on the specific circumstances. How much does actor want what other has to give, how important is the avoidance of embarrassment, how influenced is the audience by other, how distracting is the situation? Only when such questions are answered will it be possible to make a prediction for a given encounter.

Characteristics of the Behavior on which the Evaluation is Based

In deciding what weight to give a received evaluation, actor will take into account, in addition to everything else I have noted, certain characteristics of the behavior being used by other as a basis for the judgment. Of particular relevance would be actor's view about how typical that behavior is and how responsible he or she is for it. The postulate is that opinions of actions viewed as atypical or beyond actor's control are given low weight, all other things being equal.

Even if other is simply reporting upon his or her reaction to a specific act, actor is interested in developing a general view of his or her standing on the trait represented by that act, and it would seem "natural" that actor would not want to allow reactions which are based upon atypical behaviors to have a major influence on that general view. If a reaction is made to a behavior which actor considers atypical, that reaction would not be viewed as contributing much to knowledge of the "real" self and it would, therefore, by given a low weight. That action does not reveal what we "really" are, and so other's evaluation is not relevant for the bigger picture. As Turner puts it: "Some emanations I recognize as expressions of my real self; others seem foreign to the real me. I take little credit and assume little blame for the sensations and actions that are peripheral to my real self. Others are of great significance because they embody my true self, good or bad" (Turner, 1976: 989).

Turner further suggests that there are two "character types" which can be distinguished in terms of the kinds of behavior which they recognize as being authentic.

> To one person, an angry outburst or the excitement of extramarital desire comes as an alien impetus that superficially beclouds or even dangerously threatens the true self. The experience is real enough and may even be persistent and gratifying, but it is still not felt as signifying the real self. The true self is recognized in acts of volition, in the pursuit of institutionalized goals, and not in the satisfaction of impulses outside institutional frameworks. (Turner, 1976: 991)

In contrast to these "institutional" types who feel their behavior is authentic only when they are doing what society says should be done, only when they are resisting temptation, only when they are in full control of their faculties, only when their eyes are on the future, are the "impulsive" types, to whom:

> The outburst of desire is recognized—fearfully or enthusiastically—as an indica-

tion that the real self is breaking through a deceptive crust of institutional behavior. Institutional motivations are external, artificial restraints and super-impositions that bridle manifestations of the real self. One plays the institutional game when he must, but only at the expense of the true self. The true self consists of deep, unsocialized, inner impulses. Mad desires and errant fancy are exquisite expressions of the self. (Turner, 1976: 991–92)

Thus we would expect that people would differ in regard to which received evaluations they would downgrade on the grounds "that I wasn't really being my self," and most people would tend to fall into one or another of Turner's categories.

Lucky, Aided, and Coerced Actions. There are, of course, other reasons why people may get a feeling that a particular behavior is "not really them." For example, it would seem that for most people actions which involve achievement and failure would not be seen as revealing the "real me" if it were recognized that there was a considerable element of luck involved. This would hold whether the outcome was desirable or undesirable; whether it was caused by good or bad luck. There is, of course, evidence that we are more likely to think that luck played a big part when we fail to achieve what we had hoped to (Streufert and Streufert, 1969), but that is not the issue here. The point is simply that *if* we believe luck was involved, we tend to assume that behavior is not revealing of self.

We also tend to give low weight to evaluations of behavior when we believe our actions were influenced by others. If third parties helped us, we would be less willing to accept praise. If we believe the outcome was caused by "circumstances beyond our control" or if we think we were coerced, we are less willing to accept blame.

There are, in addition, utilitarian implications to each of these situations. If other agrees that the behavior is atypical, a result of luck or coercion, he or she is less likely to apply sanctions to actors who refuse to accept the evaluation.

The consequences of these tendencies can be frightening. According to the stories they tell, at least, seemingly ordinary people can arrange cover-ups or murder helpless civilians and feel no loss of self-esteem even as the world reacts with horror, because they simply tell themselves they were following orders. They believe they had no choice, and that the reactions of others tell them nothing about themselves.[11]

The reader probably has no doubts that actors downplay their responsibility for negatively evaluated actions, but do they also refuse credit when they think they were helped by others or by favorable circumstances? If we judge by the frequent statements to the effect that "I couldn't have done it without the help of. . .," it

---

[11] It should be understood that both institutional and impulsive types may consider their behavior to be inauthentic when they are following orders. In fact, most of the people involved in the incidents referred to seem to be institutional types. A person of this type believes his or her behavior to be authentic when he or she *chooses* to follow the dictates of others. Regardless of personality type, behavior defined as coerced is likely to be thought of as not revealing the true self. Of course, an institutional type is less likely to define conforming behavior as coerced, but if so, he is as likely as an impulsive type to deny responsibility for it.

would seem that the answer is yes. It is not clear, however, to what extent such statements are largely the presentation of a modest self. We certainly cannot take them at face value.

The evidence on this matter resembles the material on luck. If the outcome is good, people are more likely to take responsibility than when it is bad. Teachers do this, for example. When a child does poorly the teachers in one study tended to attribute performance to low intelligence or low motivation. When the child improved, it was due to good teaching (Johnson et al., 1964). But in general, if a person believes that coercion or assistance were involved, the tendency is to weight a received evaluation less than when those factors are thought to be absent.

SUMMARY

Interactionist theory suggests that the evaluative part of the self-concept is created from two elements—(1) the perceived social definition, which is actor's view of how others evaluate him or her, and (2) a tentative personal definition, actor's own reaction to his or her behavior based upon personal standards and comparisons with the actions of other people. In this chapter we considered how people know the opinions of others, why they are inclined to adopt those opinions, and how they develop a coherent view of how they are seen by others from the often conflicting opinions they receive.

It is suggested that we learn the opinions of others regarding our behavior through the process of role taking—the same process that enables us to know other views held by our interaction partners. We tend to adopt those views because to do so is often profitable for us. The major rewards associated with the acceptance of others' views are smooth interaction and self-knowledge. Under some circumstances, the expressive reward of high self-evaluation will also be forthcoming.

The basic postulate regarding the development of a perceived social definition out of many received evaluations says that the actor will average all the ratings received after he weights them. Thus, some definitions will have a greater effect on the perceived social definition than others. The theory states that particular definitions are weighted heavily if accepting them is conducive to the achievement of utilitarian, knowledge, or expressive goals. Variations in these three goals are tied to variations in the traits of the participants, the nature of the evaluation, the conditions under which the rating is given, and the actor's definition of the behavior on which the evaluation is based. The specific variables which affect these rewards are summarized in Table 4.1, which follows.

TABLE 4.1 FACTORS RELEVANT TO THE WEIGHT ACTOR GIVES OTHERS' EVALUATIONS IN FORMING HIS OR HER PERCEIVED SOCIAL DEFINITION

I. **Characteristics of the Participants**
1. Variables related to utilitarian rewards:
   a. Degree to which other controls utilitarian rewards which are desired by actor (High status others, others with whom actor will have extensive interaction, others who are liked by actor*)
   b. Extent to which other is willing to use his power (Other's degree of interest in the interaction)
2. Variables related to actor's need for self-knowledge:
   a. Actor's perception of other's ability to judge (Actor's perception of other's: expertise, knowledge of actor, intelligence, lack of bias, interest in actor and the interaction, fairness)
   b. Extent to which actor feels he can believe other's evaluations (Actor's perception of other's truthfulness)
   c. Extent to which other's evaluations are interpretable by actor (Others who give unambiguous and consistent** evaluations)
3. Variables related to the expressive functions:
   a. Actor's perception of the degree to which other's evaluation will contribute to the satisfaction of actor's need for a positive self-view (Others who actor thinks like him. Others who are expected to give positive evaluations)
   b. Actor's perception of the degree to which other's evaluations will contribute to his or her need for consistency (Others who give consistent evaluations. Others who give evaluations which are consistent with the existing self-view)

II. **Characteristics of the Evaluations Received**
1. Variables related to utilitarian rewards:
   a. Extent to which evaluation is associated with reward (Favorable)
2. Variables related to actor's need for self-knowledge:
   a. Extent to which the evaluation is thought to be deserved and accurate (Perception of other's competence; consistency of received evaluation with actor's existing self-definition;** consistency of received evaluation with previously received evaluation**)
   b. Extent to which the evaluation is interpretable by actor (Unambiguous evaluations and evaluations which are consistent with others previously received)
3. Variables related to the expressive functions:
   a. Actor's perception of the degree to which the evaluation will contribute to the satisfaction of actor's need for a positive self-view (Positive evaluations; evaluations which are inconsistent with existing self-view when they are negative**)

b. Actor's perception of the degree to which the evaluation will contribute to his or her need for consistency (Evaluations which are consistent with existing self-view)

III. **Aspects of the Situation in which the Evaluation is Received**
1. Variables related to utilitarian rewards:
   a. Evaluations by multiple others who agree versus evaluations by multiple others who disagree (Evaluations which are agreed to by all the evaluators; the majority opinion when there is variation)
   b. Evaluations given to a group whose members have received homogeneous ratings vs. evaluations given to a group whose members received heterogeneous ratings (Evaluations in heterogeneous groups)
   c. Evaluations which are the same as the evaluations received by most other group members vs. evaluations which differ from those of the other group members (Evaluations which differ)
   d. Evaluations which actor receives as an individual vs. evaluations which are directed to the group to which actor belongs (Individual evaluations)
   e. Public vs. private evaluations (Depends upon conditions)
2. Variables related to actor's need for self-knowledge:
   a. to d. the same as in III–1, above
   e. The timing of the evaluation (Recent evaluations and first evaluations)
   f. Public vs. private evaluations (Depends on conditions)
3. Variables related to expressive functions:
   a. Public vs. private evaluations (Depends on conditions)

IV. **Characteristics of the Behavior on which the Evaluation is Based**
1. Variables related to utilitarian rewards:
   a. Behavior viewed as typical vs. behavior viewed as atypical (Typical behavior)
   b. Behaviors viewed as being influenced by luck vs. behavior viewed as involving achievement (Behaviors involving achievement)
   c. Behaviors viewed as coerced vs. behaviors viewed as voluntary (Voluntary behaviors)
2. Variables related to actor's need for self-knowledge:
   a. to c. the same as in IV–1; above
3. Variables related to the expressive functions:
   none

---

*The specific category listed tends to be associated with high weight.

**For these variables, the mentioned category tends to be associated with high weight, but the relationship varies considerably depending upon other factors.

CHAPTER 5

PERSONAL DEFINITIONS AND SELF-EVALUATIONS

Exhaustive as the foregoing material may be, it does not represent a complete explanation of the development of an individual's self-evaluation. We now know how actor develops a coherent view of how others see him or her, but this *perceived social definition* is not equivalent to the self-definition. The perceived social definition interacts with what we will call the *tentative personal definition,* and it is from this interaction that self-conception per se arises. In this section there are three tasks:

1. to describe how these personal definitions are formed,

2. to describe how a general personal definition emerges from the many specific personal definitions that a person will form of his or her behavior in any given area,

3. to describe the way in which the perceived social definition and the personal definition will be combined into a self-definition.

DEVELOPING A PERSONAL DEFINITION

There are probably two basic processes by which actors arrive at personal evaluations of their actions. They measure their perceptions of their own behavior against standards which they have internalized, and they compare their behavior with that of "comparison others." Comparisons of some sort are necessary. One cannot reach a personal definition simply by observing one's acts. It is a basic assumption that "one's

120

own behavior, in itself, is not informative because it provides raw sensation that has no inherent meaning. Whatever meaning is found in the behavior must essentially be 'read into' it" (Gergen, 1977: 150). Meaning emerges when the comparisons are made.

The Nature of Internal Standards

Traditionally, interactionists have paid little attention to the development of personal definitions, perhaps because the matter was thought to be outside their area of interest. They were, after all, focusing on the *social* sources of self-evaluations. Social psychologists whose roots are in psychology have, however, been interested in personal definitions for years. William James, for example, expressed his view in the famous formula: Self-esteem = Success/Pretensions. "Self-feeling. . . is determined by the ratio of our actualities to our supposed potentialities" (James, 1952: 200).

Although even today it seems as if James had caught the essence of the matter, his formulation is clearly inadequate. For one thing, he is describing only one of the paths to the development of a personal definition, and in his formulation it is not clear what the denominator is. He is saying that we measure our performance against a personal standard, but the nature of that standard is ambiguous. In the illustrations he gives, it seems that the comparison is with our view of what the ideal, or best possible performance, would be, but his use of the term "pretensions" seems to suggest that we compare our actions to what we believe we are capable of achieving—or to what we have announced we are capable of. The task, here, is to specify the nature of personal standards, and then to discuss ways of arriving at a personal definition which do not involve the use of internalized standards.

Personal Standards.   To my mind it is misleading to suggest that the touchstone for our behavior is some single level of performance. In areas that are not new to them, people have in mind a continuum along which are ranged various outcomes. If an outcome reaches level I, it would be viewed as awful, and a behavior which attained level II might be defined as poor, and so on. Each possible level would have attached to it an evaluative statement which would allow actor to get a feeling of how well he has done "by his lights." By no means the only example, but perhaps the one most familiar to the reader, are the evaluations that students associate with the points on the grading scale. Students assign a meaning to each of the possible grades: an "82" is good or it's an unmitigated disaster.

Grades are, however, a somewhat special case, for typically an other is involved who reports the level of performance attained. The student still must interpret the meaning of the report, but in the case of an examination or term paper, actor is usually not capable of determining his absolute level of performance. A runner, however, can time himself and then interpret his time. A baseball player can figure his own batting average. As long as actor has some *subjective* scale there can be a personal definition. It doesn't matter much whether actor or other determines where the performance falls on the *absolute* scale.

I have still not, however, specified what the points of the continuum will be. What will people consider to be an acceptable performance? Do people accept only a perfect performance? Are most satisfied only when they do as well as they think they are capable of doing?

I would suggest that no general answer can be given to these questions since it varies considerably from person to person. Some are merely satisfied when they reach what they consider to be their maximum potential. Others are ecstatic when they do that well. Others ask no more of themselves than that they "pass."

In addition, of course, there will be variations within a given person. Usually, we do not use the same scale in all contexts. The evaluation associated with any given grade will in most instances depend on the particular course involved. There are, no doubt, some who use the same standards for all courses, or more generally, for all activities which are viewed as being in the same general area. Most of us, however, define a "C" in our major in quite a different way than we evaluate the same grade in a course we define as uninteresting or irrelevant to our goals. An olympic-level decathlon athlete might be satisfied with nothing less than 850 points in his specialty, but would consider 750 points as totally gratifying in some other event.

There is no general rule. The scales used by people are derived from their previous experience and that experience varies. People are taught what an acceptable performance should be and the lessons are different for different people. Some have it drummed into them, perhaps to their misfortune, that they must always "shoot for the stars," while others have learned that much less strict standards are appropriate or acceptable. Furthermore, all the standards we are taught are specific to particular situations. This kind of answer is perhaps not very satisfying, but the nature of the case does not allow for greater specificity.

Learning Standards

Given this conceptualization, it clearly becomes incumbent upon me to explain, in more specific terms, how actor comes to know other's standards and why he adopts them as his own. We turn to that next.

Much of our instruction in this regard is direct, conscious, and intentional. Others explicitly and directly suggest that particular standards should be used. Some children are told by their parents, for example, that anything less than an "A" is unacceptable while others are taught that a passing grade is fine. In addition to this kind of teaching, there is somewhat more indirect instruction. The child learns a scale by noting his parents' reactions to the evaluations he receives from others. Many parents would never think of telling a child he or she must never be satisfied with less than an "A." That would be pushing the child and exerting too much pressure. However, they convey that only an "A" is acceptable to them by their reactions to the grades the child receives. As I learned with my own children, a parent who shows any disappointment when his children come home with B's is teaching them that B's are not fine, even if he constantly tells them "all I ask is that you do your best." As in so many things, our actions speak louder than our words.

In the situations described above, three people are involved—actor, a rater, and a third person who interprets the rating. Of course, the same process can be carried on by two people. It is quite common that the person making the rating also offers an interpretation of it. Teachers do not simply give out grades; they also express pleasure or displeasure about "how the class did." The three person and two person situations are for present purposes the same. Also, it is accidental that the examples refer to children; the same process continues throughout life.

Finally, actor can learn personal standards even if other does not react to him. In fact, it is not even necessary that actor act. The first time that he receives a particular rating, he may find that he has internalized standards with which to interpret it. The process underlying this phenomenon is also a familiar one. It is based upon our tendency to observe other people and to model our behavior on theirs. Thus, we see how other people react to the ratings they and third persons receive in various situations, and we adopt and use those definitions when we find ourselves in a comparable situation. By observing the reactions of his parents to an older sibling, a child can enter school with standards which allow him to interpret the grades he receives.

What has been described thus far involves the interpretation of an absolute rating received from an other. But, as was noted above, actor can often make the original rating which he or she later interprets. The point here is that the ability to make the original rating is also learned. In some cases, all that that actor has to do is to learn some technical skill, such as reading a stop watch. In other instances, a more complex set of criteria must be learned. Others teach actor these criteria every time they rate him or some other person. Other's ratings are of necessity based upon his standards, and actor will come to know what those standards are through role taking. The question in actor's mind is not simply, "How will he rate me?" Actor also wants to know, "Why does he rate me that way?" Only by learning other's standards can the second question be answered. When it is answered actor can use the information for self-ratings. He will now know what merits a "B." In some cases he will never be competent, or feel competent, to make the basic rating and thus he will require "help" in arriving at a personal definition. Often, however, his socialization will prepare him to carry out the *whole* process independently.

I have now described how actor comes into contact with the information necessary for a personal definition. It still remains to be explained why he adopts other's rating scheme and interpretation. Why doesn't he simply decide on his own what deserves a "B" and that a "B" is fine? Why does he adopt as his own someone else's definition of that grade?

In the previous chapter I used the basic assumption that actors often have something to gain by accepting other's evaluations of them. Now I would add that there are similar reasons for actor to adopt the standards that other uses to make that evaluation. Accepting other's standards is a way, for example, to win approval and to gain knowledge. To insist on a standard which is not accepted by others will lead us into conflict with them. And even if that were not so, how could we decide on our own what deserves a "B" and what a "B" means? The grade has no inherent meaning. It is a symbol and its meaning comes from social usage. It is an oft-repeated point by now;

actor learns the meanings that he or she applies to things from other people. What actor is being taught in this situation are the meanings that should be applied to various actions.

Comparison Others

In all these cases the process involves learning a standard which has been used by an other. One can, however, judge one's action without having an internalized absolute standard. Actor can do this by adopting a *comparison other*. He can observe other's performance, and when actor performs he can get an indication of the value of his performance by noting the direction and magnitude of the difference between his behavior and that of the other.

  The answer that is obtained may not, however, be as informative as actor would like. The comparison may tell him that he is a little better than "X," but it does not tell him whether being a little better than "X" is a great accomplishment or something to be ashamed of.

  The usual way to answer such questions is to utilize other knowledge about "X." If I know that I beat "X" in a race and I also know we are about the same age, I can take some pride in my accomplishment. If I know enough about him, I might be able to guess how he would have been evaluated, and this can also make the comparison more informative. I don't have to know what the record is for the mile; if I know that "X" was a member of the last Olympic team, I can take pride in whatever my time was since it was better than his.

  A standard developed using comparison others will differ in form from those developed by the other methods. It would say, for example, anything better than "X's" behavior is good, anything equal to it is acceptable, and so on. Standards developed by the earlier methods would lack that element of comparison. They would simply equate particular outcomes, stated in absolute terms, with particular evaluations. In one case the statement would be, "I beat X and therefore I did well." In the other case it would be, "I did the mile in 4 minutes 5 seconds and that is very good." The forms of the standards differ, and they develop in different ways, but they function in exactly the same manner. They are both standards, but to keep them separate I will limit my use of the term internalized standard to the kind which is expressed in absolute terms and developed by "adoption." When the standard is developed by comparison of self and other I will speak of the use of a "comparison other."

  Diggory (1966) suggests another form of internalized standard that may be used. Here the touchstone is not some absolute level of performance, nor the comparison between one's achievement and someone else's. One evaluates the performances in terms of their instrumentality. A performance is good if it is sufficient to meet a particular goal, excellent if it helps us achieve a higher goal. To return to our track example, a third possibility would be "I did well, because I did well enough to reach the finals."

  It should be made explicit that this view of how we arrive at standards for personal evaluations suggests that despite the relevance of such evaluations, the self-concept is completely social in its origins. The comparison of actions with standards is the act of an individual, but I have shown that, if one scratches the surface, the social roots of those standards are quickly revealed. They are certainly ours in the present, but it is almost equally certain that directly or indirectly we learned them from others in the past.

Also, this focus on standards should not be construed as meaning that we always bring criteria for personal judgments to our interactions and it does not suggest that when we do bring such standards with us we are "wedded" to them. The standards we bring to a situation can be, and often are, altered and when we do not have standards we can often devise them "on the spot" utilizing the same processes I have just described.

Studies of Personal Definitions

This analysis leaves several questions unanswered which we will consider soon. Before going on, however, let us look at the somewhat limited systematic evidence bearing upon the assertions made so far. Do people make personal evaluations of their own behavior independently of those made by others? Do they do this by comparing their behavior to internalized standards and are these standards derived in the ways described? And do they also arrive at personal evaluations by comparing their actions with those of others?

A study by Stotland et al. (1957) demonstrates that we make comparisons with internalized standards and that these standards have social roots. One group was told that they had voted, as the group norm, that each member should be expected to complete the task that they would be given. The other group was led to believe that all they would expect was that each group member would do his best. They were then given two tasks, one of which was impossible to complete. On the "failure task" those from the group with high expectations rated themselves lower than those from the low expectations group. It would seem that the people did take on the group's expectations as their own and that they measured their performance against those norms.

Morse and Gergen (1970) illustrate quite vividly the strength of the tendency to form a personal evaluation by comparing one's personal traits to those of others. They arranged it so that male undergraduates who believed they were applying for a job waited in a room with one of two confederates, who was described as being "another job applicant." One of the confederates, called Mr. Clean, had a personal appearance and manner which most would find desirable. He was well-dressed, businesslike, well-organized, and so forth. Mr. Dirty, on the other hand, was slovenly, rather dazed, and ill-prepared. Despite the very limited contact with the confederate—he and the subject were together for only a minute and a half before the subject was asked to fill out some forms—and despite the fact that in half the cases the confederate was not applying for the same job as the subject, it seems that a comparison was made by the subjects and their self-evaluations were affected by the results. Those who met Mr. Clean showed a decrease in self-esteem and those who waited with Mr. Dirty showed an increase. Since the subjects were randomly assigned to the two conditions, the only plausible explanation is that their self-views were influenced by what they perceived to be the differences between them and the confederate.

A study by S. C. Jones (1968) also shows that we compare our actions with others, and that the results of those comparisons affect our self-conceptions. In a group discussion experiment, some subjects were told only their own ratings and others were given ratings of their own performance and evaluations of the contributions of the other group members. Among those who knew only their own ratings, the differences in self-rating for those who had received high evaluations and those who had received low ones were smaller than were the differences when the subjects knew both how they had been evaluated and how the others had fared. It would seem that the high and low ratings they received had little meaning for the subjects *unless* they could compare them with those received by others. They needed to know the ratings of others before they could create a scale which would give meaning to the feedback they had received about themselves.

Thus there is experimental evidence to indicate that evaluations of self are made in the absence of direct, meaningful evaluations from others, and that the general processes I postulated are used to make those judgments. People measure their behavior against internalized standards which have a social origin and they compare their behavior and the evaluations they receive with those of others.

With the basic fact established we may turn to a consideration of three "second-order" questions:

1. How does actor develop a coherent internalized standard from the many varying standards he will meet?
2. What determines who he will choose as a comparison other when he has several possibilities from which to choose?
3. How does he develop a composite personal evaluation from the numerous specific judgments he is likely to make about himself in any particular area?

The answers to the first and last questions will sound familiar, for the processes are quite similar to those involved in the development of a perceived social definition. The internalized standard is the weighted average of the standards that have been suggested to actor by others, and the general personal evaluation is a weighted average of the specific evaluations that actor has given himself. The weights are applied, just as with evaluations received, in such a way as to aid actor in achieving utilitarian, knowledge, and expressive goals. Thus, the specific factors which lead to high and low weight are basically the same as those described in Chapter 4. For these questions, it is pointless to repeat all that has previously been discussed; it should be sufficient to briefly refresh the reader's memory, discuss some of the minor changes that must be made, and present the limited data which bear on the validity of the theory as applied to these materials. Let us first consider the development of internal standards.

Regarding the characteristics of the other, the situation is almost exactly comparable whether received evaluations or suggested personal standards are involved. In the first case, other is making a direct evaluation of actor and if other has the characteristics I mentioned earlier, actor will find it advantageous to accept that evaluation as his or her own. In the present case, other is—directly or indirectly—suggesting that a particular set of standards is valid and appropriate and under the same circumstances, actor will find it gainful to adopt them. I cannot discern any essential difference between the two situations.

The Stotland et al. (1957) study provides indirect evidence that two of the factors which relate to acceptance of another's evaluation are also applicable to the acceptance of other's standards. They discovered that the effect of group standards upon personal evaluation was greatest when the subject was "concerned about" the group's expectations and when actor's task was relevant to group goals, that is, when the group's solution of the general problem depended upon the subject solving his part of it.

It is certainly going beyond what the data say explicitly, but the first finding suggests to me that the tendency to accept the group's standards is greater when the actor likes the group members. An actor would be concerned about his team's expectations primarily when their disapproval would be punishing to him and their approval rewarding, and this would be the case when the actor liked the other people in the experiment. The association between concern and influence gives indirect support to the postulated relationship between liking others and accepting their views. We know from the study that when there is concern, adoption of other's standards is more likely, and I am suggesting that liking increases concern. If these relationships are strong enough, liking should also be related to acceptance of other's standards.

In addition, the finding that adoption was greater when actor's performance affected other's payoffs suggests that actor is more likely to adopt other's views when other is interested in him. When other has that interest, he is more likely to use what power he possesses. In the "irrelevant" condition of the study, actor's performance had no influence on his partners' "fate." There was no group outcome; each person was to be graded on his own performance. When this was the case, the other subjects had little incentive to pressure actor into accepting the group's standards. And the evidence shows that under these conditions the actors showed only a small tendency to accept the group's norms.

In the "relevant" condition, each had to make a contribution to the solution of a group task or all would fail. The other people had, therefore, a clear interest in actor's performance, which, we may guess, they translated into pressure to utilize the group standard as a goal and as a measure of the extent of failure. And the evidence shows that actors did show a stronger tendency to take on other's views when other had reason to be interested in actor's performance.

When it comes to the characteristics of the reaction itself, the nature of the present case does require some changes. For example, when I spoke of received evaluations, I postulated that evaluations which serve to satisfy the actor's need for a positive view of self would be weighted more heavily, which easily translated into the assertion that favorable evaluations would receive heavier weight. In regard to suggested standards, the same general principle holds, but its application is more complicated. It would appear that the lower the standard, the more likely it is to assist actor in obtaining a positive view of self, for the lower the standard the easier it is to meet. And I suspect that there is some tendency to keep standards low. Certainly all other things being equal, people are more likely to adopt the lower of two standards which are presented to them.

At the same time I say this, it is entirely clear to me that there must be more to it than this, for this postulate would suggest that people would adopt much lower standards for themselves than they normally do. The problem is not that the postulate is wrong, but rather that all other things are very rarely equal. I have no doubt that I, as well as most others, would accept a lower standard rather than a higher one if meeting the lower one would provide me with equal prestige, money, feeling of accomplishment, pride, and so forth. Unfortunately, that is not usually the case. Thus, a more realistic postulate would state that people will adopt the lowest standard that does not require them to give up other desired rewards. That is perhaps the reason I discovered, when I recalculated some of the figures in the Stotland et al. (1957) article, that people in the high expectations groups were as concerned about the group's standards as were those in the groups which had voted a lower standard. Even though the standard was more difficult to meet, they "had to" accept it or run the risk of losing group approval.

In real life I would expect that the standard which best serves actor's utilitarian *and* expressive interests would rarely be the lowest one that has been suggested to him or her. To aim for the bottom would mean foregoing many tangible rewards—prestige and challenge, for example. On the other hand, a very high standard would also be given low weight by most of us in forming our personal standards. Such a scale may doom us to failure and a negative self-view.

Beyond this it appears that the basic theory can be applied to the development of personal standards without significant alteration. The standards of other people which we weight heavily when we are "constructing" our personal standards have the same characteristics as the received evaluations which are weighted heavily in the development of a perceived social definition.

Choice of Comparison Others

The other route to the development of a personal evaluation involves comparing one's actions with those of another, and by the results of the comparison ascribing an evaluative meaning to one's own performance. That such a process does occur is indicated clearly in a study by Gerard (1961). He discovered he could alter self-evaluations by simply telling subjects their scores on a test and the general distribution of scores.

Thus, there was no direct evaluation received; the subject had to compare himself with the others in order to determine the meaning of his score. Somewhat more indirect is the finding reported by Wilson (1963) that subjects work harder when they are promised that they will be given the norms for the test they are taking. The implication is clearly that actors wish to make comparisons with others and that they are willing to "pay extra costs" when they think they will be able to do so.

Gerard (1961) also reports that there seems to be variation in the extent to which people utilize comparison others. For example, the subjects who believed that their scores would be made public seemed most likely to use a comparison other. What seems to be the case is that the subjects who believed that others would know their scores expected that they would be evaluated by the others in terms of the norms they had all been given. The actors made the comparisons for themselves so that when the received evaluation was given it would not be in conflict with their self-view. The change in self-view seems to be a means of avoiding an anticipated cognitive dissonance.

Characteristics of Comparison Others. It seems in general that there is little question that social comparisons do take place and that certain conditions facilitate their occurrence. The data are not extensive, but they are convincing, especially when the evidence of everyday experience is added in. Somewhat more problematic is the question, "When there are several potential comparison others available, which will be chosen?" Let us consider that issue now.

At first glance, it might seem that an answer can be provided by applying the theory of the previous chapter. It would appear reasonable that the factors which lead a person to choose a particular other as a significant other would also be involved in the choice of a comparison other, for there are clear parallels between the two choices. Unfortunately, there are also important differences, and the theory presented in the last chapter will not provide an adequate answer unless it is altered to some degree. The previous theory doesn't lead to errors. The problem is that it must be extended if it is to apply to all the situations which require explanation.

Control of Utilitarian Rewards. One reason actors choose particular persons as significant others is that to do so often leads to their receiving utilitarian rewards from other. In some cases similar advantages accrue to actor when he uses other as a comparison other, and when that is so the previous theory has relevance. When the comparison other is seen as a potential source of utilitarian rewards, actor will choose those others who have more to give and those who will make being chosen a condition for giving the reward. Thus the powerful, the liked, the interested, and those we interact with frequently are more likely to be chosen as comparison others under these circumstances.

It is, however, not all that common for actor's actions in this regard to have an important effect on what is received from other. For other to offer an evaluation is, in some degree, a commitment to a particular position, and therefore other has some stake in having actor's agreement. Other is less likely to have an investment in being chosen as a comparison point. If he or she isn't chosen, no insult or contradiction is given. In such cases, utilitarian rewards would not be influenced by actor's choice.

If the search for utilitarian rewards is often irrelevant to the choice of a comparison other, what are actor's goals in making such a choice? The answer, I believe, is that actor will choose primarily with a view to increasing the likelihood of receiving knowledge and expressive rewards. Thus the differences between this situation and that of choosing a significant other lie not in the general goals and principles, but in the details. Both processes are directed by reward seeking, but the rewards sought differ somewhat. Let us see how this works out in concrete cases.

Self-Knowledge. Above anything else, the choice of a comparison other is motivated by the desire to increase self-knowledge. We wish to answer the question, "How am I doing?" and though almost any comparison will give us some self-knowledge, some will give us more than others. Therefore, I would postulate that we choose the comparison other in a manner designed to give us the maximum amount of useful self-knowledge. What, then, will we consider to be the most informative comparisons?

If I compare my racing performance against that of the Olympic star, I am likely to end up with very little useful information. Of course, if I beat him or her I will know that I am very good; in fact, if I come close I will know that. But that is hardly likely to happen; the chances are that my performance will be very much inferior, and I won't know much more than when I started. I won't know that I am a poor runner, for to be unable to keep up with such a person is not equivalent to doing poorly—any more than beating a five-year-old would lead me to evaluate myself favorably.

The situation becomes clear when it is realized that for most of us, "How am I doing?" means, more specifically, "How am I doing in relation to what may be reasonably expected of me?" Few of us wish to be measured against perfection; that is why we reject some evaluations given by others on the basis that an unfair scale is being used. The other who evaluates us is expected to utilize an appropriate scale for people like us.

When a comparison other is being used, however, there is no scale. We attempt to learn "how we are doing relative to reasonable expectation," by seeing how others are doing. In order for the comparison to provide the answer we are seeking, the other who is chosen must be someone who resembles us. We choose a particular person to tell us, by his or her behavior, how people "like us" do. That is the kind of comparison that will give us a feeling of self-knowledge. Thus I would hypothesize that all other things being equal, we tend to choose as comparison other people who resemble us in what we consider to be relevant ways, for such comparisons will usually give us the kind of information we want.

Although they do not relate to judgment of ability, a number of studies in the reference group tradition produce results consistent with this idea.[1] For example, it

---

[1] As with many other concepts in social psychology, the term "reference group" is used in different ways by different authors (compare Shibutani, 1955; Turner, 1956; Kuhn, 1964a;

was found, somewhat surprisingly, that during World War II better educated, white-collar soldiers were more accepting of having to serve than were those of the blue-collar class (Merton and Kitt, 1950; Stouffer et al., 1949). The reason seemed to be that each group compared its fate with those of similar occupational background. Since almost no white-collar jobs were defined as essential, the better educated were not likely to know people *like them* who had received occupational deferments, but the former factory workers could point to people they viewed as comparable who had escaped the draft. Similarly, black soldiers stationed in the South were at least as satisfied as those stationed in the North, apparently because each group compared their situation with that of the black civilians in their area. In the South the comparison indicated their situation was not all that bad.

In addition, the literature from experimental social psychology shows a strong tendency to choose similar others as a basis for comparison because such comparisons are thought to be more informative. Hakmiller (1966), for example, found that when people were unsure of their ability they tended to choose to know the responses of others who had previously performed like them. When they were rather sure they were good at the task, they did not show any preference. The indication is clear that only those who were unsure needed to know "how they were doing," and they attempted to discover that by comparing themselves with people of similar ability. (For several other studies along this line see Latané, 1966.)

There are other indications that actors think they get "better" information when they compare themselves with people they believe are similar on the task they are involved in. Zanna et al. (1975), for example, discovered that people tend to choose people of their own sex and major subject as a comparison when they are trying to make sense of their score on a supposedly sex-linked trait. Only one student chose a nonstudent as the first choice. Similarly, Samuel (1973) reports that the subjects in his study who thought they were at the extremes tended to choose people who they believed had similar ranking, and, in addition, they favored people with similar traits even though those traits were supposedly not relevant to the test they were taking.

Schachter's (1959) studies on the affiliation motive are also relevant in this regard. Ability evaluations were not at issue—the goal of the subjects was to find out if they were "right" in being afraid of participating in a study which involved electric shock. To do this, they chose to be with others when given the chance. The relevant point here is that they preferred to be with certain others—those who were also going to be in the study. Schachter's (1959: 24) remark captures it well: "Misery doesn't love any kind of company, it loves only miserable company." And, I would add, mis-

---

Schmitt, 1972; Hyman and Singer, 1968). There is fairly general agreement, however, that a normative reference group is the source of the individual's values and behavioral prescriptions, and a comparative reference group is the "group which serves as the point of reference in making comparisons or contrasts, especially in forming judgments about oneself" (Shibutani, 1955: 56. See also Kelley, 1952; Williams, 1970). Hyman (1942) had comparison groups in mind when he introduced the term and this is the type which is presently of interest.

ery loves miserable company because other supposedly miserable people provide one with a basis for evaluating the appropriateness of one's own misery.[2]

Our desire for simplicity is again going to be frustrated, for the tendency to compare oneself to similar others is not absolute. This tendency arises from the fact that such comparisons *often* lead actor to feel there is a chance of obtaining the most relevant information. Under some circumstances, however, comparisons with similar others are not viewed as the best ways to get the desired information. The governing principle is that people seek relevant information, but this does not always lead to comparisons with similar people.

In some cases, actors feel that they will get more relevant information by choosing a dissimilar person as a touchstone. This is illustrated in a number of studies which have a basically similar design: a group of people engage in a task and then each subject is told his absolute score and that he ranked in the middle of the group. Half of the subjects are told, in addition, the approximate value of the scores obtained by the highest and lowest scorers. The subjects were then given the opportunity to see the actual score of one participant. After they made that choice, they were allowed to make a second choice (Wheeler et al., 1969).

The key element in these studies is that the actor knows his rank—he knows his performance was average. In this case, the comparison is useful only to give more meaning to what is already known. (In the more common examples discussed above, the comparison may be assumed to have the function of giving basic information concerning where actor stands.) Under these circumstances, what kind of information do actors seek when they try to get more details about the adequacy of their performances?

Subjects who did not know the range of scores tended to use their two choices to find out the highest and the lowest scores, not those of the people who were closest to them. Whether the high score was the best performance or the worst, the majority asked to see the highest score first, but this tendency was stronger when the highest score was the best performance.

When they knew the approximate range of scores from the outset many subjects, as above, asked for the exact scores of the extremes. But under this condition, people also showed a strong tendency to use their two choices to find out how the people closest to them had done, choosing the one who had done a little better first and the one who had done a little worse second.

These tendencies seem rather consistent under constant conditions, although the introduction of variations in the methodology changes the patterns to some extent. For example, if the respondents rated other than average, their choices change when they believe they will interact with the person they choose. They fear having to interact with someone who is much superior and they are not as likely to choose the extremes,

---

[2]The supposition that the desire for affiliation is based upon a need to compare one's emotional state with others is bolstered by several facts: (1) The desire for affiliation is greater when the threatening situation is ambiguous; (2) In these situations people with low self-esteem have a greater desire to be with others, presumably because they have a greater need for comparison; and (3) The desire for affiliation is reduced when opportunities for communication with the other are restricted (Zimbardo and Formica, 1963).

although it is still a common choice pattern. (For other relevant studies see Latané, 1966; Zanna et al., 1971; Gruder, 1971; Friend and Gilbert, 1973. Gruder, 1977, and Suls and Miller, 1977 contain bibliographies of experiments of this type.)

The reason for this pattern of choice is a matter of debate (cf. Wheeler et al., 1969 and Arrowood and Friend, 1969). Considering both positions, I would suggest that choosing to know the extreme scores is an attempt to establish just how well one did. If one scores in the middle, it is informative to know how far the middle is from the extreme. The fact that the tendency to choose the extreme was reduced when the approximate range was known would support this interpretation. That there was still some tendency to choose the extreme even when its approximate value was known suggests it is a strong tendency.

The subjects, however, thought at the outset that they could make only one choice. Thus they could only determine one end of the range. Why did they choose to set the high end rather than the low? The worst score is equally informative in setting the range, but the best score gives additional information. It tells the subject how much better one has to be in order to be the best. Few people who know they have done reasonably well are particularly concerned about knowing how much worse they can be without being the worst. Most people are more concerned about what they have to do to get better than they are about what they have to avoid to prevent getting worse (see Festinger, 1954).[3]

Reference group studies also show that the choice of similar persons is not always seen as the way to get the most relevant information. Under some circumstances, people choose as their reference, groups to which they do not belong, or, to turn it around, they do not use as a reference those who are similar to them and with whom they interact. How could making a comparison with one who is obviously different from you provide desired information? The accepted answer (Merton and Kitt, 1950) is consistent with what was suggested in explaining the tendency to choose people who did better: If a person desires to change groups he may not care at all how he compares with his peers. He wants to know what he has to do to meet the standard of the group to which he aspires, and he is interested in knowing how close he has already come. The upwardly mobile person, the person hoping for a promotion, is interested in knowing if he is as good as those he aspires to be like, and the most relevant information for him or her is contained in a comparison with the nonmembership group—the people who are dissimilar.[4]

---

[3]Even this discussion does not fully indicate the complexity involved in applying the basic principle. For example, if the subjects are told they are below average, a rather different pattern of choices is observed. Gruder (1977) and Mettee and Smith (1977) discuss some of the circumstances which lead people to compare themselves with persons who are not similar to them.

[4]It may go well beyond this. In some cases the actor may even compare himself against an imaginary person (Shibutani, 1961; Kemper, 1968). Under some circumstances, actor will feel he knows himself best when he knows how he stands up against the "average person" or against some "ideal person." All this notwithstanding, the strongest tendency is to compare oneself against inter-action partners who are like you. This is particularly true for children (Rosenberg and Simmons, n.d.).

Although the need for self-knowledge is an important element in the choice of a comparison other, as I have already noted, it is not the only element operating. Mettee and Smith (1977) and Patchen (1961) discuss a number of goals that are involved; we will consider only two more—the need for a positive self-image and the desire for utilitarian rewards.

Expressive and Utilitarian Reward. At first look, this tendency to compare oneself with superiors or near equals rather than inferiors may seem surprising, given that people also attempt to achieve the expressive goal of maintaining a favorable view of self. Almost by definition one is more likely to "look good" when compared to someone who is an inferior. I do not believe, however, that the results are actually in conflict with the tendency to protect and enhance one's self-esteem. In fact, the result might be viewed as quite consistent with such a tendency.

To compare oneself with one who is assumed to be superior does not really threaten the existing level of self-evaluation. In the laboratory situations, the people know—by their rank—that they did not equal or exceed the high scores. To find that they were far from admittedly superior people should not lower their self-evaluation, but to find that they come close, in an absolute sense, may make their middle rank seem better, thus increasing self-evaluation. To compare with the worst in the group can only lower one's self-evaluation. If the middle rank is close to the bottom, it will not seem so good to be average; if a middle score is much better than the worst, one will still only be average. If this is acceptable, it would seem that the subjects had only one way to raise their self-evaluations above the point that was set by knowing what their rank was. They "had to" compare themselves with the highest scorers in the hope they would turn out to be close. By making this choice they had a lot to gain and little to lose. The case of the upwardly mobile seems quite analogous.

I said at the outset that in many cases the choice of a comparison other cannot be used to obtain utilitarian rewards from the person chosen. But when it can be so used, the best plan for actor is to pick someone who is like him or a little higher. If a person of lesser stature is chosen, he may be complimented, but he also may have little of value to give to actor. A person of much higher status is not as likely to be complimented, or at least not sufficiently complimented to give up anything that actor wants. The boss may like to be used as a model by the young clerk, but unless the boss has an unusually large ego the clerk is not likely to get much for his trouble, especially since many people of high status are aware of the dangers of being "used" by underlings who make a pretense of respect. The best choice would seem to be someone who is similar; they are likely to have valued things and be sufficiently complimented by being chosen as a point of comparison.

But again this would not hold for the upwardly mobile. They would choose higher-status persons as comparisons even if to do so does not lead to *immediate* reward. As Merton and Kitt (1950) note, the upwardly mobile person will further his eventual mobility by choosing his comparison other from the group to which he aspires. By doing this, he learns what one has to be like to belong—it provides anticipatory socialization.

It should be noted, however, that this tendency to look outside the group for comparison others involves a price. Succumbing to the siren call of the outsider can be defined as desertion by all involved. Someone who takes this route had better "succeed" because there is no going back.

Because of this element of treason, it is often necessary for the upwardly mobile person to deny, even to himself, that he is choosing his comparison others from the group to which he does not belong. Norman Podhoretz (1969), a boy from the slums of Brooklyn who "made it" in the literary world of Manhattan, describes how it was possible to make the "longest journey in the world." It seems clear enough from his description that he, more than most, tried to emulate those above him. How else can one explain his excruciating embarrassment at not knowing how to act in the restaurant to which a high-school teacher had taken him as part of her campaign to "civilize" him? Why else were each of his college papers in a style resembling that of the professor teaching the course? Why was he so concerned about impressing his supervisor at Cambridge University even though the supervisor would have, at best, limited influence upon his academic fate? Though he was clearly "on the make," Podhoretz insists many years later that he was unaware of what was happening, and if he had known he could never have gone through with it.

> I have become a fully acculturated citizen of a country as foreign. . .as China and infinitely more frightening. That country is sometimes called the upper middle class. It appalls me to think what an immense transformation I had to work on myself in order to become what I have become: If I had known what I was doing I would surely not have been able to do it, I would surely not have wanted to. No wonder the choice had to be blind; there was a kind of treason in it: treason toward my family, treason toward my friends. In choosing the road I chose, I was pronouncing a judgment upon them.
>
> When I say the choice was blind, I mean that I was never aware. . .how inextricably my "noblest" ambitions were tied to the vulgar desire to rise above the class into which I was born; nor did I understand to what an astonishing extent these ambitions were shaped and defined by the standards and values and tastes of the class into which I did not know I wanted to move. (Podhoretz, 1969: 3-4)

In summary, the need for utilitarian rewards and expressive needs push in the same direction as the need for self-knowledge—horizontally or up. People tend to choose similar persons as comparisons, but under special conditions they will choose those above them despite the costs sometimes involved in such a choice.

Combining Personal Evaluations

The key to understanding how a *general* personal evaluation is devised from a series of personal evaluations of specific acts is to realize that actors' reactions to evaluations received from themselves are like their reactions to evaluations received from others.

(As has already been noted previously, one of the qualities of human beings is that they can be objects to themselves.) Thus, an actor will give greater weight in forming his personal definition to those evaluations he gave himself which were favorable, to those personal evaluations which were consistent with other evaluations given to self and with opinions expressed by others. Recent personal evaluations will count more as will those which have primacy, and so on.

What may not be clear is how the characteristics of the other could be pertinent since the other is always the same person—the actor himself. Let me show that these factors are in fact relevant.

The other may be the same person in all cases, but people are different at different times. Even though only one person, the actor, is giving the evaluations, that person will have somewhat different characteristics when he is giving different evaluations. For example, the extent to which we are honest with ourselves will vary. Just as actor will give greater weight to an evaluation which he receives from an other that he believes to be truthful, so actor will weight more heavily those evaluations he gave himself when he was being most honest with himself. Also, people have an awareness that sometimes they are more competent to judge themselves than they are at other times. Some personal evaluations may be based upon more information than others are, for example. Again, just as we will give greater weight to those of our evaluations made by credible judges, we will give greater weight to those of our evaluations which we believe were made under circumstances of greater competence.

In summary, in addition to developing a view of how he is defined by other people, actor makes a personal evaluation of his specific actions, and from these he develops a general personal view of his ability in a particular area. The specific personal evaluations are made by comparing one's actions with internalized personal standards and by comparing one's actions to those of selected others. The internalized standards, though they are "actor's" in the present, are usually taught to him by others, either directly or indirectly. The many standards that are suggested to actor are combined and the weighted average is the standard used. The weighting factors closely resemble those used for received evaluations.

The choice of a comparison other is influenced in large part by the desire to obtain the greatest amount of relevant knowledge about the self. The implications of this will vary depending upon circumstances. When actor knows nothing about where he ranks, the "best" information is obtained by comparing himself to similar persons; when one knows one's rank, the best way to obtain additional information is to compare against the best. Expressive and utilitarian needs are also served by choice of similar or superior comparison others.

After a series of evaluations of specific acts in a particular area, a general personal definition is arrived at by weighting and averaging. Some of our own evaluations of self are given more weight than others in a manner similar to the weighting done to form a perceived social definition.

The Combination of Personal and
Social Evaluations

Now that I have described the ways in which the ingredients of the evaluative component of the self-concept are prepared, there is only one task remaining—to discuss the way in which they are combined into a self-evaluation. The actor, we may assume, now has a coherent view of how he is viewed by others and he has a personal definition. How will he create a self-conception?

The answer is the same as the one I suggested when the problems were how several evaluations from others are combined into a perceived social definition and how several specific personal definitions are combined to form a general personal evaluation. The actor weights each of the elements and then takes the average as the self-evaluation. A self-evaluation will take into account the perceived social definition and the personal definition, but they will probably not contribute equally. The factors that determine the weight to be given to each component will be essentially the same as those which were discussed previously when I was considering how the components are developed.

The characteristics of the evaluator will, as before, be of major importance. Without oversimplifying the matter, we may think of the situation as though there were two evaluations vying for influence—one contributed by actor and one contributed by others. The attitudes of actor toward the others and toward himself will influence the weight he gives to each. How much does he need or want the utilitarian rewards that will be forthcoming from other if he gives greater weight to their evaluations? Does he believe that their evaluations or his own will contribute more to his self-knowledge? That is, who does he believe is more competent to judge, who is more informed, who is more objective?

Just as always, the characteristics of the evaluations themselves will also be relevant to the weight assigned them, and the needs that actor will attempt to satisfy are the usual ones. For example, if the personal and social definitions differ in the extent to which they are favorable or consistent with the existing self-definition, the actor will tend to give greater weight to the one which is more favorable and more consistent, for it better serves expressive needs. Also, the two evaluations may differentially serve actor's need for self-knowledge. One may be based upon the performance of a group; this will be weighted less heavily than one which was influenced solely by actor's own performance. If the personal and social definitions differ in the extent to which they are based upon actions which actor considers volitional, they will be weighted differently; if actor feels that one is more accurate than the other he will weight that one more heavily.

Actor's weighting of the two components will also be affected by the degree to which others control his rewards, the extent of his need for those rewards, and the extent to which reward is made contingent on accepting their viewpoint. Thus utilitarian rewards are also considered in the construction of the self-concept just as they are in the development of the self-concept's components.

Finally, the timing of the evaluations will influence the weight they receive. The principles of primacy and recency will apply to the composite definitions just as they applied to the elements which went into the construction of the composites.

In general, then, the theory which has been used throughout is also applicable to the present case. A few of the postulates may not be relevant here, but no new principles are required.

Inners and Outers

Now let us consider some implications and extensions of what has been said. The position being taken here suggests strongly that for a given person the relative effect of the personal and social definitions will vary depending upon circumstances. The same person who yesterday was shaken to the quick by a negative remark, may today take a "public be damned" attitude. It would depend of course on who is saying what about what. This notwithstanding, it does seem likely that people can be ranged along a continuum in terms of their relative sensitivity to personal and social definitions (see Silverberg, 1952; White, 1963; Rosenberg, 1979; Boudreau, 1980; see also Franks and Marolla, 1976). No one will consistently favor personal evaluations over social ones or vice versa, but some people show one pattern more often than they do the other. Adopting Boudreau's (1980) terms, those who tend to weight personal evaluations more heavily will be referred to as *inners* and those most influenced by the perceived social definition will be called *outers*.

That there are inners was suggested as long ago as 1902 by Charles Horton Cooley (1964). It is not true, as some believe, that sociologists have seen the self as a simple reflection of others' views, although it is true that they have emphasized the reflected self. In Cooley's view it is the "best," the most ambitious and most productive people who are relatively immune to others' praise or deprecation. "They necessarily build up in their minds a self-image which no ordinary social environment can understand or corroborate, and which must be maintained by hardening themselves against immediate influences, enduring or repressing the pains of present depreciation, and cultivating in imagination the approval of some higher tribune" (Cooley, 1964: 258).

It would seem, to elaborate on Cooley's point, that the avant-garde in the arts, the saints, and such others, would be particularly likely to show the pattern he describes. The major source of their self-evaluations should be from comparisons of behavior with internalized standards and nonmembership reference groups. The reason for this is fairly clear and hinted at by Cooley. Such people would not be concerned with the utilitarian rewards that could be provided by "normal" people. They want their page in the history books or their reward in heaven and are "playing," therefore, to an audience not composed of their contemporaries. Furthermore, the evaluations received from others would not be viewed as providing self-knowledge. How can mere mortals judge the "Gods?" Mortals cannot understand the accomplishments of such people, and if they did they wouldn't have a scale against which to measure them. All the average person could use would be the standards which were current in the society, and those would be, almost by definition, inapplicable. The more modest of these people would admit that a few chosen others could make evaluations worth listening to, but in the extreme case even that would not be conceded. For the same reasons, there is little to be gained from using a real life comparison other. Against whom can you compare yourself if you are incomparable?

It may appear that this is simply a "cop-out," a way of avoiding evaluations, or a way of maintaining an enormous ego without doing anything to deserve it. And, certainly, this view makes it possible for some to congratulate themselves when no one else will do it. Their great willingness to accept the praise of the rest of us, if it should be forthcoming, is an indication of this. Some self-proclaimed geniuses seem to say, "you are unfit to judge" only when they are judged negatively.

Cooley (1964: 258-59) suggests that is exactly the danger:

> If a man succeeds in becoming indifferent to the opinions of his neighbors he runs into another danger, that of a distorted and extravagant self of the pride sort, since by the process of gaining independence and immunity from the stings of deprecation and misunderstanding, he has perhaps lost that wholesome deference to some social tribunal that a man cannot dispense with and remain quite sane. The image lacks verification and correction and becomes too much the reflection of an undisciplined self-feeling. It would seem that the megalomania or delusion of greatness which Lombroso, with more or less plausibility, ascribes to Victor Hugo and many other men of genius, is to be explained largely in this way.

But that is certainly only one possibility. Very often the rejection of others' views does not lead to a positive self-concept. Though they reject other people's standards, many of these people are constantly measuring themselves against their own standards, and typically these standards are not easy to meet. More than this, there are always the doubts. The life of a genius is a lonely and insecure one. How can one be sure of the validity of one's standards if by their very nature they cannot be externally validated? How can one be sure that he or she is meeting, or failing to meet, those standards when there is no one with whom one can check one's judgments? Again, the problem is eased by recognizing a small group as competent, but in the face of rejection by the rest of the society that may not be enough.

Perhaps I have spoken for these people too much already. Let us hear what they, and those who know them better than I, have to say.

An apt example of the extreme case is Friedrich Nietzsche, who shows in his *Ecce Homo* (1969) megalomania, a denial of others' ability to judge him, and supreme confidence in his own judgment. He is the ultimate inner.

> Seeing that before long I must confront humanity with the most difficult demand ever made of it, it seems indispensable to me to say *who I am*. Really, one should know it, for I have not left myself "without testimony." But the

disproportion between the greatness of my task and the *smallness* of my con-temporaries has found expression in the fact that one has neither heard nor even seen me. I live on my own credit. (217)

Hear me! For I am such and such a person. Above all, do not mistake me for someone else. (217)

With that [*Thus Spoke Zarathustra*] I have given mankind the greatest present that has ever been given to it so far. This book, with a voice bridging centuries, is not only the highest book there is, the book that is truly characterized by the air of the heights—the whole fact of man lies beneath it at a tremendous distance—it is also the *deepest*, born out of the innermost wealth of truth, an inexhaustible well to which no pail descends without coming up again filled with gold and goodness. (219)

When I now compare myself with the men who have so far been honored as the *first*, the difference is palpable. I do not even count these so-called "first" men among men in general: for me they are the refuse of humanity, monsters of sickness and vengeful instincts; they are inhuman, disastrous, at bottom in-curable, and revenge themselves on life. I want to be their opposite. (257)

Having understood six sentences from [*Zarathustra*], that is, to have really experienced them—would raise one to a higher level than modern man could attain. *Given this feeling of distance, how could I possibly wish to be read by those "moderns" whom I know*? (259, emphasis added)

Can this be serious? Is it simply self-satire, or the kind of outrageousness people use to attract attention to themselves? My philosopher colleagues assure me that Nietzsche was entirely serious—within a few weeks of the onset of madness—but nonetheless at this point sane and serious. Satirical, intentionally exaggerated? Most probably. Mocking? Yes, but probably more an attempt to mock his critics than himself. Perhaps it should be read as something other than a literal description of self-evaluation, but there seems to be little doubt that under the style is his perception of the truth.

But Nietzsche is, when you get down to it, a rather simple case who fits easily into Cooley's mold. Walt Whitman is much more complex. To specialists, and to this nonspecialist who has merely dipped into works by and about him, Whitman remains a fascinating and enigmatic character. In regard to his feelings about the sources of his self-concept, Whitman authorities give directly contradictory answers (Carlisle, 1973; R. W. B. Lewis, 1965). Whitman himself seems to be saying in the following passages that neither he nor others are capable of understanding him.

I charge you forever reject those who would expound me,
    for I cannot expound myself. (Whitman, 1949: 255)

I give you fair warning before you attempt me further,
I am not what you supposed, but far different. (Whitman, 1949: 162)

Even while you should think that you had unquestionably
    caught me, behold!
Already you see I have escaped from you. (Whitman, 1949: 162)

To that last statement I would say "Amen," for in his work we seem to have all the possible combinations. However, perhaps in this confusion lies the answer. Part of the problem is that Whitman seems to have been a different person at different times. He was "always going out and coming in." But it is more than that. Unlike Nietzsche, there seems to have been a basic ambivalence within him. He may illustrate the alternative I spoke of earlier—the rejection of other's standards associated with the lack of a dependable and acceptable substitute. In Whitman, the result was self-deprecation ("The best I had done seemed to me blank and suspicious"), great swings in self-feelings, the desire for solitude alternating with an enormous and never totally satisfied need for intimacy. "Whitman was a poet of comradeship, perhaps above all else, but his notebooks show that he was a lonely man who never found the ideal comrade in life" (Allen, 1961: 19). And when he did "connect" with people, it was as a giver rather than as a taker.

There is no doubt that Whitman rejected conventional standards. Carlisle (1973) puts it as follows:

> The poem implies that the "published standards" are clearly repressive and alienating. Not only do the prevailing sexual and social values fail to express the poet; they would destroy him besides, either by converting him into a conventional man or by forcing him to feel guilty and ashamed and to question and despise his own personal nature. *So to find the real "me". . . Whitman must follow the path seldom taken by others.* (122, emphasis added)

There are several passages which suggest that path would be solitude in which he could look within himself:

> . . .his emotions &c are complete in himself, irrespective (indifferent) of whether his love, friendship, &c are returned, or not. (quoted in Carlisle, 1973: 79)
>
> He grows, blooms, like some perfect tree or flower, in Nature, whether viewed by admiring eyes, or in some wild or wood entirely unknown. (Quoted in Carlisle, 1973: 79)
>
> I exist as I am, that is enough.
> If no other in the world be aware I sit content,
> And if each and all be aware I sit content. (Whitman, 1949: 110)

If this were all there were to it, there would be no problem. Whitman would simply be repeating the Nietzschean pattern without the egomania. At one point, that is what Carlisle suggests:

> He is 'complete in himself.' Evidently, he recognizes neither the need or essentiality of relationship, and he possesses such self-assurance that nothing seems to challenge or threaten him. The wholeness he presumably achieves results from exclusion and withdrawal rather than from a realistic encounter and participation in the complexities of life. (Carlisle, 1973: 79)

But this is not all there is to it:

Later Whitman seems to qualify and revise this initial image in two ways. (1) He begins to imaginatively identify himself with other individuals and thus recognize their concreteness and independence. The actuality of their situations. . .(2) He also speaks of a basic interaction between himself and the world—an interaction upon which his identity depends and through which he comes to know the essential inner reality of himself. (Carlisle, 1973: 80)

O the joy of my soul leaning pois'd on itself, receiving identity
    through materials and loving them, observing characters and absorbing them,
My soul vibrated back to me from them...(Whitman, 1949: 210)

When he whom I love travels with me or sits a long while
    holding me by the hand,
When the subtle air, the impalpable, the sense that
    words and reason hold not, surround us and pervade us,
Then I am charged with untold and untellable wisdom,
    I am silent, I require nothing further. (Whitman, 1949: 165)

It appears to this reader that Whitman's need for others did not involve a need to receive definitions from them. Rather, he seems to feel that he can *discover himself* only through his relations with others. Be that as it may, he does illustrate the case of the person who rejects other's standards and at the same time feels he cannot totally depend upon internalized ones.

Not too different, but more clear-cut, are the demons with which Lawrence of Arabia grappled on the occasion of his thirtieth birthday.

. . .On this birthday in Bair, to satisfy my sense of sincerity, I began to dissect my beliefs and motives. . .There was my craving to be liked—so strong and nervous that never could I open myself friendly to another. The terror of failure in an effort so important made me shrink from trying. . .There was craving to be famous: and a horror of being known to like being known. Contempt for my passion for distinction made me refuse every offered honour. I like the things underneath me [socially and intellectually] and took my pleasures and adventures downward. There seemed a certainty in degradation, a final safety. . . . Indeed, the truth was I did not like the "myself" I could see and hear. . . .It was part of my failure never to have a chief to use me. . . .Allenby came nearest my longings for a master, but I had to avoid him. . . .lest he show feet of clay with that friendly word which must shatter my allegiance. (Nutting, 1961: 149-50)

It is little wonder that Lawrence was on the brink of madness when those feelings were experienced. What could be more hopeless than to want, above all else, to have the good opinion of others and yet not be able to seek or to accept such opinions? Unlike some, he believed that the standards of others are in principle, valid; his great desire was to truly deserve other's favor. But he believed that only those beneath him could admire him and their esteem had little value for him. In fact, it was impossible for him to benefit from praise from anyone, because a profound self-hatred led him to interpret all favorable evaluations as evidence that their givers were incompetent to judge. What could be more destructive of self-esteem?

The reader should not be misled by the focus upon extraordinary people; they are not the only ones who emphasize personal evaluations over received evaluations. They may be the extreme cases, but they are not the only ones. It would seem, moreover, that the average person who depends mostly upon personal evaluations does so for reasons which are moderate versions of those used by the person who is "not of his time." Most people do not believe that no one is capable of judging them, but many think that they themselves are in most instances more competent than others to do so. Most people have some interest in and concern about the rewards that others can provide, but it seems that some people are less dependent on external rewards than are others. Such differences should produce general differences among people in the extent to which the perceived social definition and the personal definition are weighted in forming a self-evaluation.

There is possibly another factor operating. Some people who give little weight to other's evaluation do so almost as a matter of necessity. I would postulate that some people are socialized in a way that leads them to believe, "This above all, to thine own self be true." They are taught that they alone are responsible for their actions, and that they must follow the dictates of their consciences. If one is enjoined to follow where conscience leads, what criterion can be used to judge actions other than some internalized standard? A person who acts from conscience cannot turn around and allow someone else to tell whether he behaved wrongly or correctly. The measure of that has to be, "How true was I to my 'inner voices'?"

Traits of Inners. To take it one step further, let us consider what kinds of people would be most likely to have one or more of these general characteristics which lead to greater weight for the personal evaluation.

In regard to views concerning the relative competence of self and other, a rather obvious factor would be the actor's general self-esteem and the level of self-evaluation in the areas under consideration. If we believe we are good, or good at something, we tend to think we are good judges of performances. Thus people with high self-evaluations are more likely to weight the personal definition heavily. This is, of course, equivalent to saying that those who received positive evaluations from others in the past are the ones who are most likely to weight their personal evaluations heavily in the present. In childhood, about the only way to develop a positive self-view is to receive approval from others. Children feel they lack competence, so their favorable personal evaluations won't be given much weight. But once a positive self-evaluation is built up it becomes the means to freeing one from dependence upon other people for evaluation.

The actions of others can help us to become independent of them in other ways. For example, although they don't get weighted very heavily in the balance, actors, even in childhood, will develop personal evaluations, and in one way or another make those evaluations public knowledge. If others accept them as valid, and if other's evaluation of actor is based upon or consistent with actor's personal evaluation, then this will ultimately lead actor to assume his personal evaluation is a competent one, even when it disagrees with a current other's. In general, then, we have a paradox that it is often through the efforts of others rather than through our own efforts that we are set free from psychological dependence upon others.

People who do not depend upon others for utilitarian rewards are also likely to be inners. If people's wants are small or if they can provide themselves with all that they require, they can afford to ignore other's views. Ascetics are traditionally unconcerned about what people think, and so are those who have great control over resources. It is no coincidence that John D. Rockefeller was the one to announce the "public be damned" policy. Great wealth does not insure insensitivity to the opinions of others, but general observation suggests that it certainly contributes.

If a person has a strong conscience, his personal definition will be more important than other's opinion. And a strong conscience seems to develop when:

> 1. people are rewarded rather than punished for autonomous behavior, that is, when there is specific socialization for autonomy;
>
> 2. they have opportunities to practice autonomy (for example, when they are given opportunities to act on their own rather than being required to follow specific directions);
>
> 3. there is a social structure which has a "minimum of obvious constraints and. . .many and increasing options for conduct" (Riesman, 1968: 446);
>
> 4. they are held personally responsible for their actions and begin to accept that responsibility;
>
> 5. they are trained to be introspective, or, in a more contemporary idiom, when they are in touch with their feelings.

As Riesman (1968: 461) puts it, autonomy "depends. . .upon the success of his effort to recognize and respect his own feelings, his own potentialities, his own limitations."

In general, then, one's self-concept depends more upon one's own judgments than on the opinions of others when one is *taught* to be independent, and when the conditions are conducive to the expression of that approach to life. It seems again that we end up asserting that actions which seem to deny the influence of others upon actors are, in fact, made possible by the prior actions of others. That is unlikely to be a popular contention in a society such as this, but it seems inescapable.

One final point in concluding. I have assiduously attempted to keep value judgments out of the discussion, but in this case most readers have probably come to the conclusion that it is preferable to weight the personal definition more than the perceived social definition. That is typically viewed as being true to oneself, and the general assumption is that we would all be better off if we were truer to ourselves. I am sufficiently a product of my time and place that I would probably agree, but it does appear appropriate to suggest that the matter is by no means simple. Riesman's (1968: 448) comments on the relationship between autonomy and morality seem applicable to the present issue. He asks whether spontaneity and creativity, which most people would associate with autonomy, are morally valuable per se, and he answers, "Autonomy can have moral value in itself insofar as it expresses and reveals the extent of human possibility. This can be balanced and overbalanced by the evil consequences such expression can often have." He goes on to suggest that people are quite variable in their moral endowments. "I would not today contend that spontaneity or creativity are morally valuable per se; this depends on the context, on the total moral setting." It seems to boil down to the question, "Autonomy for whom, to do what?" Regarding self-evaluations, that would suggest that autonomy is good insofar as it leads to self-knowledge rather than to self-deception, and it can lead to either, just as adoption of the perceived social definition can.

Other Dimensions of the Self-Evaluation

The theory I have been presenting is designed to account for the content of the evaluative self—its direction and level. A few of the ideas contained in that theory, are, however, relevant for an understanding of two other dimensions of self-evaluations—their stability and the certainty with which they are held. Before concluding, let us briefly consider these matters.

Stability. The stability of the evaluative self refers to the extent to which it resists change in the face of new personal definitions and received evaluations. The basic assumption of this theory is that all relevant experiences have an influence upon the self-conception, but the extent to which a given evaluation will change the self-concept is variable.

The amount of change a new evaluation will cause is partly dependent on the "nature" of the existing self-concept. As with any average, stability is greater when the average is based upon a large "N." In this case, that means that self-concepts based upon many previous evaluations will be less influenced by new evaluations. A simple mathematical example will illustrate this. If the existing self is strongly positive, say +10, but that value is an average of two previous evaluations, a new evaluation with a value of −4 will reduce the self-evaluation to 5.3 (e.g., 5 + 15 − 4 = 16/3 = 5.3). If, however, a person with a self-evaluation of +10 has it because he or she has received 10 previous evaluations which average out to 10, a new evaluation of −4 would make less change (100 − 4 = 96/11 = 8.7). Only if the self-concept was the arithmetic *sum* of all evaluations would an evaluation of a particular weight have the same effect on all people. Thus, I would postulate that the self-concept becomes more stable as it is based upon an increasing number of evaluations.

To define stability of the self-evaluation in terms of the absolute amount of change brought about by a given new input seems to be the most relevant way to define the concept. However, a case could be made for defining the concept in terms of how heavy new evaluations must be before the valence changes. According to this definition, a stable self-concept is one which can absorb a heavy infusion of new evaluations without changing its direction.

The determinants of stability in this sense are the value of the average and the size of the "N." The closer the self-evaluation is to the zero point, the less it takes to change it from plus to minus or vice versa. But as before, an average of a particular value will be more difficult to change, the greater the number of cases on which it is based. A slightly positive evaluation can more easily be made negative, all other things being equal, than a strongly positive one. And if the number of previous evaluations is small, revising the direction of the self-evaluation is easier.

Of course, the characteristics of the existing self-concept are not the only determinants of the degree to which it will change. All that has gone before suggests that the amount of change will be influenced by the number, weight, and direction of new evaluations. The self-concept will be stable if the actor receives a small number of new evaluations, if he gives low weight to them, and if they are consistent with the existing concept. A consideration of the factors which influence the number and direction of the new evaluations is beyond the scope of this theory. The factors that influence the weight given to new evaluations have been discussed in depth and tested against data from studies which are, essentially, investigations of the conditions under which self-evaluations change most.

Certainty. Empirically there is probably a strong correlation between the certainty with which a self-evaluation is held and its stability. If we are relatively sure that we have a certain characteristic, we are less likely to change our minds than if we are uncertain about it. Conceptually, however, the dimensions are distinct. Certainty refers to an attitude of actor to the self-concept; stability is a property of the self-concept. We can learn about certainty only by asking actor about his or her feelings; stability is determined by measuring the self-concept at different times.

The distinction between the two dimensions can be seen if we return to the mathematical analogy. Stability, as we have seen, is a function of the number of evaluations received, and I would now note that certainty is also affected by that. Intuitively, it would seem clear that a person who has received two positive evaluations would be less certain that he or she is good than would be the case if there had been a hundred evaluations of the same value.

A person's certainty about the self-concept, is, however, also affected by the degree of variability in the evaluations that comprise it. With frequency of evaluation held constant, there should be more certainty if all the evaluations were the same than if the average was arrived at by combining some very favorable evaluations and some negative ones. One hundred +10 evaluations should produce greater certainty than fifty +20 evaluations and fifty zeroes. In both these cases, the self should show considerable stability and the level of self-evaluation would be the same, but the feeling of certainty should vary.

SUMMARY

In this chapter, the second ingredient that goes into the construction of a self-evaluation —the tentative personal definition—was considered. The basic postulate is that in addition to receiving evaluations from others, actor makes a personal definition of his behavior by comparing his actions with internalized standards *and* with the behavior of others.

The personal standards that actor uses in the evaluation of his behavior have, however, social roots. We measure ourselves against standards that we have been taught by others. The development of personal standards is basically similar to the other processes described. We form a general standard by developing a weighted average of the standards we have been exposed to. The weight assigned to a "suggested" standard depends upon profit we gain by accepting it. As before, knowledge, expressive, and utilitarian rewards are relevant.

Similar gains are realized when we use comparison others, but here the general theory must be extended to explain why a particular other was chosen. Nonetheless, the same principles apply. We choose a comparison other who will increase our rewards.

The personal evaluations of actor's several performances in a particular area are combined, by means of weighting and averaging, into a general personal evaluation for the area. The factors which determine the weight given to a specific personal evaluation are similar to those which affect the weight given to evaluations received from various others. Thus, for example, in developing a general personal evaluation in a particular area, a specific personal evaluation will be weighted heavily if it is favorable, recent, thought to be deserved, thought to be based on a typical performance, and so on.

The final step in the development of a self-evaluation involves the combining of the perceived social definition and the personal definition. This process is the same as those involved in the development of social and personal definitions. The self-evaluation is the weighted average of the perceived social definition and the personal evaluation. The factors which affect the relative weight given to these two elements are, again, essentially the same as those discussed in the previous chapter. The weighting process is structured to increase the likelihood that actor will receive knowledge, expressive rewards, and utilitarian rewards. Thus, if actor believes he is more competent to judge himself than others are, he will give heavier weight to the tentative personal definition. If the personal definition is favorable and the perceived social definition negative, the former will be given greater weight. If others control actor's rewards and they make these rewards contingent on his accepting their view, the perceived social definition will be heavily weighted, and so forth.

CHAPTER 6

THE DEVELOPMENT OF IDENTITIES, ROLES, AND PRESENTED SELVES

The next task is to account for the development of the remaining central variables—the identity set, role definitions, the presented self, and the roles associated with the presented self. The basic assumption is, of course, that these mental structures develop in a manner basically the same as the one which leads to the development of the evaluative self. Therefore, most of the groundwork has already been laid. The theory presented in the last two chapters should, with minor modifications, apply to these variables. In this chapter I will note the changes that are required and evaluate the theory's applicability by considering the available empirical data.

THE DEVELOPMENT OF IDENTITIES

At first glance it might seem that an explanation of how people develop identities need not be as complex as the theory which has been presented thus far. Identities are labels which people use to describe themselves to themselves. Isn't it simply that people think of themselves as having certain identities when they possess the social traits that go with those identities? Isn't the reason why I have a father identity in my identity set simply the fact that I *am* a father?

For some identities the answer is, in fact, not much more complicated than that. Whether or not a person has an identity is a function of whether he and others define him as possessing a particular social characteristic. For many traits there is a clear-cut criterion, and almost inevitably, the person who meets it will be defined both by himself and by others as possessing that trait. Thus, the person adopts the identity because of social and personal definitions that it is appropriate for him or her, and since all the definitions are consistent there is no need for the complex weighting process that constitutes the heart of the theory.

This does not say that the theory presented in previous chapters is incorrect regarding the development of such identities—it is simply that much of it is irrelevant because of the tendency toward consistency among the definitions. It will be recalled that when I spoke of self-evaluations I noted that the extended theory was needed only because evaluations do *not* tend to be consistent.

Many identities are not adopted so simply, however. People often find that there is disagreement about whether or not a particular identity is appropriate for them; they are often unsure about which identity should be used in a particular situation, and when they do know what the "right" definition is, they may not be able to think of themselves in those terms. Under such circumstances they often develop a feeling of unreality or alienation from self. Olesen and Whittaker (1968: 263–64) describe the plight of the nursing student as follows:

> Through these cycles the process of socialization moved forward. Confronting one identity predicament after another, bridging identity discrepancies raised by these predicaments, moving through cycles of depression and relative elation, meeting agents of legitimation, the student attempted to, and was forced to, integrate self with role. She was forced into viewing herself in new and different ways. Some of these ways were so discordant that she could only feel alienated. This sense of alienation. . .could signify that the student has somewhat lost sight of who she was and groped, often painfully, to weld her former self with the new self handed out to her.
>
> "Do you ever get the feeling that you can't quite recognize yourself?. . .It suddenly hits you that this is you in a way that it's never hit you before. You sort of drift off for a moment. . .I suddenly realize that this is me, Elfriede, and I almost cannot recognize myself."
>
> Other students talked about a sense of "playacting" and forcing themselves to perform the actions and mouth the words nurses were known to use, of going onto the wards as if they were going onto a stage.

Becoming an Adult

Another identity which is not simply "taken on" is that of the adult. When a person achieves a certain chronological age, it does not follow automatically that the actor and all others will immediately begin to define him or her as an adult. The criterion for adulthood is not universally agreed upon. As many of the readers of this book may know only too well, reaching the legal age of majority does not lead everyone to define you as an adult. In fact, this is an identity in which personal definitions and social definitions are likely to be in conflict, particularly when the others are parents.

In such cases, the theory presented previously becomes relevant and applicable. When there is disagreement about whether the actor belongs in a particular category, the determination of whether or not the actor possesses the identity will be the balance between the definitions. The actor will determine whether the balance of other peoples' opinions suggest actor is or is not an adult, and in determining that balance the various definitions will be differentially weighted according to their source and nature. If the other is a significant other, his or her definition will count more. If the identity is one which actor desires to hold, definitions which suggest it is appropriate will be weighted more heavily, and so on.

A perceived social definition will emerge from this process, and the actor will also develop a personal definition. As with self-evaluations, the actor will compare his behavior and characteristics with internal standards about what qualifies a person to be an adult, and he will compare himself with those people he believes fall into the category. The social definition and the personal definition will then be combined, with appropriate weights assigned, and the actor will or will not embrace the identity depending upon the outcome. The only difference between this process and the development of self-evaluations is that evaluations can be conceived of in numerical terms and identities tend to be an either/or matter. Because of this, we speak of the balance of opinion rather than using the analogy of calculating an average. If the predominant opinion suggests the identity is appropriate, we will adopt it.

An excellent example of how all this works is provided by Ladner (1971) in her discussion of the coming of age of lower-class black girls. The achievement of womanhood is highly desired among these girls, but they realize that "wishing won't make it so." Certain behaviors are required before others—or the girl herself—are willing to bestow the status of "woman" on her. Both personal and social definitions are dependent upon giving up "girlish" ways. In this group, that involves (1) acting in a decorous manner, (2) developing realistic expectations for the future, which often means giving up the hope for marked social mobility and a willingness to settle for less than was dreamed of when younger, (3) independence from parental control, and (4) relating to men in a mature way. In most cases, this last requirement meant engaging in sexual behavior, but sexual experience, although necessary, was not sufficient to attain womanhood. Immature girls might be sexually experienced; but a young *woman* would handle a sexual relationship differently. For one thing, she imposed obligations upon her boyfriend. He would, for example, have to give up other women, and he had to be willing to marry her if she became pregnant and she wanted marriage. Other aspects of her relationships with men were also important. A mature lower-class black woman does not have her head in the clouds; she has a realistic view of men. She realizes that in this society, a black man's chance of being highly successful is limited, and she understands that this is something largely beyond his control. She knows that men can be exploitative, and can cause her much grief, and she knows how to protect and "handle" herself.

The female who fits this description will be defined by her elders, her girl friends, and most important, by her male friends, as a *woman*—for these are the criteria they use. In addition, her tentative personal definition will also put her in this status because these represent her internalized standards for womanhood. These behaviors will also tell her she is a woman when she compares herself with females who are unequivocally women.

This is not to say that the definitions she receives will consistently define her in this way. Her teachers and other representatives of the larger society will undoubtedly use different criteria—giving, for example, a much greater emphasis to actual age. This notwithstanding, the girl herself is almost certainly going to adopt the adult identity if she exhibits the aforementioned behaviors. The definitions she receives from the larger society are unlikely to be weighted very heavily in forming her perceived social definition. Certainly, the representatives of the society have power over her, but the rewards and punishments with which she is most concerned are at the disposal of her peers—particularly if she is by this time "turned off" by school. And, perhaps most important, she is likely to believe that she, her friends, and the adults of her community are the ones who have the competence to make the judgments in this area.

Other Identities

Throughout the life cycle people find that its stages are not clearly marked. When does middle age begin? When I was a child, ads for a laxative called Serutan were ubiquitous, and they proclaimed that it was for "all those over 35." Those ads served to define the onset of middle-age for me and for many of my generation. (A soap opera heroine by the name of Helen Trent served a similar function in defining the end of middle age. She proved that it was possible to find romance in life at 40 and *even* beyond!) By the time I reached those ages, other socialization had been added, but the lessons I had learned after childhood failed to save me from "identity-confusion."

The problems associated with the "elderly" identity have been systematically studied, and the data show the applicability of the theory. Actual age is, of course, not totally irrelevant. In a sample of people over 60, Blau (1956) found that as age increased the proportion who defined themselves as old also increased. The correlation was, however, not very strong. Among people over 70, 60 percent defined themselves as old, and about 20 percent of those under 65 did.

The definitions of others and the occurrence of events which meet internalized standards seem to be quite important. Blau's data can be read as suggesting that people begin to define themselves as old when other people define them in that way, and also when certain other events occur—retirement, widowhood, and isolation from friends. The strongest effect is associated with others viewing actor as old, but for technical reasons it is not certain that this is the major factor[1] (see also Phillips, 1957).

The professional identity is another which does not have a simple clear-cut criterion of applicability. When does one become a physician? When one enters the

---

[1] The difficulty is that a multivariate analysis is not provided. The correlation between each variable and the dependent variable is given, but we are not told what the correlation is for each with the others held constant. The most highly correlated variable when other variables are not controlled, need not be the one which is most strongly correlated, with all other things being equal.

clinical years of medical school? When the MD degree is awarded? When one is finished with the internship? With the residency? When one enters practice? When people start calling you doctor? When does one become a professional musician? When the first paid performance is given? When one finishes the course at the conservatory? When one's studies are completed? Is a graduate student with full responsibility for a course a student, a teacher, or a student-teacher?

Studies which have addressed these questions have been done on medical students (Huntington, 1957; Becker et al., 1961; Preiss, 1968) and on students in music conservatories (Kadushin, 1969). With the exception of the Becker et al. study, they all show that the professional identity—physician or musician rather than medical or music student—is well-established in a number of the subjects before they have finished their course of study. They also agree that the closer the students come to graduation, the more likely they are to think of themselves in professional terms.

It is clear, however, that at the same level of advancement some students think of themselves in professional terms and others retain their student identities. By looking at the development of professional identification, we can further "test" the applicability of interactionist theory to the case of identity learning.

The importance of role playing for the development of an identity comes through clearly. Normally, we explain role behavior in terms of identities; actors are behaving as they do because they are defining themselves in a particular way and they believe that is proper behavior for persons so defined (see Chapter 7). However, it also works in the opposite direction. When we find ourselves playing a particular role, we begin to define ourselves in terms of the identity which goes with the role. Thus Preiss (1968) finds that in the third and fourth years of medical school, when the students have extensive contact with patients, the proportion who see themselves as doctors shows a marked increase—particularly if they believe they have been doing well. Similarly, in the two music conservatories studied by Kadushin (1969), the proportion who thought of themselves as being more like professionals than students increased as the number of professional performances increased. The proportion of "professionals" also tended to be greater among those who had been successful in music competitions. Membership in the musicians' union and "hanging around" with professional musicians also contributes to the professional identity, but having informal contact with their teachers and fellow students does not.

These data take on meaning when they are considered in the light of the theory. The basic idea is that people will think of themselves as professionals when others react to (define) them in such terms and when their behavior squares with the criteria they themselves hold regarding the circumstances which warrant the use of the label. Each of the factors mentioned should contribute to one or both of these.

It would seem that when people engage in the activities associated with the professional role, others begin to define them as professionals and such performances also meet the requirements of actor's internalized standards. Thus, playing the professional role influences both the perceived social definition and the personal definition.

The importance of the perceived social definition may be detected in Kadushin's (1969) finding that association with one's teachers outside the classroom does not contribute to the early development of the professional identity. Teachers, even when they are friendly, typically view their students as students and are perhaps the last people to convey to them that they are full-fledged colleagues. This is one of the problems faced by people who teach in the institutions from which they received their degrees. Even though they have all the credentials and are "regular" members of the department, their former teachers often do not validate their identities. In other cases, after twenty years' experience, to meet one's former professor at a convention can make one feel like a student again.

Huntington (1957) shows the importance of the perceived social definition in another way. She explicitly recognizes that people's ability to identify themselves in a particular way will vary depending upon the circumstances. Although she suggests, as do the other studies, that it is meaningful to ask, "Do you think of yourself primarily as doctor or student?" she also asked which identity predominated in various relationships. The subjects were first-year med students, but the school in which they were enrolled was unusual in that there was contact with patients from the very beginning. Almost none of the students thought of themselves as physicians when they interacted with classmates and faculty, and very few felt that way in their encounters with nurses. About 30 percent, however, thought of themselves as doctors when they were dealing with patients. It seems clear enough that only a patient would think of a first-year medical student as a doctor, but Huntington shows this directly; 75 percent of the students said that they thought that patients were defining them as doctors, but almost none believed this to be true of other students, faculty, or nurses. And, if there is any doubt, almost all the students who identified themselves in professional terms thought that patients also identified them as such.

This same study also shows that it is not simply a matter of taking on an other's definition. Most of those who said patients identified them as physicians still thought of themselves as students. Obviously, they were rejecting this social definition. Other people's definition of them or their personal definitions were more influential than the definition by their patients.

Certainly these studies provide a very weak test of the applicability of interactionist theory to the learning of identities; they are relevant only to the barest outlines of the theory. Nonetheless, as far as they go, they are consistent with expectations.

THE PROMINENCE HIERARCHY

As I noted earlier, identities are arranged along a hierarchy of prominence (McCall and Simmons, 1978; Stryker, 1968); some are obviously more important to actor than others. To use an "operational" definition—all other things being equal, an identity which is high on the prominence hierarchy will be chosen in preference to one which is lower when the actor is in a situation which permits use of either one. And, if actor has a choice of two encounters equivalent in everything but the identity that each calls forth, the actor will choose the encounter associated with the identity which is higher on the hierarchy. To understand actor's behavior, we need to know more than simply whether or not a particular identity is in his or her repertoire. It is often equally important to know its position on the hierarchy. We will see why this is so in a later chapter, but for now the question is what determines the position that an identity occupies on the actor's hierarchy of prominence?

To handle this issue, I must make a number of changes in the theory which was presented in the earlier chapters. The same basic ideas hold, but they must be applied somewhat differently if they are to be useful in this case.[2]

We may, however, start out with a few very familiar ideas. The first postulate would be: All other things being equal, the position of an identity on the hierarchy is a function of the frequency with which actor has been defined in terms of the identity. Identities which we and/or others use frequently in defining ourselves will tend to be more prominent. And, of course, the definitions of some others will be given greater weight in determining our perceptions of how frequently the identity has been used.

Relative frequency of use is, however, only one factor involved and very likely not the most important. The extent to which rewards have been associated with the various identities in the repertoire will also have a major influence upon the place they occupy.

With this postulate, my analysis of the issue is joined to McCall and Simmons' (1978) and Stryker's (1968) discussions of the specific factors which affect the ordering of identities on the hierarchy. McCall and Simmons (1978: 75) state, to start: "Those identities that, from our egocentric perspectives, we more nearly manage to live up to are, in their rarity, very dear to our hearts." I would agree, and suggest that such identities will be high on the hierarchy. This occurs because fulfilling the role demands we believe to be associated with a given identity is rewarding. It helps us to satisfy our need for a positive self-image. The internalized criteria used to develop personal evaluations are often simply role definitions. If we can meet the requirements of the role attached to an identity that identity will, in our minds, be associated with reward.

McCall and Simmons also suggest that the extent to which we have been positively evaluated by others when a given identity was being used will influence its location on the hierarchy. The reason for this is obvious; such identities have also been rewarding because they also have aided us in achieving a positive self-view.

Stryker's (1969: 561) major hypothesis is that "the more extensive and/or intensive the network of relationships into which one enters by virtue of a given identity, the higher will be that identity in the. . .hierarchy," and this too is easily handled within the present framework. In fact, Stryker himself uses such an explanation. Identities which involve an actor in a network of relationships are likely to be perceived "as instrumental to 'wants' of the person" (562).

In the language of this theory, some identities are highly valued because they

---

[2] The reader will recall that this was also the case when I moved from a consideration of the content of self-evaluations to a discussion of the structure of the evaluative self. In general, the theory is more directly applicable to the learning of content than to the development of structures.

bring us into relationships which provide us with expressive rewards. Included here would be the pleasure most people get from attachments to others and the sheer enjoyment we get from some activities—for example, the joys of meeting challenges, having interesting conversations, getting physical exercise, obtaining sexual release, and so on. In addition, identities may involve us in relationships which provide utilitarian rewards—such as money, power, prestige—and such identities will rank high.

Of course, involvement in a network of relationships does not always prove rewarding. Thus, Stryker adds that an identity which is a passport to a network of relationships is most likely to rank high on the hierarchy when the other people in the network share actor's role definitions and when the identities which brought the others into the relationship are also high on their own hierarchies. It is under such circumstances that rewards are most likely to be forthcoming.

I would note, in addition, that the roles associated with different identities vary in their difficulty, and the same role will be more difficult for some than for others. Since difficulty in performing a role is a cost, it would follow that the better actor knows the role associated with an identity and the easier it is for him or her to perform it, the higher it will be on the hierarchy.

Thus several of the specific factors which are believed to be associated with position on the hierarchy of prominence are easily explained in terms of past reward. But there is a problem. McCall and Simmons also postulate that identities will rank high if they were difficult to achieve. If one has to put in a lot of time, energy, and resources before the identity can be incorporated into the repertoire, it is likely to be a prominent one. This seems intuitively correct, but it is not so easily explained in terms of a past reward framework. In fact, it would appear to oppose much of what has been said because such identities were, in the past, associated with high costs.

The solution is, I believe, that in regard to the previous matters there was an implicit and justified assumption that past experiences would be repeated in the future. If an identity was associated with enjoyment in the past, it is expected that enjoyment will also be experienced when the identity was used again. In regard to a large investment, actor does not assume that when he or she again utilizes that identity, a similar investment will be required. In fact, the assumption is just the opposite. If a large investment has been made to obtain the identity, once it is in the repertoire, the payoff on the identity will start coming in. And this too is a reasonably justified assumption.

Thus I would postulate that difficult to achieve identities will be prominent *if* actor believes that once such identities are achieved, the costs are reduced and large rewards are likely to follow as repayment for the original investment. If the actor believes that the costs will continue as in the past, the identity will not be high, all other things being equal.

To summarize these points, I would postulate that an identity will be high on the hierarchy of prominence, all other things being equal, if it has been previously associated with reward and if it is expected that this will continue, or if large future profits are expected from playing the role associated with it.

In general, the theory does not seem to require basic change. All that is necessary are alterations in the application of the basic ideas due to the focus on structure rather than content.

ROLE LEARNING

A role, it will be recalled, is the set of behaviors an actor considers appropriate when he or she is utilizing a particular identity and interacting with an other who is using, or should be using, a specified identity. Roles are the game plans we bring to our encounters. This suggests that frequently our actual behavior is not a reflection of the role definitions with which we start. The circumstances of the ongoing interaction may suggest that we act out of role and/or we may alter our view regarding proper role behavior during an interaction episode. These matters will be considered in the discussion of interaction. They do not deny, however, that we bring to interaction conceptualizations of proper behavior which have some stability and generality. At this point, the problem is to account for the development of the generalized role definitions.

The most general answer is that these definitions are largely a reflection of the definitions received from others—the basic interactionist view. Illustrations of the validity of this assertion abound in the sociological literature. For example, Teevan (1972) found a strong correlation between college students' premarital sexual behavior and their perception of the extent of their friends' sexual experiences. He also found that students who were strongly tied to their parents had less sexual experience, which suggests that such students were accepting the usually more conservative norms that parents hold. Similarly, students' occupational and educational plans and aspirations have often been shown to be importantly influenced by the attitudes of their parents and friends (Bordua, 1960; Ellis and Lane, 1963; Kahl, 1953; Simpson, 1962; Alexander and Campbell, 1964; Otto, 1977; 1975; Astin, 1965).

There have been studies of the role definitions of college undergraduates, and they also suggest the social sources of roles. The following is a catalog of a few of the more interesting findings. (For a more complete summary, see Feldman and Newcomb, 1969.)

1. When freshmen enter college, they consider grades more important than they do after they have been there for a few months, and this attitude increases their similarity to upperclassmen. That the change is due to accepting the role definitions of the older students is indicated by the fact that the drop in importance is greater for those freshmen who know many nonfreshmen and who care a great deal about being liked. If the nonfreshmen known deemphasize grades more than the typical upperclassman, this also increases the likelihood that the freshman will come to give less stress to grades (Wallace, 1964; 1966).

2. The likelihood that high ability students will want to—and do—go on to postgraduate education is affected by the extent to which they perceive that there are pressures among their peers favoring aestheticism, reflectiveness, and intellectualism (Thistlethwaite, 1965; Thistlethwaite and Wheeler, 1966).

3. Women who entered college holding attitudes which were deviant, from the perspective of the general student body, showed less change in the direction of the majority if they developed friendship groups with others who held similar views (Newcomb et al., 1967).

Given this, the major questions to be answered are: "How do actors learn what others' role definitions are?" and "How do actors handle the often contradictory definitions they receive?"

In regard to the first question, I would note, to begin, that role definitions are often conveyed to actor through direct intentional teaching by other. "Listen to me carefully, because after I show you how, you will have to do it on your own." In addition to this, others teach actors role definitions without consciously intending to do so. The phrase commonly used is that others serve as "role models" for actor.

Role Modeling

When actor interacts with other he or she has to take other's role, which is the same as saying that actor rehearses mentally the behaviors which other is likely to use. These imaginings are then checked against other's actual behavior and "revised" if they prove to be incorrect. Role taking is an important means by which we learn from our models. Because actor is actively engaged in the process, he or she is more likely to retain the information gathered about how this other plays a particular role. If other's current identity is also a part of actor's repertoire of identities, actor's interaction with other will help to teach actor how to play one of his or her roles.

In addition, actors have opportunities to observe others play their roles when they are not in interaction with each other. This too will be a source of information for actor concerning the "appropriate" way to play roles. Observational learning should, however, be less effective than the other forms because actor is not as likely to be involved in what is going on. Social learning theory (Bandura, 1969a; 1969b) tells us that the extent of actor's attention is an important factor in the acquisition of all kinds of knowledge.

This notwithstanding, the amount of attention required for some role learning to occur seems quite low. Lefkowitz et al. (1955) and Freed et al. (1955) show that a simple rule, such as waiting for the "walk" sign before crossing a street, is more likely to be violated if a model is seen to violate it first. Socially useful behaviors can also be increased by the observation of models. Bryan and Test (1967) devised a situation in which passing cars would come upon a young woman standing next to a car with a flat tire. For half the time, it was arranged that some time before they got to the woman, the cars had to pass another woman whose car also had a flat tire. At the first car it was clear that a man had stopped to help the female driver. For the rest of the time there was no first car.

Only 93 out of 4,000 cars stopped to help the woman in distress, but 58 of these stopped after seeing the model of helpful behavior and only 35 stopped when it was not present. In a similar fashion, they found that a model putting a coin in a

Salvation Army kettle led to an increased likelihood that someone else would do the same. It seems clear that even in the rush of everyday events, people's attention to their surroundings is sufficient for them to pick up suggested behaviors which they then make their own. (See Blake (1958) for several additional studies along these lines.)

If we now take it as given that actor tends to adopt role definitions held by other people, we can consider the next question, which is how he or she develops a coherent image of other's role definitions in the face of the fact that the information is likely to be quite contradictory. If I suggest that actor develops a perceived social definition of the role, the basic outlines of the answer should become clear, because it is the same process used in developing a perceived social definition of the self in evaluative terms.

The perceived social definition of a role represents an amalgam of the various views held by the others that actor has known, and the contribution of various definitions to this amalgam will vary. Bandura et al. (1963a) found such a pattern when actors had an opportunity to observe several potential models who acted in somewhat different ways. In such a situation "observers may select one or more of the models as the primary source of behavior, but they rarely restrict their imitation to a single source, nor do they adopt all of the characteristics of the preferred model. Rather, observers generally exhibit relatively novel responses representing amalgams of elements from different models" (Bandura, 1971: 11).

Beyond this, the question becomes what determines the contribution made to this perceived social definition by the various definitions received, and the answer is quite similar to that for received evaluations. The contribution of a particular viewpoint to the amalgam is a function of characteristics of the other who presented it, the nature of the view itself, the conditions under which it was presented, and so on. Just as with self-evaluations, the acceptance or rejection of another's viewpoint may lead to rewards or costs, and actor will attempt to maximize rewards when formulating role conceptions. The potential rewards are of the same types that were relevant when the focus was on self-evaluations, that is, the satisfaction of utilitarian, expressive, and knowledge needs.

Choosing a Role Model. The generality of interactionist theory becomes even clearer when we face some of the specific issues in this area. For example, the answer to the questions "Who will be chosen as a role model?" and "Whose direct teaching will be most effective?" is to be found in the earlier discussions of how comparison others and significant others are chosen. I will illustrate the matter by considering studies which relate to a number of key hypotheses. I will begin with a consideration of the effect of other's power upon role learning.

If we extend the previous material to the case of choice of a role model, we come up with the hypothesis that people will be more likely to choose a person as a model when that person has control over their fate than when he does not. More specifically, people who are perceived as controlling rewards and punishments are more likely to be imitated by actor. In regard to the first part of the hypothesis, there is little question. Several studies show that people who are seen as controlling rewards are more likely to be used as models—at least when actor is a child. (See Mussen and Distler, 1959; Hetherington and Frankie, 1967; Bandura, 1969a; 1969b; 1971; Mussen, 1969; Gewirtz, 1969; Mussen and Rutherford, 1963.)

We can be less certain that punishment and/or the tendency to punish has a similar effect upon modeling behavior. Mussen and Distler (1959) provide data which show, at least indirectly, that a punishing father is more likely to be modeled than one who is not seen as a potential source of punishment, and Hetherington and Frankie (1967) got similar findings. Mussen and Rutherford (1963), however, get mixed results.

In the studies just considered, there is a single basic methodology. There is one potential model and they attempt to determine if his characteristics influence the likelihood of his being imitated. The general considerations upon which this discussion is based would also suggest that if actor has the *choice* of two models, he or she should choose the more powerful one, and actor's tendency to model in the future should be influenced by whether he or she was rewarded or punished for previous modeling behavior. Unfortunately, in view of the ambiguity of the previous findings, these hypotheses have not been treated in regard to punishment, but there are a number of interesting studies that relate to the importance of reward.

Bandura et al. (1963a) show in an experimental study involving young children, that a rewarding model is more likely to be chosen than one who does not reward. The procedure was as follows: A child observed an adult give another adult some toys, candy, etc., or the child received such items from one adult while another adult looked on. Then, each adult performed a task and the child had an opportunity to imitate the particular way that each carried it out. As our theory would predict, the adult who had been the dispenser of the "goodies" was imitated much more frequently. When they have a choice, children model themselves after people who control rewards.

Support for this hypothesis is also indicated by a study of adolescent boys conducted by Payne and Mussen (1956). If the father was perceived as being more rewarding than the mother, the likelihood was increased that the boy would show a high degree of identification with the father. A similar finding is reported in the Hetherington and Frankie (1967) study in which children had an opportunity to imitate their parents in a laboratory situation. If the father was warmer than the mother, he was imitated more often; if the mother was warmer she was the one more frequently imitated.

Regarding the second hypothesis, Shein's (1954) study directly shows that reward for the act of imitation increases its frequency among adults. But he also sees signs that they experience inhibitions to imitation under some circumstances—it's cheating; you can't beat someone if you copy them; you can't get the satisfaction of solving something by yourself if you imitate; and so on.

Other studies show, however, that these barriers to imitation can be removed when the probability of reward for imitating is high and the social conditions are such that no sanctions seem likely if the subject does imitate (Kanareff and Lanzetta,

1958; 1960). In our terms, that would mean that imitation is facilitated if it is likely to bring forth reward but no punishment. Another study by these authors (Lanzetta and Kanareff, 1959) shows that if the potential reward is increased, that is, if a small monetary prize is offered, imitation will occur even when the instructions suggest that it is inappropriate.

Considerations of model power and differential reward for imitation also help to explain changes in role models or, as they are often called, normative reference groups. For example, although parents remain important to their adolescent and young adult offspring, the influence of the older generation does decline as the age of the children increases. This seems associated with increased attachment to the peer group which lessens the value of the rewards and punishments that the parents can control. An excellent illustration of this is to be found in a classic study by Theodore Newcomb (1958) of attitude change of students at Bennington College during the 1930s. He discovered that "the general trend of attitude change for the total group is from freshman (political) conservatism to senior nonconservatism" (266), and he explains this as a result of a shift in reference groups. The freshmen tended to reflect the values of their well-to-do and conservative parents, but as they went through the college years they began to take on the attitudes of the more advanced students and the extremely liberal faculty. The reason for this shift in reference groups seems clear. In a community such as Bennington was during the 1930s, prestige from peers required liberal attitudes; as the students aged, the rewards of their peers became more important than those of the parents. This led to the political conversion of many of the students. The validity of this interpretation is indicated by intensive study of some students who managed to reach their senior year with their conservatism intact. Almost all of them were characterized by strong ties of dependency to their parents, and in some instances this combined with few friendships on campus.

Parallels to all this were seen in earlier discussions, but a full consideration of role modeling requires some additions to the theory. In most cases, however, all we have to do is to apply an old principle in a new way; new principles need not be added.

An important change of this type involves the recognition that in role modeling there is often *vicarious reinforcement*, that is, behavior tendencies are strengthened when actor sees others being rewarded for that behavior but receives no reward himself. Vicarious reinforcement does not involve the operation of a new principle. I have already discussed a number of conditions which will lead actors to believe that they will be rewarded and I suggested that role modeling is facilitated by the assumption of reward. All that has to be added here is the assertion that actors are likely to believe that they will be rewarded for modeling other if they see that the behavior of other has been rewarded. Actors do not have to receive direct reward from the model or from third parties. They seem to assume "if it works for him it will work for me."

That actors are more likely to model behaviors of other when other is rewarded seems beyond doubt; this has been demonstrated many times (Bandura, 1965; Bandura et al., 1963b; 1963c; Walters et al., 1965). One of the details, however, is worth mentioning. The effects of vicarious reinforcement are largely upon performances rather than acquisition. If the model is not rewarded, the subjects are less likely to imitate; but this doesn't mean they haven't learned the behaviors. Bandura (1965) showed that when children who had observed a nonrewarded model were given an incentive to do so they could reproduce the model's behavior as well as the children who had seen the model rewarded. This seems to be consistent with the theory's postulate that all experiences have an effect upon actors, and that the effect of reward is to increase the weight given to a received definition when actor develops a personal definition of appropriate behavior.

It should also be noted that reward increases the tendency to imitate; imitation does not *require* reward. Several of the studies mentioned earlier show this, as do several investigations of children's modeling of aggressive behavior. There is evidence that mere exposure to aggressive models increases the likelihood of aggressive behavior. When there are no consequences attached to the model's aggressiveness, there is considerable imitation, and even when the model is punished there is still a small increase in imitative aggression and some preference for the aggressor. These effects are seen when the models are presented on film and even when the aggressor is a cartoon character (Bandura et al., 1963b; 1963c). The relevance of these and the previous findings for the debate over violence in television seems quite clear (see also Goranson, 1970).

Another nonbasic change is required in the postulate which says that heavy weight will be given to received opinions which further actor's desire for a positive view of self. That principle also holds for role definitions, but unlike the case with received *evaluations* from others, this does not simply mean that actor will give greater weight to favorable role definitions, because, actually, it does not make much sense to speak of favorable role definitions. We can say, however, that actor will give greater weight to a definition held by an other when actor feels competent to live by that definition. Actors evaluate themselves favorably when they live up to the role definitions they hold, so a received definition which is perceived as achievable will be weighted more heavily because by doing so actor increases the likelihood of having a favorable self-evaluation.

In addition, roles involve activities, and these activities are defined by actor as more or less enjoyable, and as more or less likely to lead to outcomes which actor desires. A role definition which prescribes activities which actor defines as enjoyable or as likely to result in a desired end are going to be weighted heavily because they are seen as the means to expressive and utilitarian rewards.

When self-evaluations and identities are involved, actor gains self-knowledge when he or she accepts the definitions of others, but when it comes to roles a somewhat different kind of knowledge is obtainable. Most people assume that there is a right and a wrong way to play many roles and they would, therefore, give greater weight to a definition received from some "who should know," because accepting such a definition gives the feeling that now "I know, too." Thus, just as with self-evaluation, people who are viewed as competent, interested, or truthful, will have their role definitions weighted more heavily. And, as was the case with comparison others, role models should be chosen from among those who are similar, and/or somewhat "better" than actor. Such persons illustrate how someone like actor should play a role or they show the more desirable ways of enacting it.

The effect of similarity is to be found in several of the studies of imitation by children, for when there is more than one possible role model, the tendency is to choose the model of the same sex (Hetherington and Frankie, 1967; Bandura et al., 1961; 1963c). Similarly, Burnstein et al. (1961) show that describing an adult as having a similar background to a group of children leads them to accept the adult's preferences about the best way to play as exotic a role as deep-sea diver. People do seem to believe that the ways of people like them are the ways that they, themselves, should act.

The effects of presumed competence upon choice of role models is shown by studies which suggest that actors choose different role models depending upon the issue involved. Thus Brittain (1963) found that adolescent girls tend to follow parental guidelines regarding dilemmas that involve such issues as honesty or job choice, but peers were chosen as models when the issue involved dress. Other studies showed that parents have a greater influence than peers on occupation and vocational plans and other "serious" matters, while peers exert their greatest influence on matters of style and "manners" (Remmers and Radler, 1957; Simpson, 1962).

Some of the data on the relative influence of teachers and peers on the attitudes of college students also bear on this issue. Teachers are used as models in some areas; peers are more important in others, and the differences make sense in terms of assumed differences in competence. By their own testimony, students are more affected by the faculty in their intellectual development and occupational and career decisions. But when it comes to their social life and interpersonal and personality development, other students are seen as more influential (Feldman and Newcomb, 1969).

Experimental data also show the effects of competence. If the subjects of a study are led to believe that a potential model has been successful in performing the task facing them, his or her behavior is more likely to be imitated (Mausner, 1954; Rosenbaum and Tucker, 1962). And the study by Lefkowitz et al. (1955), showed a clear tendency for people to imitate high status models more readily than they do persons of apparent lower status. The experimenters varied the clothing of a male confederate who crossed a street against the "wait" signal and counted the number of other pedestrians who followed his lead. Though most did not follow him, the proportion who did was greater when he was well-dressed than when his clothing made him appear to be a low-status person. This effect may not be exactly a "competence" effect, but it comes close. We can't tell exactly what was in the pedestrians' minds, but it seems plausible that many of them said to themselves, "If a person who is a person of some worth is breaking a rule, it is probably OK to do it."

Practice Effects

Because roles involve activities, the effects of practice become more important than they were previously. In many cases, full role knowledge is not acquired until the actor has an opportunity to actually "try out" newly acquired information. There are, of course, technical skills involved in the playing of many roles, but they are not the focus of interest here. My concern is with the social aspects of role performance— the ability to respond in a particular way, knowledge of which social actions will lead to the attainment of goals, the internalization of the proper attitudes, and so on. The acquisition *and* retention of these things is facilitated by practice, no less than the acquisition of, for example, typing skill. In many instances, in fact, these social aspects of roles cannot truly become a part of actor's repertoire without practice. The kind of instruction that has been considered may be a prerequisite, but it may not be sufficient. In a sense one does not really know a role until one can play it almost automatically, and that is not likely to occur from "book learning" alone.

There are no systematic data that show directly that practice is necessary, but general observation would indicate that as people gain experience in a role, their performance of it becomes "smoother," and they find it easier to live up to its demands. Compare, for example, the average person on his or her first date with the person who has a long dating history. There are, in addition, studies which show that engaging in certain activities leads people to take on the attitudes associated with those activities. This even occurs when the actor is just pretending; playing a role that he or she has been instructed to play, as in psycho- and sociodramas. Such techniques are used to inculcate roles in leadership training programs, in marriage counseling, and in some forms of psychotherapy. The evidence is weak, but there are indications that the techniques are effective (Mann, 1956; Lippitt, 1943; Zander and Lippitt, 1944; Shoobs, 1944).

Moreover, the effect of this kind of role playing upon attitudes has often been demonstrated in laboratory experiments (Elms, 1969; Janis, 1968; Mann and Mann, 1959). The most striking of these investigations is the one conducted by Mann and Janis (1968). They found that women who smoked heavily "cut down" rather considerably after they played the role of a patient who is being told that she has lung cancer. Moreover, the effect was long lasting; 18 months after the experiment, they were still smoking less than the control group which listened to a recording of a role-playing session but did not play the role.

These effects are, of course, to be seen outside of the laboratory. Without actually presenting systematic data, Waller and Hill (1951) speak persuasively of the changes that occur in the value systems of people when they take on the roles of a married person. Although there is a long period of anticipatory socialization for married life during which people have many opportunities to learn the proper roles, much of the key learning and practice does not occur until the position is actually attained. It is only after marriage that the young spouse gets "on the job training" and it is only then that he or she has the opportunity to learn and to use the basic concerns, world views, and value system of the married group. The changes are often drastic; the wild young man becomes the responsible husband and the glamour girl becomes the efficient housewife. Whether these changes are desirable or undesirable is not the question. The fact is that they often occur.

More systematic is Lieberman's (1950) longitudinal study of changes which occur in the values of workers as they change their status from worker to foreman or shop steward. He found that as the men played their new roles, their attitudes changed in the "proper" directions; foremen became more pro-management and stewards became more pro-union. He also discovered that the foremen who left this status showed a tendency to revert to their old attitudes regarding management. The reason for this, however, is not clear. It may have been caused by the return to the old status or it might have been due to resentment about being demoted.

Another finding from the Mann and Janis (1968) study suggests that role taking alone has an effect, though it is not as strong as actually playing out of the role. The women who had heard the recording smoked less than a group of women who had not been exposed to the scene at all. This effect seems to be due to human's ability to rehearse events in their minds without actually "going through the motions." The women who heard the recording were no doubt saying to themselves, "I wonder how I would feel if I were in that situation?" and these imaginings served to fix the "proper" responses in their minds. This study supports two of the propositions I have offered; namely, role taking leads to the learning of roles, and overt practice enhances that learning.

The Personal Role Definition

In role learning there is nothing directly comparable to a personal evaluation developed by comparing behavior against internal standards. There is also no process quite analogous to developing a personal evaluation by comparing one's performance against that of a comparison other. There is, however, some element of individuality in the formation of actor's role definitions.

This comes in largely because role behavior is goal-oriented, and actor may in fact hit on, or figure out, a way to build the social equivalent of the "better mousetrap." It is not uncommon that the ways we are taught do not lead to the achievement of our goals—for example, a young military officer finds that his men do not "follow" when he applies the lessons he learned at the Academy, and a father finds he cannot control his child by doing what his parents did. In such situations, and in innumerable others, most people would attempt to redefine their roles so that in the future the chances of reaching their goals would be increased.

Thus, for roles, as for self-evaluations, there is a personal definition as well as a perceived social definition. This personal definition is not formed in the same way for roles as it is for self-evaluation, but they are similar in most other respects.

One of the similarities is that when one looks below the surface of personal definitions of roles, it is often discovered that there is a social source to much of the "individuality." Personal definitions of roles often turn out to be cases of *role assimilation*—applying a role definition learned from others to a new and "inappropriate" context. When this occurs we can hardly say actor has come up, independently, with a new definition for a role. He or she has simply transferred information from one situation to a new one. Let us consider this process a little more deeply.

Role assimilation was first described in a classic article by Orville Brim (1958). In reanalyzing data gathered by Helen Koch, he discovered that in families with two children, young children who had opposite sex siblings were more likely than other children to exhibit behaviors which were traditionally considered inappropriate for people of their gender. That is, boys with sisters were more "feminine" than boys with brothers, and girls with brothers were more "masculine" than girls with sisters.[3]

The children who were playing a role usually associated with the opposite sex clearly had, and were using, a personal definition of sex role. It seems likely that no one ever told them they should act that way. At the same time they could not be credited with having made a basic invention. Brim suggests this process: If a child has an opposite sex sibling, he or she will take the role of a child of the opposite sex, since we may assume to have a sibling means that one will interact with him or her frequently. In the process of taking the other's role the child learns, as we all do, the role of the other. But these children did not simply file this information away; they *assimilated* the other's behavior into their own role repertoire. They acted as the other did.

Other studies in the area of sex role learning also illustrate the operation of role assimilation in a somewhat different context. Studies of boys from middle-class white homes in which a father is not present generally show that they are, by traditional criteria, somewhat less masculine than comparable boys from "complete families" (Biller, 1971; Burton and Whiting, 1961; Kagan, 1964; Leichty, 1960). Part of the explanation seems to be that in the absence of a father, a boy's interaction with his mother is increased in frequency and intensity. He has more opportunity to take, and learn, the masculine role. Such conditions would seem ideally suited for role assimilation.[4]

A second process which results in apparent innovation in role definitions is *role extension* (Brim, 1960). In this case, the actor utilizes a role that he or she has been taught for a particular actor-other combination in another situation. In further explaining the data we have just considered, Brim suggests that part of the femininity of boys with sisters may be due to role extension.

> Where the boy has only one sister, he learns peer level interaction patterns appropriate to a male-female relation. Certainly the expectations of his sister,

[3] Rosenberg and Sutton-Smith (1964) in their study of 9 to 12 year olds also found more femininity among boys with sisters, and Sutton-Smith and Rosenberg (1965) found the same thing for college men, particularly when they were younger than their sisters. Leventhal (1965; 1970), however, reports that college men with sisters show less femininity—again, particularly if the sister was older. Thus it seems fairly clear that the effect found by Brim holds for young people, but it is not certain that it persists throughout life. Leventhal (1970) suggests several reasons why an opposite pattern may be found in adulthood. Among them is the possibility that social pressures may later lead the boy with a sister to give up his imitation of her and adopt a "super-masculinity" to prove to himself and to others that he is not effeminate. The validity of this speculation cannot be judged until more information is available.

[4] This assumption has been uncritically applied to lower-class blacks, but there are no data which show that the extension is justified. In fact, Heiss' (1975) data suggest that the idea is not applicable to this group. As Hannerz (1969) argues, the conditions which facilitate role assimilation in white middle-class "fatherless" homes, are not present in similar lower-class black homes.

and those of his parents for him toward her, include less aggression, less anger, and so on, than if another male (a brother) were involved. In the first-grade classroom he would tend, through [role extension] to respond to his peers as he did to his sister, and hence would receive a lower rating on aggression and similar traits (Brim, 1960: 155).

Again there is innovation here. Actor is playing a role in a manner that he was never taught. But, as before, it is socially based. The role definition is clearly and unequivocally a personal one, but the existence of such definitions hardly make role definitions anything but social products.[5]

Most readers, I believe, will have no difficulty in accepting the existence of role assimilation and extension in children, but many may feel it is unlikely that these processes are important sources of role innovation in later life, particularly when they learn that one of the factors that lead to their occurrence is role confusion. People assimilate roles when they don't understand that the role of the other is not appropriate for them, and they extend roles when they are unaware that the behavior appropriate for a particular other is not appropriate for a different other. In the first case, a boy may assume that the behavior of his sister is the way *children* should behave, and in the second he may believe that the way he is supposed to act toward his sister is the way he should act toward *all* children. Very immature people are probably the only ones who would fail to make the appropriate distinctions.

Confusion is, however, only one source of assimilation and extension. If one considers the other causes, it seems quite plausible to postulate the existence of these processes in adults. For example, assimilation and extension are often conscious, goal-oriented processes. Brim (1958: 2) suggests that if a particular behavior of an other has been successful to a high degree, actor may "consciously transfer to his own role such behavioral elements for trial. To the extent that they prove successful for him, in his performance, and are not eliminated through punishment from others for being inappropriate, he will adopt them." For extension, this would suggest that if a behavior "works" for actor vis-à-vis one kind of other, there would be a tendency to try it out with different others. The personal role definition may not be equivalent to the invention of a better mousetrap; it may simply involve using a trap which has been successful with other animals to catch a mouse.

Brim describes a third, and similar, source of role assimilation as follows:

Faced with novel situations where "his" own behavior fails, the elements of others' roles are already learned and available for trial and hence would tend

---

[5] The reader must be cautioned that what may appear to be a personal definition often turns out to be a social definition learned from a group whose viewpoint is not the dominant one in the society. Many uninformed people assumed that the hippies of the 1960s were "doing their own thing"—that more than most, their role definitions were personal creations. To the contrary, even the originators of the hippie-ethic were influenced by the role definitions of earlier "bohemian" groups and the rank and file who adopted the ethic learned it in a manner exactly comparable to that used in the teaching of any role. There is likely to be as much conformity in "nonconformist" groups as there is in "straight" groups.

to be tried prior to the development of totally new responses; again, if success-ful, they tend to be assimilated to the role (Brim, 1958: 2).

For extension, this postulate would suggest if actor finds that in a given situation he or she doesn't know how to act vis-à-vis X, he or she will do what is known to be appropriate relative to Y in that situation.

After this expanded discussion, role assimilation and extension should be seen to have the character of adult behaviors. They are not simply a result of confusion, but are designed to solve interaction problems with a minimum of effort—a very common adult tendency.

Turner's (1978) discussion of role-person merger is also worthy of mention here. This phenomenon is quite similar to role extension, although perhaps more extreme. Two of the criteria of role merger show the similarity: "The. . .actor is demonstrating role merger when there is a failure of role compartmentalization, when he continues to play a role in situations in which it does not apply, and when he resists abandon-ment of a role despite available, advantageous, and viable alternative roles (Turner, 1978: 3). I do not wish to get involved in the question of where extension ends and merger begins. The important point is that a person who engages in role merger is acting inconsistently with the behavior he or she has been taught is appropriate in a particular situation. To that extent, actor is using a personal definition of the role.

Turner's discussion is of particular importance because he considers the inter-active determinants of merger as well as those characteristic of the individual. What he seems to be saying is that in some cases people continue to play a role in a situation in which the role does not apply because other people expect it of them. Others come to the conclusion that a particular role reveals what the actor is like as a person, and therefore they expect his behavior in another role to reflect elements of the first role even though the second role "should" be played differently. To avoid problems, actor gives them what they want. If this is the source of a particular role merger, the distinction between social definition and personal definition breaks down. In this case, actor is giving a role a personal twist by playing it in a way that was not taught, because others are suggesting he or she do so. In this borderline case, the language of personal and social definition leads only to confusion.

Combining the Personal and Social Role Definition

Borderline cases aside, actors will often be faced with situations in which their per-sonal role definitions are different from their perceptions of the social definition of the role. And when this is so, they must arrive at a resolution of the discrepancy. For obvious reasons, the solution will not simply be to accept the personal definition. Even if the personal definition is viewed as a more effective route to the achievement of some of the goals of the interaction, to ignore "public opinion" is to open oneself up to punishments inflicted by self and others for deviating from "proper behavior." A young man may figure out a better way of winning women, but find out his vic-tories are hollow because he and others view him as a "cad."

What usually happens is similar to what we saw occurred in combining personal and perceived social evaluations. The working role definitions will be an amalgam of the personal and social role definitions, differentially weighted, in terms of principles which are basically the same as those described in the section on the evaluative self. For example, to follow the personal role definition is likely to have associated with it certain utilitarian rewards and costs, and the acceptance of the perceived social definition is also likely to have its advantages and disadvantages. Actor's judgment about the desirability of the consequences which will follow from emphasizing one over the other will determine which will have the greater influence on the working definition.

Similarly, actor will judge whether his or her own definition or that of other people will better serve expressive and knowledge needs. Which definition is more correct? Which can be followed successfully? Which is more pleasurable to follow? The answers to such questions will also influence the weight given to the definitions which are awaiting combination.

Although many of the major points of interactionist theory about the learning of roles have not been tested, what is available tends to support the basic contention that the theory presented in previous chapters is applicable, although some alterations are necessary because of the differences between this mental construct and the ones discussed earlier. In general, these changes are not basic. Details aside, there are clear indications that actors develop a perceived social definition of what others consider to be appropriate behavior and this definition represents an amalgam of received definitions weighted in such a way as to increase utilitarian, expressive, and knowledge rewards. There also appears to be a personal definition developed for social roles. These two elements are then weighted and combined into a working definition of the role.

THE PRESENTED SELF

My treatment of the process of learning presented selves will be relatively brief since no additional changes are required in the theory and there is little relevant research. A definition of a proper presented self says that when you are in a particular situation it is appropriate, acceptable, or "wise" to convey a particular image of yourself, and our ideas about what is appropriate are learned by familiar mechanisms.

In learning presented self definitions, there is direct conscious teaching; the learning that comes from reactions of others which are not consciously intended to teach; the instruction that comes from role taking, observation of models, and practice. Just as with roles, many of these lessons will contradict each other, and actor will develop a general impression of the social definition of proper presented selves by forming an amalgam through the differential weighting of various received definitions. The weighting process will be governed by the same principles used so often already. In addition, actor may develop a personal definition of what is the proper image, perhaps because he finds it works better for him. Then actor will blend the social and personal definitions into a working definition, again giving differential weights to the elements.

Learning Presented Selves

Unfortunately, these contentions will have to rest on their plausibility because there are no systematic data which show how, and from whom, actors learn what self-images should be presented in given situations. And there is no evidence to show how contradictions are resolved. I can, however, give some illustrations of how we "pick up" the necessary information. For example, the nursing students in Olesen and Whittaker's (1968) study were very interested in presenting a proper "front," but before they could do that they had to learn what the desired image was:

> To do this the students became sensitized to a variety of occurrences not only between themselves and faculty, but between faculty and other students. They watched closely for faculty reactions to all potentially revealing situations, such as the way a classmate handled equipment around a patient's bed, or talked to him. In the conference, they made mental notes of the manner and tone in which the instructor commented upon another's presentation, the fleeting expressions on her face. They became cognizant of the style in which each instructor herself played the nurse at the bedside. (Olesen and Whittaker, 1968: 161)

In this case, the students' problems were increased by the fact that the faculty, who knew best what would make the proper impression on them, were unusually loathe to give direct instruction in the matter.

> "Psyching out" was complicated by the type of self-management affected by the faculty, where great importance was placed upon the studied avoidance of direct criticism, upon commitment to permitting the student to discover the appropriate nursing style on her own and upon wearing on the face, at all times, the controlled mask of passivity and impartiality. (Olesen and Whittaker, 1968: 161)

Although exaggerated here, this is probably a fairly common pattern; the relevant others will not explicitly tell the actor what self should be presented to them. There are exceptions, of course. Others will often "dress down" inferiors if they fail to show proper respect. However, there are restrictions on this kind of instruction. (You can't demand respect or love. If it is not given spontaneously, it is not worth anything.) In most instances people will get little direct instruction from other.

However, the actor does not have to depend solely upon observation and imitation. Third parties are frequently able and willing to instruct actor:

> Reference persons emerge. These people, in a sense, assume the guise of legendary figures who have confronted unknown dangers, and, by doing so, have cast

light upon the nature of reality. Their trials and feats become the substance of a folklore that, passed from mouth to mouth, helps to clarify an environment and a process, which have heretofore defied pragmatic surveillance. Thus for each student there is a frame of reference, partly made up of the experiences of others, by which maneuvering through the school is facilitated. (Olesen and Whittaker, 1968: 166–67)

In our specialized world we even have books whose function is to play the part of the third party and teach us what selves should be presented. Quaint as it may seem now, not too long ago adolescents were being treated to advice of the following kind in guides to good manners:

Don't show your scorn of dominoes, even if you would rather play rummy. It will not hurt you to look as if you were having a good time even when you are not, and it will make things jollier for you and everybody else. (Boykin, 1958: 190–91)

It is better for a girl to make the mistake of seeming to have too little rather than too much affection, unless she is sure that he has at least as much as she. (Landers, 1936: 94)

Illustration is not proof, but it does seem likely that the processes of information gathering used for presented selves are the same as those used for the other central variables.

Adopting Presented Selves

To know that others believe that a particular self should be presented does not explain why an actor accepts that view. The explanation is, however, easy to provide. We adopt particular presented selves as our own because to do so is rewarding. And the rewards we obtain are the familiar ones.

For example, nursing students seem to present certain self-images because they hope to receive positive evaluations from others:

In her opening remarks, Rosa Mallard indicated that it was quite possible for a student to more or less "psyche out" an instructor and act in a particular fashion as to maximize the possibility for a favorable evaluation (Olesen and Whittaker, 1968: 161).

Many students whose clinical performance is only mediocre manage to get very good grades because they're skilled in putting on a good front before instructors (Olesen and Whittaker, 1968: 175).

The students had psyched out. . .that in the conference active and frequent participation was most desired (Olesen and Whittaker, 1968: 176).

"I do hate to be late for things and I don't like to miss out on things and I really don't want to create a bad impression here at the school by not showing up for these things, so I guess that I'll have to come around tomorrow and make amends" (Olesen and Whittaker, 1968: 179).

"You remember how dull conferences with the instructors were and the instructors would sit around waiting for us to say deep and profound things. Lots of times this made me so uncomfortable that I would act real interested and enthusiastic. . .when all along deep inside me, I was feeling that it was just a lot of baloney" (Olesen and Whittaker, 1968: 179).

In and of itself a favorable evaluation from others is a utilitarian reward, but it is also a means to other utilitarian rewards. In the case of the student nurses it was the means to graduation and a good job. And, of course, it goes well beyond this; the utilitarian rewards which may be obtained by presentations of particular selves are extremely numerous and obvious. Perhaps these few will do to suggest the range: the appearance of contrition is rewarded by forgiveness; the appearance of honesty is rewarded by trust; the appearance of interest, sympathy, and sacrifice, are rewarded by gratitude; the appearance of love is rewarded by love; the appearance of loyalty by loyalty.

Presented Selves and Expressive Needs

Since presentations of self can produce favorable evaluations from others, they can also serve the expressive need for favorable self-evaluations. The evaluations from others which are based on presentations of selves may not be weighted very heavily, for actor may consider them undeserved. But they do count even when actor knows that the self being presented is false. In fact, it is not uncommon—although it is rather self-deceiving—for actors to present false selves primarily so that they may raise their self-evaluations. Somewhere between the received evaluation and the weighting process actor seems to "forget" the evaluation was obtained "under false pretenses."

It seems, then, quite clear that particular self-presentations can be used to give actor the expressive reward of a favorable self-evaluation by putting him in a good light in the eyes of others, and by this means improving the perceived social evaluation. It also seems that a favorable presentation of self can increase actor's *personal* self-evaluation. In one experiment, two groups of subjects were asked to formulate a talk about themselves which would put forth a positive image of self that would impress a prospective employer. Both those who actually delivered the speech and those who did not showed enhanced states of self-esteem as compared with a control group (Gergen and Taylor, 1966). "In effect, the subjective rehearsal of a given presentation, whether or not actually buttressed by active behavior, may alter a person's feelings about himself in a situation" (Gergen, 1968: 306). In the terms of relevance here, when actor presents a favorable self he is likely to convince himself that it truly represents him— even if it was done "on order" with no positive feedback from others because of it.

Gergen (1971) explains this rather interesting finding as follows:

A person may harbor a variety of concepts of himself which differ in salience from moment to moment. When a particular role is used in a particular situation, the salience of certain concepts may increase and others may be lost from awareness. Thus, self-presentation may convince a person. . .that he is indeed what he says he is. To be sure, not all presentation is accompanied by feelings of "true self." Highly learned concepts of self may be continuously salient and nag one when he violates them. However, there is a strong tendency in social relations for the person to become the mask. (Gergen, 1971: 86)

When I was young it was often said, usually by a girl about a boy, "He is so far gone that he believes his own lies." I think we must accept that they were often right, for it is not an uncommon occurrence.

Presented Selves and Knowledge Functions. With this explained, it can be seen how self-presentation can lead to "knowledge" for actor. Just as presenting a favorable self-view can contribute to a positive self-view, presenting any kind of self leads actor to think that he is the kind of person portrayed in the presented self. Actor gains the feeling of self-knowledge and identity. The fact that I acted kindly, even if deep down I know it was an "act," will lead me to feel I know the answer to the question "Am I kind?" This would be particularly true if others were led by my self-presentation to define me as kind, but it would happen even if there were no feedback. I would repeat that the basic principles of the theory would suggest that the gain in feelings of self-knowledge may not be great because such experiences have characteristics which lead them to be given a low weight. However, they would have some influence.

In sum, then, the presentation of self can lead to satisfaction of needs in all three categories, and though it has not been shown directly that we tend to accept definitions of presented selves because they produce these rewards, it does seem likely that that is the case. The material hardly represents a test of the theory's applicability to the learning of the presented selves, but it does give hope that more searching tests of the crucial hypotheses will provide support.

THE ROLE ASSOCIATED WITH THE PRESENTED SELF

The presented self role is that set of behaviors which actor believes will lead other to view actor in the way actor wishes to be viewed. Its development is barely distinguishable from that which leads to definitions of presented selves. In fact, the two elements are usually taught at the same time. A particular encounter is likely to give instructions on both the proper image and how that image will be achieved. "When you go for the interview, you want to look like you don't need a job, so I would suggest that you. . ."

Perhaps the only difference of note is that practice is of greater importance in regard to the presented self role than it is in regard to the presented self. This is just as it was when I was discussing identities and roles. The more often we do it, the easier it is to think of ourselves in a particular way, but practice is even more important for carrying out requisite activities in a smooth and convincing manner.

With this said, there is nothing more to do than to illustrate how people are instructed in the proper behavior for the selves they wish to present. (See Chapter 2 for a discussion of the general mechanisms used in the presentation of self.)

The learning of presented self roles is clearly seen in the apprenticeship undergone by novice call girls. During this time the woman is "taught the ropes," and that includes learning how to present the proper self-image to the customer. When things get slow the women solicit over the phone. The trick there is to present oneself in a way that will engender sympathy and a willingness to help out. This is apparently an impression that inexperienced women have difficulty in presenting, and they are specifically taught how to do it by means of direct instruction and observation:

> [Do they [pimps] teach you during the turning out period how to make a telephone call?] Oh, usually, yes. They don't teach you, they just tell you how to do it and you do it with your good common sense, but if you have trouble, they tell you more about it (Bryan, 1965: 293).

> I used to listen to my girl friend [trainer]. She was the greatest at this telephone type of situation. She would call up and cry and say that people had come to her door. . .She'd cry and she'd complain and she'd say "I have a bad check at the liquor store, and they sent the police over," and really. . .a girl has a story she tells the man. . .Anything, you know, so he'll help her out. Either it's the rent or she needs a car, or doctor bills, or any number of things (Bryan, 1965: 292).

For more respectable "pitches," there are books to instruct the inexperienced in how to achieve their aims of impression management. Let me quote again from a book on adolescent etiquette:

> And, last but not least in the ways to attract a boy is the party method. It's simple and appears so undesigning. Entertaining at home offers a good opportunity for one to show her qualities. . .as hostess, a girl is very much in the center of attention. . .By organizing games and stunts, she has every opportunity of showing qualities of leadership and finesse. Boys are attracted to girls who are fine hostesses (Bryant, 1960: 43).

Presenting Favorable Selves

It is possible to be somewhat more specific about the techniques which are used to present a self leading to favorable evaluations from others. In general, of course, the point is to make other aware of one's good points and to hide one's bad points. In addition one can create good points when they don't exist. For example:

> Lisa claims that those who can do little things for the patient and somehow tell the instructor they have done this—those are the students who do well. This does not mean that they go up to her point-blank and inform her of the little extras that they have undertaken for the care of the patient, but somehow or other they manage to get this across in conferences (Olesen and Whittaker, 1968: 176).

Kelly pointed out that very few students bring their mistakes up at conferences (Olesen and Whittaker, 1968: 177).

The evidence indicates, however, that the matter is not all that simple. There are conditions which limit the extent of positivity that actors put into their self-presentations. The rule is not that one presents oneself in the best light, but rather that one acts in a way that will bring approval from others. In some instances actors seem to believe that in the long run a little humility will get them further.

The amount of humility which will be used is determined in part by whether or not actor will find himself in a situation in which he may have to "live up" to his self-created reputation. It would seem much better to admit faults than to deny them if other is likely to be able to validate your self-description.[6]

It would also seem wise for actors to show humility by aggrandizing potential opponents in their public statements. If they later win, the victory becomes all that more valuable; if they lose the defeat has fewer negative effects on third persons' evaluations of them. Of course, if the evaluation of the competition will have no effect on third parties' views because the estimation is given in private, additional considerations come into play. On the basis of this reasoning, Gould et al. (1977) predicted that subjects would present themselves in a way which indicated respect for the other's ability when they evaluated a competitor in public, but when the evaluations were private the opponent would be denigrated. No one who has ever read a pregame statement of a college coach need be told that their hypotheses were supported. In fact, it seems that modesty is taken on even when there is no expectation of competition. The expectation of future contact can by itself lead to admission of negative traits. This seems a clear case of confessing before you get caught.

It would also seem to be good strategy to assume a modest air in the presence of someone who is extremely modest and to become more egotistical in the presence of an extreme egotist. Gergen explains this as follows:

> The egotist creates a power problem. By accentuating his virtues he implies that others are not equal to him. His manner bespeaks his assumption that he deserves status, a greater share of whatever rewards are available, and the right to lead in decision-making. Skillful self-presentation may be helpful in dealing with this kind of person; in particular, we might well react in kind, accentuating our assets and hiding our shortcomings (Gergen, 1971: 83).

With an extreme egotist, there is perhaps little chance of favorable feedback, but there is clearly none unless we put our best foot forward.

With a person who is very self-deprecatory, the problem is quite different. To be too self-laudatory would be cruel, to deprecate ourselves to the same extent as he or

---

[6] Although this seems plausible, as yet there is no evidence to support it. In fact, Archibald and Cohen (1971) did not find clear-cut differences in the direction predicted by the hypothesis. There seem, however, to be questions concerning the effectiveness of their experimental manipulations.

she does would be inconsistent with our self-image and nonproductive. It is best in this case to admit some faults, but to indicate sufficient good points so that the other will have to recognize your superiority.

Gergen and Wishnov (1965) provide evidence that this happens. Female students who interacted with an egotist increased the favorability of their self-descriptions as compared with the ones they had given a month earlier, and those who had contact with someone who seemed to think she had no good points didn't make much change in the number of positive traits they mentioned, but they did increase their admission of negative traits.

Another situation in which actor might get more favorable evaluations from other by presenting a modest view of self is when he is so much superior than the others that admitting a few faults, particularly on rather irrelevant traits, will not jeopardize his standing in the eyes of the others. In fact, by showing his humanity it might even enhance his standing. This is what Jones, Gergen, and Jones (1963) found to be the case. Juniors and seniors in a Naval ROTC unit were told to try to win the liking and respect of freshmen, and this led them to describe themselves in less favorable terms than a control group of upperclassmen who were not under "ingratiation instructions" (see also Gergen and Taylor, 1969). Moreover, this modesty effect was greater for items they did not consider to be important.

LEARNING ABOUT OTHERS

Throughout the last two chapters the focus has been on the ways that actors learn about themselves. But if there is to be accurate role-taking (see Chapter 2) and adequate interaction (see Chapters 7 and 8), actors must have similar information about the others with whom they interact. Actor must know how others identify and evaluate themselves, what they consider to be proper role definitions, what selves they may present, and how they are likely to go about it. Actor must also identify and evaluate other, and develop his own definition of other. Of course, in regard to a specific other, this information will emerge in the processes of role-taking and interaction, but for that to happen actor must enter the situation with some idea of the likely possibilities. Before going on to a consideration of interaction, it is necessary to consider how this information is obtained.

The basic theory will apply here, for it is again a matter of learning meanings about objects, and the other is as much an object as is the self. There are no basic differences. From direct instruction, observation, and role-taking actor will obtain information which will be combined, by weighting, into a generalized view of what most people expect of others in particular situations. This could be called the perceived social definition of others. This definition will be of the kind; in this situation most people seem to believe that the other with whom they are interacting will define himself in this way.

The information involved here is not based upon direct observation of the relevant others. It is developed from what people "say" the relevant others are likely to do. If someone else tells actor, "If you are not tough with them at the beginning they are going to think they are the bosses," that would contribute to the perceived social definition. It tells actor what third parties think the relevant others do in a particular situation. This suggests to actor how other will define himself and how actor should define him.

Personal Definitions of Others

In addition, actor will develop a personal view of how others define themselves. This will be based upon the actor's personal experience with the relevant others. (Thus its source is different from the personal component involved when the self is the object of interest.) If I see that others, in fact, accept my or somebody else's authority when kindness is shown at the beginning, I have information which will contribute to my personal definition of what others do. Simply stated, the difference between social and personal definitions of others is that the social definition is based upon what third parties "tell" actor about others and the personal definition is based upon his direct experience with relevant others.

As may be seen from the examples given, the social and personal definitions of others may be different. What people tell us about others often conflicts with our personal experience. Actor will again be faced with the job of developing a working definition from them. Just as before, this will be an amalgam of the two with differential weight applied to each.

Hopefully, all that is unclear at this point is: how do we create a social and a personal definition of others from the conflicting definitions we possess? And, how do we combine the personal and the social definitions of others into a coherent self-definition of others? The answer is, in general terms, as it was before. First, weights are assigned to each definition in a manner designed to produce utilitarian, expressive, and knowledge rewards; we then adopt the predominant view. Let us see how that works out for the development of a perceived social definition of others from the multiple definitions received from third parties.

We start with the familiar notion that if an other controls utilitarian rewards, he is more likely to give them when we accept his view than when we don't. The acceptance of a third party's view about other is a means to utilitarian goals, and the view of people who control utilitarian rewards will be more influential. Acceptance of a third party's definition of other can also satisfy our need for knowledge. Not only do we want to have accurate knowledge about ourselves, but we also want to know about others. Thus, considerations of competence, interest, and so forth will come in. Definitions of others can also serve a number of our expressive needs. If we come to believe that others hold a particular set of definitions, we may be helped to a positive view of self if, when we compare our conceptions to theirs, we conclude that ours are superior. There is, then, something of a tendency to think the worst of others. Certain beliefs about others can also permit us to justify our actions. If "they deserved it" because of what they are or believe, behavior which would normally lead us to feel contempt for ourselves can be made acceptable. And, to give just one more example, certain beliefs about others serve our need for cognitive consistency, whereas others do not. Thus, all other things being equal, we will tend to give greater weight to definitions of other, from third parties, which square with what we already believe to be the case.

SUMMARY

In this chapter the theory which was developed to explain the development of self-evaluations was applied to the other central variables. There is much less relevant data available for these variables, but what there is suggests that with relatively minor alterations the theory applies.

For example, other people will suggest to us that we do or do not have the traits associated with a particular identity, and we will compare our traits with those of people who possess that identity and with our personal view of what qualifies one for holding it. From the various suggestions presented by others we will decide whether people in general consider the identity proper for us. In making that decision we will give greater weight to some opinions than to others. Those opinions which are rewarding will be given heavier weight. By a similar process, our several comparisons of ourselves with others and with our standards will be combined into a tentative personal definition. Then the two parts will be combined into a self-definition. When the perceived social definition and the tentative personal definition do not agree, our decision about whether or not the identity is appropriate to us will depend upon the weight assigned to each component. The more rewarding component will predominate.

This is essentially the way that self-evaluations are developed. The major difference is that evaluations are matters of more or less and an identity is appropriate or it is not. Thus, it is not meaningful to talk about averaging after weighting. For identities, the hypothesis is that actor will view the identity as his own when the predominant opinion says it is.

It is further suggested that the theory can be extended to account for an identity's position on the prominence hierarchy. The determinants are the frequency with which actor has been defined in that way, and, more important, the extent to which the identity is associated with reward.

It is asserted that roles, presented selves, roles for presented selves, and definitions of others are all learned in basically the same way that identities are. There are, however, differences to be found in the specific nature of the rewards involved, and some processes, such as practice, efficacy, and transfer effects, are relevant only to some of the mental constructs.

CHAPTER 7

ROUTINE AND PROBLEMATIC INTERACTION

An interactionist theory must, above all, describe and explain human interactions. It's not that excuses have to be made for the extended discussion which has preceded this point; an important part of the social psychologist's job is to account for the content of the human psyche. Nonetheless, the previous material takes on greatly enhanced significance if it can be shown that the abilities and mental structures which were the focus of previous chapters have a key role in determining how actors relate to others. That is the task of this and the following chapters.

To begin, the two major types of interaction must be distinguished. The first type Hewitt (1976) calls the *routine* situations of interaction:

> These situations are routine in the sense that they are familiar to us: they can be readily named; the objects to be dealt with in them can be easily anticipated, the roles represented are known in advance, and frequently we know who will make these roles; and, in general, a more or less patterned set of activities will occur, often strongly resembling activities that have taken place on previous such occasions (Hewitt, 1976: 110-11).

In such situations actor can perform with relatively little effort, and if these situations were less common than they are, human life would be exceedingly wearisome. They are, however, not the only kinds of interaction situations we face. To a greater or lesser degree, all people find themselves in encounters in which the interaction is *problematic*: things are not familiar, the other seems to be operating on a different wave length, innovation is required, and so on. These situations are also common, and much effort will be devoted to considering the nature of the problems which emerge in interaction and the ways they are solved. It must be emphasized, however, that routine and problematic interaction are basically the same. The same principles apply to both; they differ only in terms of their complexity. In fact, it is often the case that interaction is routine simply because the problems associated with it were solved at an earlier time.

ROUTINE INTERACTION

Before going into the details, I will present a general overview of the course of non-problematic interactions.

1. The actor enters the situation with long experience in interaction behind him. This experience will have provided him with the capacity to interact and with the tools needed for interaction. The latter would include identities, roles, etc., for himself and other, and knowledge of the meanings of many objects—such as words, physical entities, and so forth. The capacity to interact also implies that actor can take the role of the other, and can devise ways of acting and reacting that promise to lead him in the direction of his goals.

2. On the basis of the cues available, actor develops a preliminary definition of the situation. This is actor's attempt to make sense of the situation. As Weinstein (1969: 755) puts it, a definition of the situation is actor's "best guess as to the nature of the reality with which he is currently engaged; his answer to the question, 'What is going on here?'"

3. This preliminary definition of the situation will suggest to actor what his first act should be. Certain behaviors will fit in with his understanding of "what's up" and others will seem inappropriate. His tendency will be, of course, to choose the former.

4. Before putting his plan into action, actor will consider the effects his acts will have upon other by taking the role of the other and "determining" what other's definition of the situation is. This information will make it possible for him to predict other's reaction to his action.

5. In a routine interaction, the other's probable reaction is one which actor considers desirable and therefore actor can go ahead and do what he planned to do. Thus actor acts.

6. While actor was working out his definition of the situation, other was doing likewise. Actor's act will be taken as another cue, and other will reconsider his definition of the situation in the light of this additional information. In a routine interaction, this information will serve to support other's definition; he will find that it does not require alteration.

7. On the basis of his definition of the situation, other will decide what kind of response is appropriate to actor's behavior. Before reacting, other will take actor's role and determine how actor will react. (He should be somewhat more accurate than actor was because he has an additional bit of information upon which to base his guess, that is, actor's first act.) If other feels that actor's reaction will be what he wishes, and in a routine interaction this would be the

case, other will put his plan into action. Thus we get other's first act and the completion of the first interact.

8. Actor will respond after reconsidering his definition of the situation on the basis of the new information provided by other's action. Then the process will continue with each responding in turn until the encounter is completed.

That, in brief, is a typical interactionist view of the interaction process: noting cues, definition, plan of action, consideration of consequences, possible revision of plan, action by actor; noting cues, definition, plan of action, consideration of consequences, possible revision of plan, reaction by other, etc.

Now for the all important details. First, what is involved in a definition of the situation? What is its content, and how is it formed?

The Definition of the Situation

Definitions of situations contain several interrelated elements which combine into a description of the key characteristics of the interaction situation. Using Stebbins' (1969) discussion as a base, I would suggest that, typically, actor's definition of the situation would include:

1. A perception of the relevant traits of the participants, including actor himself. Who am I and who are they in this encounter? What are our relevant identities, qualities, self-evaluations, presented selves?

2. A perception of the participants' evaluation of the situation. What are "the moral, emotional, or sentimental connotations of the immediate setting?" (Stebbins, 1969: 198). What do I and they think about the situation itself? Do we welcome the opportunity to be here? Do we feel that there is anything wrong about being here? Do we see this encounter as an opportunity or as a chore?

3. A perception of the goals and intentions of the participants. What do we hope to accomplish by the interaction?

4. A perception of the actions which are suitable. What behavior is appropriate and useful in our attempts to achieve our goals? What should my game plan be? What is theirs likely to be?

5. A perception of the participants' justifications. These justifications are often attached to the goals; they legitimate the participants' desire to accomplish a particular end, or they may be tied to the planned actions. In this case, they may simply represent explanations of how the projected means will lead to desired ends. They can also serve as justifications in a moral sense. They can defend the acceptability of planned actions.

A quick perusal of this list will suggest the connection between the present discussion and the material presented in earlier chapters. The mental constructs I considered in such detail are among the key building blocks of preliminary definitions of situations. The definition of the participants involves choosing, for actor and other, the self-concepts and presented selves which will be operant in the encounter. The perception of the actions which are appropriate involves determining what roles go with the chosen self-concepts and presented selves. In general, *the process of setting up a preliminary definition of the situation involves using the cues in the present situation as the basis for selecting the proper elements from one's stock of previously learned definitions.*

This list of the content included in definitions of the situation gives some idea of how complex they can get. There are five general elements, each has several parts, and each has to be supplied for actor and for one or more others. This in itself can become quite complicated, but it goes beyond that. Answers to questions of the type, "Who am I?" or "What are they going to do?" are usually not enough to ensure smooth interaction. These "first order" questions are usually followed by "higher order" questions, that is, questions which involve asking about two or more definitions. For example, if actor is to predict other's behavior, it is useful for him to know what other's definition of himself is—actor's definition of other's self-definition. And why not push it further? When actor tries to figure out what other thinks actor thinks of himself, we are at a third-order level: actor's definition of other's definition of actor's self-definition. The logical extensions are endless, but, of course, matters soon get so complicated that the exercise is ended. I would doubt that it often goes beyond the third level. That is, however, enough to justify the statement that definitions of situations can be, and often are, quite detailed and complex.

On the other hand, they are often a lot simpler than this discussion would suggest. Stebbins (1969: 198) captures the essence of the matter when he says: "We may not need or desire the kind of knowledge contained in each of these perceptions. We, as social persons, require only *adequate* knowledge. . .so that we can act; additional information, while perhaps desirable, is less essential."

The amount of detail that is required before a definition will prove adequate will vary greatly depending upon circumstances. In general, however, the higher-order questions would be the "first to go." In many simple interactions, we can get along very well without worrying about what he thinks, I think, he thinks, I think. . . . Justification may also not enter into consciousness when the behavior is of a rather ordinary everyday kind. And, in many instances, the definition is rather light in regard to those parts which require actor to figure out what is on other's mind. This may be due to time constraints, lack of information, or simply lack of interest. The complexity of definitions of situation varies greatly. The trick involved in smooth interaction is to know how much one must know for any given encounter.

Developing a Definition of the Situation

Now that we know what goes into definitions of situations, we can consider how actors arrive at their definitions. Before we get into the details, however, let me make explicit the several simplifying assumptions that are implicit in what follows. It should be reiterated, to begin with, that I am dealing with routine, rather than problematic, situations and that the focus is on the preliminary definition which is required to get the interaction underway. Even in routine situations this definition is not fixed.

It will be expanded and very likely altered as the interaction progresses and goes down new roads. *The course of any interaction is* not *set by the original intentions of the participants.* Those intentions are likely to change as new opportunities open up and barriers are discovered. And, even if the basic intentions do not change, interactions go through phases (Bales, 1950). The ultimate goal may be utilitarian, but there will come a time when business is suspended for awhile and tensions are eased. When that happens, the actor must be flexible enough to alter his definition to avoid being out of phase.

In addition, it will be assumed that preliminary definitions cannot be worked out beforehand. In many instances, of course, this is not so. We plan for many of our interactions, and that often involves doing much of the defining before arriving on the scene. To make this assumption realistic, I will work from the premise that actor did not initiate the interaction.[1]

Categorizing Situations. The first phase in defining a situation involves categorizing it as a specific example of some more general category of situations. We apply a label to the encounter; it is a social occasion, a therapy session, or a work situation. When this is done, some of the answers we need are immediately supplied. Recurrent or routine situations have associated meanings. "They do not occur as neutral, uninterpreted happenings. In the very process of identifying the category of setting we are in, we have also selected a portion of our cultural or habitual definition because [the definition] is associated by means of socialization with the events at hand" (Stebbins, 1969: 199). Once we have identified a situation, we know a lot about its meaning, for we assume that it has the same or similar meaning that we worked out for it in the past. "When a situation has once been seen in a particular configuration, it tends to be seen in that configuration ever after, and it is very difficult to see it in any other" (Waller, 1932: 294).[2]

More specifically, the labeling of the situation helps provide the first three elements. The label suggests the appropriate identities, evaluations, and goals for the encounter.

The working out of a plan of action and a set of justifications may also follow rather directly from the process of labeling. The tendency is to plan to do what we did before in successful encounters of this type. In addition, however, the first three elements will prove of value in working out a plan, for, as has been noted several times, roles are associated with identities. Once we know the relevant identities, we will have strong hints about what we should do.

All this, however, somewhat begs the question. As I have shown, if we assume

---

[1] It should be understood that if actor did initiate the interaction, the processes would be the same. They would, however, be somewhat simpler since there would be time to prepare beforehand.

[2] Of course, objective situations and their definitions are always unique if taken as a whole. They do have commonalities, however, and these commonalities are the basis for the preliminary definitions. We can usually wait until later to make the adjustments required by the fact that the present encounter is of necessity a special case of the category into which we have classified it. In fact, in most instances it must be done this way for the information available at the start is usually sufficient only to put the situation into a general category.

that actor can categorize the situation, it is easy to explain how the definition of the situation is formed. To leave the categorization of the situation as an unexplained given is, however, to avoid an important and difficult question: "How does actor place the situation into a category?"

There is, to be sure, an easy answer to this question, but it is rather unsatisfactory. Actor categorizes the situation by a simple process of associative learning. He will recognize certain cues as having been present in some previous encounters and absent in others, and he will classify the present situation with those in which the cues were present.

The difficulty with this answer is that in any situation there are innumerable cues present. Actor could not possibly take note of them all, and if he did, he would be likely to find that the present encounter has *something* in common with every previous interaction he has experienced. If the simple existence of a common cue was the basis for classification, there would be no classification, because every social situation resembles every other one in some way or other. The classification must be based upon a common cue which is important and relevant. The problem is, therefore, what to look for among the innumerable features of a situation and how to know when one has found an important and relevant similarity.

Although it may not be totally satisfying, I would suggest that the answer is that we take note of the cues that we have been taught to note. Previous socialization and experience will teach that certain things are of significance and others are trivial and can be practically ignored. We may assume that in the past actor did note the wrong things and that this led him to make an improper categorization—a fact which probably became clear as the interaction proceeded. The costs associated with that "error" would fix in actor's mind that he should not take note of those features and that he should look to other things. The importance of experience is twofold. It teaches us what to look for in order to categorize the situation, and we learn what definitions are appropriate for that category of situation.

The problem with this is fairly obvious. We do not learn a rule to the effect that one should *always* take note of particular aspects of the situation. What is relevant to note varies depending upon the situation, but how can one know what is likely to be relevant unless the situation is classified? And the problem I am trying to solve is, "How does actor classify the situation?"

There appears to be a possibility of getting into an infinite regression here, and I wish to avoid that. Perhaps I can break the chain by simply suggesting that before actor begins the *focused* cue seeking that leads to a firmer classification of the situation, there is a period of *scanning*—an unfocused taking in of the surroundings in order to develop an extremely tentative and imprecise categorization. This provides a basis for a more focused search for the cues which will permit the situation to be classified with greater precision.[3]

[3]It should be noted that some of these difficulties are caused by the assumptions under which I am operating. In many instances, for example, actor knows what to look for from the start because he has initiated the interaction with a particular goal in mind. And from his previous experience, he may be aware of the aspects of the situation which hold the answer to the question, "Will I be able to achieve my goal, and what must I do to achieve it?"

Cues for Categorizing Situations. With this said, we can briefly consider the major kinds of objects which will be available for consideration. First, physical aspects of the situation will provide a number of clues which help categorize encounters. I am, at the moment, in my office, and my knowledge of this will help me to make sense of any interaction I am likely to have. The fact that I am here markedly reduces the number of categories into which interactions may be placed. When someone comes in, I can immediately rule out some possibilities: the interaction which follows is unlikely to involve religious observance, physical exercise, buying and selling, and so on. It may very well be concerned with scholarly activities, teaching, counseling, sociability. Physical surroundings suggest some possibilities and indicate that others are highly unlikely.

Physical surroundings help us to categorize a situation, but generally a classification based simply upon physical aspects of the situation is too broad to be of much use. In most physical settings, there are many different situations that could occur, and even the more specialized "containers" may be the site for several possibilities. In a classroom, classes are usually taught, but the rooms are also used for public lectures, movies, faculty meetings. Physical setting must normally be supplemented by other cues before a situation can be adequately categorized.

The supplement is, of course, the cues provided by the other person in the situation. These cues often represent the key to the categorization of the situation. Human beings give off innumerable cues. Their appearance, as conveyed by dress, gestures, and grooming, is often so informative that it alone provides an adequate basis for classifying a situation and determining several elements of the definition. Uniforms certainly do that, as do other stylized forms of clothing. Stone (1962) suggests that appearance can bring forth at least four forms of reaction—the placing of identities, the appraising of values, the appreciation of moods, and the anticipation of attitudes. When appearance is combined with a perception of the physical surroundings, the information provided is even greater. It is quite likely, but by no means certain, that a person who is dressed in tennis clothes, carrying a tennis racket, and on a tennis court has a plan of action which involves playing tennis.

Revealing as appearance is, the most valuable aid to categorizing the situation provided by the other participants is what they say and do. It may be interesting to figure out other's suggested definition of the situation from nonverbal cues, but in actual interaction first place is likely to be given to explicit statements and physical acts which convey other's intentions more unequivocally.

Other may direct actor's attention to specific aspects of the situation which he feels are important and thus lead actor to the "proper" classification of the situation. "Look out, he's got a gun," for example. Other is even of more help when he offers his own definition of the situation with the suggestion that actor adopt it. "I'm a student in your methods course, and I would like to go over the test with you." When this is done, and it is obviously a rather frequent occurrence, all actor has to decide is whether or not other is telling the truth and if he (actor) wishes to accept other's definition as his own. If actor decides to reject it, or even if he wishes simply to modify it, the interaction is removed from the routine category and new processes—which will be discussed later—come into play. If actor is willing to accept the suggestion, the interaction can get underway, assuming that the suggestion is sufficiently informative.

Once a routine situation has been categorized, the remaining elements in its definition are easily supplied. By their nature, routine situations are familiar to actor, and therefore, filling in the details is simply a matter of retrieving the necessary information from memory. He or she will utilize the definitional elements which proved to be appropriate in the past when a similar situation was faced.

When the definition of the situation is sufficiently complete, the real business of the interaction can get underway. What will happen in the interaction is a function of the definition of the situation, and for the most part it is an easy matter to explain the actions of the participants if we know what their definitions are. Their guidelines for action are to be found in the role prescriptions which they associate with the identities for self and other they have chosen for the interaction and in the roles associated with the selves they wish to present. Since the interaction is routine, there are no barriers to acting consistently with these guidelines. Other will accept such actions and will react in ways which mesh.[4]

There is, however, one connection which is not at all obvious. The definition of self which is part of the general definition of the situation includes a self-evaluation, and this self-evaluation also affects what actor does and thinks. It is not immediately clear, however, what the effect will be. The preceding material suggests, in a general way, that a person who evaluates his or her performance in a particular role favorably will act differently from one who has a negative self-evaluation. We now must specify the nature of the differences.

Let me repeat. The effect of identities upon behavior is clear. Identities have clear-cut roles associated with them. Therefore, an explanation of the effect of an identity upon behavior has the general form: Actor behaved as he did because he defined himself as X and other as Y, and he believes that when he is an X and other is a Y, he should. . . . Self-evaluations also contain suggestions for proper behavior, but it is not immediately obvious what these suggestions are. In the following section, I will lay out the implications of variations in self-evaluations.

The Effects of Self-Evaluations

At a very general level, the answer to the question being considered here is comparable to the answers I have offered above. Self-evaluations affect behavior in two ways. First, they influence other aspects of actor's definition of the situation. The actor's

[4]This does not mean, however, that the action will simply spin out and actor can, in effect, sit back and act in a semiautomatic way. As long as the interaction remains routine, something approaching that *may* be possible, but there is no guarantee that the interaction will remain nonproblematic. What worked before in a *similar* situation may not work this time. The unexpected may occur; a third person may become involved; needed resources may run out; new information may become available. Definitions of situations must always be tentative. Actor must constantly ask himself whether or not he wishes to change the course of the interaction, and he must be sensitive to signs that other wishes to do so. At any point in the interaction, the participants may have to work out a new design.

self-evaluation will, for example, affect his choice of goals. Second, self-evaluations have behavioral implications. The connection is not as clear-cut as it is when identities are involved, but there certainly is one. It may not be going too far to say that there are roles attached to self-evaluations. A person who thinks he is good at the activity involved in the interaction may, for example, think he should take a leadership position while a person with a negative view will conclude he should "hang back" and be a follower.

For many of this book's readers, the brief, general comments which have just been presented will be sufficient. I wish, nonetheless, to go into the matter more deeply. For one thing, this will permit me to add detail and specificity to our understanding of an important issue. In addition, our knowledge of this matter is sufficient to allow me to present a formal, "semideductive" system,[5] and this form of theory, which is considered to be highly desirable (see Chapter 1), has been notably missing in the previous pages. Even when the earlier material could have been presented in this form I have avoided doing so, primarily for reasons of style. But one such presentation seems necessary as an example of the type.

The starting point for a theory of self-evaluation effects is implicit in the discussion of the development of the evaluative self. If *self-evaluations are in large part based upon the appraisals that actor receives from others* (Postulate A) it is only a short step to the postulate: *If a person possesses a positive evaluation of self in regard to a given identity, it is probable that when he used the identity previously he received positive evaluations from others* (Postulate A'). If we add another postulate to the effect that: *People assume that similar situations produce similar experiences* (Postulate B), the first hypothesis is suggested.[6] It would state: If a person has a positive self-evaluation regarding a given identity, he is likely to expect to receive positive evaluations from others when he performs its role again under similar conditions (Hypothesis 1). Thus, a person's self-evaluations influence his expectations regarding other's responses.[7]

The contention that people desire a positive view of self (Postulate C), is, of course, also a part of my earlier argument, and it leads, for a time at least, down a somewhat different path. When combined with a new postulate (D), which states: *People know (or believe) that the achievement* and *maintenance of a positive self-*

---

[5] Although the presentation has the appearance of being a deductive system, it isn't really. We would need many more, "all other things being equal," "if A were the only way," "if all A wanted was," etc. It does not seem necessary at this point in the development of the theory to formalize it to that extent. The *tendencies* referred to in the hypotheses are, however, suggested by the postulates.

[6] In order to simplify matters somewhat, the focus will be on those who have positive evaluations and the implied comparison is always with those who have negative evaluations.

[7] This hypothesis is likely to be correct only when the person bases his or her self-evaluation primarily on the perceived social definition. If the major source of self-evaluation is the tentative personal definition, the hypothesis does not follow. It should be noted, however, that an analogous hypothesis is easily developed for such people. By a simple change in Postulate A, we could arrive at the idea that such people would expect to equal or exceed their personal standards and their comparison others when they play a role that has a positive self-evaluation.

evaluation require positive evaluations from others, we get Hypothesis 2 which states: People desire to receive positive evaluations from others.[8]

The argument to this point has rested heavily on the assumption that people who have positive self-evaluations have received positive evaluations from others. If we assume further that usually *others give actors positive evaluations only when actor's performances are successful* (Postulate E), whatever that might mean in a particular case, it follows that *actors with positive self-evaluations for a given identity have been successful in the past when they played its role* (Postulate E'). And if *people expect their previous experience to be replicated in new situations of a similar kind* (Postulate B), Hypothesis 3 would follow: People with positive self-evaulations for a particular identity expect to succeed when they again play its role.

Furthermore, since *success often brings utilitarian rewards—such as pay increases, advancement, etc.—*as well as positive evaluations (Postulate F), I would also suggest that: People expect utilitarian rewards when they play a role whose identity has a positive evaluation associated with it (Hypothesis 4).

The hypotheses which have already been derived have additional implications. For example, Hypothesis 1 states: People expect to receive positive evaluations from others when they are performing roles which are associated with positive self-evaluations, and Hypothesis 2 states: People desire to receive positive evaluations from others. If we combine these two hypotheses, and assume all other things are equal, several additional hypotheses are suggested. For example, when people are in a situation which allows them to choose among several identities, they will choose the identity which has the highest self-evaluation associated with it (Hypothesis 5A). (This is so because they believe to do so increases the likelihood that they will receive the positive evaluations they desire.) Also, (Hypothesis 5B), if people know several roles for a particular identity, they will use the one which has the most favorable evaluations associated with it. Furthermore, (Hypothesis 5C), if people have a choice among situations, which call for different identities, they will choose to be in the situation which "permits" them to use the identity which has the highest self-evaluation associated with it, for by so doing they again increase the likelihood that they will receive desired positive evaluations from others (see Rosenberg, 1968).

The postulates also imply that if a person has a choice among several encounters all of which involve the same role, he will choose the interaction partner who has previously given him the most positive evaluations and the interaction setting in which he has received such evaluations (Hypothesis 5D). Finally, a person who is playing a role is more likely to want to continue to play that role when the associated self-evaluation is positive than when it is negative (Hypothesis 5E).[9]

---

[8] This hypothesis has an analogous form for people who do not base their self-evaluations on the evaluations they receive. It would say that such people wish to equal or exceed their internalized standards and the achievements of their comparison others.

[9] This is perhaps a good place to illustrate the fact that the rules of formal logic would not necessarily lead to the conclusions which are being suggested (see Footnote 5). In this case we are saying that if a particular end is desired, the means to that end would also be desired. But suppose those means also lead to another undesired consequence. Then the means might be avoided because

Confidence in the hypotheses is strengthened by the fact that they are also suggested by Hypotheses 3 and 4 if we assume that *people wish to succeed and desire utilitarian rewards* (Postulate G). If this is so and it is also true that people expect success and rewards when they use identities with positive evaluations, people should prefer to use positively evaluated identities.

If we add a few additional postulates which seem, like the previous ones, to be self-evident, additional implications of Hypothesis 3 emerge. For example, let us assume that *people tend to reject influence from others when they believe their own plan will succeed* (Postulate H), and that *people are more likely to attempt to influence others when they believe that their own ways of thinking and acting are likely to result in success* (Postulate I). When these postulates are combined with Hypothesis 3, which asserts that people with positive self-evaluations expect to succeed, it follows that people with positive self-evaluations are more resistant to influence from others (Hypothesis 6) and more likely to attempt to influence others (Hypothesis 7).

Part of what has gone before shows how parts of the definition of the situation are interrelated; if the self-evaluation is positive the situation will be defined as one which is likely to be rewarding—actor's self-definition influences his view of other's probable behavior. With the hypotheses we already have and some additional ideas, it is possible to show a connection between self-evaluation and another part of the situation's definition—the goals of actor.

The new ideas are, in fact, not totally new; there are hints of them in the discussion of comparison others. For present purposes, the relevant notions are that people do not set goals for themselves which they believe are likely to be beyond their reach, but at the same time they aim for the highest level of accomplishment of which they think they are capable. These ideas may be combined into Postulate J which says *people choose the highest goal they think attainable—all other things being equal;*[10] that is, a person who "knows" there is no way for him or her to be first in the graduating class is unlikely to set that as a goal, but at the same time most students who think they are capable of getting A's won't set for themselves the goal of merely passing, all other things being equal.[11]

This postulate can be combined with a slightly reworded version of Hypothesis 3. It states that people with high self-evaluations are more likely to believe that they will succeed, and that is almost the same as saying that persons with high self-

---

on balance the desired ends are "not worth" the undesired consequences. Furthermore, there are other means to the same end which may be chosen. Obviously, there are a number of unstated assumptions and much loose reasoning. There is also a problem caused by the fact that the basic postulates refer only to tendencies. As has been shown (Costner and Leik, 1964), if A tends to lead to B and B tends to lead to C, A will lead to C only under some circumstances.

[10] The reason for this is that achievement of high goals brings high rewards.

[11] These ideas also have implications for long-term goals. Their significance goes beyond the immediate interaction situation. People will not, for example, set their life goals high if they believe their performances in the preparatory roles are poor. A person who fails biology is going to give up the idea of being a physician.

evaluations will expect to "do better," "score higher," achieve more, and so on, than will persons with low self-evaluations (Hypothesis 3A). If *high self-evaluation people expect to score higher and if performance expectations influence performance goals,* (Postulate J′) people with high self-evaluations should have higher goals than those who do not view themselves as favorably (Hypothesis 8).[12]

The goals that we set for ourselves, or adopt from others, act as internalized standards by which we evaluate our own actions. As we have already discussed in Chapter 4, *to fail to achieve an internalized goal is likely to have a negative effect on the actor's self-evaluation through its negative effect on the personal self-evaluation* (Postulate K). Given that *people desire a positive self-evaluation* (Postulate C), it would follow that a failure to reach an internalized goal should involve cost (distress) for any actor regardless of the level of self-evaluation (Hypothesis 9). Moreover, even when a goal is externally set, and *not* internalized by actor, there should be some cost if it is not met. *When an actor fails to meet an externally imposed goal, the other is unlikely to give positive evaluations* (Revised Postulate E), and if people desire to receive positive evaluations from others (Hypothesis 2) it would also follow that *the failure to reach externally set goals leads to distress* (Hypothesis 10).

Here, however, the question of interest is, "Will the level of distress experienced when goals are not reached vary in an orderly way with actor's original level of self-evaluation?" I believe the answer is yes, and that there is a direct relationship between level of self-evaluation and amount of stress experienced when actor fails to reach a goal (Hypothesis 11). This hypothesis is not directly derivable from what has gone before, however; therefore, additional postulates are necessary.

The needed assumptions are that *the amount of distress is related to the extent of loss that is associated with the failure to reach the goal* (Postulate L), and *those with positive self-evaluations lose more when they fail to reach goals* (Postulate M).

These two propositions are sufficient to derive the hypothesis, but the second requires some defense because its truth is not immediately self-evident. Let me now sketch out the ideas on which it is based.

As noted above, one of the major "dangers" in failing to meet goals, whether they are externally imposed or chosen by the actor, is the potential threat to positive self-evaluation. But as William James noted as far back as 1890 (James, 1952), the drive for a positive view of self is of varying intensity depending on the importance of the activity involved. This idea becomes relevant to the present concern when we add Rosenberg's (1968) finding that people who rate themselves poorly in a particular

---

[12]This hypothesis is, of course, only relevant when actor is free to set his own goals, and that is often not the case. Frequently, at least the floor for acceptable performance is set by others, and actor is constrained to accept that. Such cases would be covered by Hypothesis 3 if the wording were altered slightly. That hypothesis was originally based upon the notion that when there was previous success, future success is expected. Now that we have an additional hypothesis stating that people with high self-evaluations expect to do better, there is another way it can be derived. Expectations of success should be high when actor's expected performance level exceeds other's definition of an acceptable performance level, and this is more likely to be true of people with high self-evaluations because they have higher levels of expected performance.

area tend to disvalue that area. People who have a low estimate of their school per-formance, for example, are going to come to the conclusion that being a good student is not too important, and not meeting the goals they set for themselves is not likely to prove particularly bothersome even though it lowers their self-evaluation. They "don't care" about having low evaluation of self as student because it is not an important area of endeavor for them. For people who have high self-evaluation, a failure would lead to a decrease in self-evaluation in an area they have come to con-sider important.

Another way of looking at this is to recall the relationship between specific self-evaluations and global self-esteem. If a person suffers a lowering of self-evaluation for an identity which is negatively evaluated to begin with, the drop in *self-esteem* will be small because, according to an extension of Rosenberg's principle, the evalua-tion given to that identity is likely to have little weight in the calculation of global self-esteem. But failure for the person with a high self-evaluation should have a major impact on self-esteem because of the importance he is likely to place on the relevant identity. [13]

Given the general assumption that people are aware of the consequences of their actions, Hypothesis 11 may be easily restated to assert that *actors are aware that failure in positively evaluated roles produces more distress* (Hypothesis 11'). And if we assume that *people will make greater efforts to avoid negative outcomes, the greater the distress they expect to experience should such outcomes come about* (Postulate N) this leads us to Hypothesis 12A: A particular person will be more task-oriented in those areas in which he has positive evaluations than he will be in negatively evaluated areas—all other things being equal. A similar notion can stand as Hypothesis 12B: For a particular activity, people with positive self-evaluations are more task-oriented (work harder) than people with negative self-evaluations.[14]

[13] There are, however, considerations which lead me to present this hypothesis very tenta-tively. The basic idea behind the prediction is that failure is most distressing when it is a barrier to an important goal. However, it is not that simple, and there are factors which suggest that people with low self-evaluation should experience more distress. The memory of many previous successes certainly acts to cushion the blow of a failure, and persons with low self-evaluations would not have such memories. In addition, constant failure may have a weakening effect so that any new failure may be too much to cope with even if it is expected and not particularly consequential.

[14] This hypothesis is also somewhat tentative and perhaps it should be qualified. People with positive self-evaluations expect success and if that expectation is strong enough it might reduce effort. Similarly, if self-evaluation is not too low, there may be a belief that success is possible but not likely, and this may increase effort. Such considerations suggest that effort would be greatest toward the middle of the self-evaluation range.

On the other hand, the higher the self-evaluation, the higher the performance must be before it is defined as adequate. It could be that this pattern ensures that desires will tend to outrun expectations at all levels. Overconfidence is a fact, but it does not seem to happen that often and this may be why. It may occur only when there is a ceiling on performance that is viewed as quite low by actor. In many activities, the sky is the limit of achievement.

Again, there is no clear solution because there are opposing tendencies whose strengths cannot be judged. My inclination is to go with the hypothesis as presented.

From this point, we can derive a final set of hypotheses by assuming that with ability and other things held constant, *those who are more task-oriented, those who work harder, accomplish more than those who are less hard-working* (Postulate O). When this is added to Hypothesis 12A, which says that people are more task-oriented in those areas in which they have positive evaluations, it suggests Hypothesis 13A: People do better in areas for which they have a positive self-evaluation, in part, at least, because they have a positive self-evaluation in those areas. When we combine Postulate O with Hypothesis 12B, which says that people with a positive self-evaluation work harder than those with a negative self-view, we find that we have derived, and therefore explained, a common tenet of educational theory, that is, for a particular activity, with ability held constant, the higher the self-evaluation the higher the performance level (Hypothesis 13B).

In sum, this theory suggests that the level of actor's self-evaluation has an important influence on action. Role may tell the person what to do, but self-evaluation influences much else—including the skill and dedication with which the role is played and even whether it is played or not.

I hope that the argument just presented has been persuasive and that the reader has considered the postulates self-evident and has agreed that the hypotheses are suggested by the postulates and the previously derived hypotheses. But even one who has no objection to the theory as it stands should remain unconvinced that it is valid, for as yet no evidence has been presented which bears upon it. A theory does not stand simply on its elegance, its plausibility, or the persuasiveness of its author. A theory is evaluated by different criteria. For example, we need go no further if its hypotheses do not follow from its postulates. If it meets that criterion, however, it still cannot be accepted until it is shown that its predictions are consistent with the available empirical evidence.

I will consider that evidence next, but first I would note what will soon become very clear—much of the relevant evidence is not yet available. It is rather strange, but researchers have devoted much attention to the sources of self-evaluations without first determining if variations in those evaluations have an important influence on behavior. Thus, there will be many gaps in the material which follows. What is to be found in the literature will, however, give some indication of the validity of the theory and will indicate where future efforts should be directed.

Tests of the Theory of Self-Evaluation Effects

The literature contains almost nothing in the way of an unambiguous test of the first hypothesis which states that people with high self-evaluations are more likely than those with low evaluations to expect positive evaluations from others. Harvey and Clapp (1965) do mention in passing that people with higher self-esteem expect to be rated higher by others ($r = .26$), but these data are not quite what a test of the hypothesis calls for because they deal with general self-esteem rather than with specific self-evaluation. This difficulty will recur frequently throughout this discussion and there is not much to be done about it since few studies measure self-evaluation. However, in some instances it will not be a serious problem because, as is the case here, the same prediction would be made for general self-esteem and specific self-evaluation. At other times it will be reasonable to assume that people with high global self-esteem also have high self-evaluations, and when that is so the problem will also be less serious.

Deutsch and Solomon (1959) also present data about people's expectations concerning the feedback they will get from others, but here too there is a problem which occurs frequently. The independent variable is neither self-esteem nor self-evaluation; it is the quality of the respondent's previous performance. In studies such as this we must assume that self-evaluation reflects actor's perception of his prior performance or in some cases, his view of other's evaluation of that performance. We have already seen that these are generally valid assumptions, and they are particularly reasonable in these experiments since the task is frequently an unusual one. The subjects are likely to have faced the task for the first time in the early stages of the experiment so they had no preexisting self-view which could complicate matters. Sometimes, as in the Deutsch and Solomon study, it is even shown that self-evaluation is related to success or failure on the pretest. Nonetheless, the value of these data is somewhat reduced by the fact that they do not provide a direct measure of the key variable.

With these caveats in mind, we may note that Deutsch and Solomon's (1959) results are consistent with the hypothesis. Those who had failed previously said they expected lower ratings from their teammates on such matters as their intelligence, team spirit, and their desirability as a friend and coworker.

Despite the paucity of "direct" evidence, it does seem appropriate to accept the hypothesis tentatively, for there are a number of indirect indications that it is true. For one thing, it is based upon the postulate that people with positive self-evaluations have received positive evaluations from others in the past, and we saw earlier that there is much reason to believe that this is so (see pages 86–87). Also, the other postulate which is needed to derive it seems rather self-evident. All of us seem to assume that life is orderly, and that the same conditions will produce the same effects.

One of the reasons that we lack a direct test of the idea is that many researchers simply assume that it is true. Rather than finding out whether subjects are "surprised" when they receive evaluations contrary to their self-views, investigators assume this will occur and focus their attention on the subjects' reactions to this assumed disconfirmation of expectations. Many studies in the cognitive dissonance tradition are of this type. (For a summary and bibliography, see Shrauger, 1975.)

Of course, the fact that researchers assume that the hypothesis is true doesn't prove anything. The relevant point is that the subject's actions make sense if one assumes it is correct. What happens is that people who receive feedback which is inconsistent with their self-views tend, to a greater or lesser degree, to reject these evaluations. People with high self-evaluations reject low evaluations and people with low self-evaluations reject or give unusually low weight to high received evaluations. With all other things being equal, consistent evaluations tend to be preferred.[15]

The standard explanation of this consistency effect is that the expectation that one will receive evaluations which are consistent with the self-view is so strong that people cannot make sense of the situation if the expectation proves to be wrong. Their attempts to reject or change this inconsistent information are efforts to make sense of the senseless by denying and altering unexpected and inexplicable "facts."

Let me repeat that the relevance for all this for the hypothesis under consideration is quite indirect. The hypothesis says that people expect evaluations that are consistent with their existing self-view; for example, people with high self-evaluations expect people to give them positive evaluations. Their actions if they do not receive such evaluations make sense if we assume that the hypothesis is valid which suggests that the hypothesis is, in fact, valid.

Hypothesis 2. When we turn to the literature bearing on Hypothesis 2 which states that people, regardless of their level of self-evaluation, desire to receive positive evaluations, we find a situation comparable to the one that pertains to the previous hypothesis. There is little or no direct evidence bearing upon it, but a considerable body of indirect evidence is consistent with the idea. This evidence has been discussed in considerable detail in my discussion of the desire for a positive view of self (see pages 102–05), and it should be sufficient to remind the reader that most studies show that positive evaluations are weighted more heavily; negative evaluators are devalued, disliked, and avoided, and negative evaluations are remembered less accurately.

In addition, if we use a different perspective in looking at some of the data in studies of the consistency effect, we often see clear evidence of a positivity effect, that is, a preference for positive evaluations. For example, in the Deutsch and Solomon

---

[15] A few investigators have reported very strong consistency effects. Deutsch and Solomon (1959) found, for example, that women who presumably had low self-esteem liked those who gave them positive feedback no better than they liked those who gave them negative evaluations, and on some indices they rated the latter more favorably. In a study which has been the subject of great attention, Aronson and Carlsmith (1962) reported that people with low self-evaluations actually changed many of their responses when they had a chance to, if they had been told they had done well. Those with low self-evaluations who had done poorly changed fewer responses.

It must be stressed that attempts to replicate these extreme findings have not been very successful. Most studies do, however, show more modest consistency effects. For example, Lowin and Epstein (1965) found that among those with low expectancies, those who had done poorly changed more responses than the lows who had done well, but the people in this latter group did change many of their responses. They changed almost as many as the high expectancy subject who had done poorly, and more than those who had high expectancy and had done well (see also Shrauger, 1975; Brock et al., 1965). Thus, the low-high group's actions suggest they were not as satisfied with their high scores as they "should have been." There are also indications that information which is consistent with self-perceptions is more accurately perceived and remembered; people with high self-evaluations (but not those who are low) ascribe greater validity to evaluations received when they are consistent with their self-views; consistent evaluations have greater effects on self-esteem, etc. (Shrauger, 1975).

(1959) study there was a strong consistency effect, but for those who received consistent evaluations, the positive evaluator was liked better than the negative evaluator and the same was true for those who received inconsistent evaluations. Thus, there was a positivity effect with consistency controlled. Even in the Aronson and Carlsmith (1962) study, which found a very strong consistency effect, direction has a significant influence. In studies which fail to replicate the Aronson and Carlsmith consistency findings, the relevance of direction is also seen. (See, for example, Lown and Epstein, 1965.) Finally, the study by Harvey and Clapp (1965) also shows clear direction effects; deviations from expectations in a favorable direction caused greater changes in the dependent variables than discrepancies in the unfavorable direction. (See also Sigall and Aronson, 1969; see also page 196.)

The matter cannot be left at this, however. Although the hypothesis seems to be valid as a generalization, one must make some important qualifications. For one thing, other characteristics of the evaluation also influence its reception. As has been noted, important among these is the degree of consistency between the received evaluation and expectations. Furthermore, for people with low self-evaluations, there is a conflict between the consistency and direction effects and for them the direction effect is going to be reduced. This means that the strength of the desire for positive evaluations varies "across persons."

Hypothesis 3. The next hypothesis speaks of expectations of success, but this is a rather vague phrase if it is not specified. The term will have two meanings as used here. A person will be said to have a higher expectation of success if he expects to do better or to achieve more than another person. (This is the sense used in Hypothesis 3A.) Expecting success also may mean that if two persons have the same goal, the person with the higher expectation of success is the one who is more confident of reaching that goal. Let us consider the data which bear upon both interpretations of the hypothesis.

Gordon's (n.d.) study shows clearly and directly that adolescents with higher self-esteem expect to achieve more in the occupational world. With several other variables controlled, global self-esteem is positively correlated with the level of the job the respondent expects to have after finishing school. Rosenberg (1965) also finds support for the hypothesis in the occupational expectations of young people. Adolescents with high self-esteem are more likely to expect to be successful in their jobs, and they are more likely to say that their job will be at the level they wish it to be.

There are also laboratory studies which present data of a very different kind to support the hypothesis. In one study by Diggory (1966), students were asked to estimate their chances of passing a screening test for a "space science program" and they also rated themselves as good or poor candidates for the position they were seeking. In another study he had the subjects evaluate their psychomotor ability and estimate their chances of passing a test in that area. In both studies, estimated probability of success and self-evaluation varied concomitantly. In fact, the correspondence was so great that Diggory felt justified in adopting estimated probability of success as an index of self-evaluation for the rest of the study.

Feather's (1966, 1968) findings are even more impressive. Two groups of subjects did five trial anagrams and then ten others. Half the subjects were given very easy trial problems, while the other half got very difficult ones. Given the differential success rates that occurred during the trial period, it seems likely that the two groups differed in their self-evaluations at the time that they started the group of ten. Before they attempted each of these they were asked to estimate their chances of getting it right. Throughout the experiment those who had early success placed their probability of success at a higher level than those who had been in the group whose trial anagrams were unlikely to be solved in the time given. (See also Brickman, Linsenmeir, and McCareins, 1976; Feather and Saville, 1967.)

At first glance, some of Ryckman and Rodda's (1972) data seem to oppose the hypothesis, but on closer inspection this turns out not to be the case. Their design is quite comparable to Feather's and they also find that early success leads to an expectation of success. But they also relate general level of self-esteem to predictions of success and find that the low *self-esteem* people had higher expectations. This is one of the cases, I believe, in which self-esteem cannot substitute for self-evaluation. The hypothesis implies that people expect to do well in areas which involve abilities they think they have. General self-esteem can be used in studies of occupational success because self-esteem probably says something about self-evaluation as worker, but self-esteem tells us little or nothing about evaluation of the somewhat special ability of anagram solver.[16] Of course, it is not clear why low self-esteem people said they would do better; the authors' discussion is not convincing. At any rate, however, the findings do not clearly oppose the hypothesis.

Hypothesis 4.   I have found no data on Hypothesis 4, which deals with expectations of utilitarian reward, but it is closely related to the one just considered. Let us go on, therefore, to the next hypothesis.

Hypothesis 5.   The several versions of this hypothesis have in common the notion that people prefer to use identities for which they have positive self-evaluations. The assumptions upon which it is based suggest that the reason for this is that by using such identities they expect future rewards—utilitarian rewards and the rewards of being favorably evaluated and of having a positive self-evaluation.

One kind of data bearing upon the hypothesis is to be found in the literature on school dropouts. I would interpret the reported association between a low academic self-concept and early leaving of high school (Malec et al., 1969) as evidence for the form of the hypothesis which states that people are less likely to remain in a situation if they have a low evaluation of their ability to play the role called for by the situation. The same interpretation would seem appropriate for Coombs' (1969) finding in his longitudinal study of dating couples that there is a direct relationship between self-evaluation of self as a date and number of dates. It is clear in this case, however, as Coombs notes, that self-evaluation is both cause and effect of dating experience.

---

[16] This wouldn't be true if they took skill at anagram solving to be an index of an ability such as I.Q.

In addition, it is quite obvious from general observation that people quit, that is, stop playing certain roles, when they fail and have low self-evaluations. If there is any doubt about it, it may be noted that Hoppe found that tendency in the laboratory as long ago as 1931 (Diggory, 1966), and Diggory's (1966) data also show it clearly. Also relevant is S.C. Jones' (1968) finding that when given an opportunity for further association with a group, those who were positively evaluated while in the group were more likely to accept the invitation.

In other versions, the hypothesis is stated slightly differently. It is postulated that when a person is faced with a choice between using various identities, he will choose the one that has previously been associated with success and/or a high self-evaluation. Also, if there is a choice between using or not using an identity, those with positive self-evaluations and previous success are more likely to choose to use it.

The evidence of everyday observation is so strong in this area that the relative lack of formal evidence may be forgiven. Students do not typically choose a subject for a major if they have failed the introductory course in it; the people who sign up for competitions are more likely to have done well in such contests in the past as compared with those who do not enter—assuming, of course, that all other things are equal. In fact, the preference that low self-esteem people have for cooperative rather than competitive activities possibly stems from their probable lack of previous success in competition (Pepitone, 1964).

Another form of the hypothesis states that if people can play a particular role in any one of several situations, they will choose the setting and interaction partner which have been associated with success and positive evaluations. For example, an actor who can play tennis at Court A or B with opponent C or D, will choose on the basis of previous experiences in those places and with those people.

One source of support for this hypothesis is found in the literature on affiliation and interpersonal attraction. It has often been noted that people like and prefer to associate with people who like them in return (Dittes, 1959; Backman and Secord, 1959; Jones, Gergen, and Davis, 1962; Aronson and Linder, 1965; see page 193). To be liked is a goal most of us have, so it would seem that if we are liked by a person we would define our interaction with him as successful, and thus we would wish to continue the association. Also, since people who like us are likely to give us positive evaluations, our experience with them is likely to have been associated with positive self-evaluations—another kind of success.

It has also frequently been noted that people with high self-esteem show a general tendency to like and accept people, and wish to associate with them (Fromm, 1939, 1956; Rogers, 1951; 1961; Rosenberg, 1965; McCandless, 1967; Baron, 1974). This is also consistent with the idea being considered here. A person with low global self-esteem has probably not had much in the way of successful interaction, and generalizing from his experience, he assumes that he will have as little success in future interaction. Such a person tends to reject people in general, because he assumes that things will probably turn out badly regardless of whom he chooses.

As it is derived and stated, the hypothesis suggests the decision among alternatives will be based upon previous direct experience. The data show that is so, but in concluding I would also note that in some instances people believe they can predict the likely outcomes of their choices even when they have not had direct experience, and they decide on the basis of these predictions. In other words, actual self-evaluation and previous success affect choice, but so do anticipated self-evaluations and success.

The validity of this notion is indicated by Backman and Secord's (1968) finding that students prefer marital and occupational roles for which they believe they possess the required traits. Similarly, people in majors such as nursing, education, and engineering tend to say they have the traits that are generally associated with the occupations one enters with those majors. Their decisions are not based on having previously experienced positive self-evaluations and success as nurses, teachers, or engineers. Because they are students they have never used the identities, and therefore they have no directly relevant previous experience. My assumption is that they assume their experience and self-evaluation will be positive because they believe they have the necessary traits for success in the roles, and it is this belief that explains their choice.

Hypothesis 6. The evidence bearing upon the relationship between self-esteem or self-evaluation and conformity in social situations is quite extensive (see McGuire, 1969 and Marlowe and Gergen, 1969 for summaries). And, as is usually the case when there is a quantity of data available on a particular topic, the results of the various studies are in conflict with each other. The most frequent finding is that people with low self-evaluations are more subject to social influence, as I hypothesized earlier. (See, for example, Janis, 1953–54; Janis and Rife, 1959; Divesta, 1959; Hochbaum, 1954; Rosenberg, 1965; Diggory, 1966; Cohen, 1959.) Other studies, however, do not find such a relationship or find it only for certain parts of the sample or only for some of the measures. Janis and Field (1959), and Silverman, Ford, and Morganti (1966), for example, found the inverse relationship only for men. Among the women in the latter study those with a medium level of self-esteem showed the most suggestibility (see also Cox and Bauer, 1964). Lesser and Abelson (1959) report varying patterns depending on the measure of self-evaluation used (see also Berkowitz and Lundy, 1957).

The explanation offered by McGuire (1969) accounts for most of this variation in a plausible way and it does not require major alterations in the theory. He suggests that the degree of persuasibility is a function of two factors: the subject's tendency to yield after perceiving a stimulus to do so and the likelihood that the subject will "receive" the message that attempts to bring about change. This latter factor will be related to motivational factors, attention span, learning ability, etc. He further postulates that people with low self-esteem are more likely to "yield" but are less likely to "get the message."

If this is true, people with low self-evaluation would turn out to be more conforming only when the situation was simple and no one could miss the suggestion. In this situation message reception would be constant and their high tendency to yield would be discernible. *When* it was possible to fail to receive the message, people with low self-evaluation would be likely to do so and therefore they would not change much. In terms of their definition of the situation they would be under no pressure to change. Those with high levels of self-evaluation would feel the pressure, but they would also show low rates of change because of their low yielding tendency. Those with moderate levels of self-evaluation will feel the pressure and will have less resistance to it and therefore will show the greatest change. If the message is extremely complex, only those with high self-esteem will perceive it, and though they may not change much they will change more than the others—producing a positive relation. Several studies (Gelfand, 1962; Gollob and Dittes, 1965; Nisbett and Gordon, 1967; Silverman, Ford, and Morganti, 1966; Gergen and Bauer, 1967) varied characteristics of the message and produced findings generally consistent with this interpretation.

My earlier theoretical discussion was clearly focused on the yielding factor. It was implicitly assumed that the actor would be aware of the efforts to gain his compliance and that still seems to be a reasonable assumption for the majority of real life situations. But be that as it may, the results of the empirical tests show the need for sharpening the hypothesis. It is now clear it must be limited. It might better be stated as: Assuming that all subjects are aware that others wish them to conform, people with low self-evaluations are more likely to do so; or, people with low self-evaluations are more likely to yield to *felt* pressures to conform.

Some of the studies which were contrary to the hypothesis as originally stated now become irrelevant because it seems clear that message reception was not constant. It is not clear, however, that all negative evidence can be explained away in this manner. Differences in reception are not normally measured, and thus one has to judge whether "everyone must have known." At any rate, the rewording does make it possible to rule out much of the contrary evidence, and thus we may have reasonable confidence in the validity of the hypothesis.

Hypothesis 7. In contrast to the situation regarding self-esteem and conformity, there is consistent evidence that the higher the self-evaluation the greater the attempts to influence others (Hypothesis 7). Apparently, the major factors which lead a person to exert influence are related to self-evaluation in a consistent way.

Studies of young people show, to begin with, that those with high self-esteem tend to be leaders in their groups. Coopersmith (1967) reports that people with high self-esteem are more likely than those with low esteem to be active participants rather than listeners in group discussion and they are more willing to say unpopular things. Rosenberg (1965) reports similar patterns. Adolescents with high levels of self-esteem are described by others as having those traits associated with assertiveness, and they themselves report that they are leaders in their schools—they participate more extensively in extracurricular activities, they belong to more clubs,[17] they are more likely to have held office in a school organization, they say they are active participants in school discussions, they see themselves as opinion leaders, etc. Rosenberg also shows that at least part of the reason for the low participation of those with low self-esteem is due to their low opinions of themselves and their belief that others do not like or respect them (see also Thompson, 1972).

As with much of the self-report data in this area, it is not always clear in the

---

[17]Coopersmith's (1967) study fails to replicate this finding.

material just presented whether self-esteem is the cause or the effect. This problem is reduced to varying degrees in the several laboratory studies which bear upon the matter. S.C. Jones (1968), for example, shows that under appropriate conditions people who are given positive evaluations in a group increase their rate of participation. Though self-evaluation is not measured directly, the implications are clear.

Particularly important are studies by Hastorf (1970) and Gergen (1971). They show directly that events during an interaction can alter people's evaluation of self and this change can increase their attempts to influence others. There were several experiments, but let us consider two of the most successful ones. During a preliminary period (Gergen, 1971) all participants were given a signal which meant they should feel free to participate in the conversation. Then in the second period the person who had been quietest in the first stage was given the signal to participate and, without his knowledge, the others were 'told' to refrain from talking. Thus, the quiet person was forced into being the center of attraction. In a third period all were given the "go-ahead" signal and the originally quiet person turned out to be one of the most active contributors, and on the testimony of the others, one of the most influential. The opportunity to be a "star" in the second period apparently had an ego-boosting effect which turned the retiring person into a dominant one. In another experiment (Hastorf, 1970) a similar effect was obtained on the person who was originally ranked next to last in leadership by the other group members. His status was raised by giving him positive feedback when he spoke and the others negative feedback when they contributed.

There are also experiments which use pairs of people who have known levels of self-evaluation. Both Thomas and Burdick (cited in Cohen, 1959) and Cohen (1959) report that the participants perceived more efforts at influence when people of high self-evaluation were paired than was the case for pairs composed of low self-evaluation people. In the Cohen study, there were also low-high pairs and in these the persons with high self-evaluations always had a greater effect on the outcome. In general, the hypothesis receives overwhelming support.

Hypothesis 8. It has already been established that people with higher self-evaluations expect to do better at relevant tasks than persons whose self-evaluations are low. The question now to be faced is whether high self-evaluation people also aspire to greater achievement. Clearly, one does not directly follow from the other. In order to derive the hypothesis regarding aspiration it was necessary to postulate that those who are capable of high achievement come to desire high achievement. This is not necessarily so, and thus the aspiration hypothesis requires its own test. The evidence bearing upon expectations does not settle the matter.

Direct evidence bearing upon the hypothesis is presented by Gordon (n.d.). He finds that there is a relation between several measures of self-evaluation and measures of educational and occupational aspirations among black and white students even with other variables controlled. Cohen (1959) and Coopersmith (1967) present confirming evidence. It must be noted, however, that despite the consistent general trend, in the

Gordon study the correlations tend to be rather low and vary depending on the measures and subgroup involved.

It will be recalled that I earlier discussed experiments in which subjects were told how a group of people ranked and then they were permitted to choose which person's exact score they would be told (see pages 131-33). Implicit in these studies is the idea that the standing of the person chosen tells something about the actor's aspirations. Actors tend to choose people they wish to resemble, and if an actor chooses the highest ranking person it suggests that his aspirations are high. Actor's choice of a "comparison other" tells us something about what he thinks he should be accomplishing and what he hopes to accomplish. If this is so, and if the hypothesis under consideration is also true, it would follow that people with high self-evaluations should choose high-ranking people more often than those with low evaluations do. People with high evaluations should want to know what it takes to be high ranking. Those with low self-evaluations should be less interested in doing very well, and they should, therefore, have little need to know what an excellent performance is.

Wilson and Benner (1971) found that this derived hypothesis does hold as a general rule. In their sample taken as a whole, those with high self-esteem did show the greater tendency to choose the top-ranking person as their comparison other. However, there were some exceptions, some of the differences were not statistically significant, and under some conditions the expected differences were not found. When differences were not found for males, the "problem" tended to be that the low self-esteem group was showing "too strong" a tendency to choose high-ranking persons. When the prediction was not supported for women, it was apparently due to high self-evaluation women picking lower-ranking people more often than would be expected.

Given the general support it received, I am inclined to accept the hypothesis as stated. Nonetheless, these findings do remind us again that all of the hypotheses are certainly not universal truths; there are exceptions to all of them. In this case, it seems that Shibutani (1961) may have been right if he had men in mind when he suggested that "excessive ambition" may be a way of compensating for a low level of self-esteem. While certainly this is also the case for some women, Wilson and Benner's (1971) results suggest it is not as common for them. For women, the common deviation from the trend is that high self-evaluation women will not take a chance and act consistently with their self-view. This is particularly likely to be so, this study finds, when the women had to make their choices known in public. (As might be expected, low self-evaluation men were more likely to set their goals "inappropriately" high when their choice was a private one.)[18]

Hypotheses 9, 10, and 11. The hypotheses that people who do not meet goals suffer costs will not be evaluated here. They do not predict differences between people with different levels of self-evaluation and serve largely as an introduction to Hypothesis 11 which states that the amount of stress experienced is directly related to actor's

[18]Coopersmith's (1967) findings also remind us that the effect should be expected only when the choice has some significance for the subject. He expresses no surprise that there is no relation between self-esteem and the goal set for a beanbag toss.

level of self-evaluation. In general, it is predicted that people with high self-evaluation would have more of an investment in succeeding, would lose more if they failed, and thus would suffer more distress if they did fail.

The evidence bearing upon this issue is rather mixed. For example, Van Ostrand (1960) and Harvey and Clapp (1965) report that people who had *low* expectations were apparently more hurt when they got feedback which was worse than they expected, and Coopersmith's (1967) low self-esteem subjects report they are more sensitive to criticism (see also Jones et al., 1959). On the other hand, Diggory (1966) concludes that people who originally had a high self-evaluation lose confidence in themselves at a faster rate after failure than do people with low self-evaluations. However, though Diggory uses it as such, a loss of confidence is not quite an index of distress. Another study (Solley and Stagner, 1956) measures distress by measuring perspiration rates when the subject faces an insoluble task and comes to the conclusion that distress is unrelated to self-evaluation. But Feather and Saville (1967) find that as amount of failure goes up, anxiety and disappointment go up faster for those with higher expectations.

In regard to the corollary to this hypothesis, which states that people with high self-evaluations *expect* to feel more distress *if* they fail, the evidence is not much more consistent. Several studies (Thompson, 1972; Fitts, 1971; Coopersmith, 1967) show that people with low self-esteem are more anxious. This may, however, not be due to their fear of feeling distress if they fail, but rather due to their tendency to expect to fail. Much clearer in their implications and *contrary* to the hypothesis are findings reported by Modigliani (1968) and Rosenberg (1965). The former showed that low self-evaluation subjects are more likely to say that they would experience embarrassment under particular circumstances and Rosenberg found that people with low self-esteem were more likely to say they were easily embarrassed, that they were very bothered to learn that others had a poor opinion of them, etc. However, several of Modigliani's correlations were not statistically significant and Horowitz (1962) found that high self-evaluation people remembered more embarrassing incidents, suggesting they were more affected by them. Archibald and Cohen (1971) report no significant relation between self-evaluation and embarrassment, and the relation of embarrassment to self-esteem varies markedly depending on the conditions.

With evidence of this kind it is difficult to reach even a tentative conclusion. Certainly I would not begin to suggest that the literature provides support for the hypothesis. At the same time, it does not seem appropriate to accept that the association is opposite to that hypothesized. More research is necessary before a decision can be reached, but it should also be noted that the early returns would probably not lead a betting person to put his money on the original hypothesis. The doubts about it expressed earlier seem well-founded (see footnote 13).

A further consideration of the literature leads to some additional thoughts as to why the hypothesis is not faring well. The prediction is partly based upon the assumption that if there is a failure, people with high self-evaluations stand to lose more and therefore will experience more distress. However, if people with high self-evaluation are less likely to perceive that they have failed when they have in fact done so, the predicted greater distress would not necessarily follow. Denial of failure can actually prevent the occurrence of some of the painful experiences which usually accompany failure. Lowered self-esteem would fit here. Other consequences of failure —for example, the loss of utilitarian rewards—will occur whether or not the failure is recognized. However, if one does not perceive that failure has occurred, the distress associated with these consequences may not be felt at the time of failure. It will be delayed until there is awareness that these consequences will occur or have occurred. This may happen some time after the actual failure, and thus the studies which measure distress at time of failure may not pick them up.

Several authors have suggested that low and high self-esteem people differ in their reactions to and perceptions of failure situations. Cohen (1959) suggests for example, that:

> Those with low self-esteem characteristically expecting failure, may be more vulnerable to the effects of failure experiences. (104)

> Persons of high self-esteem appear to take on early in life a defensive mode which handles challenging experience by a strong self-protective facade. They repress, deny, ignore, or turn about their potentially disturbing impulses. (116)

> Persons with avoidance defenses can turn away from experiences which reflect unfavorably on their self-picture. Such persons may emphasize enhancing experiences thereby preserving an insulated but positive self-picture. Persons [of low self-esteem] whose defenses are more expressive may not be able to deal so selectively with external stimuli. (117)

There is considerable empirical support for these notions. Stotland et al. (1957) and Cohen (1959) report evidence that suggests that people with high self-esteem tend to minimize the extent of their failures. For example, people were asked to rate their own performances after they had been told that they had failed a task. The results show the higher the original level of self-esteem, the higher the self-rating on the task that had been failed. Also relevant are the following findings:

> 1. Subjects who perceived themselves as having high competence overestimated their performance relative to that of their partners when their partner had actually done better than they. People with low self-estimates tended to recall that their partners had done better than they regardless of who had actually done better (Shrauger, 1975).

> 2. When faced with an insoluble task, high self-esteem people's comments focused on difficulty of the task, "lows" referred to themselves. This suggests that those with high esteem saw the difficulty as external to themselves and the others attributed the problem to their own inadequacy (Solley and Stagner, 1956).

> 3. Under some conditions, at least, high esteem subjects were more influenced by potentially gratifying and self-enhancing communication while people with low self-esteem were more affected by self-threatening messages (Leventhal and Perloe, 1962).

> 4. Once they had made a choice, people with low self-evaluations were less likely to avoid information which would indicate their choice was a poor one (Malewski, 1962).

5. High self-esteem people are more affected by success; "lows" react to failure more strongly (Shrauger and Rosenberg, 1970).

I don't mean to suggest that there is any certainty that low esteem people suffer more distress when they fail or that if they do it is because of their inability to deny failure. Future research will provide the answer. It is clear, however, that this research must attempt to handle the problem of differential perception by using perceived failure as a variable. In anticipation of such research, however, it is also clear that the original hypothesis should be reworded: When people perceive they have failed or believe they are going to fail, those with high esteem will experience more distress.

Hypothesis 12. Since we cannot at this time assume the validity of Hypothesis 11, the major prop is removed from Hypothesis 12 which states that people work harder in those areas for which their self-evaluations are higher. I will, however, test Hypothesis 12 anyway. For one thing, if it proves to be valid it will reflect back on the question of the correctness of Hypothesis 11, since an hypothesis which is valid suggests that the hypotheses from which it is deduced are also valid. Of course, this will not settle the question of the validity of Hypothesis 11. Hypothesis 12 could be true even if the motivation for the greater effort were not the fear of distress. There may be other ways of deriving Hypothesis 12 which I have not presented. However, "favorable" evidence for Hypothesis 12 will, to some degree at least, increase our confidence in the earlier hypothesis and negative evidence for Hypothesis 12 would suggest strongly that Hypothesis 11 should be abandoned.

Contrary to what is probably the intuitive expectation, the data generally show that people with high self-evaluation do put out more effort. Hypothesis 12 does receive support. For example, after failure on an anagram test people with low self-esteem showed less persistence during the rest of the experiment (Shrauger and Sorman, 1977). Also, though the matter is complicated, as a general rule it appears that as probability of success and self-evaluations decline, so does effort as measured by time required to complete a task and by muscle action potential (Diggory, 1966; Diggory et al., 1964).

However, despite its general support by the literature, the hypothesis seems to require some qualification. To begin with, it would seem that the predicted relationship will be seen only if the task offers some challenge. If the task is too easy, those with high self-evaluation will feel—probably correctly—that they can master it with little effort. On the other hand, those with low self-evaluations will view an easy task as an opportunity to finally get some positive feedback, and they will work hard to succeed at what is likely to be defined by them as a task that can be mastered *if* they work hard at it.

The validity of this idea is indicated by Sigall and Gould's (1977) findings. Subjects were allowed to decide how many practice problems they would work on before taking a test, and the number chosen was taken as an indication of how hard the subject was willing to work. When the researcher was described as someone difficult to please, the people with high self-evaluations chose to work on more problems than did those with low evaluations, but when the investigator was easy to please those with low self-esteem chose to practice more.

What it seems to add up to is that people are willing to work only if they think it is necessary to do so to achieve goals[19] and only if they believe that to do so will increase the likelihood that they will succeed. Thus it would seem appropriate to limit the hypothesis to tasks of some difficulty, because if the task is too easy people with high self-evaluations will consider it a waste of time to work hard. This limitation of the hypothesis does not represent a significant loss of generality. Most of the situations which would be of interest would fall within the purview of the hypothesis as limited.

Hypothesis 13. The final hypothesis follows rather directly from the notion that high self-esteem leads people to work hard, for it simply states that the hard work pays off. It predicts that people of equal ability who differ in self-evaluation will differ in achievement because self-evaluation influences effort, and effort affects achievement.

Because of the specific nature of the hypothesis, much of the evidence which is usually cited in its support turns out to be irrelevant under closer scrutiny. Many studies show a correlation between self-concept and achievement measures such as academic grades (Bachman, 1970; Coopersmith, 1967; Brookover et al., 1964; 1965; Rosenberg, 1965; Coombs and Davies, 1966; Borislow, 1962; Rosenberg and Simmons, n.d. See Hamachek, 1971; and Johnson, 1970 for discussions of other studies). Those with high self-esteem also do better at learning to pair digits with arbitrary symbols (Shrauger and Rosenberg, 1970), and they even count clicks more accurately (League and Jackson, 1964).

These studies are all consistent with the hypothesis but they are inconclusive. For one thing, both self-evaluation and performance may reflect differences in ability— the correlation between performance and self-evaluation may be spurious. Some of the studies do not control ability, and therefore they produce ambiguous results.

Equally important, it is not clear from these studies that self-evaluation has any causal significance. We know performance affects self-evaluation and it may be that the reported correlations are *solely* due to this. For the hypothesis to be accepted it must be shown that there is also an effect of self-evaluation upon performance.

A number of studies whose results are relatively unambiguous suggest that self-evaluation *does* have an independent effect. Most convincing are the several studies which show that people who are *given* success in early trials of laboratory studies do better in later trials. (Shrauger and Rosenberg, 1970; Shrauger, 1972; Ryckman and Rodda, 1972; Feather, 1963; 1966; 1968; Brickman et al., 1976). Since the succeeders and the failures were arbitrarily chosen, the differences in later success could not be due to differences in basic ability, and the time order ensures that self-evaluation could not be the effect of performance in the later trials. What must have happened was that their early success increased their self-evaluations, which caused the greater success at the end of the experiment. There is also evidence that low self-esteem people react less well to "failure stress" (Miller and Worchel, 1956–57; Schalon, 1968), although the studies disagree as to whether high or moderate self-evaluation people react best.

---

[19] See footnote 14.

At any rate, this would suggest that the ultimate performance levels of low self-esteem should be low.

With the verification of this final hypothesis, I can now turn to an evaluation of the theory as a whole. The first thing that must be noted is that the "test" has been a weak one. This is true in a variety of senses. Many of the data cited are only indirectly relevant to the hypothesis, and in many cases the literature bearing upon an hypothesis is sparse even when indirect evidence is used. Methodologically, most of the studies are weak—very few of them are multivariate analyses which control relevant variables. And finally it should be noted that each hypothesis was tested separately; it was not possible to test the system of hypotheses. We know that self-evaluation affects performance, but we can't be sure that the theory is correct when it suggests that this relation is due to the action of the intervening variables suggested. To fully test the theory would require a specially designed study utilizing the method of path analysis.

While recognizing that because of these problems any conclusions must be extremely tentative, I would contend that the theory stood up rather well. Certainly, the data made clear that some of the hypotheses were stated too baldly and that some of them hold only under particular circumstances. Nonetheless, with the possible exception of Hypothesis 11, they seem to be valid as general rules. The data suggest the system needs refinement—clearly, in some instances relevant considerations were not taken into account. But the evidence does not show that the postulates require major revisions.

PROBLEMATIC INTERACTION SITUATIONS

Given the complexity of the material in the preceding pages, it may be necessary to remind the reader that the routine interactions I have been considering can usually be easily handled by actors. The decisions to be made usually cause no problems, for the issues themselves are simple and actor is likely to have faced them frequently. In many of these situations, actor may have little conscious awareness that the processes I have described are going on. *It is much more difficult to describe and analyze a routine interaction than it is to engage in it.*

This is not true, however, for problematic interaction situations. In such cases, the issues tend to be complex, the actor is unlikely to have ready-made solutions easily available, and the encounter will be unsuccessful unless the actor is highly aware of what is going on and skillful in handling the situation.

It should be emphasized that the difficulties of problematic situations do not arise from lack of experience with them. The reader should not think of routine situations as normal and the problematic as the exceptions. Both types are encountered with great frequency. The interaction difficulties associated with problematic situations are not due to a lack of acquaintance with this *type* of encounter. They are difficult to solve because the issues they raise are inherently more complicated, and because they involve actor in complex processes that do not emerge in routine situations.

In this chapter I will attempt only an introduction to problematic situations, describing some of the major kinds of problems that occur in interaction. In the following chapters, I will consider three issues:

1. What specific circumstances tend to produce each of the problems?
2. What problem-solving techniques are typically used by actors for each?
3. What are the factors which influence the technique chosen in a particular case?

Problems of Definition

Numerous problems can arise at the earliest stage of interaction at which point actor is attempting to develop a preliminary definition of the situation. In routine situations each element of the definition is easily determined; in problematic situations each element is a potential source of difficulty. For example, nothing might seem easier than to define the self for an encounter, but frequently this can cause actor great difficulty. In some cases, the cues are insufficient or actor is unable to decipher them, and as a result he has "no idea" regarding which identity is appropriate. In other instances there are many cues, but some point toward one identity and others to a different one, and thus there is no clear basis for choosing among several identities in the repertoire. In interaction with a younger superior, it may not be obvious to some whether the occupational or age identity is called for; a graduate assistant may have difficulty choosing between a colleague and student identity when interacting with the full-time faculty, and so forth.

The opposite situation can also cause difficulties. Rather than having a plethora of apparently applicable identities, actor may not have the appropriate identity in his repertoire. This is not the same as the first case mentioned. Here actor knows what identity is called for, but he cannot apply it to himself. The "immortal sergeant" syndrome is of this type. Lifetime followers are often unable to take on the role of leader in an emergency because all their previous experience makes it "impossible" to think of themselves as anything but the transmitter of others' orders. It may not even be a matter of not knowing what to do. Actor may have had ample opportunity to observe the role being played. The difficulty is that actor cannot adopt the identity which would allow him to put that knowledge into practice.

Similar problems can arise when actor attempts to identify other. There may be no cues as to other's identity, the cues may suggest several identities, or actor may be unable to conceive of other in the terms suggested by the available cues, as, for example, the older person who cannot define "that kid" as the boss.

Problems of other-definition and self-definition are likely to go together, of course. If actor cannot define himself, he is unlikely to be able to define other. Or, to put it the other way, once other is defined it will be easy to define self. Certain pairs of identities go together, and to decide on one suggests what the other should be. If I decide that I should use my friend identity, it is clear to me that other should also use the friend identity.

Deciding on an identity for self and other is only part of the task. If actor is to act with any confidence and if interaction is to go smoothly, identification must be beyond this. Actor must, for example, discern what identity other has chosen for himself and for actor. Given the fact that determining these aspects depends upon role taking, which is, we know, an error-prone process, this element of the definition is likely to cause actor difficulty. The problem is often increased by the fact that other frequently attempts to hide his identity choice from actor, and if other has chosen to present a false self he will make positive efforts to mislead actor about his "real" identity.

It must be emphasized, as Strauss (1969) does, that this process of identifying is not simply a matter of deciding who the persons "are" in some objective sense. Actor may have no doubts that he is a teacher, a male, a father, an American, and many other things as well, and he may have a comparable list for other. The difficult task is to decide which of these identities is the right one for the current encounter.

When it comes to roles, goals, and the other elements in the definition of the situation, similar problems can occur. Even when actor has no difficulty defining the identities to be used, complications may arise over defining roles, goals, presented selves, and so on. First, I will consider problems of role-definition, a topic of major interest to scholars in the field.

Roles are, of course, learned, and it is usual that a person is taught the proper roles at the same time that he or she adds the associated identity to the repertoire. And when identities for others are learned, appropriate roles are similarly learned. But this is not always the case. People can have identities for self and other for which they do not know the roles. These would be cases, to use the jargon, of "incomplete socialization." And in such cases the interaction is likely to be complicated. Roles do not provide detailed instructions on how to act, but they do provide guidelines. In the absence of such guidelines, actor's job is made markedly more difficult. In many instances, of course, he will be able to make a go of the interaction, but in contrast to routine situations there is likely to be a lack of confidence, considerable tentativeness in his actions, and undoubtedly, missteps.

An incident from *The Killer Angels,* a novel about the Civil War, illustrates this situation. When faced with mutinous soldiers, Colonel Joshua Chamberlain had no doubt that he was an officer and a leader of men. His commission from the Governor of Maine and the behavior of all those around him took care of any identity problems he might have had. But in this situation, he had to sit "for a long moment trying to function. He was thirty-four years old, and on this day one year ago he had been a professor of rhetoric at Bowdoin University. He had no idea what to do" (Shaara, 1975: 19).

Although it has been given less attention by interactionists than problems associated with roles and identities, the defining of goals is equally important and equally problematic. The nature of the problems are, however, analogous to those associated with identities and roles, and so I need not devote much discussion to them. Let me simply note that actor must decide what goals are legitimate and attainable for him, given the particular circumstances of the encounter; and he may see no feasible goals or too many possibilities. And, similarly, to interact effectively he must know what other's goals are, and this too may not be clear.

The final elements in the definition of the situation involve decisions concerning the self to be presented and the actions to be undertaken to convey the image. The problems associated with the other elements of the definition of the situation can also occur for presentations of self, and I will not cover that ground again. However, there is a special issue which requires some consideration.

In practically all interaction situations, actor has to decide whether to present a true or a false self—whether or not to convey an image that is consistent with his self-view. I would consider a decision in favor of a false self sufficient to make the interaction problematic.

The reason for this classification is that in a routine situation the definitional elements are congruent with each other. For a situation to be routine the various parts of the definition must mesh. By definition, when a false self is presented there is inconsistency in the elements; the identity does not correspond to the presented self. Furthermore, situations which involve the presentation of a false self should be classified as problematic because they are usually complicated. It may not be easy to get people to see us as we see ourselves, but for most of us it is even more difficult to get others to see us as we know we are not.

By now, it should certainly be clear that social life can be difficult. What has been presented thus far, however, is by no means the end of it. Even if actor and other can each define the relevant elements of the interaction to his own satisfaction, the encounter need not be routine. If at the outset actor and other define the same element of the situation differently, this would make it problematic. The differences may, and probably will, be resolved during the course of events. But if consensus is not present from the start, the situation will be problematic because the absence of immediate agreement leads to processes such as negotiation which are not to be found in routine encounters. A lack of congruence can occur on each element in the definition, and agreement on one element in no way insures agreement on the others.

As before, it must be emphasized that the focus is on the current interaction (Strauss, 1969). The interactants may agree that actor is a female teacher—and yet their interaction may become problematic because one believes that the sex-role identity should be used, and the other may consider the occupational identity relevant. On the other hand, they could have basically different views of the world and still have a routine interaction if they have achieved a working consensus on the relevant matters at hand. There need not be basic and deep-going agreement. It is not necessary that there be "the kind of consensus that arises when each individual present candidly expresses what he really feels and honestly agrees with the expressed feelings of the others present. This kind of harmony is an optimistic ideal and in any case not necessary for the smooth working of society" (Goffman, 1959: 9).

Performance Problems

The chief problems which may occur because of difficulties during the defining process have now been listed, and it would be nice if the discussion could be concluded at this point with a simple statement that once the problematic aspects of the situation's definition are worked out the encounter becomes routine and proceeds in the manner described at the beginning of this chapter. However, that is not the way it is.

For one thing, no definition of the situation can ever be considered final. As the interaction proceeds, any number of things can occur which require the participants to go back to the drawing board—the intrusion of third parties, interaction events which make doubtful the attainment of the goals originally decided upon, the discovery of previously hidden incongruencies, alterations in mood, and others.

If this was all there was to it, I would not need to introduce any new material. All that would be necessary would be to remind the reader that interaction can alternate between the problematic and routine during the whole of its course. There is, however, a further, and very important complication. The process of defining a situation and achieving a working consensus may not lead to a definition which all participants can live with. In many instances, the demands of other or of society can lead actor into accepting a definition which he knows will cause him problems when he attempts to act in accordance with it. Moreover, even when actor gets what he thinks he wants, he may find that it is not what he needs. A definition of the situation is a design for social action, and just as with mechanical devices, some designs that look beautiful in the blueprint stage prove difficult to execute, and others which can be implemented do not work well when one tries to use them. Actor may face the problem of role strain—a felt difficulty in fulfilling role obligations (Goode, 1960a).

Following general practice (Secord and Backman, 1964), I will distinguish between two forms of role strain. First, there are the problems that arise because actor lacks the resources, time, energy, motivation, ability, and so on, needed to meet the requirements of an adopted role. This form of role strain may be called *role overload* (Sieber, 1974). When the problem emerges because it is difficult or impossible for actor to play a role adequately because the demands associated with it are incompatible with the demands of other roles or subroles he must play, we have the form of role strain known as *role conflict*. Role overload would be illustrated by the person who feels strain in playing the breadwinner subrole because of an inability to hold a job. Role conflict is typified by the individual who finds difficulty in adequately playing the spousal role because of heavy demands associated with his or her job.

The catalog of the vagaries of interaction is now concluded. In the next chapter I will discuss the conditions which lead to each problem and the ways that each may be solved. However, before turning to that task some comment is necessary on one additional matter. I have been using the term "problematic" in its technical sense which simply implies that an interaction is complicated and involves processes that are not found in all interactions. It should be noted, however, that interactions which are problematic in this way may or may not cause problems in the popular sense of the term. Problematic interactions are sometimes trying and sometimes not, and their results may be good or bad. Let me illustrate this by considering interactions which are problematic because of a lack of consensus.

Other Consequences of Dissensus

To begin with, when there is no consensus between the participants, role taking is likely to be hampered. Under these conditions actor cannot project from his own definition of the situation and arrive at an accurate prediction of other's behavior. At best, a lack of consensus makes role taking more difficult, and under some circumstances it can lead to very low accuracy. It is not too bad if actor is aware that other's definition differs from his own. Then he can take that difference into account and make the necessary corrections. It is well within the capacity of all of us to reason: "I feel he should be acting like a friend, but he defines himself as the boss and therefore he will. . ." Such judgments are perhaps somewhat more difficult to make, but they can be reasonably correct.

A lack of consensus will, however, be quite destructive of accuracy in role taking when actor is not aware that disagreement exists. Although there seem to be situations in which it is better not to know that other disagrees (Stryker, 1957), when it comes to matters which have to do with mutual interaction it would seem that awareness is preferable. An assumption of consensus in its absence, or a lack of knowledge concerning the nature of the dissensus, will lead actor to base his predictions on false premises and the actions of other are likely to come as a surprise. Although there are certainly such things as pleasant surprises, one would assume that most of these will be unpleasant.

When we consider why these surprises are likely to be unpleasant, we see why dissensus may lead to dissatisfaction and conflict. In fact, it becomes clear that these events would have made actor unhappy even if he had predicted them.

When there is a lack of consensus, when perspectives are not shared, other's actions are unlikely to mesh with actor's. For each action there is a proper reaction— friendliness should call forth friendliness, a particular task-oriented act should call forth a certain reciprocal act. It is in this way that each helps the other to the mutual achievement of desired ends. But this will happen only when there are shared perspectives. If definitions are not shared and if people act consistently with their differing definitions, joint action will not occur. The actions of others will act as a barrier to actor's achievement of his goals rather than as an aid. Thus, there will be frustration rather than satisfaction. Actor will want to relax and he will find that other is continuing the business.

Thus, a lack of consensus can be punishing since it can be the source of barriers to cooperative action. This is not all, however. When other does not act consistently with actor's definition, actor is likely to think poorly of him. Our assumptions concerning the proper definitions for particular situations take on a quasimoral character for most of us, and others who reject these views are not simply sources of surprise and barriers to the achievement of our goals. They are people we come to actively dislike for at best we come to define them as people who don't know how to behave (Haas, 1964). At worst, they are "evil" and "sinful." Regardless of anything else, interaction with people who are viewed in this way is unlikely to be satisfying.

Differences in definitions may, to take it one step further, lead to interpersonal conflict. Most people are not content to merely dislike interaction partners who act inappropriately. They are inclined to attempt to change their definitions or behavior. Some such attempts may be simply attempts at negotiations, which are usual and acceptable parts of interaction in problematic situations. They will not cause the actors any great unhappiness. However, when there is dislike between the participants there is likely to be an unwillingness to negotiate change, and if the issue is important enough, they may resort to condemnation and attempts to force compliance. It is then that arguments, interpersonal conflicts, and hatreds emerge. In marriage, for example, much of the conflict arises from a lack of consensus. Given our general definition of marriage, its importance to us, and the frequency and depth of our interaction with our spouses, it is very likely that attempts will be made to change the other's definition of the situation when it disagrees with our own. It is difficult to tolerate basic differences in a marriage system such as ours. Although at the beginning there may be strong motivation to work out a compromise, that motivation is likely to wane, and even if it doesn't, it may be very difficult to change views given the fact that they may reflect central elements in value systems. If that is the case, conflict is likely to result because each partner is likely to attempt to force a consensus.

With all this said, I must be careful to reemphasize that dissensus need not lead to conflict and dissatisfaction. The absence of an initial consensus perhaps always complicates the interaction to some degree, but such interaction can go as smoothly and be as personally satisfying as any other. Other factors must be present to turn a lack of consensus into conflict.[20]

Furthermore, situations in which there is a lack of consensus at the start can, in the long run, serve positive functions for the society and for the persons involved, even if they do involve conflict. As Lauer and Handel (1977) note, under some conditions the resolving of differences in definitions of situation can be a source of important social change. During this process, deviant perspectives can be institutionalized if the deviants succeed in bringing a sufficient number of the nondeviants around to their point of view. Even more than this, the process can lead to true social innovation. The resultant definition of the situation is likely to be a blend of the original positions of the participants, and thus it is different from all the definitions brought into the situation. "The working consensus. . .is a product of interaction. It is achieved through negotiations and need not have existed in the minds of the participants in advance" (Lauer and Handel, 1977: 123).

This is not to say that social change is invariably good. It obviously depends on what is being changed, in what direction, and what the evaluator's values are. My only point is that the effort and pain associated with problematic interaction may prove to be a good investment, and an unwillingness to pay such costs may lead to a greater loss caused by the perpetuation of undesirable practices.

The recent history of race relations in this country may be viewed in these terms. For many years, the relationships between blacks and whites were generally governed by a working consensus which had great disadvantages for blacks. It seems probable that many, if not most, blacks did not truly accept the definition under

---

[20] In some cases, in fact, role dissensus may not complicate the relationship very much. For example, if one of the participants acts with greater kindness than the other believes is called for, it will have an influence on the course of the interaction, but it may not cause much of a problem. However, if the definitions are conflicting—if the preferred behavior of other is not an acceptable response to the preferred behavior of actor—smooth interaction is unlikely to occur. There will be unpleasant surprises, disapproval, attempts to alter the other's behavior, difficulties in cooperation, etc.

which they operated, but the costs of any attempt to renegotiate were so enormous and the chances of success so small that few were willing to do much about it. Thus, relations between blacks and whites went fairly smoothly, and few questioned the working arrangement. Those who did were likely to conclude that it was the best deal that could be achieved.

Beginning with court cases in the 1930s and culminating in the activism of the 1960s, increasing numbers were involved in an effort to redefine the situation. It was, of course, extremely costly for the pioneers, but gradually, important changes were brought about. That much remains to be done does not gainsay the fact that a willingness to pay major costs resulted in a net gain in the long run.

SUMMARY

Routine interactions—encounters which are simple and easily handled—are distinguished from problematic interactions which require actor to devise solutions to problems that do not occur in routine encounters.

In a routine interaction, the first task is to define the situation, a process which involves categorization and interpretation of the situation on the basis of the cues provided. More specifically, those cues lead us to conclusions about the proper identity for self and other, the appropriate roles, and so on. On the basis of this preliminary definition, actor decides what the first act should be, assesses the likely reactions of other, and if those are acceptable, acts. Other follows the same process before acting, but has the use of an additional cue—the first act of other. An interaction is a series of such acts and reactions.

The person's self-evaluation has an influence on his actions by (1) influencing other aspects of the definition of the situation, such as goals, and (2) by suggesting actions to him. The assumption is that we learn that certain behaviors are appropriate or acceptable for a person who is good at the activity and ill-advised for those who are not. Those "role-definitions" influence what we do. A detailed, formal theory is presented which leads to a number of hypotheses which are supported by the empirical literature. Included are the predictions that people with high self-evaluations expect to be favorably received, expect to succeed, are resistant to influence, are more hard-working, and are more successful.

In this chapter the general nature of the difficulties found in problematic interactions is also discussed. These difficulties include an inability to define the situation, a lack of consensus between the interactants regarding the definition, and an inability to engage in the actions called for in one's definition. A discussion of the personal and social consequences of dissensus is presented, and it is concluded that dissensus can produce desirable as well as undesirable outcomes.

CHAPTER 8

INTERACTION IN PROBLEMATIC SITUATIONS: DEFINING THE SITUATION

Now that the major problematic aspects of normal interaction have been outlined, the other questions posed in Chapter 7 can be answered. When are these problems likely to occur. That is, under what conditions is there likely to be a lack of defining elements? When are actor and other likely to disagree over definitions? When will actor have difficulty in living up to his definitions? Also, how may people solve the problems? And, what determines which reaction will be chosen in a particular case? Given the present state of theory and research in this area, we are entering somewhat uncharted waters. A full answer will not be possible in every case, but we will go as far as is possible in each of the major areas.

As I have already noted, problems of defining roles, identities, and goals are usually quite similar. Thus, I will attempt to discuss these three aspects of the definition as though they were one, making distinctions only when the nature of the element being defined becomes significant.

The Lack of Defining Elements

The first definitional problem occurs when actor finds that early in the interaction he is unable to define himself because none of the elements in his repertoire seems to fit. None of the identities, roles, and goals which he is accustomed to using seems appropriate. Sometimes that is all he knows—there is no clear understanding of what is appropriate. In other instances, he knows what is appropriate, but this additional

213

knowledge does little good because he cannot utilize it. He knows "X" is called for, but he cannot conceive of himself as an "X"; he doesn't know the details of the "X" role and/or he cannot imagine himself working toward a goal like "X". There are obvious, and important, differences among these situations, but at the moment their commonalities are more significant. In each case, actor does not have clear guidelines for action. We will now consider the circumstances under which this will occur.

Conditions Leading to an Inability to Define the Situation. To begin with an obvious point, I would suggest that actor is most likely to be unable to define a situation if he has had little previous experience in the situation. Much of our ability to define ourselves develops during actual interaction. As was noted in the discussion of socialization, we learn self-definitions largely by taking on the definitions we receive of ourselves from others, and most of these definitions are presented to us on the job, so to speak. This would again reinforce the contention that problematic situations are normal and common. An inability to define oneself is likely to be a concomitant of entering a new situation.

These comments suggest another condition which will increase the likelihood of these kinds of interaction problems. If actor is helped in his efforts to think of himself in appropriate ways by taking on the definitions he receives from others, it would follow that actor may have these problems even when he has had previous experience in the situation, *if* his interaction has been under conditions which lead to a low weight being given to received definitions. Under such circumstances, he may not have learned the definition despite the fact that there was an opportunity to do so. The conditions under which this will happen have been discussed in great depth in Chapter 4 and I need not go into them again.

The above notwithstanding, people are not always faced with problems of definition when they enter new situations, because the processes of anticipatory socialization frequently provide them with the mental equipment they need. We are prepared for many of our interaction experiences by informal and formal training programs, by observation of others, by role taking, role assimilation, role extension, etc.

If this is so, it would follow, further, that the likelihood of definitional problems is increased when opportunities for anticipatory socialization are at a minimum. One of the conditions likely to reduce such opportunities is rapid social change. When the social order is being transformed, when people find themselves in situations they were never expected to be in, their anticipatory socialization is likely to be rather incomplete. Society usually does not consciously prepare people for positions unless there is some expectation that they will be able to use the training. For example, when turmoil occurs in newly founded countries it is sometimes a result of processes of this kind. In many cases, the new leaders were never given the opportunity to learn how to govern or even a good basis for viewing themselves as governmental officials rather than as revolutionaries and outsiders. Thus, rapid personal changes and/or social change can produce these problems.

Although social change and personal change decrease opportunities for effective anticipatory socialization, I must emphasize before closing this section that the *absence* of these conditions does not ensure that such socialization will take place. Society seems somewhat careless about providing adequate training for a number of important, commonly occurring situations. For example, the normal expectation has been that almost all people in this society marry at some time in their lives, and although there is considerable anticipatory socialization for the marital status, it is by no means complete. For most people, there is a complete absence of formal training, and although we all have ample opportunities to observe spouses in interaction, some parts of the roles are hidden from outsiders. This has been clearly the case regarding marital sexuality, but is only slightly less true regarding matters such as money management, decision making, or the exercise of power, for example.

Moreover, observation is not a very good basis for learning, particularly when learning identities is involved. It is much more effective to allow actor opportunities to play aspects of the role or to participate as an other with a person occupying the status. Leaving quasi-marriages such as cohabitation aside, there is little opportunity in this society for such experiences.

Another way that actors can receive anticipatory socialization is for them to play parts of a future role when in another status. This would be seen in the transference of a skill learned in one role to another—for example, using social skills learned in the family on the job. This is, however, often not possible, because aspects of some roles have no direct parallel in other roles. I would argue that this is true regarding the sexual part of marriage. Certainly, premarital sexual experience contributes extremely useful information, but the conditions of marital sexuality are somewhat different, and the lessons learned in other relationships are likely to be in need of modification.

In concluding, I should emphasize that there is, of course, rarely a full-blown definition at the start of an interaction—indeed, the whole argument of this book supports that idea. The focus here has been on those times when actor's difficulties in defining himself, his role, and his goals are particularly acute and not easily remedied. These occasions are extreme cases of the routine experience. They are most likely to occur when there has been little or no prior experience in the role and inadequate anticipatory socialization. Rapid personal and social change increases the likelihood that they will occur, but they are found even under conditions of relative stability.

Handling Definitional Problems. When actor finds himself in a situation for which his repertoire provides no definitions, a number of actions are available to him. One, which is used with some frequency, is simply to withdraw from the encounter. Interactions of this kind are likely to lead to confusion on the part of actor and to engender a feeling of being in over one's head. He does not know what to do, and when he does act, probably using elements from his repertoire as a guide even though he knows they do not quite fit, other's responses are unexpected and undesirable. Such situations are likely to be viewed as hopeless and to be left as soon as possible.

In fact, however, they are not hopeless, and if actor does not give up, in many cases he will find that he can get along quite well. If actor "plays for time" and does not commit himself hastily to an inadequate definition, a helpful other may begin to fill in the gaps in actor's socialization during the course of the current interaction. The processes by which this will be done are essentially those which were discussed in Chapter 7. That is, other's words and actions may suggest to actor, after an initial period of confusion, what actor's identity should be, what the associated role involves, and so on. This may be done by direct instruction, by role taking, etc.

It does seem likely, however, that in many of the situations we have in mind, other will not define the situation as one in which his responsibilities involve the socialization of actor. From other's perspective, the fact that actor is in the situation may be taken as a cue that actor is, or should be, properly prepared for the interaction. If this is so, other will not do much conscious teaching and thus actor's opportunities to be socialized may be reduced. Furthermore, other is likely to be impatient with, and somewhat confused by, actor's interaction errors. Actor may obtain instruction, but he is likely to find his education rather trying.

There is, of course, a way out for actor. He can admit his ignorance and attempt to redefine the situation for other so that the latter will be more giving of information and more tolerant of mistakes. This would represent a gain for actor, but there is an obvious risk. If actor is supposed to be prepared, an admission that he is not may call forth abuse from other and possibly termination of the relationship. Consider for a moment what an employer is likely to do if a new employee admits he does not have the knowledge which the boss assumed he had when he was hired. In fact, even if actor does succeed in changing other's definition, there is a cost to be paid—the embarrassment of admitting ignorance. The cost of this embarrassment may, however, be low relative to the gains achieved by successfully altering other's definition.

In sum, though encounters which actor cannot initially define involve a number of potential costs, these situations are by no means hopeless. If actor stays with them he may find that other will provide the socialization he needs to carry the interaction to a successful conclusion.

Cue Problems. In the situations just considered, actor cannot find an appropriate identity, role, and/or goal, because they do not exist in his or her repertoire. Before going on, let us consider the situation in which actor *does* have the appropriate element in his or her repertoire but is unaware that this is so. It is quite possible, and not at all uncommon, that the cues in the situation do not lead actor to the realization that he or she can, in fact, define the situation.

The "fault," in a sense, may lie with actor. The cues which should, on the basis of previous learning, call forth a familiar identity, are present, but, through inattention perhaps, actor is not picking them up. However, this is not likely to remain a problem for very long. The difficulties I described earlier will serve to lead actor to a search for meaning in the situation, and if the cues are there, they are likely to be discovered.

More commonly, cues are not available for actor to use, or (and this is for all practical purposes the same thing), the cues being given off are not decipherable by actor. The latter situation is most likely to occur when actor and other come from different traditions. When abroad I have often missed signs which were intended as proffers of friendship. I took them as simple politeness, or else I did not know quite what to make of them.

The absence of cues is frequently engineered by other and since other is often the major source of guidance in interaction situations, a skilled and devious person can frequently leave actor quite at sea. Other may, for example, disguise his or a third party's identity: "Why didn't you let me know he was your husband? Why did you let me make a fool of myself?" Other can also hide his or her definition of actor's identity or role: "How was I supposed to know that you thought I should go easy with you because we are friends?" Other effective ploys include other hiding his own role definition and disguising the goals of one or more of the participants: "Why didn't you say you felt you had a right to do that?" and "Why didn't you let me know she was thinking of offering me a job? I would have been on my best behavior."

As perhaps these examples suggest, other will often believe that the withholding of cues will lead to an advantage. For one thing, it gives other more opportunity to define his or her own identity in a desirable way, and it helps in presenting false selves. If other can hide from actor the knowledge that other defines himself as actor's inferior, for example, other may be able to avoid playing a role of subordination. As is often said, knowledge is power, and if other can control actor's information he may gain from it.

In most respects, not knowing that one has the necessary defining elements in one's repertoire is the same as not having them. The same confusions and errors are likely to occur in both situations. The solution, however, may be somewhat easier when the elements are in the repertoire. In this case, actor does not have to learn new ways of thinking about things. If he can learn to read the cues or if he can penetrate other's attempts to hide information he can solve the problem. Of course, this is not to deny that these tasks can be quite difficult. If the traditions are sufficiently different or if other is particularly skilled at deception, the deciphering of the cues may be beyond actor's ability. This is particularly so because other may not be able, and in the latter case won't be willing, to give much assistance.

Multiple Definitional Elements

The obverse of the situations I have been discussing can also cause difficulties. Rather than lacking identities, roles, or goals for a particular encounter, actor may, for example, find himself in an interaction for which several of the identities in his repertoire seem appropriate. Commonly, this occurs when actor and other have a multiple relationship to each other. A particular person may be both friend and subordinate, employee and lover, sibling and business partner, and it may not be clear which elements should be used to guide behavior in the present encounter.[1]

[1] Two other situations are often considered to be the equivalent of this one, but in actuality they are not. In some instances, actor is faced with the difficult task of interacting at the same time

Solving Problems of Multiple Definitions. One would expect that when this type of confusion exists at the outset of an interaction, actor's reactions are going to be the same as when there is no appropriate element in his repertoire. First of all, he may give serious consideration to terminating the encounter. Given the problems of defining the situation, it may very well appear that continuing in it is unlikely to result in much personal profit. In this case, however, there are strong pressures to see the encounter through. The fact that actor and other stand in a multiple relation to each other suggests that they are not strangers and that they are likely to have further encounters. To end the present interaction might preclude having future contacts and that might be seen as a great cost, particularly if previous meetings have been rewarding. Furthermore, it seems likely that a multiple relation is more likely than most to be less than completely voluntary. The costs of leaving the relationship may be so great that actor feels that withdrawal is not really one of the options.

If termination is ruled out, actor is likely to try to gather additional information about other's definition of the situation. If useful information is forthcoming, the problem may be solved. Often, other's definition will be embraced eagerly if it is consistent with one of the possibilities actor is considering.

This solution to the problem requires, however, that other be able to help, and it is not at all certain that this will be the case. Other may also be having difficulty defining the situation and if other doesn't know who he is, he is unlikely to be able to tell actor who actor is. If actor expects to solve the problem in this way he requires an other who is knowledgeable.

In addition, actor has to believe the information he gets from other and often he will not. Situations such as these are particularly likely to be ones in which other will wish to hide his true identity and goals in an attempt to get actor to commit himself to an identity he would not utilize if other's ultimate goal was known.

This possibility is illustrated by cases in which other attempts to have actor believe that he is using the friend identity so that actor will adopt the same one, thus making it easier for other to achieve his goal of transacting business. (For example, businessmen take clients out to dinner, students drop in their teacher's office just to say hello and have a chat, etc.)

Actors are aware of such possibilities and it may lead them to reject the information they were so anxious to get. Actor may be afraid that other is hiding his true definition or he may suspect that other will change that definition as soon as actor uses it as a basis for choosing his own. It is clear that additional attempts at gathering information may help actor make a choice among competing definitions, but it is also clear that this will only happen if the conditions are right.

To move the discussion along, let us now assume that actor does not terminate the relationship and that he does not get information which clears up the confusion. What possibilities are then open to him or her?

---

with several others, each of whom stands in a different relation to actor. In another case, actor has difficulties because meeting his obligations to X conflicts with fulfilling his obligations to Y. Both of these situations can cause serious problems, but neither of them involves the kind of *definitional* problems of concern here.

A common decision is to embrace one of the definitions which is considered among the possibilities and to eliminate the other or others. Actor may, for example, choose to play a friendship role and forget about the requirements of the teacher role. The difference between this choice and the one previously discussed should be made clear. When the search for additional information is successful, actor also chooses one of the possibilities; but then he is doing it because it has become clear that it is the "right" choice. In this instance, the choice is made because actor must "do something," not from any confidence that this choice is the most appropriate of the alternatives.

This is not to suggest, however, that actor simply makes a choice on the basis of the "toss of a coin." Even though suitability or efficacy cannot be the basis for the decision, it is not a random choice. Definitional elements, and identities in particular, are arranged along a hierarchy of prominence; certain identities are preferred to others, and under the present circumstances the choice would be made to favor the element which is higher on the hierarchy.

To say that actor chooses an identity which is high on his hierarchy of prominence is simply to say that actor chooses the identity he "prefers," and that does not go very far to explain why the choice is made. In fact, there is a considerable element of circularity in such a statement. However, if we recall some of the factors that lead an identity to be high on the hierarchy, it will become clear what potential benefits lie behind the tendency I am postulating.

Prominent identities, for example, are likely to have been used often in the past and actor will have a firm grasp of the roles associated with them. Thus actor will be able to play the role easily, introducing a desired element of simplicity into a complicated situation. Furthermore, if the identity is high on the hierarchy, his previous performances in the role were likely to have been successful; he is likely to have received positive evaluations when he used it, and it is likely to be associated with a positive self-evaluation. Obviously, there are advantages to using identities associated with such roles again.

Aside from how well we do them, different activities carry with them differing degrees of intrinsic satisfaction. We simply enjoy some activities more than others, perhaps because they are more congenial to our personalities. Some activities involve behaviors which are more congenial to our basic needs, and at times of confusion the choice will go to such activities. It is easy to imagine someone who can play a submissive or a dominating role equally well getting more satisfaction from one rather than the other.

The case of the military chaplain provides a clear illustration of these processes. Burchard's (1954) research shows that the chaplain has a problem of multiple identities because in his interaction with enlisted men, he is at the same time a minister and a superior officer. Clearly, these identities call forth incompatible roles. "A good chaplain must be accessible; he must not be too distant from his flock; he must be on good personal relations with those he is leading. A military leader, however, must not be familiar with his men. His ability as a leader is presumed to depend, in part, on his ability to keep at a distance from his men" (Burchard, 1954:532). And to make the problem real, there is no clear objective basis for choice. The regulations apparently do not help much and the other is not likely to be able to help solve the difficulty. He is likely to be even more confused by the situation than actor is.

The typical response to the dilemma is to choose the religious role in preference to the military role. When it comes to relations with enlisted men, the chaplain tends to see himself as a pastor—not as an officer. The response was so extreme that in these encounters they tended to deny the reality of their status as officers despite the fact that they utilized that identity in numerous other encounters. The officer identity was clearly a part of their repertoire, but its prominence was low. It could not compete with the ministerial role which was a key one because of previous training, experience, and satisfaction. In fact it may be—the sources are not clear on this—that after a time the problem really disappears for most chaplains. Many of them, after some experience with it, turn the situation into a routine interaction. According to the chaplain's perceptions of it, the situation comes to have only one possible definition.

Military teachers at the Command and Staff School also serve to illustrate the choice of an identity high on the hierarchy of prominence. For them, the conflict is between the college teacher and military officer identities. They are both teachers and officers at the school, and the role prescriptions for each are quite different. Many of the elements in the college teacher's role—academic freedom in the classroom and outside, informality with students, faculty participation in academic decision making, avoidance of indoctrination, etc.—were in conflict with elements in the role of military officer—obedience, acceptance of authority, formality with those inferior or superior in rank. Clearly, one would want to be able to choose between these roles, for they call out quite incompatible actions. The decision is based on a number of considerations, but an important element is the fact that the officer-teachers are officers first and teachers second. The tendency is to choose the officer identity because the teacher role is temporary and not particularly significant to most of them. They are professional military men who have been assigned to teaching duties; the military identity is a central one and they choose it when it is a possibility, in the absence of strong counterindications.

In all that has just been said, there is an unspoken assumption that the decision will be based on considerations intrinsic to the relationship between actor and other, but sometimes this may not be the case. The interests and pressures of third persons and the requirements of other relationships may tip the scales.

Such considerations seem to enter into the decisions made by the military teachers discussed above. Even a man who places importance on the teacher role will typically use the officer identity, for to do otherwise would simply get him into trouble with third persons, that is, his superiors. "None of the Air University officer-instructors, *whatever his personal predilection* may with impunity overlook the fact that he is part of a military organization" (Getzels and Gruba, 1954: 174, emphasis added). To act as a teacher might make him more effective and might even give him personal satisfaction, but it is also likely to be a barrier to promotion and it could result in a new assignment. Few seemed willing to take the risk.

Actor may also find that general societal values may give him cues regarding the way out of the dilemma of "too many identities." As Merton (1957) and others have noted, certain identities are expected to take precedence over others and this may be the basis on which he decides. To do so, of course, is a means of protecting oneself against criticism from third persons; thus this notion is not totally distinct from the previous one. Despite this, the present point is not simply a restatement of what was said before. Even when there is little danger of sanctions from third persons, actor may still use society's preferences as a guide, because he believes that to do so is to act "correctly."

Thus far in our discussion, actor's decision was to favor one of the definitional elements already in his repertoire. There are, however, other possibilities. For one thing, actor may reject all the elements originally considered possibilities, and he may attempt to devise, and get accepted, a new identity or role. Usually this is done by combining aspects of the definitional elements in conflict. Thus, rather than deciding between being a friend or teacher, actor may "compromise" and behave as a friendly teacher. He may still insist upon performance as a teacher should, but he might temper it with the extra attention, understanding, and "mercy" that we owe to friends.

As Turner (1962) suggests, when a particular conflict of definitional elements occurs quite frequently, the compromise may become established and in the future it would be available to guide action just as any other identity or role. This is, of course, another example of the transformation of problematic situations into routine ones.[2]

Burchard (1954) suggests that the development of a new composite identity and role is also a part of the solution of the officer-minister dilemma. In fact, a composite role has become institutionalized. The military officially recognizes that the chaplain is a special kind of officer. For example, it permits chaplains to fraternize with enlisted men in ways that are not permitted to regular officers. It is also significant that chaplains are referred to by that title rather than by their military rank. The official exemptions given to chaplains do not, however, seem to be a total answer to the dilemma; they cover only some of the potential conflicts. If the compromise role were adequate to its purposes, the chaplains would not have to fall back, as we have seen them do, into a straight minister role. They would not have to deny the relevance of their officer status. Nonetheless, the official compromise role is of some value. It helps avoid some problems, and it can be a base upon which a more adequate solution is built.

Another example of the development of a composite identity is described by Perry and Wynne (1959) in their discussion of problems faced by physicians who do research. They note that it is unusual for medical researchers to use their own patients for studies, but when this is necessary it is likely to cause problems. Normally, a physician should not use unproven therapies on patients, but a researcher must do so with his or her subjects. The problem can be solved in a variety of ways, but one

---

[2] It should also be emphasized that the process of melding roles and identities when they are in conflict is merely a special case of the general process of role making (Turner, 1962). Even when actor can define the situation early in the interaction, it is likely that that definition will develop and change as the interaction progresses.

possibility is to recognize the position of physician-researcher and allow a new role definition for it. The physician-researcher, for example, might be permitted any action he had reason to believe might help even if there was no firm evidence to back up that belief. This would allow more freedom than the normal physician has, although there would be less freedom than the researcher enjoys, and it could represent an adequate solution to the conflict experienced by the person who occupies both positions in relation to a single other.

A final possibility open to actor is to vacillate between the various definitions in different episodes of the encounter. When a student-friend asks for an extension on an overdue paper, one may grant it readily because he is a friend (and because one would probably do the same for a non-friend student after some discussion), but if he asks for a better grade, one is likely to revert to the teacher role and refuse.

In general, such a solution is unlikely to prove very satisfactory. In many instances it would be difficult for actor to know when a particular definition should apply and if he feels he does, there is a good possibility that other will not agree. It is difficult to get a general agreement; it may be impossible to get the multiple agreements required here. Furthermore, there is a good chance that other will not be able to detect any pattern to actor's varying behavior. Other may see it as disturbingly inconsistent. "I don't understand you. A minute ago you seemed so compassionate. Now you are acting like a bureaucrat."

Moreover, when actor adopts this stance he really doesn't have a general guide for the encounter. Each act and each reaction must be thought out carefully, and this makes interaction a much more difficult process than it usually is. There are no ready-made answers, or, at least, there are none until actor decides what definition is to hold for the moment. And, of course, there will come a time when something happens which puts actor back where he started. Actor will find himself faced with an event for which several definitions seem appropriate.

These difficulties notwithstanding, this solution may be the most appropriate one in many cases. If the interaction is, in fact, going to be multifaceted, it may be better if actor adopts this kind of shifting definition rather than settling on a single one or a composite. The latter strategies will provide the needed answers more easily, but they are also likely to increase the number which turn out to be incorrect.

Choosing Among the Solutions. Given that there are various ways to confront problems of multiple definitions, a question naturally arises regarding which is likely to be favored. As the preceding discussion should suggest, a simple answer to this question cannot be given because the "solution of choice" depends so much on the particular circumstances. Of course, the usual general rule still applies: actor will act in ways which promise to give the greatest rewards and the least cost. The implications of that rule for the present case are, however, not immediately obvious. Rather than attempting to describe all the possible situations and the ways they will tend to be resolved, I will try to handle the issue by suggesting some middle range rules which can be applied to specific cases.

It would seem that actor's best interests would be most easily served if he first directed his attention toward choosing a goal from among the possibilities. To choose an identity or role without knowledge of one's goal would under most circumstances be a difficult task, but at least a tentative choice of a goal can be made without having settled on an identity and role. In fact, unless the cues of the situation clearly suggest a particular identity is appropriate, it is probable that normally that is the order in which actor proceeds.

In this case, where the information actor has leaves open several possible goals, the first step in making a decision would involve a consideration of actor's current need for the kind of reward associated with the attainment of each goal. Actor's current need for a particular kind of reward would be a function of the general desire for that reward and the extent to which it is has been satisfied. (One may need love more than money, but if one has all the love one wants, the tendency will be to seek money in situations which seem to hold out the possibility of attaining either but not both.)

Need will, however, not be the only consideration. The possibility of satisfying the need will be noted. In this case, however, this factor is not likely to be crucial. If actor's problem is, as here, to choose a goal from several possibilities, it may be assumed that each of the possibilities is in fact viewed as a possibility. Of course, actor may not view them as equally probable, and the difference in probabilities may very well tip the scales when the need levels are close. In most cases, however, need will be the key consideration.

Implicit in all this is the notion that actor will prefer to choose a single goal rather than to attempt to achieve some kind of composite goal or to alternate among different goals. For most people this appears to be a reasonable assumption. In general, when elements for defining a situation are in competition, most people would opt for one of the elements currently in the repertoire rather than attempting to innovate or alternate. The latter two would be used only if the first does not work out.

This contention is based upon an "economy of action" principle; people will do what is least costly to them in terms of effort. In this sense, the choice of a single goal has clear advantages; actor has previously been socialized to the ways of attaining it, so action should be easier. It is not new so other may also know it; he is likely to be familiar with it and with his counter-role. Actor does not have to resocialize other to the same extent that would be necessary if an unfamiliar composite were used. And, as was noted above, alternating among the possibilities requires a vigilance which is not needed when a simpler game plan is used.

If actor is successful in choosing a goal, his attention will then usually be turned to choosing an identity and role for the encounter. As suggested before, he may now find that the problem has disappeared. In many instances, the choice of a goal will indicate that he should use one of the identities and roles originally considered to be in competition.

If that does not happen, if several roles seem to hold promise of achieving the chosen goal, further decisions will have to be made. I would suggest that the tendency will be to give first place to considerations of efficacy. The identity and role which is used will be the one which seems to hold the greatest promise of leading to the attainment of actor's goal.

This basis for making the decision will, however, not be available to actor in many instances. It could be, for example, that several identities or roles appear equally likely to lead to the goal. If that is so, actor would use another basis for his choice. The relevant consideration would probably be the place of each identity on his hierarchy and this in turn would be related to his skill at playing it, the extent to which it has been associated with reward, and so on (see Chapter 6).

It could, of course, turn out that none of the identities and roles that actor is considering holds promise of leading to the goal that actor has chosen. This is, however, not too likely to happen. In actual interaction, the choices that actor must make are not as discrete as they seem to be when they are described. The same cues which lead actor to choose a particular goal are probably also used in the tentative choice of identities and roles, and it is improbable that none of the identities and roles being considered would be seen as a means to the chosen goal.

If this does happen, however, actor will be faced with an extremely complex situation for which the possible solutions are numerous. Actor could search his repertoire for other identities and roles which appear likely to lead to the goal, or he might change his goal to fit in with the identities and roles suggested by the cues in the situation. If he decides to stick with the chosen goal and he cannot find a "proper" identity and role in his repertoire, he would at this point again reconsider changing the goal he seeks.

If this possibility is again rejected, then actor will have to attempt to develop a new identity and role. If actor can do this, and gain acceptance for his "innovation," that might settle the issue. There would, however, be costs involved. Simple and familiar roles are likely to be preferred and these new identities and roles are likely to be neither, particularly if they are composites. If they are efficacious, however, and the actor sees no simpler efficacious possibilities, they are likely to be used because the gains of a successful encounter will be likely to exceed the associated costs.

A somewhat less drastic solution may work, however. It may be that an existing identity and role hold promise of leading to the goal *if* actor could be freed of some part of the role requirements. Under these circumstances actor's salvation may lie in obtaining an *exemption*. Actor may accept the role definition, in principle, but attempt to get himself freed from some part of it at this time. For example, he would accept that to be a judge requires that he rule on cases, and he agrees to do that in all cases "except those in which. . ." In cases of partial exemption, the responsibility is not totally given up, but permission is sought to fulfill it at a lower level under these circumstances: "I will do the cooking, but you can't expect fancy meals when I'm working."

The distinction between a redefinition of the role and exemption is, I admit, a subtle one, particularly if the claimed exemption applies to most of the relevant encounters. Nonetheless, there seems to be a difference at least in terms of the likelihood that others will accept the desired change. For example, most traditionalists would not accept a definition of the citizen role which did not include the require-ment that the citizen be willing to serve in the armed services. But even such people are usually willing to accept that some should be deferred or exempted from such service because it would cause unusual hardship. And when an exemption is granted, those who receive it are not likely to lose status because they are not considered to be shirking their responsibilities.

Actors' chances of solving their problems in this way will be markedly increased if they have available to them the mechanism of delegation (Goode, 1960a). If actors are to be permitted to slough off what is considered to be one of their responsibilities, someone else will probably have to be found to take over. Another judge will have to hear the cases from which the regular judge wishes to be disqualified; colleagues will have to read and grade the papers the professor feels he cannot grade fairly. There has to be someone available who is willing and able to do the job.

The chances of winning exemption are, in addition, influenced by what it is actors wish to be exempted from. As Goode (1960a) points out, others and third parties are easily convinced to grant exemptions from the responsibilities of certain parts of roles and are quite adamant about others. If fact, the activity may be con-sidered so unimportant or so optional that exemptions are given almost automatically. When this is so, actor may feel free to drop the activity without permission if he feels a need to. In many universities, service of the faculty to the larger community falls into this category. Beyond these "automatics," activities are sometimes finely graded in terms of the ease with which people may gain exemption from them. Professors can usually have graduate students grade papers, but only under special circumstances may a professor be exempted from lecturing to his classes, and under no circumstances are they supposed to allow others to write their scholarly papers for them.

Throughout this long process it is quite probable that actor has often considered terminating the interaction. In such a difficult situation it would certainly be an ever-present possibility. In the usual case, however, it seems reasonable to assume that actor will choose to remain in the encounter until all the possibilities I've discussed have failed. We are socialized to desire interaction and since interaction is a necessary means to many of our goals, the basic tendency will be to continue rather than to terminate a problematic interaction.

This tendency can, however, be overridden. In general, termination will be chosen when the rewards likely to be forthcoming from the interaction do not seem likely to equal or exceed the costs associated with continuing. This would be the case, for example, when actor does not place great value upon the rewards associated with the goal and when actor does not think he is likely to achieve his goal.

The rewards associated with the goal are, however, not the only relevant re-wards. In many instances, as suggested above, the intrinsic rewards of interaction are important to actor, and thus it would follow that termination is likely to appear attractive when actor's need for interaction is approaching satiation. To put it in other terms, if actor has, even prior to the appearance of problems, approached the point of desiring a respite from others; if he is beginning to covet some privacy, he is not likely to be willing to tolerate an interaction which seems likely to be difficult. Under this condition, noninteraction would seem—given the total picture—to hold greater promise of reward.

I would also note that each interaction is in potential competition with other interactions. Omitting the possibility of carrying on several interactions simultaneously, time spent in one interaction has to have counted as one of its costs the gains that might be had from other interactions. The general postulate is that the tendency would be to terminate a problematic interaction and engage in an alternative when the perceived satisfaction derivable from the alternative exceeds that perceived as obtainable from the problematic one (see Thibaut and Kelley, 1959).

DIFFERENCES IN DEFINITIONS

Let us now assume that the participants have each worked out, *with the help of the others, to be sure,* a definition of the situation which, though tentative, seems to hold promise of being adequate for the task at hand. Let us also assume, in order that the discussion may progress, that there is a lack of congruence between them on one or more of the elements in that definition.[3] Four questions about this situation will be considered:

1. Under what circumstances is such a lack of congruence most likely?
2. What are the participants likely to do when this lack of congruence is discovered?
3. Under what circumstances is the lack of consensus most likely to be reduced or removed?
4. What factors determine which of the participants will have the greater effect on the form that the agreement takes?

The Sources of Dissensus

The answer to the question, when are the preliminary definitions of interaction partners likely to be in conflict, is implicit in material presented earlier and all that will be done here is to make the relevance of that material clear.

The first point is a simple one: When entering an interaction situation, actor will tend to define it in the ways that he has previously been taught to define it. Our first definitions of situations are largely a function of what we bring to the situation and what we bring to the situation is a function of our previous socialization experience. We tend to assign particular meanings to the available cues because our previous socialization has led us to believe that those meanings are the correct ones. Anything which increases the likelihood that actor and other have had similar socialization, will

---

[3] A lack of consensus between interaction partners may involve any or all of the elements in a definition of the situation, and a lack of consensus over goals is obviously different from disagreement about identities. These distinctions need not concern us here, however. At a general level, the factors which lead to each kind of dissensus are similar, as are the mechanisms used in the attempt to solve the problems they cause.

increase the likelihood that they have a similar set of meanings and *decrease* the likelihood of dissensus.

This general postulate can easily be translated into more specific hypotheses. For example, since people with similar social characteristics tend to have had more similar previous experience than people with differing characteristics, it seems likely that the chances of dissensus are directly related to the extent of differences in the participant's social background. A number of social traits are potentially of relevance—race, ethnic group, education, religion, gender, occupational level, and so forth.

Of course, I am not suggesting that consensus will invariably follow when actor and other are similar in social traits. There may be a tendency for people with similar characteristics to have had similar prior socialization experiences, but given the variety that exists in all social categories this is at best a weak tendency. Its strength would, furthermore, be quite variable. Similarity on a certain trait might, for example, be relevant for a particular element in a definition and totally irrelevant for consensus on other issues.

Given this, it should come as no surprise that the data on social similarity and consensus are quite mixed. MacKinnon and Summers (1976) did find a relation between similarity of antecedent social circumstances and role consensus in a study of students and teachers in a retraining program, but beyond this the data are usually inconsistent even within a particular study. For example, Van Es and Shingi (1972) report that on eighteen attitude items, Brazilian couples who were similar in educational level showed somewhat greater consensus than couples who differed in education. But most of the relations were not statistically significant, and on seven other items the differences were not in the predicted direction. Jaco and Shepard's (1975) data also lack consistency in that they show greater consensus on family planning attitudes for couples who share a common religion and come from the same part of the country (Appalachia), but there is no relation between consensus and similarity of education. Along the same lines, Gross et al. (1958) report that school boards which were relatively homogeneous in religion and education showed greater agreement on educational philosophy. However, the education correlation seems to be partly artifactual and no association was discovered when gender and income similarity were the independent variables. Presthus (1964) found that the more homogeneous of the two communities he studied had greater consensus, but in Speight's (1968) study of twelve black communities there was no correlation between a community's ranking on several homogeneity measures and its ranking on a consensus measure.

In general, then, the hypothesis does not fare well. It would seem that either similar socialization experiences do not lead to consensus, or similarity in social traits is a very weak index of similar socialization. I would favor the latter explanation and there is some evidence that suggests its plausibility. If the members of a group have all had similar formal training, role consensus seems to be increased. Gross et al. (1958), for example, found greater role consensus among school superintendents than among school board members, and Bible and McNabb (1966) found a similar pattern when county extension directors were compared with their staffs. In both cases the higher consensus group had been exposed to a fairly standardized course of formal training and the lower consensus group had not. Not too different are Hill, Stycos, and Back's (1959) finding that Puerto Rican couples who attended meetings at which birth control was discussed showed increased consensus. There is then at least a hint here that common socialization patterns do not increase consensus, and by inference a suggestion that the results cited earlier are due to the fact that similar social traits are a weak, or not very general, index of similar socialization.

To this point, the implicit assumption has been that actor and other were socialized by third parties and the question has been, essentially, what circumstances increase the likelihood that these "outsiders" have taught similar lessons. The discussion can be advanced considerably if it is now noted that the meanings applied to a situation by actor may have been taught to him by other in *previous* encounters. Anything that would increase the likelihood that this is so would also increase the likelihood of early consensus in the present interaction.

Given this, an obvious hypothesis may be offered as a starting point: early consensus regarding definitions is more likely when actor and other are acquaintances than when they are strangers. To say that the interactants know each other is equivalent to saying they have interacted previously, and to say that there has been previous interaction is equivalent to saying there have been opportunities for mutual socialization.

It goes well beyond whether the interactants are strangers or not, however. Among those who are previously acquainted there will be great variations in the extent to which there have been opportunities for mutual socialization and perhaps equally great differences in the extent to which the available opportunities have been used. And these variations should be systematically associated with other variables.

At the simplest level, it would seem likely that the longer the prior acquaintance and the greater the frequency of interaction, the greater the likelihood of early consensus on definitions. People who have interacted more extensively have had more opportunity for mutual socialization on a wider variety of issues. Moreover, it seems probable that all other things being equal, actor is more likely to allow other to influence him when their interaction is frequent. The greater the interaction, the greater the trust we are likely to have in other. Also, frequent interaction is likely to be with people like us and with people we like (Homans, 1950; 1961). Our tendency to accept other's suggestions should be increased by these conditions.

Quantity of interaction is, however, not the only relevant consideration; the qualitative aspects of the interaction would also influence the extent to which previous interaction would lay the groundwork for consensus in later interactions. For one thing, some interactions are rather superficial and limited in scope while others are intimate, deep, and wide ranging. It would seem clear that interactions of the latter type should lead to greater mutual influence.

Along similar lines, it would seem that the "gain" from a particular interaction would also reflect the extent to which actor and other liked each other, and the degree to which they were similar. When there is similarity and liking, interaction is likely to be less superficial and efforts to influence more successful. The latter effect is due to the fact that when there is similarity and liking, there tends to be a feeling that other's opinion should be actor's also; a fact long recognized by salesmen of all kinds.

Furthermore, when there is liking there is a desire to be liked in return and a good way to insure that is to allow other's definition of things to influence one's own.

Studies of Consensus. Evidence bearing upon the prediction that people who know each other show more consensus than strangers is available in studies which compare the value agreement of members of a family with the amount of agreement shown when the responses of each subject are compared with those of a randomly selected other. As the hypothesis predicts, the associations tend to be higher for people married to each other than they are for randomly paired persons of opposite sex (Kirkpatrick and Hobart, 1954; Hobart, 1956; Ferreira and Winter, 1974). However, caution is necessary. Dentler and Hutchinson (1961) studied consensus in groups composed of father-mother-child and they found only small differences between real and created groups regarding consensus on what makes for a happy marriage. This study underlines the fact that association is not always sufficient; some issues are simply not relevant in some kinds of relationships, and nothing bearing upon them may ever come up. In other cases, the nature of the relationship is such that people resist others' attempts to socialize. If either of these is so, association is not likely to increase consensus (F. E. Jones, 1968; Gross et al., 1958).

The hypothesis that the *extent* of previous interaction relates to consensus is supported by several studies. Length of marriage is a frequently used index of extent of interaction and it tends to relate to consensus (Couch, 1958; Van Es and Shingi, 1972; Ferreira and Winter, 1974). The hypothesis receives indirect support from F. E. Jones' (1968) finding that when men work closely together and on similar tasks they show higher consensus. The assumption here is, of course, that these conditions increase the extent of interaction and communication. Also relevant is the finding of Gross et al. (1958) that if the members of school boards had served together for a long time there was more consensus among them.

An interesting and complicating finding is provided by Kirkpatrick and Hobart (1954; Hobart, 1956) who find that the length of time a couple has been at a particular level of intimacy is unrelated to their consensus. For engaged couples, for example, length of engagement is unrelated to consensus. In the sample as a whole, there is undoubtedly a correlation between consensus and length of acquaintance, but the suggestion is that if degree of intimacy is controlled the time relation would disappear.

It is difficult to know how much to make of this since the previously cited studies do not support it. *If* Kirkpatrick and Hobart's findings are correct, it would mean that in relationships of this kind, length of acquaintance has its effect on consensus through its effect on level of intimacy. The theory, however, posits the existence of a direct effect of length of acquaintance upon consensus.

There are also data which suggest that consensus is greater between parent and child of the same sex than it is between a parent and an opposite sex child (Ferreira and Winter, 1965; Byrne, 1965; Grotevant, 1976. Jennings and Niemi, 1968, find no difference). The exact meaning of the majority finding is not clear. It may be due to a greater willingness to accept the views of the more similar parent, it may be associated with differences in extent of interaction, or it may be due to a combination of both. All of these are, however, consistent with the hypothesis.

To conclude, I would note that other studies which correlate direct measures of communication with measures of consensus do not find associations, possibly because of the weakness of the self-report communication measures. For example, Jennings and Niemi (1968) found no correlation between the reported number of parent-child political conversations and parent-child political consensus, and Hobart and Klausner (1959) found no relationship between consensus and their measure of openness of communication.

In general, then, the data suggest that extent of interaction has some effect on consensus. At the same time, however, it is clear that this relationship is limited and complex.

Moving on to other matters, I would suggest that regardless of who is involved in them, certain kinds of encounters would be more likely to be characterized by dissensus. For example, on the basis of general observation, it would seem that encounters which take place in specialized locations such as those which occur in courts, classrooms, or religious edifices, are *less* likely to be characterized by dissensus, and the same would be true for encounters which are products of written contracts or formalized rules. On the other hand, interaction episodes which occur only rarely in a society and those which are associated with recent social change would be associated with more dissensus.

In large part, these differences can be understood in terms of the principle that dissensus is more likely when the participants have had disparate socialization. When this is so, they are likely to assign different meanings to the available cues and thus define the situation differently. The link is that for some kinds of encounters it is likely that the participants have had similar socialization and for other encounters the chances are low that the interactants have had similar preparation. For example, when there is a written contract we may assume that the participants have had a common socializing agent. The contract itself would teach them what cues are important and what their meanings are. Of course, as Strauss (1958) notes, we should not exaggerate the extent of consensus in formal situations. Contracts are open to varying interpretations, they do not cover all aspects of the interaction, and people differ in the extent to which they accept the provisions of contracts to which they have agreed. Nonetheless, I would expect a somewhat greater likelihood of consensus in formal interaction situations, all other things being equal.

Interactions which are not covered by contracts and formal rules vary in the degree to which their definitions are generally agreed upon in the society. The definitions of some situations are institutionalized; there is something approaching a society-wide consensus about the meaning of the cues associated with them. If there is societal consensus, it is likely that actor and other would agree, for in such cases, no matter who the socializing agent was, the same lesson is likely to have been taught (Van Es and Shingi, 1972).

This postulate is the basis for several of the previous assertions. It seems likely, for example, that encounters which take place in specialized settings are likely to have definitions which are matters of societal consensus. Most people agree on how one should act in a church or courtroom. And it would also seem that situations which occur rarely in the society would be less likely to be institutionalized, although certainly the correlation between frequency of occurrence and degree of institutionalization is not strong. In a similar manner, it would seem that situations which are new in a particular society would not have generally agreed upon definitions.

To this point, I have been assuming that the cues available to each participant are the same, but there are times when this assumption is not valid. Chief among those times would be the occasions when one of the participants is attempting to control the cues available to the other. In fact, under those circumstances, actor is often attempting to lead other to define the situation in a way which is different from actor's. When a con man (the actor) hides the facts from his victim, when a person making a sexual advance makes an ambiguous statement, when an athlete tries to "fake out" an opponent, the whole purpose is to have other define the encounter in a way that actor does not. Thus I would postulate, to conclude, that dissensus is likely when different cues are available to actor and other, and that the latter condition is most common when one of the participants believes there is something to gain from dissensus.

Reactions to Dissensus

There is a wide range of possible reactions to a lack of consensus regarding definitions of situations. Under some circumstances whose nature will be discussed below, there are not attempts to reduce the dissensus. Each participant simply maintains his own definition and acts upon it. More commonly, though, the existence of dissensus is defined as dissatisfying and the actors attempt to reduce the disagreement and move in the direction of consensus. Their efforts may take a variety of forms. Strauss (1978) lists some fourteen specific options ranging from requesting to killing, and his list is probably not exhaustive. These specific reactions may, however, be reduced to six general categories—persuasion, education, manipulation, appeal to rules or authority, coercion, and negotiations (or bargaining). Though each of these is used in the resolution of differences of the type under consideration here, negotiation seems to be used most often, and, in common with most social psychologists, I will focus my attention on it.[4]

Negotiations. Given how frequently people speak of negotiation, it is surprisingly difficult to find a clear-cut definition of the term. One author, in fact, managed to write an entire book on the subject without ever formally or explicitly defining the concept. I will base my definition on a discussion by Chertkoff and Esser (1976), because they seem to me to have caught the essence of the matter.

The first requirement for a negotiation situation is that the "parties have diver-

---

[4]Most social psychologists do not make a distinction between the terms "negotiations" and "bargaining." I too will use them interchangeably.

gent interests, at least to a certain extent." Typically, in negotiations over definitions of situations, the divergence of interests comes from the fact that each participant has a stake in his or her own definition; it is preferred to the alternative held by other. Actor will usually assume that it is to his advantage, psychologically and/or tactically, if other drops his definition and embraces actor's.

Second, negotiations require that it be possible for actor and other to communicate with each other. Negotiation is an interactive process and in order for there to be interaction there must be communication. This may seem to go without saying, but it happens that many of the laboratory studies included in the literature on negotiations do not meet this requirement. In many studies, communication is not possible or is severely restricted. The subjects are not permitted to make offers and counteroffers, they cannot defend or explain their suggestions, etc. Such strictures change the situation in basic ways and such studies will not be considered here.

These two requirements are obviously not sufficient to define negotiations. Several other "consensus seeking" techniques meet them. Chertkoff and Esser (1976: 464) suggest three additional conditions are required and I would add another. First, there must be the possibility of compromise. It may work out that the original suggestion of one of the participants is adopted without change; one person may gain a complete victory and the other may be totally defeated.[5] But this is rare, and if a situation is to be considered a negotiating situation the "rules" must permit the emergence of a solution which is different from either of the original definitions. To this I would add that there must be the possibility of "no agreement." If they are required to agree upon a common definition, a set of pressures which are basically different from those normally found in negotiating situations would result. Again, one or both of the participants may feel that they "have to" reach agreement, but that cannot be part of the ground rules.

Negotiations, Chertkoff and Esser (1976: 464) suggest, must also permit the participants to make provisional offers. I would interpret this to imply several things. First, offers may be hedged by qualifications. A participant must be allowed to make a suggestion which is conditional upon some action by other. Actors must be permitted to say, "If you will agree to X, I will do Y." Furthermore, actors must be permitted to send up "trial balloons." They must be allowed to make tentative suggestions without committing themselves. They must be permitted to say, in effect, "I'm not sure I'm willing to, but. . ." Finally, no acceptance of an offer can be absolutely binding. Of course, once one of the participants makes a suggestion which is accepted by the other, each will feel commitment to it, and the fact that it was agreed upon will make it difficult to change. Nonetheless, everything must be, at least potentially, renegotiable at any point in the interaction.

Finally, "the provisional offers must not fix the tangible outcome until an offer is accepted by all sides" (Chertkoff and Esser, 1976: 464). To me, this seems to say

---

[5] I will usually speak of situations in which there appear to be only two persons involved in the interaction. When more people are interacting, additional processes, such as coalition formation, become a possibility, but the number of persons in the group is not a key consideration for the matters with which I am concerned.

that in a negotiation situation all must acquiesce before a change in the *status quo ante* becomes a fact. No one participant can impose a solution on the other. The other must be able to consider all the ramifications of the offer and decide whether he or she wishes to accept it. The implication seems to be that neither can claim the right to decide for both. This may seem to rule out the possibility of coercion, but it is probably wise to avoid taking a position on that matter. In practice, the line between coercing someone and making an offer "he can't refuse" is often a very fine and indistinct one.

A typical negotiating session will follow a sequential pattern. Actor will define the situation, decide what an appropriate bargaining point would be, consider other's probable reaction, reconsider his plan in the light of that, and present a proposal. Other will evaluate the proposal, decide whether it is appropriate to offer concessions, resistance, or counterproposals, consider actor's probable reaction, reconsider his decision, and then react to actor's original proposal. Actor will redefine his situation in the light of the information contained in other's reaction, decide on his options, consider other's probable responses, reconsider his plan, and then respond. A series of such exchanges will follow until a working consensus emerges or until one or both decide to break off negotiations. Thus, negotiation is simply a special case of interaction. Though the specific details differ, the interaction pattern of definition, plan of action, consideration of consequences, possible revision of plan, and action can easily be detected in this description of the negotiating process.

Mechanisms of Negotiating. Now that we have a general view of the nature of negotiations, I will discuss in detail some of the specific mechanisms actors use when they are engaged in the process. Quite commonly negotiations revolve around the question, "Is a particular behavior which actor favors right or wrong, acceptable or unacceptable in terms of conventional standards?" Often, of course, there is disagreement over what the standard should be, but in this case let us assume that all parties accept the general principle.[6] The dissensus lies in the interpretation of the principle as it applies to specific actions. At such times actors tend to resort to *accounts* in their attempts to convince other. We will consider the various forms of accounts next.

In the attempt to convince other that the behavior in dispute is acceptable, actor may resort to *justifications* which are simply statements to the effect that, appearances notwithstanding, the behavior is in fact acceptable according to the agreed-upon standards. Actor makes no apologies for his action. He simply tries to convince other that other's interpretation of the act is incorrect (Scott and Lyman, 1968). "I may not have told the whole truth, but that's not the same as lying." "Yes, I killed him, but it was in self-defense. You have no right to treat me as though I had committed murder."

[6] As Merton (1976) notes, it is very likely that there will be disagreement over the interpretation of principles, since it is normal that the principles we are taught contain within them mutually contradictory elements. For example, a father must put his family first and he is also expected to "give his all" to his job.

A *disclaimer* (Hewitt and Stokes, 1975) tries to characterize the actor and his or her motives in a way that will make permissible what is usually impermissible. Aggression can be justified by suggesting that the motive is not to hurt—"Let's have some fun and. . ." Acts which would be reprehensible when committed by the average person can be justified by claiming to be a special person: "I've earned the right to. . . ," "For most people this is dangerous, but I know what I'm doing." Certain phrases tip off the likely occurrence of a disclaimer: "I'm not a. . .but. . . ," "I am a. . .and therefore. . . ," "Usually I can't stand people who. . .but. . . ," "I only want to. . . ," "I won't let it go too far. . . ," "You don't understand. . ."

It should be clear that the power of disclaimers comes from the fact that the meaning that should be applied to an act depends largely on the motive behind it and the identity of the person doing it. A disclaimer attempts to control the meaning of the act by influencing other's definition of actor's motives and identity.

Another technique used in negotiations is the *claim of extenuating circumstances.* Here the focus is on the situation, not on actor or his motives. Essentially we ask other to look at the whole picture. We say, "Don't apply the conventional standard uncritically. This is a special case and the special circumstances put this act in a category into which it doesn't usually fall." The general form it would take would be, "Normally I wouldn't think of it, but in this case. . ." A common extenuating circumstance is related to the behavior of the target of the act: "After what he did. . ." Extenuating circumstances can also refer to the situation of the actor: "My kids are hungry. . ." or "It may be my last chance. . ."

Excuses are basically different from all the previous techniques, for they are arguments which flatly admit that the action in question is, in fact, unacceptable. But they ask that other accept the behavior anyway because actor "can't help" doing it. Excuses involve in one way or another a claim of diminished responsibility.[7]

Scott and Lyman (1968) recognize four kinds of excuses:

1. *Appeals to accident* are arguments to the effect that a particular action was not intended. Improper behavior was caused by or will be caused, if it occurs, by forces beyond the control of actor. "I was late because the traffic was heavy" or "This will only work when the conditions are right so please excuse me if. . .".

2. *Appeals to defeasibility* as described by Scott and Lyman seem to me to contain two rather distinct kinds of excuse:

    a. *lack of information arguments* suggest that actor does not know, and cannot know, exactly what the results of his or her actions will be and therefore if they turn out to be inappropriate, actor must be excused. "I'm willing to try it, but don't blame me if. . ." or "I've never done that before and if. . .".

    b. *Lack of free will arguments* assert that actor is not responsible for the act

---

[7]Excuses are not especially useful when the goal is to get other to accept a behavior which has not yet occurred. It is difficult to convince someone that when the time comes, you will have diminished responsibility for something you clearly foresaw was going to occur. They are more effective in the attempt to gain a pardon after an act has been committed.

because someone or something forced him to do it. "I have to follow orders. . ." or "If I don't do what he says. . ." or "I don't want to do this, but I have no choice."[8]

3. *Appeals to biological drives* are best typified in our society by the frequent use of the sex drive and psychopathology as excuses for behavior. To argue that a murder was a "crime of passion" will not usually lead to an acquittal in these times, but it is considered a mitigating circumstance. Before the fact, we sometimes warn others in terms such as, "You have to understand that I have a weakness for. . ." or "Sometimes I lose my head and. . ." The emphasis should, I think, be put on the drive part of the label rather than on the biological aspect. It is a lack of free will argument in which the stimulus is something internal to the actor. In the second form of defeasibility, the stimulus is clearly external to actor.

4. *Scapegoating* is a rather specific case which combines elements from (2b) and (3). It involves an argument that the actor acted as he or she did because of an overpowering internal drive, but the source of that internal drive is the target of the action: "If she does that again I can't be held responsible. . ." or "Something snapped when he did that."

It should be obvious that setting up these categories involves the making of rather fine analytic distinctions. In real life, arguments are unlikely to fit comfortably into one or another category and a number of accounts are likely to be offered in a single negotiation episode. Thus, it does not make much sense to ask what conditions are going to lead to the use of one kind of account rather than another, and it is equally futile to consider the relative effectiveness of the various types. It is possible, however, to discuss some of the general factors which affect the likelihood that an account will be honored, that is, that other will accept, or at least tolerate, the actions actor wishes to engage in. That question will be treated in some depth in the section dealing with factors affecting the outcome of negotiations. But before we get to that it is necessary to consider the factors which determine whether or not there will be negotiations at all.

Entering Negotiations

Because there is dissensus at the outset does not necessarily mean that the processes I have been discussing will actually be used. Actors who disagree in their definitions of a situation often make no efforts to remove the differences between them. This being the case, the next question is obvious: "Given that a lack of consensus exists, what conditions increase the likelihood that negotiations will be attempted?"

---

[8] Banton (1965) tells us that until the lords "got wise" and instituted the notion of a liege lord whose demands took precedence, vassals would swear fealty to several lords and escape fulfilling their obligations to any by arguing that they had a prior obligation to another: "I would love to serve in your army, but Lord X is likely to call and I have to be available."

Awareness and Negotiations.   Awareness that there is disagreement would seem to be a prerequisite for beginning negotiations, and though it might seem at first glance that sufficient awareness is always present, I would argue that this is not so. In fact, much of my discussion of role taking would suggest that actors may very well be unaware of how other defines the situation. Knowledge of other's view would come through role taking and as we have seen role taking is likely to be less than 100 percent correct.

Of course, it could be argued that even if the actors are not quite aware of its specific nature, when there is disagreement things will not go right in the interaction and this would certainly cause them to see that there is dissensus. I do not believe that this will always be the case, either. The basic theory certainly would suggest that the interaction will not go smoothly, but the amount of disruption may be fairly minor and the participants may not be very conscious of the fact that there could be improvement. And, more important, the interaction difficulties may be attributed to causes other than discrepancies in the participants' definitions of the situation. It could be assumed that the problem is an inability to act consistently with definitions, a refusal to do so, and so on.

All of this leads me to postulate that awareness of dissensus is a variable and that this awareness is usually a prerequisite to negotiations.

As was previously suggested, one of the factors that influences the likelihood of adequate awareness is the accuracy of the role taking of the participants. Thus, it would follow that the factors associated with accurate role taking, discussed in Chapter 2, would also be associated with the likelihood of negotiations occurring in the presence of dissensus. If there is disagreement, we would expect the chances of negotiations to be increased when there has been frequent interaction in the past, when there is a universe of discourse, when the relation is important, etc.

In addition, the extent of the disagreement is relevant. The larger the gap between actor and other, the easier it is to perceive that there is a difference and therefore the greater the likelihood of negotiations. Large differences are also more likely to cause serious difficulties for the participants and this would lead them to look for the causes of the problem. This too would increase the likelihood of their becoming aware of the disagreement.

Awareness that there is dissensus is a prerequisite for negotiations in most cases, but awareness alone does not ensure that they will take place. For one thing, if people believe that the issues are not negotiable they are not likely to make the effort. Thus in addition to an awareness of dissensus, there must also be a belief that matters can be changed. In some cases, positions are so hardened that there is in fact no use in negotiating, and if this is perceived, negotiations are unlikely to occur. In other cases, there is a possibility of change but one or more participants are unaware of this. This occurs, in part, because people have a tendency to state their definitions in rather absolute terms when they make them overt at all. This is because they believe—properly—that this is a way of gaining advantage in negotiation. Such a strategy may backfire, however; it may convince other that actor is unwilling to negotiate, and this belief can lead to withdrawal from the situation or to a hardening of other's own position. The former is often seen among travelers in certain foreign countries. Naive tourists assume that the prices of goods are normally fixed, but, of course, in many countries the answer to the question, "How much. . .?" is intended merely as a means of opening negotiations. The tourist's assumptions, and the fact that the first asking price is likely to be outrageous and stated as though it were firm, often leads the potential customer to move along, much to the consternation of the merchant.

There are other situations in which the possibility of negotiations may not be immediately obvious. For example, a charge against an accused criminal is, in essence, society's definition of him. "He is a person who. . ." However, despite the formality and specificity with which charges are stated, they are open to negotiations through plea bargaining. If the negotiations are successful, the state will reduce the charge in return for the defendant's acceptance of the new definition, indicated by a plea of guilty. In most cases, the defendant is aware of this possibility or has a lawyer who will guide him in the matter. The defendant who does not have that awareness or guidance would be in a decidedly inferior position in comparison to one who does.

Motivation and Negotiations. To know that there is the possibility of negotiating differences, still does not insure that negotiations will take place. Awareness must be coupled with motivation. Actor must be willing to pay the costs inherent in the negotiation process, and they must desire the rewards that negotiations can bring—a victory, the development of a working consensus, etc. Thus we must ask, "What are the factors which influence the extent of actor's motivation to negotiate?"

The first general postulate is that motivation to engage in negotiations is a function of the amount of stress caused by the dissensus. This being the case, the question becomes under what circumstances is dissensus going to be a major source of strain.

I have already suggested that awareness of disagreement is important because without it people would not know that there was a task to be done. Awareness of dissensus has, however, additional significance. I would hypothesize that under specifiable conditions, awareness of a lack of consensus is, in and of itself, stress-producing. Therefore, when there is this awareness, there is also likely to be the necessary motivation. Just the knowledge that he differs from his interaction partner in his definition of the situation is often sufficient to motivate actor to do something about it.

Part of the reason for this is found in a variety of cognitive dissonance theories, all of which postulate that people feel stress if they cannot maintain a simple, validated, and consistent view of their worlds (Festinger, 1954; 1957; Heider, 1948; Newcomb, 1959). The existence of dissensus between actor and other may cause dissonance for actor simply because it leads him to doubt the validity of his own definition. In addition, if actor is favorably inclined to other, the knowledge of dissensus will be stress-producing because people expect others whom they like to agree with them. Something seems wrong when a liked person does not agree about a situation's definition. Following Newcomb (1958), I would also suggest that significant dissonance would be most likely when the subject over which there is disagreement is of importance to actor and of relevance to his relation with other. These conditions are, of course, likely to exist when the matter at issue is the definition of a situation in which they are both involved.

Dissonance is, however, not the only source of motivation. Actors want more than cognitive consistency; they have other goals that they wish to achieve in their interactions. Frequently, the achievement of these goals is dependent upon coordination and cooperation between actor and other. As long as dissensus exists, the interactants are likely to be unwilling—and perhaps unable—to engage in cooperative activities. If actor needs the cooperation of other in order to reach his own goals, he would be motivated to remove any barriers to cooperation. As Scheff (1967) notes, interactionist social psychologists have usually assumed the existence of a need and desire for coordination. It is clear, however, that this is not always the case, or at the very least its extent is variable. Thus I would postulate that, all other things being equal, the extent of the motivation to negotiate is a function of the extent to which actor needs other to achieve his goals.

Motivation to negotiate should also reflect the complexity of the coordination required for the achievement of goals (Scheff, 1967). If the success of the encounter depends upon very precise responses by the interactants, as in a trapeze act, the need for consensus would be higher than when only a loose coordination is required. In the latter case, for example, small differences do not have to be negotiated in order for the encounter to be successful. In general, then, the greater the difficulty of achieving an adequate level of coordination in the presence of dissensus, the greater the motivation to negotiate.

As just stated, the absence of total coordination need not necessarily mean that goals will be missed. But it often does mean, at a minimum, that the road to those goals is somewhat less smooth than it might be. In an interaction which is of short duration, the difficulties caused by a lack of coordination may be acceptable as petty annoyances, and the motivation to remove them may be quite low. In long-range interactions these jarring elements may have a cumulative effect and become significant enough to lead actor to try to remove them. Thus, all other things being equal, the longer the interaction the greater the motivation to seek consensus in the presence of dissensus.

Assuming that the extent of consensus required to achieve goals is a constant, other factors related to the goals become relevant. For example, if the goal is very important to actor; if a failure to reach it will have significant negative consequences for him, he would be more motivated to seek consensus than if he had little investment in the outcome. However, if actor believes that the chances of reaching the goal are small even when consensus and coordination exist, the motivation to work for consensus through negotiation is likely to be low. Going beyond this, if actor believes that the chances of achieving consensus are low or that the consensus which is likely to result will be closer to other's position than it is to his own, his motivation to engage in negotiations is likely to be reduced.

The factors which lead actor to believe that other "will get his way" are quite apparent. Of special importance would be actor's view of his power relative to that of actor and actor's perception of the extent of other's commitment to his definition. Almost by definition, if actor views other as more powerful he will think that other can control the outcome if he wishes to do so. And when he believes that other has a strong commitment to his definition, he knows it will be a struggle to win concessions. When other has both power and a strong commitment, actor may believe that he has no chance.

Actor's commitment to his own view may also be relevant, but the relation is complex. In some instances the commitment to his original definition may be so strong that actor will avoid negotiations even when it would appear to an outside observer to be in his best interest to negotiate. Actor may be willing to forego the achievement of goals that third persons would see as extremely valuable because he believes that the attainment of consensus will require him to alter some aspect of his value system which he views as central. Examples of this phenomenon abound in history. All religions have their martyrs who chose death in preference to negotiating with their adversaries over basic elements in their belief systems, and spies and patriots have done the same for their secular gods.

Of course, a strong commitment to one's original definition does not always preclude negotiations. In fact, under some circumstances it leads to a strong motivation to negotiate. This will happen when actor believes it is possible to convert the other to his point of view, when he holds beliefs which require him to attempt to convert others even if the chances of success are low, and when his commitment is strong but his faith is shaky and he needs the conversion of others to validate his viewpoint. The last of these is graphically illustrated in *When Prophecy Fails* (Festinger et al., 1956), a study of a group whose prediction of the end of the world proved to be untrue. When the evidence became overwhelming that a basic tenet of their belief was wrong, they did not give up that belief, but, to the contrary, increased their proselytizing. Their reasoning seemed to be, "If we can convince others we are right, we must be right."

Actor's motivation to engage in negotiations will also tend to be higher when alternatives are lacking. All other things being equal, if interaction with this particular other represents the only opportunity to reach a goal, the motivation to engage in negotiations is likely to be increased. If other, more "agreeable," people are easily available, there is less need to pay the costs of negotiations.

Implicit in all that has been presented thus far is the assumption that actor's involvement in negotiations is completely voluntary. It must be noted in ending our discussion of motivation that actor may be coerced into negotiations—he may participate because of a desire to avoid punishments which are threatened by a more powerful other or by an interested third party. Contract negotiations under the threat of a Taft-Hartley injunction, compulsory attempts at reconciliation prior to divorce, psychiatric treatment under court orders, and much of the interaction between some parents and their children typify this situation. The line between voluntary and forced, seeking to obtain a goal and seeking to avoid punishment, is a fine one, but the distinction seems to be of importance in this case.

In addition to all this, there are probably general personality factors relevant here. Some people are more tolerant of the existence of dissensus. Some are bothered more by cognitive dissonance than others, some are very upset by disagreements and the resulting conflict; others are not bothered as much, etc. When one or both of the interactants have the characteristics which lead to a low tolerance of dissensus there would, of course, be a greater likelihood that negotiations will be undertaken.

Achieving Consensus

The fact that the actors desire to replace dissensus with consensus and are willing to engage in negotiations in pursuit of that goal does not ensure that the negotiations will be successful—as many labor negotiators and formerly married persons can testify. A consensus can be reached by negotiations—if one of the participants abandons his original position and adopts that of the other; if each changes his view and adopts a new one which did not exist at the beginning in the mind of either; or if each compromises and gives up part of his or her definition. Regardless of which occurs it is clear that a working consensus can be arrived at only when one or both parties are convinced to change their views. That both are willing to enter negotiations does not ensure that they can be convinced to accept the specific alterations in their views which are "required" for consensus. In fact, as just indicated, people may enter negotiations with such great resistance to change that there is little likelihood that anything that goes on will have much chance of moving them. Thus my discussion of the factors which lead to negotiations does not end the matter. I must now discuss the factors related to the likelihood that the negotiations will be successful, that is, the factors which are most likely to produce a working consensus at the end. Fortunately, part of the answer can be arrived at by a restatement of points already made, and thus some aspects of the problem can be handled with dispatch. Assuming that the parties have been brought to the point of negotiation, the general factors which will affect the likelihood that a consensus will be reached include the following:

1. the extent of the disagreement
2. the extent of the actors' resistance to alteration in their views
3. the effectiveness of the pressures brought to bear by the participants
4. the strengths of their arguments in support of their positions

The first factor may be passed over rather quickly. The relationship between extent of disagreement and the likelihood of reaching consensus is fairly obvious. If there isn't much difference to begin with, small changes in views will produce a working consensus, and it seems clear that small changes are easier to bring about than larger ones. We have already considered the factors which are related to the amount of dissensus present (see pages 226-31), and it is not necessary to re-cover that ground.

Resistance to Change. The relation between the actors' tendencies to resist changing their minds and the probability that a working consensus will emerge is also very clear. Certain people have personality traits which make them more suggestible than others. And, if one or both of the negotiators have the characteristics associated with suggestibility, the likelihood of a consensus emerging is increased. The problem then becomes to specify what the relevant traits are.

Following McGuire (1969), I suggest that all other things being equal, a person is more likely to be persuaded if he attends to and comprehends (learns) the arguments of the other. A person who turns a deaf ear to his interaction partners is unlikely to be persuaded by them, *and* some people are generally "better listeners" than others.

A second relevant factor would be the individual's ability to abide cognitive dissonance. As I will note again later, in some cases people will acquiesce because to do so results in a reduction of cognitive dissonance, an end which theory suggests is desired by most people. We must not, however, overlook the fact that people vary in the extent to which dissonance represents a problem for them. A person with low tolerance of dissonance would be more persuasible. Also, acquiescence is not the only way of reducing dissonance. Actor can, for example, retain his disagreement and reduce his dissonance by changing his view of other. People may have general preferences regarding the mechanisms they use to reduce dissonance, and if this is so it would again follow that there are general differences in persuasibility.

There are other factors involved in the extent to which a person is likely to be persuaded, all other things being equal. Perhaps they need only be mentioned, because their connection to persuasibility seems fairly clear. For example, people with low self-esteem, almost by definition, have less confidence in the correctness of their views, and therefore they should be more willing to give them up. Those who have a strong need for the approval of others, those who are easily frightened and less immune to threats, those who are more trusting, and those who are less analytic in their thinking should also be more likely to abandon their original views in the presence of arguments to the contrary.

Some of the data which were cited in the discussion of the effects of self-esteem (see pages 185–205) showed that in nonnegotiation situations, people with low self-esteem were more likely to be influenced by others, and that material has obvious implications for the present issue. Beyond this, however, there is not a great deal to report. Personality variables have frequently been used in "negotiations" research, but most of the studies used paradigms which do not meet the definition of negotiations being used here, and many of the other studies use a dependent variable which is not relevant for our concerns. Thus, there is little direct evidence bearing upon the hypotheses presented above.

It has been found, however, that groups composed of people who are high on dogmatism—that is, people we would normally consider to be close-minded—are less likely to be able to successfully negotiate issues and also tend to take longer to reach decisions (Druckman, 1967). The obverse of this has also been reported. In one study, McGrath (1966) found that the cognitive flexibility of the group members was correlated ($r = .31$) with successful negotiation outcomes, but an attempted replication failed. Consistent with the hypothesis is the finding by Kelley et al. (1970) that pairs composed of competitive persons reached fewer agreements than did groups who described themselves as cooperative. But this relation is also limited. The study was conducted at a variety of American and European universities, but the association was found only at those sites where competitiveness was perceived as being associated with personal strength.

Finally, I would note that persons who believed that they could control their fate were tougher bargainers than those who believed that they were at the mercy of outside forces (Hartnett et al., 1973). This would seem to suggest that if two of the former were put together the chances of consensus would be reduced.

Chertkoff and Esser (1976) suggest that all these findings can be understood in terms of a single principle. They suggest that people who are dogmatic, who equate competitiveness with strength, who believe they are responsible for what happens to them, etc., are likely to feel strongly that their selves are on the line when they are bargaining. They are unwilling to give in because to do so is taken as a personal defeat and an indication of personal weakness. They must win in order to protect their self-images.[9]

The Costs and Gains of Negotiations. The extent of difference and the general characteristics of the participants are not the only factors that determine the likelihood of consensus. The general idea that lies behind what was said before is that consensus is likely to occur when rewards for it are high and the costs are low. A small change is less costly than a large one and a change in opinion is less costly for some than for others. More generally, we can say that an actor's willingness to change is increased when he or she perceives that the gains of consensus will exceed the profits associated with the status quo *and* the rewards associated with not changing one's mind. People will change when there is something in it for them.

This situation is likely to exist when certain factors—which were considered earlier in another context—exist. I would postulate that change is likely to be defined in a positive way when coordination is necessary if the goals of the interaction are to be reached, when these goals are important to actor, when the existence of disagreement causes cognitive dissonance, when alternative attractive interactions are not available, and when actor's commitment to the original definition is low. The reasoning is that under each of these conditions actor has much to gain and/or little to lose when a consensus is achieved.

The strength of actors' prior commitments to their original positions has been well studied and we may start there. The connection is fairly obvious; if a person is strongly wedded to his own view, the cost of giving it up will be high. If both are highly committed, neither is likely to be willing to change and a deadlock is more likely. If one or both have low commitment, the chances of consensus are improved.

Commonly, commitment is manipulated by varying the prenegotiation experience of the subjects. To increase commitment, some subjects discuss and reach a decision with a partner and then they are paired with another person who has had a similar

---

[9]Druckman (1967) found, in fact, that people with high degrees of dogmatism are likely to define even a compromise as a defeat.

experience with a different partner. The idea is that the reaching of a decision in the original group increases actor's commitment to the agreed upon position. In the second group, he is negotiating for his original partner as well as for himself. He is likely to believe that changing his position will be a betrayal of his first partner. In the low commitment condition, there is either no prenegotiation session or the first session involves only discussion without an attempt to reach a common position. Studies by Druckman (1967), Kahn and Kohls (1972), Kogan et al. (1972), and Bass (1966) used this basic paradigm and produced results which clearly show the relevance of commitment.

A study along the same lines is reported by Blake and Mouton (1961). After a relatively long association, groups of varying size determined "their" solution to a problem. Then a representative from each group met in public with a member from one, two, or three other groups to choose the best solution. No compromise was possible, so the paradigm does not quite meet the negotiation definition, but it is striking to note that in sixty of the sixty-two trials there was a deadlock. Almost all the representatives stood firmly behind the solution worked out in their original group. In every case, however, impartial judges had no difficulty deciding which decision was best.[10] McGrath (1966) cites data from a study by Campbell which also suggest that a strong commitment to one's group's position stands in the way of agreement. Note should also be taken of the Kogan et al. (1972) finding that when the same people were asked to negotiate several issues, some of which had been the subject of prenegotiation discussion and others which had not, there were more deadlocks for the previously discussed issues.

High commitment is, of course, not the only thing which will influence the cost associated with giving in. For example, when the cost of negotiating is high—because it uses up a desired resource—one would want to reach agreement and do it quickly. In real life the resource is often time, and people are inclined to agree so that they can stop "wasting time" and get on to other things. In a study by Komorita and Barnes (1969), money was the resource wasted by extended negotiations. Some of the subjects had two dollars deducted from their "profits" for each offer that was made, and other subjects had no cost assessed. Time to decision was fastest when both were charged and slowest when neither was. There was, however, no clear difference in number of decisions reached.

The extent of the consequences which follow the outcome should affect the ease and likelihood of reaching agreement. Consistent with this are findings reported by Druckman et al. (1977). In a simulation, which required groups to decide which of several programs would be favored, agreement was more frequent and quicker when there was little to lose regardless of what was decided. If the money was coming from external sources and if both factions would share in the control of whatever program was funded, the decision making was easier. When the groups themselves contributed the money and the winning faction would control the program, there was more firmness.

---

[10]Impressive as these findings appear, it must be noted that there was no control group. It is possible that a like number of deadlocks would have occurred in the absence of these strong efforts to increase the subjects' commitment to their groups' solutions.

Finally, there are studies which vary the cost of failing to reach agreement and they show that the greater the costs associated with a deadlock, the lower the likelihood that dissensus will remain (Thibaut and Faucheux, 1965; Thibaut, 1968; Thibaut and Gruder, 1969). The same point is made indirectly in other studies. As Chertkoff and Esser (1976) note, in most laboratory studies agreement usually has less cost associated with it than deadlock. Thus we would expect that when subjects are aware that time is running out, they will make a strong effort to reach agreement even if it involves concessions that they were apparently not willing to make up to that point. The data support this expectation (Benton, Kelley, and Liebling, 1972; Esser and Komorita, 1975).

Threats and Promises.   The focus to this point has been on costs and gains which are not controlled by the participants in the negotiations. An interaction partner does not usually provide the punishment one gets by not standing up for one's principles, and a negotiating partner is not normally the source of the rewards associated with protecting one's vested interests. However, the course of negotiations is often importantly influenced by the participants' expectations concerning what they will get from each other. More specifically, I would hypothesize that conditions which lead other to expect punishment from actor for noncompliance will increase the likelihood of compliance as will conditions which lead other to expect a reward for compliance.

This statement sets several tasks. First, I must specify the conditions which lead other to expect reward and punishment, and then I must show that the expectation that actor will reward or punish actually influences other's reactions. The situation varies somewhat for rewards and punishments, so each will be handled separately.

Threats and Punishments.   I would start by saying that other is likely to believe that he will be punished for noncompliance when actor makes a credible threat to that effect. This statement is not as self-evident as it appears. It could be, for example, that other will expect noncompliance to lead to punishment even in the absence of a threat. Other may think that in this situation if actor can punish, he will. There is, in fact, some evidence (Hornstein, 1965) that the mere possession of power is sometimes enough to bring compliance. In most cases, however, other will assume that there will be a warning, and his or her behavior will be importantly affected only when there is, at a minimum, an implicit threat. If this is so, the focus then shifts to the conditions which will lead actor to threaten and the factors which will make the threat persuasive to other.

Actor is more likely to make a threat when he has the power to actually punish other. Of course, people do bluff; they will make threats that they have no ability to carry out. Power is not an absolutely necessary condition for the making of threats. A bluffing strategy is, however, risky, so the actual possession of power to punish will at least increase the likelihood of a threat being made.

The mere possession of power is, however, not enough. If it were, threats would be ubiquitous in human interaction, since most people have some ability to inflict some kind of cost on most other people. If nothing else, we can all apply the sanction of disapproval. None of us is totally impotent. There isn't much point, however, in making a threat which is so puny it has little chance of being successful. Threats are costly to the threatener so actor must believe that his power to punish is sufficient to compel other's acquiescence. Thus actor needs *substantial* power to punish, and the more he wants from other the greater that power must be.

It goes beyond this, however. Actor must believe that his power to punish is sufficient to gain acquiescence *and* protection from retaliation. Other also has power to punish, and if when actor exercises power in an attempt to gain acquiescence he is left open to retribution, he will probably think twice about doing it. It may not be in actor's interest to gain compliance by punishment if to do so leaves him defenseless against a counterattack by other.

In addition, the gain from other's compliance must be of some magnitude. As will be noted in more detail later, the use of threats and punishments invariably involve some cost for actor. If there is a counterattack, they will be even greater. Actor will not be willing to pay these costs unless compliance has greater value for him. Among the factors that will determine the value of other's compliance are the utilitarian rewards at stake, the likelihood that a deadlock will be a barrier to the obtaining of the reward, actor's commitment to his own position, and so on.

Thus far it seems that actor is inclined to use threats when he has considerable power, when the gains from other's compliance are high, and when other's power to retaliate is low. This boils down to the hypothesis that the likelihood of actor's using a threat is directly related to the extent of actor's power, the degree by which actor's power exceeds other's, and the significance of the issue being negotiated.

There is, however, more to it. As Tedeschi and Bonoma (1977) note, threats and punishments are usually measures of last resort. Even if conditions permit actor to use them against other, the chances are they will be used only when no alternative will work. This is because the fixed costs of coercive actions are generally rather high. In fact, Tedeschi et al. (1970) suggest on the basis of their experimental evidence that when the costs associated with retaliation are equal to those directly associated with the exercise of coercion, the latter are greater barriers to threats because they are more certain. In other words, in some cases threats are often not made because we *know* they are difficult to carry out.

The high cost of punishment is partly a function of the time and effort it is likely to involve, but even greater cost comes from the fact that punishment often conflicts with cultural values. As Tedeschi and Bonoma (1977: 228) note, "the *offensive* use of coercion is generally disapproved and resisted, and in many instances it is illegal and merits punishment." In addition to the costs of social disapproval, there are the personal costs. At a minimum, actor will have some doubts about the legitimacy of his actions and this will have consequences for his self-view.

Given this, I would expect actor to be more likely to use threats when they can be made in secret and when his relationship to other is such that offensive coercion is more acceptable than it usually is. The latter would be the case when other is disliked, when the stakes are high, when other is, in absolute terms, reasonably powerful, and when a quick response is required.

Successful Threats. Let us assume that on the basis of these considerations actor has decided that a threat is a good strategy and he has threatened other. The question now becomes, "Will the use of threat increase the likelihood of compliance and thereby increase the likelihood of consensus?" The answer is, obviously, that it depends. Some threats are successful and others are not. In general terms, the relevant considerations are clear-cut: compliance will be most likely when the threat is believable and the gains associated with submission are seen *by other* to exceed the total cost associated with compliance.

Under what conditions will a threat be viewed as believable? Under what circumstances will other assume that actor will in fact impose the threatened punishment? The relevant considerations are similar to those discussed above. Let us consider how they apply to other's perceptions of actor's probable behavior.

When other believes his or her power to punish is equal or greater than actor's, threats from actor are *unlikely* to be credible. If other believes that he can retaliate equally, if not in kind, he is going to believe that actor wouldn't dare carry out the threat. He will believe that his countervailing power will lead actor to decide, when it gets down to it, that there isn't much in it for him. As other will see it, actor will decide that other is more likely to counterattack than acquiesce. Or other may conclude that actor will realize that if other does comply, that won't be the end of it. Actor will be expected to understand that other will get back in some other way, thereby raising actor's costs to an unacceptable level. Actor won't make a threat unless he believes he is more powerful. Other won't believe actor will carry out his threat unless he (other) believes that actor is accurately assessing the power relation. And often these two conditions will not coexist. It is not at all uncommon for actor to threaten and for other to disbelieve. We now see that this will happen when actor and other have differing views of where the power is.

In the previous point, the relevant consideration was the *relative* power of actor and other. Also to be considered is other's view of actor's power in absolute terms. Because actor believes or asserts that he has the resources to do what he threatens does not mean that other will believe it. A threat to the effect that "I will ruin you financially" may not be believed because other thinks actor wouldn't dare, but it can also be disbelieved because other thinks that actor couldn't do it if he tried. Other's perception of this matter would depend upon the information he has about actor. As Tedeschi and Bonoma (1977) note, in some cases actor can make his threat more believable by concealing information about himself. In other instances, the more other knows the better it is for actor. Obviously the relevant consideration is the extent of actor's actual power.

In the absence of direct information concerning actor's power, other will depend upon indices of actor's probable power. Data show that threats received from high status persons, for example, are more likely to be believable (Faley and Tedeschi, 1971) because high status implies power. And threats from experts, in areas which their expertise has relevance, are more likely to be believed and complied with because such people have the skill needed to carry out their threats (Tedeschi et al., 1975).

Believability of threat depends on more than other's view of the power situation.

For one thing, other knows as well as actor that offensive coercion is frowned upon. The making of threats is not totally approved, but acting on them is worse, so other may not believe a threat when it is made under conditions that mean acting upon it will lead actor to suffer high costs. Thus a threat which involves illegal punishments is less likely to be believed, all other things being equal, and the same would be true for one which is defined as morally reprehensible, difficult to carry out, and so on.

Also relevant for believability is the actor's reputation. If he is known to other as a person who usually carries out his threats, he is likely to be believed in the present case (Bonoma and Tedeschi, 1973; Bonoma and Lindskold, 1972). What is not totally clear is how generalizable reputation is. Two studies are available which show that people who have a reputation for keeping promises are more believable when they threaten, but people who have lived up to their threats do not increase the credence of their promises (Heilman, 1974; Tedeschi and Bonoma, 1977). Other questions of generalizability have not even been studied to this extent.

Several other factors would enter into the believability of threats. A partial list would include:

1. Other's view of actor's general personality, specific intentions, and present mood. Is he a person who enjoys inflicting punishment? Is he really serious in his threat? Does he act "rationally" or is he willing to take a loss of utilitarian rewards to avoid loss of face? How important is it to him to obtain compliance? Is he a risk taker? Would he bluff? Does he like me? Is he in a bad mood?

2. The way in which a threat is expressed may influence its believability, perhaps largely because of the clues it gives to the issues already raised. For example, a threat may be made as "a final offer" or in a very tentative way. Has he left himself an out? A threat made in the heat of anger will have low believability if the "showdown" is some time in the future, but high likelihood of being believed if the decision on implementation will follow quickly. Even the form of the threat is relevant. Schlenker et al. (1970) threatened subjects in two ways which in fact said the same thing. However, the threat which stated what the subject must do was viewed as more threatening and complied with more than the one which said that the subject must *not* do something.

3. Although there is no adequate direct evidence which tests the point, it seems likely that characteristics of other also influence the extent to which actor's threats will be believed. Some people are simply naïve; they are unaware that actors bluff and/or lose their nerve. They tend to take actor at his word. Some others are timid; they are unwilling to take risks. If they believe that there is any chance that actor will implement his threat, they will play it safe and assume he will. Some view the world as a hostile place and assume that most actors are inclined to punish; others take a more benign view of the world and require a lot of evidence before they can be convinced that "anyone would really do that" (see also Tedeschi and Bonoma, 1977; Tedeschi et al., 1971).

To further the discussion, let us assume that other is convinced that actor means business. Under what conditions will actor's threat be effective? When will consensus emerge because other acquiesces? The general rule has been mentioned often. Other will agree when the costs of compliance are less than the costs that will be incurred from actor's imposition of the threatened punishment.

Several of the relevant considerations have been considered previously, for they are similar to the factors which make other's compliance valuable for actor. The cost of giving in will be high for other when his commitment to his original position is high, when his compliance will importantly reduce his share of the utilitarian rewards, when there is much at stake, and when he has something to gain from a deadlock.

On the other hand, the costs of nonacquiescence will be high when the punishments actor can inflict are substantial. This will occur when actor has a lot of power, when actor's power far exceeds other's, when other is unlikely or unable to retaliate, and when the matter is important to actor. Under such circumstances other is likely to comply. (See Rubin and Brown, 1975: 284, for a summary of several relevant studies.)

There is one other element which has not come up before. The fact that he has given in to a threat frequently produces additional costs for other which are quite substantial (Brown, 1968, 1977). To give in to a threat is often viewed by other as causing a loss of face. It may also lead him to view himself as cowardly, incompetent, etc. These costs must be included in the cost of giving in. The threatened punishments must outweigh the utilitarian losses *and* these intangible costs. If they do, other will acquiesce; if they do not, he will refuse.

In some instances, an increment in threat increases the cost of compliance more than it increases the cost associated with the punishment itself. When that happens, the threats reduce the likelihood of compliance. In efforts to prove that he is not a coward, other may ignore his utilitarian interests and engage in what Deutsch and Krauss (1962) call a threat-counterthreat-aggression cycle. Similarly, in both real life and laboratory experiments, people have been known to take fewer profits than they could have obtained if by so doing they also cut the profit of a punitive opponent (Rubin, Lewicki, and Dunn, 1973; Brown, 1977). There is even evidence (Hornstein, 1965) that powerful others can sometimes get more compliance when they don't threaten than when they do. Threats may not work with prideful, competitive, and aggressive types. They may, in fact, be counterproductive.

There is another circumstance under which threats will not increase the likelihood of consensus. Up to now I have been implicitly assuming that only two possibilities are open to other: comply or suffer the consequences associated with actor's punishing behavior. Sometimes, at least, there is a third option. Other can make a counterthreat, and if it is credible and of sufficient magnitude he can "force" actor to back off, avoiding both punishment and compliance. The factors which will affect other's ability and willingness to make such counterthreats and the conditions under which they will be effective, are, of course, the same as those which influence actor's decision about the original threat.

Promises and Rewards. In an attempt to gain compliance from another, the promise of reward is an alternative to the use of threats and punishments. The factors which lead to a decision to make a promise and the conditions which determine whether compliance will be given in return for the reward are, in their general form, similar to those considered above. I will therefore cover the matter very briefly.

Actor's decision to offer a reward will partly depend on whether he feels he has "enough to spare," which is related to the value he places on what he is giving up and the value that other's compliance has for him. In addition, he will consider how likely other is to accept the proffered reward. In many cases, actor's perception of how much he has, how valuable it is, and how much other wants it will be influenced by what he and other have. If actor has more than other, this will increase his propensity to make an offer.

By the same token, when other is trying to decide whether the proffered reward is sufficient to exceed the cost of giving in, his perception will be influenced by what he has relative to what actor has. The fact that he has less may increase his desire for the reward and the value he places on it. Thus, an unequal distribution of resources leads to an increased likelihood that rewards will be offered and accepted. And since I am assuming that the giving of the reward is conditional upon compliance, it would follow that unequal power to reward increases the likelihood of achieving consensus.

Again, however, the hypothesis must be hemmed in by qualifications. Simply to have more is not sufficient. The person offering the reward must be willing and able to spare more than a pittance. The offer has to be an attractive one, that is, it must be seen by other as exceeding the cost of compliance. In addition, the hypothesis must be limited to cases in which the value of the thing to be exchanged is strongly influenced by the relative amount possessed. In many cases this will not be so. For many rewarding things there is an absolute criterion of value. If I have enough to eat, an offer of food will not be made more attractive by the fact that my interaction partner has more than I. If I am at the satiation level I won't want more regardless of how much my partner has. In such cases, relative control over resources would be irrelevant to the achievement of consensus.

When the demand for a resource is not affected by other's supply, the appropriate hypothesis would be that consensus is more likely when an actor has what he considers to be an excess of a particular resource and other considers his store to be too low. When this is so, it may be that actor's and other's store of the resource may be unequal, but they need not be.

Finally, the matter is complicated by the fact that there are a variety of rewards. When actor offers a particular resource, other may reciprocate without giving compliance. An offer by actor of X in return for compliance may lead to a counteroffer of Y for X because other is well supplied with Y. Actor may have a shortage of Y and feel constrained to accept. Such an exchange will only indirectly move them in the direction of consensus. Compliance may not occur until a series of bargains has brought about mutual satiation on all but one resource. Only then would compliance be the only way that a promise could be reciprocated.

Threats vs. Promises. All that has gone before indicates clearly that both threats and promises "work." The logical next question is, "Which works better?" The previous discussion considered each separately and asked, in effect, what conditions maximize the effectiveness of each. Now I will discuss the effectiveness of one as compared with the other. However, since both threats and promises vary in their effectiveness depending upon the conditions which surround them, the question must be specified. Let us ask, "When each is used under conditions which are fairly close to being ideal for it, which is likely to be more effective?"

It is not totally clear what the answer to this question should be, for there are a number of relevant considerations and they do not all push in the same direction. It would seem that the net effect would favor promises, but let me begin with a consideration which inclines punishments to be more effective. Both threats and promises convey information. They tell the person who receives them what future events are likely to be, and they convey information about actor's preferences. Of course, actor often has a more direct way of telling other what he wants. Actor can simply state his goals or desires. But in some cases this way is not available, not used, or considered by other to be unreliable as a source for valid information. Other may believe, and properly, that people are likely to lie in a situation like this. But if they are willing to "put their money where their mouth is," they are probably not attempting to deceive.

Following Rubin and Brown (1975) I would suggest that this is relevant for the matter under consideration, because given the way threats are usually made they often convey more information than promises, and if the opportunities for communication are limited the extra information may be important (Lewicki and Rubin, 1973; Rubin et al., 1973). Assume that other has several options available, only one of which is desired by actor. If actor says "I will reward you if you do X," it is clear that X is acceptable, but there is no indication what the reaction will be to the other behaviors. Other cannot be sure that no reward will follow if he does Y or Z. Similarly, if actor says "I will punish you if you do X," little information is conveyed about Y or Z. They are perhaps more acceptable than X, but they need not be free of punishment. Usually, however, a threat is *not* stated in that way. Usually actor will say "If you *do not do* X, I will punish you." If this is the case, other knows that the consequences of Y and Z will be negative and he can presume that X will not be punished. He cannot be sure, of course, that it will be rewarded, but at a minimum he knows about more options than he would if the usual form for promises had been used. Obviously there are a lot of "ifs" here and the difference in information is largely a result of a linguistic convention which is not absolute. Sometimes people will say, "I will reward you if you do not do Y or Z," though it is more common to tie reward to a specified desired action. Furthermore, the participants will often not need to use threats and promises as a source of this kind of information, and if they do, the threat or promise will be sufficiently detailed so that either approach will give the same amount of information. In other words, the point is valid, but its significance and applicability are limited.

The other considerations would generally suggest that promises are more likely to bring about a consensus. Some of what follows will be familiar, for I have considered most of these topics in my earlier discussions of promises and threats. The basic point I wish to make is that the impact of these factors is of different magnitude in the two cases. Y stands as a barrier to acquiescence to a threat, Y′ stands as a barrier to compliance in return for a promise, but Y is a stronger barrier than Y′.

1. If other has reason to believe that actor usually does what he promises or threatens, other is more likely to comply. In other words, actor's words must be credible. But the degree of credibility required seems to differ for threats as compared to promises. In regard to threats, research shows that when credibility is low the threat doesn't increase compliance. Some of the available studies show, however, that compliance occurs even when the credibility of a promise is low. This may be interpreted as suggesting that others are more likely to believe a promise than a threat, with credibility held constant. It goes somewhat beyond the data to say so, but I would suggest that when actor is in doubt he tends to believe promises and disbelieve threats. (See Rubin and Brown, 1975, 283–84, for a summary of some relevant investigations.)

I might add that other is probably correct in operating in this way. If actor seems likely to change his mind about a threat other may assume that the threatened punishment will not be forthcoming. Certainly other won't demand that actor live up to his word. If actor changes his mind about a promise, other may, however, be able to force him to "come across."

2. Both rewards and punishments "work" when they are sufficient to balance the loss associated with compliance. However, threats encourage and discourage agreement at the same time. The discouragement comes from the fact that to comply in response to a threat increases the cost of giving up one's original position. (It implies cowardice.) Since this adds to the cost to be overcome by a threat, a threat will probably have to be quite strong to "work." Promises do not have similar effects unless the promised reward is so large that it appears to be a bribe. When this is not so, promises may in fact reduce the cost of compliance. To comply in response to a promise can be interpreted as a kindly act, as a totally voluntary one, as a smart one, and so on.

3. The focus in the previous point was on the immediate effects of threat and promise. In conclusion, I would note that the use of threat can create a general atmosphere which will make future agreements more difficult even when threats are not used regarding these later issues. Threats create stress in the relationship, and as Hopmann and Walcott (1977) show, stress is a barrier to effective negotiations. It increases rigidity, curtails problem-solving ability, affects perception, etc. Threats also reduce interpersonal attraction (Rubin and Lewicki, 1973) which should reduce cooperation and willingness to yield (see Rubin and Brown, 1975). Promises, on the other hand, have opposite effects.

This clearly leads to an hypothesis that under constant conditions promises are more productive of agreement than threats.[11] All that is necessary to tie up the loose

[11] This is part of the reason why threats are used less than promises when actors have a choice (Cheney et al., 1972; Rubin and Lewicki, 1973). In some cases, however, promises are not preferred even though they are more likely to be successful. Lindskold's and Gruder's studies (cited in Rubin and Brown, 1975) show that the "normal" pattern is not seen if other is defined as unfair

end is a study which controls magnitude and compares the relative effectiveness of the threat and promise. Unfortunately, that is not too easy to do, for it is often difficult to equate rewards and punishments. Usually the units are not commensurate. If they are both expressed in monetary terms, it might be possible to do it, but how does one decide how much approval is equivalent to a particular kind of disapproval? And the threats and punishments relevant in negotiating definitions of situations are likely to be of the latter type.

Although it involves a task which does not meet all the defining characteristics of a negotiating situation, a study by Rubin, Lewicki, and Dunn (1973) comes close to meeting our other requirements. In this investigation, the experimenter could either threaten to reduce the subjects' pay if they did not choose to work on difficult rather than easy anagrams, or he could promise to raise it, by a like amount, if they worked on the more difficult task. The results show that the promise was more effective in achieving the experimenter's goals.

This study is quite suggestive, but we must be careful not to overgeneralize from it. The major problem is that we do not know how the subjects defined the money they stood to lose by defying the threat. The subject could lose no more than sixty cents, and we cannot be sure the results would have been the same if the potential loss was large. As emphasized before, we don't expect a threat to increase compliance unless the punishment far exceeds the costs the threat adds to complying. I can easily imagine the subjects being quite willing to forego this kind of payoff in order to get back at "that threatening so and so." (It should be noted that the subjects believed their actions could influence the supervisor's pay.) On the other hand, the subjects had nothing tangible to lose by working on the more difficult task. Their payment was not affected by how well they did on the anagrams. So even if in psychological terms the reward was small, I am not surprised that it was enough to get them to "help out" the "nice" investigator. Another test is needed in which the payoffs are both equal and major.

Other studies are available which compare the effects of rewards and punishments, but for one reason or another, none of them is conclusive. All of them are, however, consistent with the hypothesis that promises are more effective than threat. Lewicki and Rubin (1973; Rubin and Lewicki, 1973) solve the problem of equating the magnitude of rewards and punishments by simply saying the same thing in different forms. For example, in some cases the statement was phrased, "I will write up the final report if. . . ." For other subjects it was stated, "If you. . . , you will have to write up the report." The data show that simply changing the form of the statement did have effects. In one study (Rubin and Lewicki, 1973) there was no actual compliance measure; the subjects simply indicated whether they would have complied with each request and rated them in terms of how effective they thought each was. In the other

---

and exploitative. When that is so, winning becomes less important; saving face and "getting back" become major goals. This latter pattern is probably limited to cases in which the rewards of winning are not very great.

study (Lewicki and Rubin, 1973) there was a measure of actual compliance. In both instances the superiority of the "promise" form was considerable.

The answer to the original question seems clear. Considering both the direct and indirect evidence it appears likely that one gets further by promising than by threatening.

Honoring Accounts. One might get the impression from what has been presented that negotiations are simply decided by the balance of power between the participants, but that is not the case. Might is not the only thing that makes right. Other can be convinced by the strength of actor's arguments. What is said in support of one's position and how it is said *do* have consequences. As noted earlier, the substantive arguments in negotiations often take the form of *accounts*—excuses, justifications, etc. Thus, the next question becomes what makes an account persuasible. What kinds of accounts are more likely to be honored and what aspects of the style of presentation affect the likelihood that a particular account will be accepted?

If an account is to be honored it must be credible above all other things. Other must believe that what actor is saying is true. What, then, are the characteristics of a credible account? First of all, it has to be internally consistent. Contradictions within the several arguments making up an account will destroy it even if each argument taken by itself seems persuasive. One cannot normally combine, for example, an account involving internal drives and one involving obedience to orders.

An account must also be congruent with the facts as they are perceived by other. A person who is known to be skilled at a task cannot use the "I didn't know that would happen" argument, and that excuse will also be ineffective if other believes that "everyone" knows, or should know, what the consequences will be. Similarly, one cannot argue for an inability to withstand the pressures of third person if other knows of cases in which such pressures have been effectively resisted. Finally, if the account is to be credible it must fit in with other's implicit theory of human motivation. Actor cannot use the disclaimer "I was trying to be kind" if other believes that anyone who did such a thing can only be trying to be cruel (cf. Blumstein et al., 1974). As Scott and Lyman (1968) put it, an account will be honored only if it fits in with the background expectancies of others.

This point suggests again the importance of role-taking ability in human affairs. If actor is to have his accounts accepted, he must be able to guess what other knows about him, what other believes is known by people in general, and what other's view of human motivation is. That information would, of course, be obtained by the process of role taking.

Credibility is necessary for the acceptance of an account, but that is obviously not sufficient. Other must consider the account to be credible *and* adequate. It must be relevant to the action, and if it is an excuse it would have to be equal to the gravity of the offense. Other must not be inclined to say after hearing the account, "I can see your point, but I don't consider it a good enough reason."

What will be considered adequate by other will vary widely. Particularly interesting, for example, are the very different points at which people are willing to accept dishonesty. All but a few will tolerate dishonesty under some conditions, but the nature of those conditions vary widely from person to person and group to group. Some will accept almost any reason as legitimate, while others would have to be convinced that there was extreme provocation, extreme need, or a strong possibility that the behavior was not in fact dishonest. Other's view of actor will also affect his response to actor's accounts. A child, for example, will need less justification, all other things being equal, than an adult would, and if other likes actor he is likely to be more easily convinced.

Since accounts frequently get their basic power from the argument of special circumstances, it would seem that each time a particular account was used by actor its chances of being accepted would be reduced, assuming, of course, that other knew about the previous uses. Special circumstances can't be special if they seem to occur all the time.

This tendency is, however, limited. Particularly if the account is not of the inadequate information or accident type, actor might be able to increase the credibility of his argument by pointing out instances in which the same thing happened. Under some circumstances it could prove very effective to say, "I can't seem to help it, but everytime I. . ."

All theorists in this area emphasize the social influences involved in determining whether accounts will be honored. We are taught that certain things are reasonable; they become part of what everyone knows and they are immediately recognized and easily accepted as adequate and credible. The clear implication is that accounts which are common in a society are more likely to be accepted, assuming, of course, that they are used in the proper situation. Lyman and Scott (1968: 50) suggest that a particular account "may be an expected excuse in some cultures so that the failure to invoke it, and the use of some other excuse, constitutes an improper account."

This, too, is probably not always the case. A person who offers an account which is different in its details may get extra credit because of that. Perhaps it shouldn't be too original; if it is, other won't be able to place it into a category of acceptable accounts and he will have difficulty judging it on its own merits. But if it is an ingenious variation on a familiar theme, it is likely to be very effective. Other will feel, "He's not just repeating the same old excuses." Originality suggests that actor is not simply using an excuse he has seen work for other people. Originality will imply some degree of credibility. In fact, actor may get the ultimate accolade: "He's got to be telling the truth. No one could make that up."

Effective Negotiations. Noting the relevance of the content of the arguments offered does much to correct the view that reason is irrelevant in negotiations, but the picture is still not complete. It should be mentioned, for example, that a person who has a good argument favoring his or her definition, may not present it in a way that makes its persuasiveness apparent. Given the nature of negotiations, arguments must be presented with some skill. Negotiations involve complex and subtle processes. Even in very formal negotiating situations, such as labor and diplomatic negotiations, definitions are usually not laid on the table in black and white. They are hinted at, presented tentatively, and perhaps withdrawn. The implications of the offer are often not made explicit and the actors have to get below the surface of what is actually being said. An other may neglect to make a counteroffer which would break an impasse because he mistakenly believes that the other would not accept it. The participants may argue past one another because neither truly understands what the other is suggesting.

From this it would follow that the likelihood of achieving a working consensus would be in part a reflection of the extent and effectiveness of the communication between the interactants. And there is some evidence that in general an increase in the available information facilitates the reaching of consensus (Bass, 1966; Druckman, 1967; 1968). Other studies, however, fail to find a difference (see Rubin and Brown, 1975). The reason for the lack of consistency is obvious. There are conditions under which it is better not to know. Certain information can be a barrier to agreement. If actor knows that other intends to violate agreements, for example, the chances of a deadlock are increased. And, in addition, information without motivation to use that information in the service of reaching an agreement is equivalent to not having information (see Rubin and Brown, 1975).

All this notwithstanding, it does seem that variations in information do have relevance. Thus, it seems worthwhile to consider how information exchange can contribute to consensus. In the course of doing this, there will be some references to the factors which relate to the extent of information exchange.

Basically, information is necessary because it improves the role taking of the participants. If agreement is to be reached through offers and counteroffers, each must know the goals of the other, their views about the relative importance of the several issues, how particular proposals will be defined, and so on. These matters are often subtle and if each can truly understand the other—if each can understand the meanings behind the overt meanings—the chances of finding a common ground are increased. This would suggest that the greater the universe of discourse, the greater the likelihood that a consensus will emerge.

The point becomes clear if one considers what is likely to happen if the tourist and foreign merchant I previously mentioned ever do get to the point of negotiating. Even in regard to such a relatively simple matter as arriving at the price of an item, if communication has to be limited to hand signs and the few words they are likely to share, the chances of reaching agreement are low. (For a discussion of the factors associated with variation in the universe of discourse see pages 47–48.)

The possession of common meanings is not enough, however. There must be adequate communication of those meanings, which implies, at a minimum, that there must be few barriers to the communication of views. A number of factors influence the extent to which there are barriers to communication. For one thing, the topic at issue is relevant. Hill et al. (1959) report, for example, that there was less consensus than there might have been among lower-class Puerto Ricans about the use of contraception because that topic was taboo even for married people. Sufficient time is also necessary if there is to be full communication, as is a willingness to expose one's embryonic ideas. The latter probably requires a certain degree of security in the relationship, and that is probably part of the reason why there is a relationship between intimacy of relationship and agreement (Kirkpatrick and Hobart, 1954; Hobart, 1956).

The conditions under which the interaction takes place should also influence the extent of communication. The peripatetic habits of foreign ministers reflect a belief that communication is better in a face-to-face situation, and their desire to keep the progress of the negotiations a secret while they are going on suggests that communication is more open when third parties are kept away.

This last point is, however, a complicated one. The presence of an audience is usually a drawback, but not always. The effects of an audience are sometimes due to their effect on communication, but again, not always. People will say things in private that they won't say in public, and that is the main point here. But sometimes when privacy is related to agreement the tie is not through increased communication. Kogan, Lamm, and Trommsdorf (1972) have found, for example, that there was less concern about loss of face when there was no audience present, which suggests that privacy also contributes to agreement by making it easier to concede. The privacy-open-communication line is not the only relevant one (see Rubin and Brown, 1975).

Furthermore, audiences can facilitate agreement under some circumstances, and again the effect may or may not be through the intervening variable of information. Audiences can sometimes facilitate agreement by forcing information exchange. The audience may be in a position to supply a participant with information if actor will not. Also, if the audience is playing the role of mediator, it can use that role to facilitate communication. Pruitt and Johnson (1970) found that bargainers are less apprehensive about making concessions if they can do so through a mediator. I would suspect that a mediator could, in a similar way, reduce resistance to certain kinds of communication (see Rubin and Brown, 1975). However, when audiences push toward agreement, information may not be the relevant intervening variable. The public can, for example, force concession when it feels its interests are being ignored.

Earlier we saw that awareness that there was dissensus and awareness that negotiation was feasible were important for getting negotiations started. Now I might add that it is not always clear to the interactants that negotiations are underway, and when one or both partners do not have this awareness the chances for successful negotiations are reduced. The reason is obvious. If the participants are not aware of the nature of the situation, communication will be hampered. The necessary information will not be presented, and if it is, its full meaning will not be appreciated.

In this case, however, the matter is quite complicated and the generalization must be hemmed in with a number of qualifications. In some instances, a lack of awareness on the part of one of the participants makes it easier to conduct successful negotiations. This would occur when the resistance of actor would be increased if he were aware that the other was consciously attempting to get him to accept a particular definition. Much of psychiatry involves getting the patient to accept the therapist's definition of the situation, that is, the doctor's view of the patient's problem and the proper solution to it. But many would argue that the patient will truly accept this definition only when he believes that he, rather than the psychiatrist, is its source. A skilled psychiatrist will, of course, have little difficulty in leading the patient to the right "insights" (Scheff, 1968).

In other cases, negotiations are likely to be broken off by one of the participants if the other comes to realize that they are negotiating. Scheff (1968) notes that lawyers often bring their clients to define their crimes in a way which will mitigate the client's responsibility without the client knowing that he is being coached. In this case the lawyer needs the protection of his client's unawareness. A lawyer is not supposed to coach his clients in this way, and if the client is aware that he has been led to a particular definition, there is always the chance that he will let this fact slip when pressure is applied. It is much safer for the lawyer to change his client's definition without the client realizing that this is happening.

It would seem, then, that mutual awareness of negotiation is not necessary if the aware participant is trained, practiced, and skillful. It is also necessary, if there are to be successful negotiations without total awareness, that the person who is aware be in control of the situation and in a position to direct it. The psychiatric situation works because the psychiatrist asks the (often leading) questions, the patient answers, and the psychiatrist subtly accepts or rejects the responses. If the roles were reversed, the chances of success would be slim indeed.

In a small number of cases, negotiations can take place only when both participants are "unaware" that negotiations are occurring. This would be so when all the participants hold the view that the issue at hand should be nonnegotiable. Some lawyers take the rules against coaching clients seriously and a few defendants do not take kindly to other people telling them what they really did and why they did it. Put such a lawyer and client together and you might think that there would be no possibility that either could successfully negotiate with the other. But, of course, there is a way out. They can define their negotiating behavior as being something entirely else and thus get around the barrier. Lawyers will convince themselves, quite sincerely, that they are merely instructing their clients in the provisions of the law and this will give them the cloak they need to hide the true meaning of their activities from themselves. And the same definition of the lawyer's activities may make it possible for the defendant to convince himself that he is coming to see the facts of his acts as they really are. Similarly, for some, nonmarital sexual relations are acceptable only if they are unplanned—only if there is a spontaneous "bigger than both of us" attraction. But there usually has to be some negotiations before a nonmarital sexual relation can be set up. How can one negotiate something which is supposed to have arisen spontaneously? The answer is by redefining the negotiating behavior. One was simply expressing feelings of attraction; one was discussing in an intellectual way one's sexual philosophy, etc. If such rationalizations are available and acceptable to the actors, negotiations can sometimes be carried on in the presence of mutual unawareness.

After all the space that has been devoted to a consideration of the exceptions to the rule, it is probably necessary to emphasize that, all of this notwithstanding, the general postulate *is* valid. Except under special circumstances, negotiations are more likely to succeed when both participants are aware that they are engaged in the process, and the reason for this lies in the fact that successful negotiations require good communication.

Without gainsaying the importance of communication, the reader must be cautioned against falling into the common error of assuming that all differences can be resolved if "only people would talk about them frankly." This is not so, even when effective communication is combined with motivation, awareness, and good negotiating techniques. It must be recognized that some differences are, in fact, irreconcilable. In some cases the interests, wants, and desires of the interactants are in basic conflict and no solution exists which will be acceptable to both. No solution will give both interactants the minimum amount of reward they require in return for their acquiescence. When that is the case, only coercion or bribery will produce a working consensus.

Winning at Negotiations

Throughout the last section, the interest has been on those factors which are conducive to the emergence of some kind of working consensus. There has been no attention devoted to the question, "If a working consensus does develop, whose view is more likely to prevail?" or to the more apt question, "Who will make the greater contribution to the compromise which is likely to be the result of the negotiations?" It should be obvious, however, that the answers to these questions are implicit in much of the material I have presented. For example, to say that the use of threats and rewards is conducive to the emergence of a consensus is to imply that the person who makes the threat or promise is more likely to have his or her view prevail. Threats and promises lead to consensus because they lead the person who is their target to compliance. Since these techniques are used to bring others to comply with actor's view of things, the person who successfully uses them will be the "winner." If this is so, all the factors that are associated with the use of threat and promise will also be associated with winning. If actor is more likely to use threats when his power to punish is substantially greater than other's, it would follow that the person with the greater power to punish will have a greater influence on the outcome. All the evidence provided which showed that consensus is more likely when there is inequality of power to punish also shows that the person with the greater power is the winner because the consensus is normally achieved by the compliance of the threatened person. The same could be said for control over rewards.

In addition to the studies cited, there are many more which show the relationship between power to punish and reward and outcome. A survey of them would simply be redundant. It may be taken as established that empirical evidence supports my position.

Many of the other issues I have discussed have equally clear implications for the present topic. For example, I have asserted that consensus is more likely to result when the parties are aware of the nature of the situation. My discussion of why this is so would suggest that when there is a difference in the amount of awareness possessed by the actors, the one with the greater awareness would have an advantage in controlling the direction the negotiations take. The aware person would be more likely to be able to marshal his arguments, to anticipate other's response, and so on. Thus, awareness should be associated with winning. Similarly, I showed that consensus is more likely when one or both of the negotiators have the personality characteristics associated with persuasibility. One does not need to dig very deeply to see that when one person is persuasible and the other is not, the consensus is going to be more influenced by the less persuasible person. To offer one final example: if consensus is unlikely when both participants are strongly committed to their original views, this would suggest that agreement is likely when neither or only one has a strong commitment. And it seems clear that the one with the stronger commitment will have more influence, as confirmed by the many studies already cited.

SUMMARY

This chapter focuses on the problematic aspects of interaction which deal with defining the situation—the absence of the appropriate elements from the actor's repertoire, the presence of several seemingly appropriate elements in the repertoire without any clear basis for choice, and disagreement between the definitions held by actor and other.

Actor may be said to lack defining elements when none of the identities, roles, and goals he is accustomed to using seem to fit the present situation. This is most likely to occur when actor has had little previous experience in comparable situations and when opportunities for anticipatory socialization have been limited. Actor will often decide that the only solution to this problem is to leave the scene as soon as possible; but if he stays the interaction itself may provide him with the instruction necessary for adequate participation.

In other situations which actor feels incapable of defining, he may actually possess the necessary elements, although he may not realize that they are appropriate. This is particularly likely to occur when other is controlling the cues present in the situation. In this case, actor's task is to learn to read the relevant cues despite any barriers.

When actor and other stand in a multiple relation to each other there is likely to be confusion regarding which of several elements is the appropriate one for the present encounter. In these circumstances, the first attempt at solution will probably involve gathering further information. Particularly valuable in this regard would be knowledge of other's definition. If this does not clear up the problem, actor may choose one of the elements and use that to the exclusion of the competing elements, he may attempt to devise new elements by combining existing ones, or he may alternate among the competing definitions. If one of the existing ones is chosen, it is likely to be the one highest on the hierarchy of prominence.

The decision regarding which possible solution is chosen will be based upon a consideration of a complex set of factors. In general, however, the choice will be made with a view to maximizing rewards and minimizing costs.

A lack of congruence between actor's and other's definitions is most common when the participants have had dissimilar socialization, and that is most likely when they have not previously interacted together. It *may* also be more common when they have different social traits and when the definitions associated with the encounter are not institutionalized in the society.

When efforts are made to resolve dissensus, negotiations are often the process used; that is, actor and other communicate with each other and attempt to reach a mutually acceptable bargain. This process is simply a special case of the general phenomenon of interaction. It involves offering justifications and excuses and applying pressure. However, the existence of dissensus does not ensure that attempts will be made to reduce it. Awareness that there are differences which can be reduced and a desire for the rewards which accompany a working consensus will increase the likelihood that negotiations will be undertaken. If negotiations are engaged in, the chances that a consensus will be reached are increased when the disagreement between actor and other is small, when one or both of the interactants have the personality traits which are associated with suggestibility, when the participants' commitment to their original view is low, when one has more power than the other, and can, therefore, effectively use threats and promises, when one or both is capable of giving strong arguments in favor of their view, and so on.

There is not likely to be a clear-cut winner in negotiations. The consensus which emerges will probably represent a compromise. However, one of the participants may contribute more to the compromise than the other. The winner, in this sense, will probably be the one who is a more effective debater, the one who has the greater power, and so on.

CHAPTER 9

INTERACTION
IN PROBLEMATIC SITUATIONS:
ROLE STRAIN
AND FALSE SELVES

As was noted earlier, the successful conclusion of the defining process simply means that the actors have arrived at a joint definition of the situation which they are willing to use as a guide to their actions, at least for the moment. At this point they are, however, not "home free." It often turns out that actor finds it difficult or impossible to fulfill the role obligations associated with the definitions that have been worked out. This condition is generally called *role strain,*[1] and we turn next to a consideration of the problems associated with it. As before, the specific questions to be considered are: What are the various forms the phenomenon can take? What conditions are conducive to its occurrence? What are the means utilized to reduce it?

The Nature of Role Strain

The discussion of role strain is complicated by the fact that the term refers to several distinct conditions (Goode, 1960a). All forms of role strain have in common a felt difficulty in meeting role agreements, but beyond this the types differ in their sources, consequences, and solutions. Thus, my first task is to provide a classification of the various types.

[1] The term "role strain" is also used by some (Secord and Backman, 1964) to include two situations I have already discussed—the lack of clear role definitions and the lack of consensus concerning roles. To my mind, to use a term to encompass all these things is to make it too broad to be useful.

261

Two major forms of role strain are generally recognized. First, there is *role conflict* (Secord and Backman, 1964). In this case, actor has trouble meeting the demands of a particular role because it calls for behaviors which are incompatible with those associated with another role he "must" play. In the other general type, the problem is not incompatibility of demands, but rather that the demands are so heavy or difficult that they exceed actor's time, energies, or resources. Secord and Backman (1964) call this *role competition*, but I feel that Sieber's (1974) term *role overload* is more descriptive. Competition seems to suggest that the problem is caused by the fact that actors must play several roles, and though it is true that this is often the source of the burden, it need not be. In some cases, a single role would cause difficulty even if it were the only one that actor had to play in a given time period.

In both role conflict and role overload caused by multiple roles, it is common to recognize subcategories distinguised by the nature of the role elements involved. Distinctions are made among difficulties caused by roles in the same role set, by roles in different role sets, and by subroles in the same role (Goode, 1960a).

To clarify, let me give illustrations of some of the major types of role strain. Conflict between roles within the same role set is well typified by the study of Gross et al. (1958) on the school superintendent role set. As the superintendents see it, their obligations to teachers require them to do their best to improve salaries, but their relations to the members of the city council require that they keep expenses down. They experience great difficulty in doing both.

Though the incident probably did not actually occur, the difficulties of the previously mentioned Col. Chamberlain (Shaara, 1975) exemplify the conflicts between roles in different role sets. According to the story, his younger brother was one of his junior officers, and when Chamberlain had to fill a gap in the line, he was faced with a conflict between his military role and his family role, which included taking care of his kid brother. In the heat of the battle, the decision was quickly made in favor of his military role set, but the memory of making such a decision was a source of great distress to him when things calmed down.

Incompatibilities among the subroles which make up a single role can easily be found in the professor-graduate student role. In many professors' views, their relationship to "their" graduate students includes the subroles of mentor, sponsor, friend, evaluator, and employer. The subroles of evaluator and sponsor often conflict. One cannot fail a student who deserves a failing grade and at the same time help him or her to find a job. There is also conflict between the mentor and employer subroles. If a graduate student is employed as an assistant on a research project, much of what he or she must do will be menial, and tasks which have educational value usually have such value only the first few times they are done. More than that, the time the professor as boss demands of his or her students makes it difficult for the student to devote time to study. Thus, if the professor acts as a boss "should," it will be difficult to play the mentor role and vice versa.

There are also a few rather special, but interesting, forms of role strain from multiple roles which deserve mention. For example, multiple roles can cause strain even if they are not played simultaneously. Because humans have histories and memories, roles played in the past may create role strain when another role has to be played in the present (Secord and Backman, 1964). In many societies there are sharp discontinuities between the behaviors expected at different times of life. In many primitive societies, for example, infants and young children are indulged and permitted great freedom, but as they get a little older they are held to strict standards and treated quite harshly (Benedict, 1938). The earlier experience makes it quite difficult to adapt to the later expectations. Analogous problems, somewhat different in content, are to be found in the transition from adolescence to adulthood. In the "old days," at least, social commentators were fond of noting that there were rather different demands made upon the unmarried and the married, and for many the "required" shift in attitudes and practices was not easily made (Waller and Hill, 1951).

In all these cases, it is not simply that new behaviors must be learned and put into practice. The role conflict occurs because the old behaviors are not forgotten and they interfere with the use of the new behaviors. A particularly poignant example of this is seen in the difficulties that former spouses and lovers experience when they try to remain friends after the old relationship is ended.

Examples of role overload caused by multiple roles should be familiar to the reader. Within some students' role set, there is both the student-professor role and the student-coach role, and this may cause problems even if the responses they call forth are compatible. There may just not be enough time and energy. Playing football and studying are not inherently incompatible, but the time spent at practice may be so great for some that they have little time to devote to their classes. A common illustration of role overload developing from the demands of roles in different role sets is the felt difficulty many men experience in trying to spend time with their families and meet their responsibilities on an exhausting job. However, in most families, the difficulties of a mother with a career are, in these respects, even more severe (Holstrom, 1972; Rapoport and Rapoport, 1976). Overload resulting from the demands of the subroles of a role would be seen in the situation of a parent who has no time to be a companion to a child after he or she has finished acting as a provider, disciplinarian, and socializing agent.

The Incidence of Role Strain

At present, there is a lively debate over the extent to which the playing of multiple roles produces role strain. No one denies that having to play "too many" roles produces strain, and all are aware that most people can, and do, play several roles during a single time period. The argument is over how many roles are likely to be too many.

Somewhat earlier work (Goode, 1960a) appears to be based upon the assumption that the average person has limited ability to play a variety of roles during the same time frame. More recent thought tends to be diametrically opposed to this view. Although they admit that the tipping point will occur at different points depending on the roles and persons involved, both Sieber (1974) and Marks (1977) argue that their predecessors have failed to appreciate that most people can play a large number of roles without strain.

Sieber and Marks come to their conclusions from somewhat differing starting points, but there are certain commonalities to their arguments. Sieber points out, to begin with, that one can occupy many positions without being required to do very much. For one thing, the roles associated with many positions require very little activity from actors. It is in the nature of many positions that there is little to be done. This would be the case for membership, or even holding office, in many associations. Thus, if he chooses well, actor may occupy a large number of positions, play many roles, and yet have little to do.

Marks (1977) goes well beyond this. He argues that it is incorrect to assume that people have a finite amount of time and energy and that each activity uses up more or less of them. He claims that many of our activities refresh and recharge us. Furthermore, he says that the difference between depleting and refreshing activities lies not in the nature of the activities themselves, but rather in the extent of actor's commitment to them. "Abundant energy is 'found' for anything to which we are highly committed, and we often feel more energetic after having done it" (Marks, 1977: 927).

This perhaps overstates the case. Marks himself suggests later that some combinations of roles cause problems even in the face of extremely strong commitment (see also French and Caplan, 1972). So it's not quite true that role strain can be totally prevented by increased commitment. It does, however, seem likely that if we are sufficiently committed to what we are doing, we will produce energy which will make it possible for us to handle a considerable number of demanding roles without strain.

Marks and Sieber are focusing upon multiple roles, but their views are easily applied to the case of single roles. If under normal circumstances a total role repertoire is not likely to be too much for actor to manage, it seems that it would be even rarer that a single role would be so. This is not to say, of course, that a single role will never cause role overload. When actor's commitment to a role is low, that is, when he does not consider it important to meet role obligations and would rather be doing something else, role overload can result from a single role. Under these conditions, there is likely to be a feeling of strain even if the actor does succeed in living up to the role bargain. In addition, low commitment and the belief that the role obligations are "too much" can turn a manageable role into one which is really beyond actor's capacities. Doing a dreaded job often proves to be destructive of energy and it often takes a long time. We may, that is, create for ourselves the conditions which make it impossible to fulfill role obligations.

Again, however, commitment is not a panacea. In some cases, a role may produce overload despite a strong commitment to it. For some roles, overload is unavoidable primarily during times of crisis. Soldiers in combat, a physician during an epidemic, or an author trying to meet a deadline may devote their full time to their occupational roles and still find that it is impossible to do all they have to do. In other instances, overload is an everyday accompaniment of the role. Jobs such as air traffic controller and President of the United States have been so described.

Beyond all this, role overload may arise from a single role because of simple incompetence. In the best of all possible worlds, no one would have a social trait unless he was competent to play the role associated with it, and in such a world no one would accept a definition of a situation which involves a role definition beyond his abilities. There is, however, considerable room for improvement in the world as it is, and incompetence is a common fact of life. The Peter Principle (Peter and Hull, 1969), which states that in the work world people tend to get promoted to their "level of incompetence," may not hold universally, but there is more than a germ of truth in it. Excellent vice presidents frequently make terrible presidents, highly skilled ball players are often flops as managers, and world renowned scholars have been known to create havoc as deans.

It is important to note here that incompetence is not limited to technical and work roles. Role strain of this type is a possibility in all social roles. All a role may require is that the actor be considerate, for example, and it may turn out, for any number of reasons, that this proves to be beyond him under the given circumstances.

For the present purposes, it doesn't much matter why the person is incompetent, but it should be noted that the inability of the role player to meet his obligations may not be indicative of any lack of native ability. In part, the lower-class black males discussed by Liebow (1967) and Hannerz (1969) have marital difficulties because they cannot adequately play the provider subrole in the way that their wives—and they, for that matter—believe it should be played. The source of this incompetence is, however, largely external to them. It comes from their low levels of training and bias in hiring. In a true sense, they lack the necessary supporting structure. In order to fulfill the terms of their role bargains with their wives, they require the cooperation of a third party—an employer—and they have difficulty finding one.

By definition, if an actor feels that meeting the demands of a particular role is difficult or impossible for him, he is feeling role strain. However, it should be understood that the existence of role strain does not necessarily mean there will be significant psychological stress. We must be careful not to equate role strain with negative psychological states. They are often connected, but they are not the same thing and they do not always go together.

This distinction is particularly important in discussing commitment and role strain. As noted above, low commitment is likely to produce role strain, but at the same time it is likely to be a barrier to stress. If commitment to a role is low, not meeting its requirements is unlikely to be defined by actor as a personal failure and the rewards which will be foregone are unlikely to be seen as a great loss. Under these circumstances, role strain is likely to result in distress only if others apply significant sanctions to actor when he does not meet his role obligations.

When commitment to a role is high and motivation is low, both role strain and stress are likely to occur.[2] Because of his low motivation, actor is likely to have

---

[2] Motivation and commitment are similar and highly correlated but they are analytically distinct. An index of actor's motivation is the extent to which he is willing to incur costs in order to carry out an activity. Commitment is the importance actor places on the activity.

difficulty in meeting his obligations, and because of his high commitment, he is going to be in the situation of failing to meet obligations he considers important. This combination of high commitment and low motivation is, of course, quite common. Many students, for example, strongly feel that it is important to complete their assignments, but at the same time they are unwilling to pay the costs they incur by not devoting their time to other activities. Such students are likely to experience the stress produced by feelings of guilt.

Antecedents of Role Strain

Given the variety of forms that it can take, it is no surprise that if one gets below a rather general level, it turns out that the antecedent conditions which lead to role strain are quite numerous. If, however, the issue is discussed in fairly general and abstract terms, it is possible to delineate some conditions which are common to the several forms. That is what I will do here.

The fact that actor is experiencing role strain is *prima facie* evidence that the negotiations process has not worked well for him. At a minimum, actor hopes that he can live with, and by, the definition of the situation which emerges from negotiations. If role strain occurs, it is clear that that goal has not been reached. This being the case, it would seem that we can find at least some of the sources of role strain if we consider the circumstances which might lead actor to leave negotiations with a "bad deal."

If we assume that in most cases actors will not intentionally accept a definition of the situation which will be difficult to abide by, it becomes obvious that role strain is more likely when actor has a limited influence on the shape of the agreement which emerges. I have already discussed the factors which influence the extent of actor's control over the defining process; a full discussion is not required here. Suffice it to say that the relevant factors would include differences between actor and other in power and negotiating skill. Power is in turn related to differences in such factors as access to resources, need and desire for the interaction, availability of alternatives. Negotiating skill is a function of such things as role-taking ability and persuasiveness.

This is not the whole of it, however. Actor may accept an unfavorable definition of a situation because he is unaware that it will prove to be such. Actor may actually control the situation and end up with a bad deal. The unfavorable definition may even have been suggested by actor. Interactionists often assume that people have an accurate view of the consequences of their actions, but that is obviously not always the case.

The circumstances which would make such "errors" more common seem fairly obvious. If actor has had little previous experience playing the role, he is less likely to see the full implications of his agreements since he would have had little or no previous opportunity to try them out in practice. Thus, the acceptance of an undesirable bargain is more likely when actor is playing a newly acquired role. This lack of experience in playing a role will be particularly important if the role is one for which anticipatory socialization is inadequate or absent. In such situations there is the likelihood that actor will not know the full implications of his commitments. Some of the campaign promises of politicians may be considered analogous to role agreements. They often say, "If I am elected I will do it this way," and their failure to live up to such promises may be evidence of duplicity. In some cases, however, it is due to the fact that the difficulties of dealing with an entrenched bureaucracy cannot fully be understood until they are experienced.

In addition to making his own errors, actor can be led into error. Others can lead actor to the unwitting acceptance of a strain-producing definition. Other can use the negotiating process in such a way that actor is not totally aware of what he is agreeing to. The role definition actor thinks he agreed to might not have been productive of strain, but it may turn out that he has, in fact, agreed to something quite different. Salesmen of encyclopedias, dance lessons, and courses at health spas are fabled for their abilities in these matters, and the psychiatrists and lawyers I spoke of earlier go them one step better by getting their clients to accept an agreement without the client's even knowing they are negotiating. This would suggest that role strain is more likely when actor is inexperienced in the role and other is not, when actor's role-taking ability is low and other's is high, when the situation is not conducive to the full exchange of information, when other controls the flow of information, and when other stands to gain from actor's role strain.

Society and Role Strain

Up to this point there has been little explicit recognition given to the possibility that the cause of the "bad" situation is to be found in forces which are largely beyond the control of the interactants. What has been said thus far has focused on the negotiations between actor and other, and this might seem to suggest that actor and other are free to work out whatever arrangement they want. If this impression has been given, I hasten to correct it. The negotiations between actor and other take place within a structure which is largely beyond their control. Thus, there are limits on the issues which can be negotiated and the agreements which can be reached. In some cases, the role strain is not a result of ineffective negotiating by actor. He may not have had a chance. Limitations, whose basic sources are to be found in the larger society, may have given him little maneuvering room. He may have had no real opportunity to work out a good deal for himself because societal definitions of his statuses and roles were relatively fixed.

Actor will have great difficulty in negotiating a favorable definition if societal definitions support an opposing view. For one thing, other is unlikely to look favorably on such a definition. If a particular definition is widely accepted, the chances are that other will also accept it and be less than willing to agree to actor's request to alter it. More than this, other will be in a very good position to refuse to change. He or she will probably be able to call upon third persons for support or, equally effectively, can resort to the general value system of the society.

In fact, when the societal definitions are unfavorable and institutionalized, it may never really come to the point of negotiations. Actor may let opportunities for negotiation go by because he accepts the institutionalized view as an unalterable given or because he realizes that in the face of such a situation, he would have to give up a great deal before other will acquiesce. Both of these possibilities are illustrated by the men described in Tally's Corner (Liebow, 1967). Some of them seemed to pass up opportunities which might have led to a definition which would have better fitted their circumstances. In part, this was due to their acceptance of the mainstream view of husband-wife relationships as a given which was not open to negotiations. In addition, they failed to negotiate because they realized that if they succeeded they risked a loss of self-esteem, and their wives, who were strongly committed to the standard marriage model, would have exacted a heavy price before acquiescing. More specifically, if the women agreed to playing the breadwinner role the men were likely to lose much of their power over family relations, for in part at least, power flows to the source of the money.

The intrusion of society into the "private affairs" of interactants goes beyond this, however. Even when actor and other might both be willing to accept an agreement which is to their mutual advantage, they may be unable to do so if that agreement is contrary to societal norms. In many instances, society has to ratify the results of negotiations. Goode's (1960a) example of the society, in the person of the law, acting to prevent a policeman and a criminal reaching a role bargain which involves a bribe is only an extreme case of a common phenomenon. The agreement does not have to be illegal, of course. There is no law that says that the traditional husband and wife roles cannot be reversed, but such role bargains are not viewed as appropriate by most people. The fact that they exist is, of course, evidence that societal opposition is not always effective. I would suspect, however, that many more couples would adopt such an arrangement if they could do so without constantly having to explain and defend their decision.

The Intrusion of Institutionalized Roles. Now that it is established that the existence of institutionalized norms can and does interfere with actor's ability to negotiate a strain-free definition of the situation, it must be noted that the extent to which this will occur is quite variable. For one thing, there is variation in the extent to which the societal definition is likely to cause role strain for actor if it is accepted as the governing definition, and there is also variability in the likelihood that such definitions will be accepted in "preference" to a private agreement. I will end this section with a brief discussion of the factors which affect variation in these matters.

Obviously a number of actor's individual characteristics will be related to the extent to which acceptance of institutionalized role definitions will create a strain for him. These would include such things as the extent to which his previous socialization has been typical of that society, the extent to which his collection of roles is typical, etc. In other words, the assumption is that societal definitions are more likely to be suited to the average person than to the unusual or deviant one.

In addition, the amount of strain created by accepting institutionalized rules will vary depending upon the nature of the rules themselves. If they are strictly defined and permit no "personal touches," they will be more troublesome than if they are loose and permit alternative, equally acceptable variants. The degree to which the norms are institutionalized will also be relevant. Because a rule is generally accepted does not mean it is universally accepted, and if there are significant numbers who subscribe to alternative patterns, actor may find that he is damned, by some, even if he accepts the established rule. The opposition of these "deviants" may mean that actor experiences difficulty in playing his roles even when he is playing by the rules. This is, in fact, the normal case. Rarely, if ever, is there is society-wide consensus. But the greater the consensus, the less strain associated with playing institutionalized roles.

Assuming, for the sake of continuing the exposition, that the problems caused by accepting societal definitions are constant, the amount of strain that will be caused by such norms is a function of the likelihood of their being followed by members of the society who would prefer another arrangement. Societies would, clearly, differ in this regard also. In some, third parties are rather accepting of private agreements; in others, a strict adherence to institutionalized ways is demanded. At least by reputation, complex, rapidly changing, modern societies would seem to typify the first type and simple, stable, traditional ones the second.

In addition, of course, any given society or subgroup will be differentially tolerant of deviant private agreements, depending upon a number of factors. For one thing, societies are more interested in maintaining preferred patterns in some areas of social life than in others. Deviations in some areas are viewed as minor peccadilloes hardly worth noting, whereas others are viewed as heinous crimes. In very general terms, it appears that activities viewed as essential to the perpetuation of the society, those that have to mesh with the activities of others not party to the private negotiations, and those touching the basic values of the society, are more likely to be subject to restrictions on private negotiations. In addition, the extent to which the actors wish to deviate from the established pattern should be related to the ease with which they can do so. Private arrangements which deviate only slightly from the institutionalized norm should be more acceptable than those which differ in major ways from the standard.

In fact, provision is made for this in the institutionalized norms. They rarely say that one must play a role in one way and one way only. There is frequently a range of behaviors which are almost equally valued and also a group of less accepted, but still acceptable, alternatives. Beyond this, the society may even have a ranking for the different unacceptable arrangements that may be worked out. Thus in the more traditional parts of this society, legal marriage is the accepted arrangement in which to carry on a sexual relationship. Discreet sexual relations between consenting adults are not severely condemned, though they do not have complete approval, and public announcements of nonmarital sexuality, such as in cohabitation, remain beyond the pale.

A society can, however, act to oppose a private arrangement only if the members know of it or if the interactants believe they may learn of it. Thus, a key factor in determining the restrictiveness of institutionalized norms is the extent to which the negotiations and/or role behavior are carried out in public. What I said regarding deals between policemen and criminals is true, but it obviously would be much truer if those deals had to be made in a glare of publicity. And, as every student who knows the ropes is aware, exemptions from general rules are much more likely to be granted when the request is made in private and when the behaviors involved will not be observable.

Earlier I described a number of mechanisms used by actors when they are trying to convince their interaction partners to accept certain behaviors which are not clearly in accordance with conventional standards (see pages 233-35). Here I would note that these accounts are also used by interaction partners in their relationships with outsiders. They can be used in an attempt to get third parties to accept private agreements. Thus it would follow that institutionalized norms are most restrictive when acceptable justifications and excuses are not available. If I ask when that will occur, we will find that we are back to material already covered. It would seem more difficult to get an account accepted when, for example, the desired deviation is large, when it is a matter of wide public knowledge, when the matter involved is defined as important by the society, etc.

The focus here has been on the ways that societal definitions stand in the way of individuals working out their own destinies, and that is appropriate given the matters under consideration. For our present concerns, it was not necessary to discuss whether or not there were advantages to having institutionalized norms. But before I go on to the next topic, I would like to consider this matter, because the association between societal norms and role strain has led many to what I consider to be an erroneous conclusion. Particularly during the 1960s, but still today, many seem convinced that we would be better off if there were no *societal* norms, at least in some areas of social life. The notion seems to be that if we could get society off our backs, if we could do "our own things," we would all be happier.

It is rather difficult to conceive of such a society; it seems likely that if existing norms were abolished they would soon be replaced with others. But if such a society could exist, I suspect it would be one that most of us would want no part of. It would be characterized by confusion, disorganization, unpleasant surprises, and very stressful social interaction. Social norms may cause problems, but they also aid role-taking, serve as mechanisms of societal integration, provide solutions to some of the problems we face each day, and so on.

In my view, the goal should not be the elimination of societal norms but rather the reform of the existing norms. A desirable society is one whose norms are consistent with most peoples' needs, flexible enough to change with changing conditions, and loose enough to permit "costless" deviations by those who wish to deviate—particularly when the deviations do not cause difficulties for others who are following their own bent. Such a society is perhaps as utopian as a normless one, but it seems a more appropriate one to work for.

Reducing Role Strain

Given that these are the sources of role strain, we can next consider what people are likely to do when they are faced with it. Though the chronology is by no means fixed, it seems that a logical first step would be to make attempts to change the definition in an effort to get better terms.[3] Perhaps actor will attempt to utilize a different identity, or the key may lie in changing the role definition which goes with his identity or in altering the goals of the interaction. If things get too hot for a department head he may resign, and as the formula goes, return to teaching and research; or he may attempt to have his duties redefined so that he can pass on some of the more onerous tasks to an associate department head; or he may convince himself and others that it is really impossible to make the department the best in the country.

All of these issues have been met before. In the original setting up of a definition of the situation, actor had to decide what identity to use, what role to play, and what goals to seek. Now he has to remake those decisions in the light of the fact that his original decisions proved to be unwise. And, just as before, if his new definition is not acceptable to other, there will be an attempt to renegotiate a working consensus. All of the mechanisms and considerations previously discussed will be used again.

Beyond this, there is little that can be said about the process of redefinition and renegotiation that was not previously said about definition and negotiation. There is, however, one important point that should be made. In general, the factors discussed in the section on negotiations will also determine whether a new consensus will be reached and what form it will take. However, the course of the renegotiations will be affected by the fact that a previous consensus was reached. If the existing agreement is still viewed favorably by other—the interactant who is not suffering the role strain—actor will find that the previous consensus will be a weapon available to other in his attempt to maintain the negotiated status quo. Other will now have available the argument, "You agreed to this and now you want to go against your word. That's not fair." Since it is possible that actor got himself into the situation of role strain through an inability to control the course of the original negotiations, his chances of changing the situation through renegotiations seem slim given the fact that this opponent is likely to be even stronger than he was previously.

Despite this, actor might be able to improve his or her position through more effective use of the negotiating process. For example, a plea relating to "how much I have suffered" might work. However, actor's best chance of obtaining a redefinition would seem to reside in other's becoming disenchanted with the previous definition. This, of course, frequently happens. If actor is having difficulty playing his roles, those with whom he is in interaction are also likely to be experiencing costs. In many cases, when actor is suffering role strain, others are, from selfish interest, very anxious to renegotiate his situation. The subordinates and superiors of officers who have cracked under pressure are, for example, usually quite cooperative in arranging a change of status even if it means "kicking him upstairs."

Thus, renegotiations are not futile even though their success may depend more

---

[3] Here, as throughout this book, the mechanics of language require me to present in a linear-fashion, processes which do not progress in a straight line. Techniques are used, dropped, and then returned to. Issues are never totally settled. What appears to be a resolution soon crumbles. A deadlock breaks. Neither victories nor defeats are total. This is all in the nature of interaction, but to describe it as it really happens would involve a degree of complexity that would make the presentation incomprehensible.

on the disposition of other than on the actions of actor. Let us assume, however, in order to continue the discussion, that the attempt at renegotiation fails and that path seems closed at least for the time being. At this point, actor is in a situation in which he cannot get agreement to a change in a definition with which he finds it difficult to live. What can he do now?

Undoubtedly, at this point actor is going to give serious consideration to the alternative of breaking off the interaction. The decision as to whether or not to continue will be reached on the basis of the same factors which were mentioned when I discussed whether termination would be chosen when consensus was not quickly reached (see page 218). I will not repeat that material. All I would say is that the existence of an apparently unnegotiable strain-producing role definition is likely to lead actor to the conclusion that termination is the least costly of the available steps. We will, however, assume that the decision is to continue the interaction and again the question becomes "What is he likely to do next?"

Reducing the Costs of Role Strain

The basic motivation, it would seem clear, is to reduce the strain of acting, and there would be two general ways of accomplishing this. Actor could attempt to reduce the perceived discrepancy between what he "should" do and what he "can" do and by this means reduce the sanctions applied by other; and/or he can attempt to blunt the effects of the sanctions he experiences. Again, these approaches to the problem are separate only for analytic purposes. In actual interaction, they will go on apace. But here I will of necessity consider them separately.

The notion of a "perceived discrepancy" noted in the previous paragraph is important, for a major way in which actors reduce the externally imposed strains involved in role playing is to arrange things so that other does not see the degree to which the behavior is deviant. An obvious way of doing that is to hide the facts.

In the service of hiding the facts, there are a number of techniques which can be used. Lies are common: "It wasn't really a vacation. I spent the whole time working on the book"; but often one doesn't have to resort to such gross methods. All the mechanisms useful in the presentation of a false self (see pages 74–82) would also be useful in presenting one's behavior in a "respectable light."

In other cases we don't attempt to deny our actions, but we do try to get our behavior defined more favorably than it would be without any efforts on our part. Just as in the original negotiations, the major techniques used in the attempt to influence other's definition are justifications, disclaimers, and excuses; attempts to convince other that our behavior is not as different from his preferences as he thinks, and attempts to get him to believe that "under the circumstances" the behavior is acceptable or unavoidable.

In fact, as Scott and Lyman (1968) note, the original negotiations and the attempt to mitigate consequences are very much the same. The kind of arguments given and the circumstances under which they will be accepted would be the same regardless of whether the goal is to reach consensus or obtain "mercy." This material is discussed in Chapter 8 and I will not repeat it here. I will, however, briefly recall some of the points made earlier as I describe the one study which bears directly on some of the theoretical ideas I am offering.

The relevant study (Blumstein et al., 1974) is a pioneer effort and it is not surprising, therefore, that it has important limitations. Most important, peoples' reactions to accounts were not actually observed and they were not even asked what they would do. Rather, students were presented with several vignettes which described a common violation of conventional standards, a demand for an account, and the account. The nature of the offense, the nature of the account, and the status relationships among the participants were systematically varied, and the students were asked several questions including, "Do you believe the person in the story will honor the account?" The assumption is clearly that the students would project onto the person in the story the response they would give, but as in all studies that use projective devices, this is a moot point.

One of the more relevant findings deals with the relationship between the perceived credibility of the account and its likelihood of being honored. It was suggested earlier that an account must be credible to be honored, and the data do show a correlation between believability and the likelihood that an account will be honored. However, there is also an indication that credibility is not enough. The strength of the justification must be judged to be commensurate with the extent of the transgression. It seems that most believable accounts are considered to be adequate in this sense, but when an account is not considered equal to the offense it tends not to be honored— whether it is believable or not.

The reaction to the account also seemed to be directly related to the subject's view of the actor's moral worth. In the Blumstein study, a subject who saw the actor as sincere, trustworthy, valuable, and responsible was more likely to see the account as credible, adequate, and likely to be honored. The content of the account was important largely because it influenced the subject's perception of the actor's moral worth. Thus the full causal chain seems to be: content affects perception of actor, perception of actor effects credibility, credibility affects estimate of adequacy, and adequacy affects honoring. The problem is, however, the subjects almost *had to* base their estimate of actor's character on the content of the account, because they knew little else about him. In real life, the content of actor's account would be only one of several bases for judgment.

Reducing Self-Inflicted Costs.   The focus has been on actor's attempts to reduce the punishments received from other, but much of what has been said above is also pertinent to the reduction of self-inflicted costs. Actor may, for example, engage in what I would call—extending Scott and Lyman's (1968) concept—"self-justification." One may admit responsibility for one's failure, but argue internally that the deviation is of a minor kind—a technical violation perhaps, but not a fullblown crime. In a true sense, an actor doing this is engaging in interaction with himself. He is being an object to himself, that is, he is being *both* actor and other. The ability to do this is, of course, within the capacity of all socialized humans.

The second technique used by actors to reduce their feelings of guilt is "self-excuse." This is directly comparable to the offering of excuses to "real" others. Again the difference lies only in the fact that in this case actor and other is the same person. The form of self-excuse is the same as in all excuses: "There were mitigating circumstances." "I really didn't know what I was doing." "He got what he deserved."

Essentially, the factors which make an account acceptable to an "external other" will make it acceptable when the other is the self. These are discussed in Chapter 8 (see pages 253–54), and I will not consider them here. I should note before we move on, however, that the processes of negotiating with self and with others are not the same in all respects. Some of the techniques used in convincing others do not make sense "when the enemy is us." Bribery and retaliation, for example, do not have clear relevance when actor and other is the same person.

Reducing Deviations from Expectations. Another general way to reduce the perceived distance between expectations and behavior is, in fact, to reduce it. I have been assuming that actor is experiencing strain despite the fact that he is doing his best to fulfill all his obligations, and undoubtedly actor assumes the same. However, actors often find that when role strain hits them, they can rearrange their situations so that what seemed impossible becomes possible. The specific nature of the required changes will vary depending on the situation, but a few examples may be offered.

If the problem is an inability to meet the requirements of a single role, there is frequently the possibility of obtaining additional training. In some cases, this may involve formal training; one takes a refresher course or learns a new technique. Overburdened researchers usually find that the time spent in learning to use computers is well spent in the long run. Less formal "training" may also help. Authors of scholarly works who get "stuck" and are in danger of missing a deadline, which would be a violation of a role agreement, often find that a little more digging in the library will unearth a solution to the problem. In more general terms, when anticipatory socialization for a position has been inadequate, there is often a possibility of on-the-job training.

Along somewhat similar lines, when a person finds himself in a position he cannot fill, there is often the possibility of obtaining direct assistance from others. As noted above, a complete delegation of a responsibility with an attendant change in the operant role definition is a possibility with the concurrence of the other, but here I have in mind less sweeping action—the hiring of an assistant, for example.

Of course, there are dangers in getting such help. A researcher who hires an assistant with skills the researcher does not—but should—have, will lose status in the eyes of his colleagues *if* they know about it. Certain other kinds of assistance are considered even less legitimate, and if discovered, they bring great costs. The student who buys a term paper because he "can't write" is running a great risk because he is doing something which is not an acceptable solution to role strain. This notwithstanding, the use of assistants is a common way to reduce strain. It is often acceptable, and when it involves costs they may be neither great nor likely to be imposed. Actor may consider them trivial relative to those associated with failure.

When the strain arises from an overload caused by multiple roles whose demands do not conflict, the problem is by definition one of a lack of time and/or energy. The actor has the skills to live up to each of his roles, the actions demanded by one are compatible with the demands of the others, but the actor feels unable to do it all. His total role obligations seem to represent too great a burden. What can be done?

The two solutions previously discussed would also be useful here even though the problem is not one of competence. With better training and assistance, more can be accomplished in less time and an apparent role overload can be made manageable.

In addition, there are other possible solutions. My conceptualization of the problem is that actor views himself as being overburdened by two or more roles which he wants to keep and cannot alter. He may discover, however, that other roles which were giving him no trouble and were considered irrelevant to the strain can be abandoned with little cost, thus freeing up time and energy for the strain-producing constellation of roles. Students, for example, will often analyze their problems in such terms as, "I can't get everything done because I have a job and I'm taking five courses." On occasion they can be brought to see that sloughing off some of their recreational activities is one way to solve their problem.

Marks' (1977) discussion, which was considered earlier, also contains within it implicit suggestions about how actors may reduce role strain. If certain conditions increase actor's energy store, it might be that actor can arrange for those conditions to exist. Paradoxically, this might mean that actor can reduce his role strain by increasing rather than decreasing role activities. Marks suggests that, "Perhaps some roles may be performed without any net energy loss at all; they may even create energy for use in that role or in other role performances" (Marks, 1977: 926). Of course, not all roles would do, but if some roles do in fact expand our energy, taking on those roles would represent a way out for actor.

There are no systematic data which bear upon Marks' contention, but it does fit in with the evidence of general observation. We have all experienced, I am sure, exhilaration rather than tiredness after some activities. Recreational activities are the ones which come most immediately to mind, but any interaction which provides support, emotional release, relief from boredom, and the like would do. Therefore, the correct prescription for the overburdened student I referred to above might not be that he stop "wasting time" and give more time to work. It *might* be that he is working too hard and not having enough fun. The solution might be to spend more time interacting with others in a way that will bring him back to work refreshed and "rarin' to go."

Marks (1977) would also suggest that an increase in commitment will sometimes make it possible for actor to meet role demands which appear beyond his time and energy. This notion has a touch of the "Pollyanna" about it. It suggests that if you want something badly enough, you will be able to accomplish it. Pollyannaish or not, the idea does have considerable plausibility, if it is understood that there are definite limits to its applicability.

When actor's problem is that several roles are in conflict, that is, when the demands of one subrole or role are incompatible with the demands of other roles that he *must* play, his options are much more limited. He may be able to hide the fact that he is not meeting his agreements, but most of the other possibilities I have discussed are not much use if there is a true incompatibility between the demands of "required" roles. If a good solution is to be found, it has to be found at an earlier point in the interaction.

Reducing the Costs of Role Strain. For the purposes of this discussion, I will again assume that none of this has worked for actor. He has found that he could not live by his original role agreement and his efforts to change that agreement, to justify his failures, and to improve his performance have all failed. At this point he must realize that he is going to pay considerable costs. These costs are of three kinds: (1) utilitarian goals not reached; (2) externally inflicted punishments such as negative evaluations and ostracism; in general, the refusal to grant nonutilitarian reward; and (3) self-inflicted punishments such as guilt and shame which result from a failure to perform up to standards. There is nothing left for actor to do but to take his medicine; however, I believe he is unlikely to simply give in, even at this point. If he can't avoid the medicine he will at least try to reduce the dose and/or to take a palatable kind. Given that costs are inevitable, his goal will be to reduce their size.

If cooperative efforts are necessary for actor to achieve his utilitarian goals, and if such efforts are precluded by his inability to play his roles adequately, there is little actor could do at this point to increase his chances of obtaining the rewards he hoped to get from the interaction. He can, however, change his goals so that he feels the loss of the original utilitarian goals less keenly, or he may attempt to achieve his original goal in another interaction. Perhaps, given what he has learned in the present interaction, he will be able to strike a better deal with another interaction partner.

Actor may also be able to reduce his costs by influencing the kinds of external and self punishments he receives. This can be done, in part, by choosing the nature of his failure. If he cannot meet the demands of all his roles or, to put it somewhat differently, if he cannot meet his own expectations and those of all his role partners, he may be able to decide which he will meet and which he will fail to meet. The neglecting of some roles may ensure success with the others, and if actor makes wise decisions about where to fail he may keep his losses small.

It may not be saying very much, but one of the factors that will affect the choice among roles is the extent of the actor's commitment to the roles in contention. He will choose the role he considers most important, and this is likely to be the one associated with the identity highest on the prominence hierarchy. If a teacher is more committed to his teacher role than to his friend role, he will grade his "graduate-student-friend" objectively; if the family role is more important than obligations to the "boys," a man will pass up that late-night poker session. This will lead to less guilt and less external cost. Granted, actor may still want to have the best of all worlds, and there may be attempts to straddle the fence. A husband/father may go to the poker game but leave early or set the limit on his losses lower. If there is a tilt in favor of one of the roles, however, commitment will influence the direction of choice. To do the opposite would simply be masochistic because it would create greater costs than there have to be.[4]

In some instances, particularly when actor's commitments to the roles in question do not differ, the decision will be based upon characteristics of the role partners. To reduce guilt, actor will decide in favor of the partner whose demands he considers more legitimate (Gross, Mason and McEachern, 1958). If actor believes that the definition of one of the contending parties is closer to what actor believes other has a right to expect, all other things being equal, that person's expectations are going to take precedence.

Taking that tack will certainly result in less guilt, but actor also has to consider the possibility of externally imposed sanctions and he will try to minimize them also. The way to do that, of course, is to follow the wishes of the partner with greater effective power. Actor will obey the other who has greater control over the punishments he wishes to avoid, and he will try to please the one who is most likely to impose those punishments. The man who thinks that he is in danger of being fired will obey his boss if he believes his wife is unlikely to leave him, as will the man who thinks he will feel the loss of his job more than he will the loss of his wife. The student who cannot do all his assignments will devote more of his efforts to the course taught by the toughest grader, and so forth.

In concluding this discussion, I will note again that there is always the possibility of terminating the relationship, and this, of course, is a very effective way to avoid the imposition of sanctions. If one drops out of school, the power of one's teachers is effectively blunted. Though this possibility has frequently been mentioned, the suggestion was always that actor did not choose it. In one sense, this was realistic. The costs of termination are likely to be high. Most readers, though, have probably realized that I "could not" permit actor to make that choice anymore than a screen writer could permit the star to be killed off in the first reel. We are, however, coming to the end so it is possible to suggest that under some circumstances the costs of termination may not be that great. Certainly, if actor's need for the potential rewards of the interaction is low it would not be costly to leave.

Moreover, even when actor has a great need for the reward that the interaction might bring, having an alternative source would reduce the costs of leaving a particular interaction (Thibaut and Kelley, 1959). In fact, if he thinks that he can get those rewards on his own terms from somebody else, he is likely to terminate the encounter at the first sign of trouble. And if he cannot physically leave the situation, he may be able to do so psychologically, by continuing to go through the motions without being much affected by the situation. A classic illustration of this is to be found in Cohen's (1955) analysis of the delinquent subculture. The goal of the lower-class adolescent male is status, but because of a trained incapacity he cannot live up to the middle-class view

[4] It must be recognized that this description is somewhat simplified, implying as it does that these decisions are easily made. Clearly, actor is often going to judge wrongly, and even more important, he or she will often feel that no reasonable decision can be made, given the available options and information.

of acceptable behavior—a prerequisite for enhanced status. Because there are others in a similar situation who are willing to give him status for the delinquent behavior he is capable of, the adolescent terminates, in so far as he can, his interaction with representatives of middle-class society and finds satisfaction and reward in his interaction with his delinquent peers. He cannot completely end his interaction with middle-class people, but he alleviates his role strain by reducing his contact with them to a minimum and by giving such contacts little importance.

In conclusion, I should note that almost everything said in this section remains hypothetical. The few paltry bits of empirical evidence scattered through these pages pretty much exhaust the evidence bearing upon these issues. None of the ideas presented here is, to my knowledge, contradicted by the available evidence, but almost none of them is supported by data either. Again, theorizing has far outrun research.

THE PRESENTATION OF A FALSE SELF

It may seem rather odd to suggest that interactions in which a false self is presented become, because of that fact, problematic interactions. The presentation of a false self is certainly not a problem in the same way that dissensus and role strain are. The presentation of a false self is not something to be solved; it is something that actor chooses to do. The justification for this label is to be found in the basic definition which says, essentially, that a problematic situation is one in which the interaction is more complex than it is in routine situations. In problematic interactions, distinctive processes develop which require actors to give more care and attention to their actions than is necessary in nonproblematic encounters. Practiced as actor might be, an encounter in which he presents a false self is likely to be characterized by these traits—a fact that should become clear as I progress.

Although the presentation of a false self is a common occurrence in interaction, it appears that the basic tendency is to present a true self. Most people attempt to convey impressions of themselves which are consistent with their self-definitions. My main concern is to specify the conditions which increase the likelihood that false selves will be presented, but before that can be done, we need a general discussion of the gains and costs associated with such presentations. We turn to that next.

Rewards of Presenting a False Self

There are considerable gains to be had from a successful presentation of a false self. For one thing, if other accepts the false self it may permit actor to behave in ways that he could not if other had a true picture of him, for what other will "permit" actor to do depends on other's definition of actor. And, to look at the other side of the coin, other's "erroneous" definition of actor may free actor from doing things which he does not wish to do, but would be expected to do if other really knew who he was.

Numerous examples from everyday experience come to mind. For example, if a person is young, to present himself as being older than he actually is permits him to enjoy those pleasures reserved for the mature. To disguise low status frees a person from the necessity of being subservient. To make a successful claim to the possession of particular formal training may allow a person to play an occupational role which is within his ability but which would otherwise be closed to him.

False selves can also be used to obtain desired responses. Certain identities call forth respect, others lead to contempt. Respect can be obtained and contempt avoided by the skillful presentation of a false self in those cases in which the real self does not produce the desired reaction. Thus somewhere between the city and the summer resort, the shipping clerk becomes at least a salesman, and the typist a junior executive.

It is obvious that certain reactions from others are desired because they are in themselves valuable—it's nice to be liked—and because they are means to desired tangible gains—companionship, power, perhaps even wealth. They also can lead to somewhat less obvious gains. Sometimes actor tries to get others to see him in a particular way so that they will treat him as though he were that kind of person *because* he wants to see himself in that light and cannot do so unless others see him that way. This would hold both for identities and self-evaluations. A person may exaggerate his accomplishments so that others will admire him, which permits him to have a positive self-evaluation in accordance with the principles underlying the development of self-evaluations. Similarly, a person will make a claim to a particular identity, say that of adult, not simply in order to be able to buy a beer, but also, or perhaps primarily, because he wants to be able to consider himself an adult. Of course such people are "fooling themselves," but such behavior is quite common and it often achieves its desired end.

Paradoxical as it may seem, actors are often led to present false selves because in a real sense others demand it of them. This does not mean that other is asking actor to deceive him. What may happen is simply that other's definition of actor is different from actor's definition of himself, or it may be that though other does not know what identity actor actually has, other has a preference as to what it should be. To answer the question, "Do you love me?" in the affirmative may involve actor in the presentation of a false self. But that query is not simply a question. Usually it involves a hope or a suggestion, and actor may be led to the false self by other's unspoken wish.

Various motives can lead to such compliance. Actor's goal may be simply to please other. On the other hand, his motive may be purely selfish. Such a motivation was reflected in a bit of street lore that every adolescent male of my era had drummed into him: "Always say you love her. It works wonders."

Costs of Presenting a False Self

Along with the gains to be had, there are also costs associated with the presentation of false selves. Many of these derive from the simple fact that the norms of society are generally opposed to them; such behavior is defined as deceit. Thus, a "properly" socialized individual who presents a false self is likely to suffer, to a great or lesser extent, because of it. In some cases guilt may result, and in other cases, self-contempt; or at least the loss of an opportunity to add to self-respect. At a minimum, there will be a feeling of inauthenticity (Turner, 1968; 1976)—a dull feeling of unease at not being ourselves.

If it is discovered that actor is attempting to mislead, additional costs will be incurred. Other is also likely to be socialized to look with disfavor on the presentation of false selves; the discovery that actor is doing this will call forth all the usual sanctions which other uses when actor behaves in an inappropriate way—criticism, dislike, withholding of rewards, and the assignment of an undesirable identity (liar, cheat, faker), etc.[5]

Performance Costs. From this it is clear that actor "must" avoid being caught in a false self-presentation. It is difficult, however, to perform convincingly, and that makes such presentations costly. Let us consider what is required. First, the performance has to be internally consistent. Spy movies are full of scenes in which "a cover was blown" because a spy inadvertently did some small thing which was inconsistent with the self he was presenting. The "bad guy" in a James Bond movie who is posing as a British agent gets tripped up because he orders a red wine with fish—something Bond is quick to perceive no properly raised Englishman would ever do. In a World War II movie the good guy gets caught—temporarily of course—because he eats his slice of pie from the point out, revealing he is an American rather than the European he is pretending to be. The slips involved in everyday life may be less dramatic and they are certainly less dangerous, but they are equally destructive of self-presentations. When other assigns an identity to actor, or in this case when he is led to a particular view of actor, he expects a pattern of behavior, and if that pattern is broken he becomes exceedingly suspicious.

In addition to internal consistency, other kinds of consistency are necessary for effective self-presentation. The actor's appearance, known history, and associates all must mesh with the presented self.

Consistency is important, but it is not enough. The actor's performance must be seen as correct by actor. Essentially, what I have been saying is that a lack of consistency will lead other to see the performance as wrong. The present point goes beyond that; the performance can be totally consistent and yet convey to other that it is false because it does not coincide with what he believes such a person would do. As I have defined them, role definitions and performances cannot be judged in terms of right and wrong. They are what people believe is appropriate under particular circumstances. Nonetheless, particularly if the role is an institutionalized one, people believe that there is a typical way of playing it, and if actor's way of doing it does not

---

[5] There are, of course, exceptions to this. Under some circumstances, politeness or kindness may even "require" actor to present a false self. When that is the case, third parties are not likely to condemn actor for his deception. Other, however, may be critical under these circumstances if he or she discovers what has happened. Even when we "plead" for it we find it upsetting to learn that actor has deceived us. Actor's motivation will, however, usually be taken as a mitigating fact.

fit in with other's view, other's suspicions are likely to be aroused. Of course, "incorrect" performances are not always assumed to indicate false self-presentation. People do recognize the fact of variation in role performance. Nonetheless, a person who is presenting a false self does not want other to look too closely, and one way of decreasing that likelihood is to present the role in a way other is likely to view as typical and correct.

The successful presentation of a false self involves the creation of an illusion that cannot be seen through—much as a stage actor does. This leads me to the notion that even if the actor has the lines of the role down pat, it is not certain that his performance will be convincing. Memorizing a script does not make one Laurence Olivier. In presenting a false self it is very important that the person appear to be unstudied. He has to convey a feeling of naturalness and a lack of prior preparation. If actor is using prepared props, they cannot appear to be prepared. If he is being coached, or was coached, other cannot be allowed to see it. If he has to think out what to do next he had better do it quickly and, if possible, before getting his cue.

The presentation of a self, whether true or false, involves "performance costs." The actor has to plan behavior, consider how other will perceive him, check up on himself to be sure that he is staying in role, etc. These costs are likely to be great when the attempt is to present a false self. The actions associated with the presentation of a true self are likely to come more easily. Actor is likely to be more practiced at them, and he doesn't have to keep reminding himself that the behavior which comes most naturally, given the definition of the self, is not the appropriate behavior. The chances of "falling out of role" (Goffman, 1959) are considerable and it takes effort to reduce them.

A final cost of false self-presentations is the extra anxiety that such performances cause most people. Whether the presented self is true or false, the goal is to have it accepted. The consequences of an inadequate presentation of a true self are not desirable—people do not see us as we think we are. But as I have indicated, there are important additional costs involved when a false self-presentation fails. For most people the fear of having to pay these costs is enough to cause stage fright throughout the performance.

Specific Conditions Favoring False Self-Presentations

With the preceding as a base we can discuss the specific conditions conducive to false self-presentations. False selves are most likely to be presented when the potential gains are high and the costs, or the likelihood of paying the costs, are low. Given what has been said about the nature of these rewards and costs, when will this occur?

If the goal of presenting a false self is to acquire the rewards associated with that self and/or to avoid the costs associated with the true self, it would follow that people who have disvalued traits are more likely, all other things being equal, to present false selves. And the lower the value of the true self the greater the tendency to present false selves. Almost by definition, people with such traits will gain from other's acceptance of the false self. Thus, we would expect that those of low status, those who are stigmatized (Goffman, 1963), and those with low self-evaluations would be more likely to present false selves than their opposites would.

This approach would also suggest that certain characteristics of the interaction situation itself would be relevant. It may be assumed that actor is, to some degree at least, loathe to initiate interaction if that interaction will call forth a disvalued identity. In an other-initiated interaction he would also try to avoid such identities, but his control over the matter would be less. Although the tendency may not be very strong, turning this around would suggest that actor is more likely to be motivated to present a false self in other-initiated interactions, particularly when actor's participation is involuntary. This certainly does not mean that we never present false selves in self-initiated, voluntary interactions. Confidence men make a profession out of initiating situations in which they present false selves, men who used to be called cads are accomplished amateurs at it, and we all do it some of the time. In fact, if actor initiates the encounter it makes the presentation of a false self easier (see below). All that is being postulated here is that there is likely to be less "need" for false self-presentations in voluntary encounters.

There is a complex relationship between the duration of the interaction and the likelihood of presenting a false self. As we will see later, there are considerations which lead to the hypothesis that false selves would be more common in short-term interaction. However, questions of motivation suggest the opposite, under some conditions at least. If the cost involved in being identified by the disvalued identity involves a single payment, length of interaction should have no relation to the issue at hand. One pays the adult admission price, and that's the cost of being defined as an adult regardless of how long the movie runs. In other instances—for example, when the cost is humiliation—the payment may continue throughout the interaction. If the extent of cost associated with the disvalued true self is a funcion of the length of interaction, the basic idea would suggest that the longer the encounter, the greater the likelihood that a false self-presentation will be attempted.

These factors, then, incline actor toward a false self-presentation. They are, however, only part of the story, for even when they are motivated to do so, actors will not present false selves unless the cost factors I spoke of are weak or absent. For example, one of the costs which inhibit the performance of a false self is the fear of discovery, and it would follow that conditions which reduce the fear of discovery are conducive to the presentation of a false self.

It has already been noted that the length of time the interaction will take is related, under some circumstances, to the strength of actor's motivation to present a false self. People engaged in short interactions should be less motivated to present a false self. The matter under consideration here, though, would suggest that there is a contrary tendency. In short-term interactions the probability of discovery is likely to be considerably lower. If "the part" is not too long, we can rehearse it rather completely before we "go on," and if rehearsal is not possible, it is certainly easier to present a consistent and convincing·ad lib performance when we do not have to keep it up for a long time. The shorter the interaction, the less the likelihood that the actor will fall out of role. Furthermore, in short-term interaction there are fewer acts and therefore a lesser likelihood that we will contradict ourselves or give information which won't "check-out." In addition, the shortness of the time span gives other less time to do the checking. Of course, the checking could be done after the interaction is over, but by then it may be "too late" for other to do anything if he discovers the deception. Moreover, in many instances other's motivation to check up will be drastically reduced once the interaction is done. About the only counterindication to the postulated tendency is that actor requires sufficient time to convey his image. If the interaction is too fleeting, actor may be rushed and not have enough time to present a false self with subtlety and shading. This would be so, however, only in very short interactions, and in any case it does not seem equal in weight to the other factors.

It seems fairly obvious that the better one knows the details of the requisite role, the better one's chances of presenting a self with sufficient skill to avoid detection. If this is so, and if we learn from our experiences, it would follow that we can do a better job as our experience increases. If the better the job we can do, the more likely we are to try it, we should be more likely to present false selves the greater our experience with the associated role. However, extent of experience is not simply a matter of counting exposures. Different kinds of experience undoubtedly have differential impact. Having played the role in the past is better experience than having been the other when it was played, and the latter is better than observing it or hearing about it. Probably the best experience is having played the role vis-à-vis the present other. It should be clear that all that I had to say in my discussion of role learning is relevant. Therefore, it should be sufficient to note here that anything which will add to actor's familiarity with the role associated with a false self will increase the likelihood that he will perform it.

From a similar set of considerations, I am brought to the notion that the availability of a so-called backstage area in which actor can prepare and/or rehearse will also increase false self-presentations. If we have to "go on cold," we are less likely to know our lines well, and our reading of them is unlikely to be smooth. In addition, the success of a performance often hinges on the messages conveyed by our appearance and by the physical props we use. They need arranging and preparing, and this cannot be done—particularly for false selves—in the presence of the audience. Thus, even when we know the role well a private area for preparation is useful. This being the case, we have a factor which opposes the tendency previously noted. An actor who initiates an *interaction* may be less motivated to present a false self, but if he has that motivation he is more likely to act on it if he initiates the interaction. When that is so, actor is more likely to have the desired rehearsal time and space.

The availability of a good, well-rehearsed supporting cast—what Goffman would call a team—can also increase the likelihood of a false self-presentation by increasing the adequacy of the performance and thereby increasing the safety of doing so. I have already discussed the uses of a team (see pages 81–82), so we don't have to go into it too deeply here. Suffice it to say that a team is particularly valuable when a false self is being presented. By providing the correct cues, they can make it easier for actor to play his part; they can, by their apparent acceptance of actor's presented self, incline the target other to accept it, and if gaffes occur they can divert attention or explain them away.

Finally, I would postulate that there is a general ability factor involved here. With all the things I have mentioned held constant, certain people would be better able to present a convincing performance than others. I seriously doubt whether this is an inherent ability. Differences in this regard can probably be traced to earlier experiences—for example, the extent to which the actor has been taught to present false selves, the extent to which they have practiced them, etc. There is no doubt that Gigi, who came from a family of courtesans, was more adept at presenting a false self than is Mary Smith down the block. It seems clear, however, that Gigi's abilities are a result of training, not genes.

Characteristics of the other and of the relationship between actor and other also relate to the likelihood that a false self-presentation will be detected. Just as there are some actors who are not very adept at presenting false selves, there are some others who are particularly poor at detecting such presentations. Some people seem to believe anything they are told. Others are constantly on the lookout for deception and are quick to discover it when it exists, because they know the ways in which it is likely to be carried out. They check their sources, they know what is reasonable, etc. Children would be a good example of the first class; good reporters and anthropologists would fall into the second group.

It is also safe to present a false self to those who are uninterested and uninvolved. This group of people may be quite able to see through false presentations—they simply lack the desire to do so. It requires extra work to detect false selves, as it does to present them, and under some circumstances people just don't care to bother. Often servants find it easy to fool their masters because the latter don't care enough to look closely.

Finally, I would note that strangers are less likely to penetrate actor's disguise. They do not have the needed information to detect that the presented self is, in fact, false, and they cannot so easily check the evidence being given by the actor because they lack the necessary supplementary information.

Even when the likelihood of discovery is quite high, actor may "take a chance" and present a false self. This would occur when the gains of success are high and the cost of being discovered are low. I have already considered the conditions under which the gain will be high. When will actors suffer little if they are discovered?

In general, this will happen when others have few sanctions they can apply. Others may have little power because they don't have an effective sanction available or because they dare not apply it; which boils down to the same thing. Humiliation of actor is one of the major sanctions that can be used under these circumstances, but if any attempt at it would lead to severe counteractions, such as being fired, other will keep quiet. Dislike is another punishment frequently used by others who penetrate disguises, but if actor doesn't care about other's opinion, other's use of this sanction will have little effect. Ostracism is often effective, but if the two will never meet again in any case, it also has no constraining power. Withdrawal from interaction is another cost that a deceived other can assess. But if the interaction by its very nature will be short run anyway, or if actor doesn't care whether the interaction continues, or if other is dependent upon the interaction for some important goal and actor is not, the threat of ending the encounter has no power.

In all these instances, other lacks power or is prevented from using it. Slightly different is the case in which other simply does not care to apply the sanctions at his disposal. One circumstance which could produce this situation would occur when other does not subscribe to the norm opposing the presentation of false selves or holds it weakly. Sometimes this is a matter of not throwing the first stone: "How can I condemn him when he is only doing what I do all the time?" The inhibition on other's part might also come from a view that the trangression is minor and understandable. He might feel that to apply any of the available sanctions would amount to overkill. This is particularly likely to be the case when other attributes benign motives to the actor: "Yes, she lied, but she just didn't want to hurt him." Transgressions are also likely to be defined as minor when the false self and the true are fairly similar. Other may then interpret actor's behavior as only a minor sin: "He didn't lie; he just exaggerated a bit." We also define as minor, cases in which we are not certain that the presentation was intentionally false. "I know now that she is a grad assistant, but I'm not sure she meant for me to conclude she was a professor when she said she taught at the University."

Even if all these barriers are down, actor may still not present a false self, particularly if the gain from it would only be moderate, for the cost of performance may be too great in relation to the gain. Therefore, to conclude this presentation, I must consider those circumstances which will tend to reduce the cost of performance.

Since one of the major costs involved in the presentation of a false self is the effort required to put it on stage, it would follow that the cost of performance would be reduced when the performance is "easy" for actor. Thus it would seem, again, that there is a greater tendency for false selves to be presented in short-term than in long-term interaction. Other factors discussed for their relevance for earlier considerations may be mentioned here as well. The likelihood of discovery, it will be remembered, is low when the associated role is familiar, and clearly, so are the costs of performing it. There needn't be so much attention paid to getting it right; it comes easier. The same may be said of instances in which a loyal and proficient team is available. Ideally, the team can take much of the burden of the actual performance from the shoulders of actor, and the presence of allies can reduce anxiety, which is another important cost. But there are dangers. Keeping the team in line, rehearsing them, worrying about defections or bloopers can lead actor into more effort than would be required for a solo performance. Under the best of circumstances, however, this would not be so, and it is under such circumstances that the presence of a team increases the likelihood of false self-presentation.

Extra effort is not the only added cost associated with the performance of false selves. I have assumed that most people feel anxiety about the consequences of being discovered. This anxiety is also properly considered a cost of performance, and thus anything which reduces it could be noted here. To do so, however, would mean repeating much of the previous discussion, for anything which reduces the likelihood and cost of discovery will also reduce the anxiety that people feel about being discovered. People are more likely to present a false self when the other is a stranger, for example, because they foresee that they are less likely to suffer negative consequences if they are discovered. This decision is based upon a nonemotional calculation of concrete gains and losses. At the same time, *because* they think they are risking less, their anxiety level will be less when the other is a stranger. The cost of the performance itself will be less, which will be an analytically distinct contribution to their decision.

I have assumed that most people feel, to some extent at least, that they are acting improperly when they present false selves. In addition to anxiety they feel guilt, and this guilt must be added in as another cost of performance. What conditions affect the extent to which guilt is felt? One factor that might contribute would be the degree to which the false self departs from the true self. If the false self is not that different from the true self, a variety of rationalizations become possible. Just as others are more likely to find this behavior minimally acceptable, so is actor.

Another basic assumption is that actor chooses to perform a false self because the rewards associated with it are greater than those tied to the true self. There may, however, be some rewards associated with the true self, the loss of which must be counted as a cost—if not a cost of performance per se. Although it is perhaps clear from what has already been said that in making a decision, actor considers the rewards associated with both the false self and the true self, it appears useful to highlight the point. A false self will be presented when the profits (rewards vs. costs) associated with it are higher than those foregone by not presenting the true self, and this is likely when the rewards associated with the true self are low.

As previously indicated, true self rewards will be low when actor and/or other disvalue the identity associated with the true self. But it also may be so when it is a valued identity which has frequently been used. If this is the case, actor may simply be satiated with the rewards it can bring and wish to increase the supply of another kind of reward. Also, though it is uncommon, the identity may be highly valued, but the self-evaluation associated with it may be low. This would be a barrier to actor's presenting it—not because he doesn't want the rewards associated with it, but rather because he doesn't think he is likely to get them.

Finally, it should be noted that there are certain advantages in the presentation of a true self just because it *is* the true self. Self-respect would be one advantage and, interestingly, so would the opportunity to gain validation for our view of ourselves. There is often some question in our minds about who we are, and other's reaction to our true self helps us to know.

If the loss of an opportunity to validate the true self is a necessary concomitant of the presentation of a false self, it would follow that the performance of false self roles would have an increased likelihood when actor does not want validation of the true self. Such would occur when actor needs no further validation because of ample previous validation, and when he doesn't want validation because he would rather not be what he thinks he is.

SUMMARY

In this chapter I concluded my discussion of the interaction process by considering the remaining two sources of problematic interactions. In the first of these—role strain—actor feels difficulty in meeting role agreements either because two or more roles call forth incompatible responses (role conflict) or because the role demands are so great they cannot all be met (role overload). Both of these forms of role strain are quite common, and therefore problematic interaction is a frequent occurrence in most people's lives. However, there is reason to believe that the extent of role overload has been somewhat exaggerated because of a failure to recognize that not all activities deplete time and energy. In fact, certain activities, such as those to which we are strongly committed, may add to our energy store.

If role strain exists, it may be taken as given that the negotiating process has not worked well for actor, and thus it follows that anything which contributes to ineffective negotiation on the part of actor will increase the likelihood that he or she will experience role strain. Included in these would be: limited power relative to other, an inability to recognize the consequences of various actions, societal definitions which support a role conception which is antithetical to actor's, etc.

When actor discovers that he or she is experiencing role strain, efforts will be made to reduce or eliminate it. At this point, actor may make renewed efforts to meet the obligations, and these often prove successful. If they are not, he or she may develop a new definition of the situation and attempt to get other to accept it. This will lead to processes which are the same as those involved in the original defining and negotiating stages. However, the specific course that they take will be affected by the existence of prior decisions and agreements. Depending upon the circumstances, these may either hinder or help actor in his attempts to renegotiate.

If the attempt to change the definition is not successful, actor will attempt to reduce the costs of failing to live up to role expectations. Since the sources of the costs are both self and other, one way of doing this is to hide the facts from himself and/or from other. In addition, he may choose to fail in ways that will produce the least cost. This would include meeting the expectations of the more powerful other and neglecting those of the less powerful.

Because they are usually complicated, interactions in which false selves are presented are considered problematic. Although they involve interaction difficulties, the presentation of false selves is quite common because such presentations are potentially productive of rewards. For example, if a false self-presentation is successful, actor may be able to act in ways that are closed to persons with actor's real traits. In addition, false selves can produce desired responses, they can be means to avoiding undesired ones, and they can be productive of utilitarian rewards.

There are, however, potential costs associated with false self-presentations, which reduce somewhat the frequency with which false selves are presented. These costs arise chiefly from two facts: such presentations involve "extra work," and if actor is discovered, he or she will be sanctioned because the norms of society are opposed to false self-presentations. From this it follows that actor will be most inclined to present a false self when it can be done easily, when the likelihood of discovery is relatively small, and when the costs, if discovered, are low. The remainder of the chapter was devoted to a consideration of the situations under which these conditions are likely to prevail.

CHAPTER 10

INTERACTIONIST THEORY AND EMOTIONS

Extensive as the foregoing material may be, it presents only the basics of symbolic interactionism. I have focused on traditional concerns and given little attention to the implications and extensions of the theory. Given the goals of the book, this is perhaps the way it should be, but it does seem worthwhile to go one step further. This chapter will test the limits of the theory by considering its applicability to emotions.

Such a test should be particularly informative, for interactionist theory is, of course, explicitly designed to explain the behavior of people when they are acting as conscious, unemotional thinkers and planners. If it turns out that the theory is useful for understanding how emotions develop and influence behavior it will become clear that the theory is much more "robust" than many have assumed it to be.[1]

Before I turn to the interactionist analysis, it is necessary to indicate what I mean when I speak of emotions and emotional states, and this is not as easy as it might seem. The words are commonly used, but their meanings tend to be elusive when an attempt is made to pin them down, and there is a notable lack of agreement among authors (Alston, 1967; Plutchik, 1962).

For our purposes, it seems sufficient to suggest that a person is in an emotional state when he is experiencing feelings which arise from his evaluation or appraisal of a

---

[1]It should be emphasized that the focus here is on conscious emotions. There is a third image of humans which views them as unconscious, emotional actors (Hochschild, 1979), but that will not be considered here. It may be possible that interactionist theory can be extended to cover this case also, but to do so would open up a whole series of issues which cannot be easily discussed in a book of this kind.

situation or event.[2] There are no emotions without feelings, but not all feelings qualify (see Alston, 1967).

For example, if I am "hot under the collar" *because* I disapprove of someone's actions, I am experiencing the emotion of anger. If, on the other hand, I am hot and tired *because* it is 120° in the shade I am not in an emotional state. Although I am experiencing feelings in the second case, they do not have the "proper" source. For an emotion term such as anger or fear to be applicable, there must be conscious feelings *and* they must have their origins in actor's definition of a situation.

With this matter settled, we may turn to the interactionist analysis of the subject. The relevant literature has grown in recent years, and it is not possible to cover it all here. (See Hochschild, 1975, 1979; Shott, 1979; Kemper, 1978a, 1978b; Heise, 1979.) Perhaps the best way to proceed is to consider the relevance of the major concepts of interactionist theory for these matters. As was the case with the central concepts, emotions are of interest as dependent and independent variables, and thus the discussion can be divided into two major sections: (1) interactional sources of emotions, and (2) the nature of emotional interaction.

INTERACTIONAL SOURCES OF EMOTIONS

Interactionism and the Etiology of Emotions

To speak of the causes of emotions is to speak ambiguously, for the phrase refers to how we learn what we should feel and to the process by which an emotion in the actor's repertoire is brought into play in a particular situation. Most of the recent discussions by sociologists are relevant to the latter question, and it seems wise, even if somewhat backward, to deal with it first. The expectation is that this discussion will contain within it the bulk of the answer to the first question.

Emotion Rules.[3]   The definition presented above states that an emotion occurs when actor's definition of the situation leads him to experience a certain feeling. Interactionists suggest that the link is through *emotion rules* that suggest the nature, extent, and duration of the emotions appropriate for a variety of situations.[4] The definition of the situation provides us with a basis for choosing the rule which applies in a particular case. When we know we are at a funeral, we know that it is proper to be sad; when we are at a wedding, we know we should be happy. And, just as we tend to act

[2] As it is used in this literature, a feeling is a perceived bodily sensation. Examples would include tension, lightness, pain, rapid heartbeat, expansiveness, and feeling good all over.

[3] All of this is borrowed from Hochschild's (1979, 1975) work on what she calls feeling rules. Given her practice of using the terms feelings and emotions synonymously, this is acceptable. In the present context, the term emotional rules is more appropriate.

[4] This is not to suggest that we must experience a single emotion, because this is often not the case (Plutchik, 1962, 1977, 1980). For our purposes, a mixed emotion is a kind of emotion.

consistently with our role definitions, we tend to have the emotions we *should* have under the circumstances as defined. Not surprisingly, our moods at weddings and funerals differ and tend to be consistent with the "demands" of the situation.

I grant that the existence of such rules is not immediately evident from casual observation. They are often latent, that is, they are not thought about unless they are probed at (Hochschild, 1979). As is the case with roles, these rules often become a "part of us," and they are applied without much thought. However, common parlance indicates that they exist and that we are sometimes aware of them. Otherwise, how could we explain why we often speak of our emotions as if they were in some way "wrong," often with some wonder that we are not feeling differently? ("I can't understand it, I should miss her terribly, but strangely enough, I feel quite happy." "Why shouldn't I be nervous? You would be too if you were facing what I am. I'm not falling apart [*that* would be wrong]; I'm just feeling a little uptight.")

These emotion rules resemble more familiar rules in other ways as well. For one thing, they are specific to situations and identities. They say that a particular kind of person interacting with a certain kind of other should feel this emotion under these circumstances. Second, there are penalties if they are broken—feeling the wrong things leaves us open to attack. Third, they are quite variable. They vary across cultures, they are different in different segments of a given culture, and not all people of a particular segment believe in the same rule. At the same time, there tend to be patterns. Particular rules are more common in some societies than in others, etc. The resemblance between these rules and role definitions is striking.

Evidence for the Existence of Emotion Rules. The previous paragraphs assert a great deal, and some illustrations of the validity of these points seems required, even if they are not the kind of statements that admit of clear-cut proof. Illustrative evidence is not difficult to find, however.

To begin, it has often been noted that people of different cultures experience different emotions in comparable situations, or, at a minimum, they experience the same emotions to markedly different degrees. There are, for example, large cultural differences in the amount of anguish felt at the death of a loved one. In fact, although apparently there is always some degree of sadness, in some cases feelings of anger and fear predominate (Rosenblatt, 1975).

The rapid mood swings of Tahitians in mourning illustrate how variable the patterns are. At one moment they are bereft; they moan, wail, and engage in self-mutilation. At the next, they are joking, laughing, and going about their normal activities. Levy (1973: 302) suggests that death "tapped some deep well of loneliness and sadness in people which sprang to the surface for a few moments and then, as a result of some combination of *inner and outer pressures,* was quickly sealed off again." [emphasis added]

The Ifaluk of Micronesia and the tribes of the Ubena area of Africa also show a pattern of extreme grief which quickly passes. Among the Kota, on the other hand, the period of mourning is quite extended and shows a pattern of stages associated with specific rituals (Averill, 1968).

Of course, emotional variation is not limited to people of different cultures. Although their extent has certainly been exaggerated, it seems probable that there are differences between men and women in our own society. For example, the expression of anger has been permitted to men, to some degree at least, but women have traditionally been expected to control it. Thus it comes as no surprise that several studies have shown that women feel more anxiety than men when they do feel aggressive. Given differential child-rearing, it is also not particularly surprising to learn that the incidence of several other types of anxiety are greater among women, women and girls generally exceed their male counterparts in friendliness, and women tend to show more fear, etc. (Mischel, 1966; Maccoby and Jacklin, 1974; Maccoby, 1966; Hochschild, 1979). It should be noted, however, that the differences are frequently not very large, there is considerable overlap in the distributions, and even the best established differences do not appear in all studies.

These examples show clearly the existence of considerable variation in the emotional reactions of people, and this suggests unequivocally that there is no necessary connection between objective situations and the emotions they engender. More than that, even situations which are defined in the same way can be tied to very different emotions. *There may be limits, but if they do exist, they are quite wide.* For example, contrary to beliefs about maternal love instincts, mothers show wide variation in their emotions toward their children, and this is true even when they define the child's behavior in the same way.[5]

The argument has been that situations involving emotions resemble "standard interaction" situations in that definitional elements are crucial, and I have also argued that a key element in the etiology of emotional states is a set of rules which are remarkably like the role definitions which are so central to the standard situations. I would now suggest that two other key elements in the definition of situations—the self-concept and the presented self—are also involved in emotion situations.

The Self-Concept and Emotions.   Certain aspects of the self-definition for the encounter are important because they provide actor with a basis for choosing an emotion from his or her repertoire. Emotion rules are tied to identities, just as role definitions are. Before actor can decide what emotion is called for, he or she must know which identity is appropriate for the encounter.

This would explain, in part, why the same event can bring out different emotions in a given person at different times. Our reactions to situations are not based simply on their details. Our definition of self will have an important influence on what we allow ourself to feel. When a student had a seizure in my class, I did not experience panic as I would have under many other circumstances. I suddenly found that because I was the teacher and "in charge," I was cool, efficient, and on top of the situation. Quite literally, there was a feeling of having "risen" to meet the demands of my position.

---

[5] See Shott (1979) and Hochschild (1979) for discussions of views which see human emotions as less plastic than I have just suggested they are.

The Presented Self and Emotions. The presented self is involved with the choice of emotions in a number of ways. For one thing, we tend to choose emotions consistent with the presented self we have selected, because if our emotions are consistent with the image we wish to convey, we increase the likelihood that other will see us as we wish to be seen. Our emotions will be taken as evidence that we are what we claim to be. Also, if we truly feel as a person with the presented identity would feel, it makes it easier to stay in role. The actor on the stage who "really lives the part" is likely to give an effective performance, as is the person who is involved in a real-life performance.

The presented self we have chosen for a particular encounter may also affect what we feel in another way. The emotion of embarrassment (Goffman, 1956) tends to occur when we have done something which leads other to see through our self-presentation (Modigliani, 1968). Of course, this emotion may be elicited by other circumstances. Gross and Stone (1964: 2) suggest that it occurs "whenever some *central* assumption in a transaction has been *unexpectedly* and unqualifiedly discredited." And Goffman (1956) notes that embarrassment can occur even when an other is present only in imagination. This notwithstanding, it seems that a frequent source of this emotion is the failure of an attempt at impression management. Thus, when we choose to present a self which is likely to be seen through, we are increasing the likelihood that we will find ourselves in a situation which leads to embarrassment.

It is now clear that definitions of situations play an important role in the production of emotions, and it also seems that the definitions which produce emotions are similar *in form* to those developed in other situations. The remaining question is whether the *processes* by which the definitions are constructed are the same. My consideration of this issue will be limited to an inquiry into the relevance of role taking for the elicitation of emotional states. Is this rather intellectual process, which is so important in the gathering of the information needed to define other situations, of relevance in situations which involve strong feelings?

Role Taking and Emotions. The answer to the question seems to be an unequivocal, "Yes." Role taking is often directly involved in the development of emotions. For example, a common stimulus for the emotion of shame is knowledge of other's opinion of actor; sympathy often results from actor's knowledge of other's feelings about himself; and fear is often stimulated by actor's assumptions concerning other's intentions toward actor. In each of these cases the emotions have their genesis in knowledge of other's thoughts, and any emotion which is based on the thoughts of another is also based upon role taking—the mechanism by which we learn the thoughts of another.[6]

[6] The examples illustrate the applicability of the distinction between reflexive and nonreflexive role taking to the present situation. When role taking is involved in the development of an emotion, actor's question may be, "What does other think of me?", and this he or she would engage in reflexive role taking. If actor's concern is other's thoughts about anything other than actor, the role taking would be nonreflexive. Shame is a reflexive feeling; feelings of sympathy are nonreflexive (Shott, 1979).

Role taking would also be involved in the choice of an emotion rule. Just as is the case with roles, after actor has partially defined the situation, he may or may not know what emotion rule should apply, and he will engage in role taking in order to determine what other thinks is appropriate. In fact, even if actor is quite certain what emotion is called for he will still want to know how other will react to his expression of that emotion, and in this effort he will also resort to role taking.

Finally, role taking is indirectly tied into emotional situations. In order to know what emotion is appropriate, actor must define his self and presented self, other's self and presented self, and so forth. Since these definitions require the use of role taking, we have an additional basis for the contention that role taking is important in the etiology of emotions.

The Problematics of Emotion Situations

The discussion thus far may be likened to my earlier one of routine interaction situations. The assumption has been that actor can define the appropriate emotion rule, and that once this is done, he or she simply experiences what is proper. In many instances this is an accurate description of what happens, but it does not hold for situations which may be described as *problematic interaction situations*—to carry over the terminology used in the rest of the book.

The problems that occur in emotion situations are comparable to the problems considered earlier. There may be problems of definition—actor may not be able to decide what emotion rule is appropriate, either because there is none in his repertoire which seems to fit or because he cannot choose among several which seem appropriate. Or, there may be problems of implementation. Actor may know what emotion he should feel, but he may have difficulty putting that knowledge into effect.

Problems in defining emotions are so similar to other definition problems that they need not be discussed here. All that was said before (see Chapters 7 and 8) would seem to apply. They tend to occur when prior socialization has been inadequate and they are solved by termination of the encounter or by attempts to obtain further socialization. Problems of implementation are not basically different from the comparable problems in nonemotion situations, but some of the details are of interest and therefore they warrant a brief consideration.

Emotion Rule Strain. In many instances actor finds that it is difficult or impossible to act consistently with the emotion rules that he or she believes apply to the situation. In other words, there is a condition which is comparable to role strain—let us call it *emotion rule strain.*

As with role strain, there are a number of subcategories within the general category of emotion rule strain. In some cases, actor cannot follow the rule because to do so would cause a conflict with other that he or she would prefer to avoid. This is often the case when there is a lack of consensus about the proper rule to be followed. ("You have no reason to be angry, and I won't take it.")

A lack of consensus is, however, not the only reason for interpersonal conflict over feelings. It may be "dangerous" to experience the emotions called for by a rule even if other accepts them as valid. Other may agree with actor that there is reason for anger, but actor may still fear the consequences of getting angry. An emotion that other considers to be inappropriate is likely to call forth stronger sanctions, but "appropriate" emotions may also bring undesired responses.

In other instances we find that the emotion rules which apply to complex situations are mutually exclusive, and we have a situation of *emotion rule conflict.* Teachers know they should feel sympathy for their students, but at the same time they may also believe that they must remain somewhat detached, and it is difficult to abide by both rules simultaneously.

I believe there is also a situation of *emotions overload,* which is comparable to role overload. Some emotion rules cannot be obeyed because actor does not have the time, energy, or "ability" to follow them. There is no basic incompatibility between love for spouse and love for one's child, but as some new parents find, the warmth lavished on the baby is so energy-consuming that there has to be a diminution of affect toward the spouse. In other cases, actor may find that he or she cannot muster up the emotion the rule calls for. For some people this is a constant problem. They know they have "every reason" to feel happy, but they constantly have feelings of depression.

When people cannot easily follow the emotion rules they consider to be appropriate they do not simply leave it at that. If the problem is a lack of agreement they will attempt to reach a working consensus with other regarding the emotions to be felt, and the process will be one of negotiations. ("What do you mean I have no reason to be angry?" "It's not an infatuation, I really love you.")

If the difficulty is incompatibility of emotion rules or fear of the negative consequences which may follow from the expression of the emotion there are a number of possible solutions; termination of the encounter, suppression of the emotion, further negotiations, a redefinition of the situation, presentation of a false self, and so forth. The basis for choice among the possibilities will be the maximization of profit rule— the principle used here so often in earlier chapters.

Emotion Work. When the problem is emotion overload the tendency is to engage in *emotion work.*[7] We try to experience the emotion we should, we tell ourselves that our emotion is correct, or we try to convince ourselves that we are experiencing what we really are not.[8]

The details of emotion work have yet to be worked out, but Hochschild (1979) makes a good start. Her discussion suggests these specific mechanisms:

[7]The idea is originally Hochschild's (1979).

[8]If none of these alternatives works, we may try to act as if we are experiencing the emotion we think we should be. This ploy is impression management rather than emotion work. There is no attempt to bring emotions into line with the rules. The goal is simply to appear to abide by the rule. Of course, as with all impression management, the "act" may become the reality.

1. *Cognitive Emotion Work.* In this type, we change images, ideas, and thoughts so that appropriate emotional states may be achieved. In some cases this would involve a change in the definition of our emotions, but perhaps more commonly, we change the definition of the situation. If we believe that we do not have sufficient reason for the anger we are feeling we can usually find additional justification if we look at the situation in a somewhat different light. We can also bring forth an appropriate, but elusive, emotion by looking for more evidence that we should feel it. We can, for example, feel sympathy when it is difficult to do so by focusing on other's present plight and forgetting the past.

When the elements in the situation are contradictory it is fairly easy to do this; we simply focus on the elements which are consistent with the desired emotion. If the current definition is unequivocal in its emotional implications the change would be more difficult to bring about, but it can be done. We might reconsider the meaning of the elements which have already been used and/or gather additional information.

In any case, it is easier to change the definition if we receive input from people who hold to the definition we seek to have. After the breakup of a marriage or love affair, one of the parties often continues to feel an unwanted and inappropriate love for the other. The cure is, of course, to see the "so and so" as he (she) "really is." Actor may not be able to manage this change on his own, but friends can help to bring it about. In fact, since actor must alter a definition which once seemed quite correct, he will probably require validation from others for any change worked out on his own.

2. *Bodily Emotion Work.* In this case we work directly on the feelings. If we want to have a particular emotion, but the proper feeling "won't occur" or an inappropriate one "won't go away," we may be able to produce it. We can try to run off tension, we can take a pill, we can try to "psych ourselves up," we can try to "get a grip on ourselves." The prescriptions are numerous, but they all involve physical or mental action in the service of changing feelings without changing definitions.

3. *Expressive Emotion Work.* This is rather similar to the previous mechanism, but it is distinctive in that the actions taken to alter the inner feeling involve the manipulation of overt expressive gestures which are usually a result of feelings. We may, for example, force ourselves to stop crying in order to feel good, or we may attempt to achieve the same goal by having a "good cry." Or, we may start crying in the hope that it will bring forth the feelings which are usually associated with crying. As these examples indicate, there are different routes to the same goal, and the same action may be an attempt to reach very different goals. The details are not important here.[9] The point is simply that any time we try to create an emotion by using an expressive reaction we have an example of expressive emotion work.

In summary, the argument has been that the emotion we experience in a par-

[9]It is not clear why this kind of emotion work is effective. Perhaps self-deception is at work, perhaps the expression of a feeling leads to feedback which produces the feeling, or perhaps catharsis and tension release account for some manifestations. Equally unclear are the conditions under which it works. What is amply clear is that it *does* work—sometimes.

ticular situation is influenced by the same mental structures and processes that are involved in other interactions. The definition of the situation is of particular importance. By interpreting cues with the aid of role taking, we define identities for ourselves and others, we define the nature of the occurrences which have taken place, we choose presented selves, etc. When this part of the definitional process is completed we know what emotions are appropriate to the situation, because these definitions tell us which of our rules for emotion should be brought into play. These emotion rules are of the following form: This kind of actor interacting with this kind of other should have this emotion to this extent when this event occurs. And when we have chosen an emotion rule we tend to follow its dictates and have the proper feelings.

This description holds for routine situations but not for problematic ones. For any of a number of reasons, actor may not know what emotion to feel in a particular situation or he may not be able to feel the emotion he believes is proper. These situations are analogous to those that involve problems of role definition and role strain and they are handled in a similar way. For example, if actor does not have the resources to experience what he or she believes should be felt, the situation may be redefined, additional attempts may be made to abide by the rule, the encounter may be terminated, and so forth. In any case, the general rule of maximization of profits will be followed.

Learning Emotion Rules

In the previous discussion the existence of emotion rules was taken as a given, but if my explanation of the causes of emotions is to be reasonably complete I must suggest how these rules are learned.

The repertoire of emotion rules is so similar to the repertoire of roles that it seems almost certain that they are learned in the same way, and a full discussion of these processes hardly seems necessary at this point. Let me simply say that in our interactions we encounter a variety of views concerning what feelings are appropriate in given situations. We receive direct instruction ("That's not funny. . ." "Don't be afraid. . ." "You're not sick, you're just in love."); we model ("Look, am I afraid?"); and we learn from general observation ("Most people don't let such things bother them.") From the rules we encounter we choose our preferred one or we fashion a personal rule. In either case, the rules we adopt will be one we believe will increase our general store of reward.

EMOTIONS AS SOURCES OF OVERT BEHAVIOR

The final topic is the connections between emotions and social behavior. The major concern will be with emotions as antecedents of behavior, but before we get to that I would note that because humans can foresee the consequences of their actions, emotions do not have to occur in order to influence what we do. Let me explain this somewhat paradoxical statement.

Anticipated Emotions and Behavior

Not infrequently, our behavior is strongly influenced by a desire to achieve or avoid emotional states: "I don't want to know, it will just make me angry." "I can't let her get too close, I don't want any emotional attachments right now." "I must see that, I think I'll really enjoy it." "I can't do that, it will make me feel guilty." (see Rawlings, 1970).

The key to understanding this is the fact that human behavior is goal-directed and a major goal is the achievement of expressive rewards. This often means simply that we attempt to create the conditions which lead toward emotions we consider pleasant and away from those we consider unpleasant. This suggests once again the applicability of the general theory to the present topic. All that has been previously discussed about attempts to structure interactions in ways which hold promise of leading to desired ends would be applicable here without change. The *fear* of guilt, shame, and embarrassment lead us to avoid certain actions and to engage in others. In fact, when it is realized that such emotions contribute to negative self-evaluations the correspondence between what was emphasized earlier and the present material becomes even clearer.

There is the danger, however, that the reader will go too far in this matter and assume a simple hedonism. I am not saying that the key human goal is to "feel good now." That is not so. Humans do not simply seek immediate bodily gratification. The goal is long-term profit and we often forego immediate emotional reward and suffer emotional costs in the pursuit of other outcomes. We may act in ways which we believe will produce undesired emotional states because those actions hold promise of giving us other rewards which we value more than we disvalue the undesirable emotional states. Many will, for example, risk anxiety, boredom, pain, and so on in their search for success.

In fact, we can be very far-sighted in these matters. We may avoid desired emotional states because we foresee that in the long run they will lead to actions which bring high costs. People who fear to love don't necessarily find the state itself displeasing. What they may fear is the vulnerability associated with it, or the time cost, or the pain they will experience when it ends, etc. And finally, even when our original goal is the achievement of an emotional state, we may abandon the effort because the costs of achieving it outweigh the payoff we see accruing to us if we are successful. Many people give up on therapy, for example, because they see it as more costly psychologically than the emotional disturbance from which they are suffering.

With this said, we may return to the major question: Given the existence of emotional state "X," what will be the effect on actor's behavior?

Emotions as a Cause of Behavior

There is little doubt that the behaviors of actors are correlated with the emotions they are feeling. This is amply clear from the most superficial of observations, and numerous systematic studies have shown connections between emotional states and

298

behavior in social situations. Altruistic behavior seems, for example, to be significantly tied to a variety of feeling and emotions. Berkowitz (1972) reports on several studies which show that people who were in a "good mood"–those who had succeeded, had been praised, etc.–were more willing to help others, and sympathy and gratitude seem to have a similar effect. It is not, however, simply that "good" emotions produce "good" behavior. Studies (cited in Berkowitz, 1972 and Shott, 1979) show that guilt and embarrassment also make actors more willing to help others. This is especially true when they can help the others without having to interact with them (Carlsmith and Gross, 1969; Friedman et al., 1967).

Emotions, of course, do not only produce socially desirable actions. It is well-established that feelings of frustration will, *under some circumstances,* produce aggression (Baron, 1977, Berkowitz, 1969); distress and sadness decrease altruism (Moore et al., 1973); distress lowers resistance to temptation (Fry, 1975); joy, *under some circumstances,* can produce addiction (Izard, 1977); shame decreases rationality (Izard, 1977), etc.

The question is not, however, "What are the effects of specific emotions upon behavior?" What we want here is a consideration of the general principles which tie any emotion to overt behavior. It is clear that when we get down to specifics, different emotions have different effects, and the same emotion produces diverse behaviors depending on the person and the circumstances involved. Are there any general patterns that can be seen under all this diversity?

The answer lies, I believe, in the realization that once an emotion is experienced, the emotion becomes a part of the definition of the situation and it also changes other aspects of the definition.

The second part of this point is not very different from that made above. Just as we attempt to achieve desired emotional states and to avoid those which we define as undesirable, once we have experienced an emotion we attempt to perpetuate or change it depending upon our definition of it. In other words, experienced emotions influence the goals we choose in our encounters.

This view makes sense of some of the data presented above. The altruistic behavior of the subjects who feel guilt does not seem to be "true" altruism–if there is such a thing. The subjects were altruistic because they expected to get something from their actions. "What seems to be common to these altruistic or reparative acts is an attempt to repair one's self-conception or self-presentation and convince others (and one's self) of one's moral worthiness or competence" (Shott, 1979). This repair of self-conception seems to be desired for itself, and also because it serves to expiate the guilt and remove the unpleasant feeling tone.

In such considerations may also lie the explanation of the superficially anomalous finding that the willingness of the "guilty" to make reparations is greater when it can be done without facing the victim. One might think that actor would foresee greater relief from guilt if he or she were present to receive the gratitude of the other. It seems, however, that the dangers of facing one's victims are weighed more heavily. Before the reparations work is done, actor will be faced by a person who is likely to be angry at him or her, and, in actor's mind, with good reason. To face such a situation is likely to be productive of anxiety, if not of increased guilt. And what if the other remains angry even after reparations have been made? This is not an unlikely occurrence, and if it happens actor may find it quite difficult to diminish his guilt feelings—especially if other has cogent reasons. If actor can avoid such counterarguments it will be much easier to convince himself that he has atoned properly.

Along similar lines, actors who are feeling frustration are quite likely to define the reduction or removal of the frustration as one of the major goals of the interaction. This would explain why aggression sometimes—but only sometimes—is a reaction to frustration. Aggression may alleviate frustration, but it is not the only way to do so; displacement (Konecni and Doob, 1972), sublimation, repression, and so forth, will also work. And in many situations aggression is so costly a way of relieving frustration that it is entirely uneconomical.

Emotional Roles. Useful as this perspective is, it does not seem to account for all the apparent connections between emotions and behavior. Let me give one example. It is often said that "he (she) did it all for love," and that may be an accurate diagnosis in many instances. We are prone to certain actions under the influence of love that do not occur under other circumstances. However, although these actions do sometimes make sense if viewed as an attempt to perpetuate the love, they often seem, at best, minimally related to that motivation. When we are in love we are willing to sacrifice our interests to those of the loved one, we tend to extol his or her virtues to others, we "foreswake all others," we do things which are "out of character." Some of these may serve to insure that the love is reciprocated and therefore perpetuated, but they are often done when they are not going to have any effect on the loved one, and particularly the last reason mentioned does not seem to be of much relevance to the matter of perpetuation. The same could be said for other emotions. We do things when we are angry, anxious, sad, euphoric, or depressed which do not seem to have much influence on the emotion either way.

Commonly, actions which are irrelevant to the perpetuation of emotion are explained as irrational or disinhibited and the implication seems to be that emotions have their own reasons; that there is some innate connection between emotions and behaviors which need not, or cannot, be explained. This is obviously unsatisfactory. To resort to a claim of innate connection is, for one thing, to avoid an explanation. The nature of the connection would have to be explicated if it is to be accepted. But importantly, such an explanation does not account for the patterned variation in emotional reaction. Are we to assume that the innate connection varies in different societies, or changes for the same person from one occasion to the next, and so on?

It would be more plausible to suggest that the emotional state becomes part of actor's self-definition and that new role definitions then become pertinent which call for behaviors which are not appropriate without that element in the self-definition.[10]

[10] As the term is used by some authors, there are no emotions unless the actor labels his feelings with an emotion term and classifies himself as being in an emotional state. The definition being used here does not make self-labeling an essential part of an emotion, but it should be clear from what has been said that I assume that labeling and classification usually accompany emotional states (see Kemper, 1978).

It will be recalled that the self-concept involves identities, evaluations, and qualities, and that among the relevant qualities is mood or emotional state. The behaviors which are defined as appropriate for a teacher are not the same as those which are acceptable for a teacher who has been insulted; the actions "required" of a man are not the same as those of a man in love; and what is understandable, if not totally approved, in a woman who is angry is not tolerable in one who is acting calmly.

The validity of this view, as of so much else in this section, cannot be adequately demonstrated. I know of no studies which demonstrate that the addition of an emotional state adjective does in fact alter the role definition associated with an identity. General observation indicates that this is so, and our frequent attempts to explain or defend our behavior in just such terms suggests the same thing, but such "evidence" is by no means conclusive. Until further research is forthcoming the point must stand largely on its plausibility.

In conclusion, let me emphasize that this "alteration of role definition" hypothesis is not intended as a complete explanation of the tie between emotion and action. For one thing, it must share the field with the "perpetuation or alteration" hypothesis,[11] and there are other ways in which the role explanation is not complete. In some instances the role implications of an emotional state are by no means clear, and when they are, they are unlikely to be very specific. Furthermore, the existence of role definitions does not, by itself, explain why they are followed. I shall not attempt to deal with these issues at all. They are discussed at great length in the general theory and that material would be equally pertinent here.[12]

On this note I would end the discussion of the application of interactionist theory to conscious, feeling beings. I, at least, am entirely convinced that although the theory starts with the image of a rational, unemotional thinker, its relevance is not limited to that type of person.

SUMMARY

In this chapter I considered whether interactionist theory applies to emotions, and concluded that almost without change it does. For example, what we feel in a particular situation is based upon rules which tell us what we should feel in that situation. Furthermore, we know what rule is appropriate by our definition of the situation which is constructed with the aid of role taking and involves such mental structures as the self-concept and the presented self. "Appropriate" feelings, however, do not always occur when they should, despite the rules, and when that happens actors often attempt to construct the feelings they seek to have.

[11] This is not to say, however, that the two processes are mutually opposed. Clearly, in some interactions they combine to produce the behavior which emerges.

[12] After this attention to the effects of emotion on social behavior, a caveat seems necessary. The fact that actor is in an emotional state does not necessarily mean that the emotion is the prime determinant of his or her behavior. As indicated above, we frequently make a concerted effort to diminish the influence of emotions. That is often what we mean when we say we were able to control our emotions.

There are two major ways that emotions affect behavior directly: (1) If an emotion is defined as pleasant, actor will attempt to perpetuate it, and if it is unpleasant he or she will try to alter it; (2) The emotions frequently have role definitions associated with them which suggest to actor what kind of behavior is appropriate for a person in that emotional state.

CHAPTER 11

THE ESSENTIALS
OF INTERACTIONIST THEORY

Given the complexity of the analysis presented in this book, there is the danger that the reader will be overwhelmed by the details and fail to see the basic structure of interactionist ideas. In hopes of preventing such an eventuality, I will devote the concluding pages of this book to a summary of the major points of the theory. Let us emerge from the thicket and look at some of the "trees."

BASIC ASSUMPTIONS

This book has presented the elements of a social psychological theory of human interaction which is a product of the symbolic interactionist tradition. As a version of symbolic interactionism it is based upon the following three premises:

1. As human beings we learn the meanings of things primarily through our interaction with other persons, that is, we are taught how to define the world which surrounds us by our experiences during social interaction.
2. Though other people are the sources of our understandings, we do not simply take on the meanings which are offered us. We select, check, transform, and so on.
3. The behavior of people arises from their definitions of their environments. Again, however, the process is not an automatic one. Previously learned meanings do not provide ready-made definitions of the situations we meet, and definitions of situations do not translate directly into action. We must *create* a definition of

a particular situation from the meanings we know, and we *develop* plans of action which seem to us to be suited to the situation as we understand it.

This theory, as do most versions of symbolic interactionism, also assumes that:

1. *Humans are unique in their ability to use a true language.* Although other animals can communicate, none can do so nearly as well as humans can. Some apes apparently have been taught a language which has many of the characteristics of human language, but this does not gainsay the point. Such languages are not normally used by apes, and even with human help they can develop only limited facility.

2. *Linguistic ability makes possible the development of several of the characteristics which are the essence of being human.* In the view of symbolic interactionists, human uniqueness is to be found in our complex social organization, in our culture, and in our mental structures and capacities—our ability to take the role of the other, our self-concepts, our role definitions, our thought processes, etc. All these things are possible because of our linguistic ability.

3. *Human development is dependent upon social interaction.* Although the potential is there from the outset, the development of human traits requires socialization, a teaching process. Maturation is not enough.

4. *Humans are purposive and rational animals.* Humans are thought to act on the basis of "perceived rationality." They have particular goals in mind when they are acting and they act in ways they *believe* will lead them to those goals.

5. *In very general terms, humans' prime goal is the seeking of rewards and the avoidance of costs.* Symbolic interactionists, as do most theorists, assume that humans seek profit. They do not, however, assume that we necessarily seek immediate gratification, and they realize that there are many kinds of rewards and costs. Furthermore, the value of a thing is not intrinsic to it. The value assigned to a thing by a particular person is a function of his or her previous experience.

6. *Humans are conscious actors.* In general, interactionists assume that humans have a great deal of awareness; they usually know what they want and they are aware of the major features of their environments, etc. Interactionists pay little attention to unconscious and automatic action.

7. *Humans are active.* As much of the above suggests, the model of humans which is used by interactionists assumes an actor who takes an active stance in relation to the environment. People do not simply take things on; they consider, and then they accept, reject, or modify. They do not react automatically; they consciously decide what they ought to do, etc.

There are several varieties of symbolic interactionist theory, but in general they share the basic assumptions I have just described. Beyond this point, however, there is less agreement between the two major groups—The Chicago and Iowa Schools. The theory presented in this book is much closer to the Iowa School whose assumptions are:

8. *Human behavior, though variable, shows considerable consistency in similar situations.* As compared with many other theories, all forms of symbolic interactionism give a large place to intraperson variability. Interactionists believe that human behavior is always subject to change; socialization is a lifetime process, behavior changes as situations change, etc. However, it does seem that members of the Iowa School believe that the situation is less fluid than Chicagoans do. Some Chicagoans have suggested, for example, that there is little carryover from one situation to comparable ones and that roles are made anew each time. Iowans would tend to suggest that though the roles may change during the process of interaction, previously learned roles serve as the starting point.

9. *Human behavior is predictable.* The two schools are also divided on the issue of determinism and predictability. The determinism of the Iowa School is much less "soft." They assume that human behavior is determined by knowable causes, and therefore, in principle it is completely predictable and explicable. The Chicagoans, on the other hand, have a place for an impulsive and basically unpredictable component in human behavior.

10. *Human behavior cannot be understood by studying lower animals.* On this point, the difference between the two Schools is relatively minor. They both assume that humans are unique, and from this they conclude that humans must be studied directly if one is to understand them. The Iowans are perhaps less adamant about this, however. At least, they seem more willing to consider psychological learning theories which trace their roots to studies of animals. Nonetheless, even the Iowans would argue that such theories cannot be applied to humans unless there are basic changes in details.

11. *In order to understand human behavior the basic methods of science should be used.* Both schools agree that the data for the proper study of people are data on human perceptions. The two Schools do not agree, however, concerning how these data should be gathered and analyzed. The Iowans favor a methodology which parallels that of the physical sciences—objective data-gathering instruments, formal theory and hypotheses, quantitative analysis, etc. The Chicagoans tend to argue for participant observation, qualitative analysis, etc.

LANGUAGE ACQUISITION AND ROLE TAKING

The theory itself begins with a consideration of the development of two abilities central to the process of social interaction: the ability to communicate through language and the ability to anticipate the response of the other (*role-taking ability*).

Interactionists use standard psychological theories in their discussions of the process by which the individual learns the meaning of symbols, which is the aspect of language development of most interest to them. They suggest that at the outset parents teach children to associate certain sounds in their children's repertoires with particular things through the use of selective reward. In later stages, the development of associations between things and "words" is aided by children's growing tendency to imitate, their increased dependence on language for the communication of their needs, and their desire to learn the meaning of words for the sake of knowing.

The development of the ability to take the role of the other begins when children learn that certain events precede other events. When this is grasped, the child can predict other's future actions from observable prior actions. Later, their own observations, projections, and instructions from others teach them to judge others' feelings, intentions, and role definitions from cues which are often quite subtle. When they can do this, their ability to predict other's actions is expanded enormously.

In essence, taking the role of the other requires actor to gather information and to draw from that information its implications for a particular case. Thus, it appears likely that variations in the accuracy with which actors take the role of the other would reflect differences in the amount of relevant information available to them and differences in their capacity to make the correct inferences from the available information. Among the factors that affect the extent of actors' store of information are the frequency with which they have interacted with other in the past, the relevance of the previous interaction, and the extent to which the available information was learned and retained. Factors which affect actors' ability to process the knowledge they have include general ability, motivation, and the extent to which they can understand the subtle meanings of others' words and acts.

THE CENTRAL VARIABLES

In order to interact, actors must have, in addition to language and role-taking ability, a self-concept, role definitions, presented selves, and roles for the presented selves.

The first of these, the *self-concept,* refers to the thoughts and beliefs that people have about themselves. It is a mutifaceted structure, but its major components are a set of *identities,* which refer to the social categories that people use to define themselves, and a set of *self-evaluations,* which are our beliefs about how good we are at what we think we are. For each identity there is likely to be an associated self-evaluation, and all the self-evaluations are combined into a weighted average which is the person's general estimate of worth—his or her level of *self-esteem.* It is assumed that the weight given to a particular self-evaluation is a function of the importance actor assigns to the identity to which it is attached, that is, a reflection of the identity's position on the person's *hierarchy of prominence.*

Roles are people's views of proper behavior for a particular type of person, interacting with a particular kind of other, in a particular situation. Normally, actor will have a set of roles for each of the elements in his self-concept. These role definitions provide general suggestions to actors concerning the ways they should behave, but they do not contain specific instructions. They are not scripts which contain lines that actors can memorize and recite. They are plot summaries which guide ad libbing.

Self-concepts are actors' views of themselves, and *presented selves* are the views that actors wish others to have of them. The presented self may or may not be consistent with the self-concept, and when it is not the actor is said to be presenting a false self. Regardless of whether the presented self is true or false, actor is going to have to behave in particular ways if the desired image is going to be accepted. The process by which this is done is called *impression management,* and the actions which actor believes will convey the desired image is called *the role associated with the presented self.*

THE DEVELOPMENT OF THE CENTRAL VARIABLES

Now that the central concepts of the theory have been presented, we may turn to the next element in it, which is concerned with the general processes by which the central variables develop and the factors associated with variations in their content. Let us begin with self-evaluations.

The Development of Self-Evaluations

In the view of interactionists, self-evaluations have two sources—the *perceived social definition,* which is actor's view of how others see him, and the *tentative personal definition,* which is actor's own reaction to his behavior based on personal standards and comparisons with the actions of others. Given this conceptualization, the first questions to be answered are, "How do people learn the opinions of others?" "Why are they inclined to accept them?" and "How do they develop a view of how they are seen by others, given the fact that they are likely to receive markedly divergent opinions?"

Role-taking represents the major mechanism by which people know other people's opinions of them. It is necessary to put ourselves in the place of others in order to determine what they "really think." This is, of course, crucial if other has any hesitancy about expressing an opinion, but even when there is no such barrier, role taking is required. An expressed opinion must be interpreted and understood, and it is possible to do this only if one takes the role of the other.

The theory postulates that we tend to accept these views of others as our own because it is profitable for us to do so in many instances. Drawing on the general literature on attitude change, the theory postulates that people seek three general forms of reward: self-knowledge, expressive rewards such as good feelings, and utilitarian rewards such as money, the esteem of others, etc. It is further argued that the acceptance of other's view often provides us with self-knowledge and the utilitarian reward of smooth interaction. Also, it sometimes contributes to our obtaining the expressive reward of a positive view of self.

The development of a general view of what others think from the many evaluations that one receives is accomplished by averaging all the evaluations received after weighting some of them more than others. Given the ideas presented above, it would follow that greater weight will be given to those evaluations which are conducive to obtaining the rewards that actor hopes to get by accepting other's view. Thus it is postulated, to give a few examples, that evaluations which are consistent with others we have received will be given a high weight because they contribute to the achievement of the goal of freedom from cognitive dissonance, and evaluations received from powerful others and from others viewed as competent will be highly influential because they contribute to obtaining utilitarian rewards and self-knowledge (see Table 4.1).

The self-evaluation is, however, not simply a reflection of other people's opinions. Actors typically evaluate their own behavior and the results of those judgments also have an effect upon their self-views. One way in which such personal judgments are made is to compare one's action with internalized personal standards. These standards are, however, not the personal creation of the person who is using them. Typically, we use standards which we have adopted from others as a result of our previous experiences. Again, there is the need to bring coherence out of heterogeneity, and this is done in a familiar manner. Actors are exposed to many varying standards and the one they adopt as their own will represent a weighted average of those to which they have been exposed. The heaviest weight is assigned, as above, to those standards which are associated with reward.

In some instances, actors do not use the absolute kind of standard that I have described. They may evaluate their performances by comparing them with those of other persons. The choice of a *comparison other* from the several possibilities that are usually available is made with an eye to increasing our profits. Thus, for example, the general tendency is to choose someone who resembles actor because such comparisons are considered more informative than those which use persons who are markedly different from actor.

These ideas do not, however, explain how a *general* personal definition is constructed. Actors' performances and their evaluations of them are likely to vary from one instance to the next, and therefore their personal evaluations are likely to contain heterogeneous elements. How are these diverse elements combined into a coherent whole?

The question is familiar and so is the answer. Actors develop a personal definition for a particular area by weighting and averaging all the personal definitions they have made in the area. And the weight given to a particular definition is determined by the same general considerations which were involved in the weighting of evaluations received from others. Of course, the details differ somewhat because the actors themselves are the sources of the definitions, but in essence there is no difference. Actors realize, for example, that they are differentially competent to evaluate their action under different circumstances and they will tend to give greater weight to those evaluations they made when they thought they were competent because such evaluations contribute more to self-knowledge.

The final step in the development of a self-evaluation involves combining the perceived social definition and the tentative personal definition. The theory which has been presented is relevant to this case also. The self-evaluation is a weighted sum of the two elements, and the weight given to each element is determined by the usual factors. For example, if the perceived social definition is favorable and the tentative personal definition is not, the former will be weighted more heavily because by so doing actors increase the likelihood that they will obtain the expressive rewards of a favorable self-image.

The Development of Identities, Roles, and Presented Selves

This theory is also applicable, with minor changes, to the development of the other central variables. Identities, roles, presented selves, and roles for presented selves are all ultimately social in origin. We are presented with a variety of definitions of what is the proper role for a particular set of circumstances. We are the recipients of suggestions that say we are, or are not, members of a particular category. People tell us, often in subtle ways, what images should be presented in various encounters. They instruct us regarding the actions that will convey those images. Through the familiar process of weighting and averaging, actor will develop a series of perceived social definitions. He or she will conclude that others say that one should do this under these circumstances, that people see me as belonging to this category, etc.

In addition, we develop personal definitions. For example, we compare ourselves with people we think possess a particular identity in order to decide whether or not we qualify; we compare ourselves to the criteria we have learned are relevant for membership; and we develop a tentative idea about whether we belong. From these comparisons we develop a tentative personal conclusion about the appropriateness of an identity for us. The self-definition, per se, is a product of the social and personal definitions.

Roles, presented selves, and roles for presented selves are all learned in basically the same way—direct instruction, comparisons with others, and the application of previously learned standards. In each case a general view of the opinion of others and a personal opinion are developed from the several opinions available, and a self-definition is developed from the personal and social definitions.

In sum, all the central variables are formed in the same way. The only differences are that some of the specific factors which determine the weight to be given to an opinion differ, and some processes—such as practice, efficacy, and transfer effects—are relevant only to some of the variables.

INTERACTION PROCESSES

Although important in itself, the theory which has been presented thus far gets its primary significance from the fact that it provides a basis for understanding human interaction. The basic idea is that the content of the central variables has a major impact on the course of interaction. The task remaining is to show the connection.

This job is simplified somewhat if we recognize two major types of interaction—*routine interactions,* which are familiar and easily handled, and *problematic interactions,* which are more complex and require actor to devise solutions to problems which do not occur in routine situations.

Routine Interactions

In all interactions, actors must start by defining the situation. Using observation, role taking, and language they take note of the relevant cues and categorize and interpret the situation. In a routine interaction this is easily done. The cues are clear and actor has, for example, little difficulty in defining the self, a key element in the definition of the situation. In routine encounters it is easy for actor to choose appropriate identities, roles, presented selves, etc., from the repertoire that he or she brings to the situation. Actor then goes through a similar process for other; he or she defines the other on the basis of the possibilities that are in his or her mind from previous experience. Again, if the interaction is routine, actor will have little difficulty in doing this.

When this defining process is complete, actor decides what the first act should be. This is done by developing a plan of action that is consistent with the definition, and by considering the consequences of the action before committing oneself to it. More specifically, the intended act will reflect the identity that actor is using, actor's definition of other's identity, actor's role definitions for people with these identities, the presented self that actor wishes to convey, etc.

In a routine interaction, all of this will cause no difficulties for actor:

1. The necessary information will be available; actor will know, for example, the content of the roles to be played by the participants.
2. He or she will find that the general plan provided by the roles is translatable into specific behavior.
3. These behaviors will be within his or her abilities.

During the time that actor was developing his or her definition of the situation, other was doing the same. Before other acts, however, the meaning of actor's first action must be considered and the definition of the situation reconsidered. After other reacts, actor reconsiders his or her definition and then reacts in return. An interaction is a series of such mutual reactions. The general process may be summarized as: noting cues, definition of the situation, development of a plan of action, consideration of consequences, possible revision of plan, action by actor, reaction by other after he or she has gone through the same process.

The relevance of the evaluative self for actor's behavior is not immediately clear from what has been presented, but this element of actor's mental equipment has similar effects. In general, self-evaluations affect behavior because actors are taught that certain behaviors are appropriate when the self-evaluation is high and others when it is low. In addition, actor's self-evaluation can influence the definition of other aspects of the situation, for example, whether it is viewed as a desirable situation in which to be.

In general terms, the difficulties faced in problematic interaction include an inability to define the situation because the cues suggest none of the elements in the repertoire or because they suggest several of them, a lack of consensus between the interactants about the definition of the situation, an inability to act consistently with the agreed upon definition, and a desire to present a false self.

In the discussion of problematic interaction the theory focuses on three questions for each of the interaction problems:

1. Under what conditions is the problem likely to occur?
2. What is the range of possible solutions?
3. What are the factors which determine which of the possibilities will be chosen in a particular case?

Definitional Problems.   Actors are most likely to feel that they lack defining elements for a situation when they have had little experience in comparable situations, particularly if opportunities for anticipatory socialization have been limited. This situation may also occur when other is controlling the cues and has something to gain from actor's inability to define the situation. In any of these cases, actor's reaction may be to leave the situation, assuming that participation is voluntary. Or he or she may depart temporarily in order to return after additional preparation. Another possibility is to remain in the situation in the often realistic hope that events that occur during the interaction will provide the necessary socialization.

The choice will be based on the actor's calculation of the costs and rewards associated with the various actions. For example, actors who believe that other has reason to "help them out" are likely to stay in the situation. They will foresee that they may obtain the rewards of the interaction without paying much "tuition" for the instruction they will be given.

The problem of having too many definitional elements which seem appropriate is most likely to occur when actor and other stand in a multiple relation to each other. When this is so, actor may be unsure about which relationship is the salient one. Again, withdrawal from the situation is a possible reaction, but if there is a multiple relation between actor and other, it would probably be a costly one because it could endanger the continuation of a relationship which is likely to be an important one. It would seem much better to remain in the situation and hope to obtain additional information. In these instances, it would seem likely to actor that information would be forthcoming which would permit him or her to decide which element in the existing repertoire is the appropriate one. If such information is not forthcoming, actor may develop new elements by combining old ones, he or she may alternate between competing definitions from the old repertoire, or a new definition may be devised to fit the situation. Again, without going into specifics, it can be said that the choice among these possibilities will be designed to maximize rewards and minimize costs.

The last problem associated with the definition of the situation—the lack of congruence in the definitions of the participants—is the subject of considerable contemporary interest. This situation is most likely to occur when the participants have had dissimilar socialization—for example, when they have not interacted together previously—and when the definition of the situation is not a matter of general agreement in the society. A common reaction to this state of affairs is an attempt to resolve the differences, and frequently this is done by *negotiations:* attempts to reach consensus through the use of justifications, excuses, and pressure.

Interactionist interest in negotiations is focused on the circumstances under which negotiations will be undertaken and a discussion of the factors which determine whether or not they will result in a working consensus. Among the factors which are conducive to undertaking negotiations are an awareness of difference in definition, a belief that the differences can be reduced, and motivation to achieve consensus. If negotiations are undertaken, they are most likely to be successful when there is only a small difference in the original definitions, when the participants have limited stake in their original views, when one is more powerful than the other, when the interactants are persuasive in their arguments, etc.

Role Strain. The existence of agreed upon definitions of the situation is not sufficient to qualify an interaction as routine. For one thing, the situation would be problematic if *role strain* occurs. That is, the encounter would become complicated if the actors are not able to live up to the agreed upon definition because of inadequate time or resources or because they are involved in other interactions which make demands upon them which are incompatible with the requirements of the first interaction.

Role strain is an indication that the negotiating process has not worked well for actor, and anything which contributes to the latter is likely to contribute to role strain. Included would be: limited power, the inability to recognize the consequences of certain actions, and societal rules which limit the participants' power to alter the definition.

When role strain is experienced, the usual reaction is an attempt to reduce it. Actors make renewed efforts to meet their obligations or they attempt to revise the working definition. If these are not successful, an effort will be made to reduce the costs of failing to meet the requirements of the definition. This may be done by choosing to fail in a way that produces less costs than alternative failures, by hiding the facts from other and self, and by meeting the obligations of interest to the most powerful others.

False Selves. When actor attempts to present a false self the situation is considered a problematic one because the presentation of a false self complicates the interaction. In general, a false self will be presented when it will produce significant rewards if it is done successfully, when there is little chance of discovery, when the costs of being discovered are low, and when little effort is required to present the false self.

A CONCLUDING COMMENT

At this point I am strongly tempted to launch into a lengthy evaluation of these ideas, and in fact, an earlier draft of the manuscript contained such material. I now see, however, that there is little point in doing that. Little would be gained if I expressed my opinions, for they would hardly be objective. The parents of intellectual offspring tend to be as biased and unseeing as the parents of real children are. Parental pride is associated with all kinds of parenthood.

Moreover, I feel that it would not be appropriate for me to judge the theory. My definition of our situation is that it is an interaction situation. What I have written represents my "first act." Now you, as other, must react, and I believe your reaction should include an evaluation of what you have read. Evaluation is part of the reader's role set. I hope that we have consensus on this definition and that you will not terminate the encounter.[1]

[1] Lest you feel role strain, let me assure you that you have the knowledge required to play the subrole of evaluator. Remember that a good theory must have certain formal characteristics, and it must be consistent with the empirical evidence. The formal criteria for theory are presented in Chapter 1 and the relevant data are scattered throughout the book. Certainly, more research is necessary before a firm conclusion can be reached, but I believe what we have should permit you to make a preliminary judgment.

REFERENCES

Abelson, Robert P., E. Aronson, W. J. McGuire, T. M. Newcomb and P. H. Tannenbaum (eds.), *Theories of Cognitive Dissonance: A Sourcebook*. Chicago: Rand McNally & Company, 1968.

Alexander, C. Norman, Jr. and Ernest Q. Campbell, "Peer Influences on Adolescent Educational Aspirations and Attainments," *American Sociological Review*, 1964, 29, pp. 68-75.

Alexander, Joe B. and Howard Gudeman, "Perceptual and Interpersonal Measures of Field Dependence," *Perceptual and Motor Skills*, 1965, 20, pp. 79-86.

Allen, Gay Wilson, *Walt Whitman as Man, Poet, and Legend*. Carbondale: Southern Illinois University Press, 1961.

Allport, Gordon W., *Personality: A Psychological Interpretation*. New York: Henry Holt, 1937.

——, *Pattern and Growth in Personality*. New York: Holt, Rinehart and Winston, 1961.

Anderson, Norman H., "Application of a Linear-Serial Model to a Personality-Impression Task Using Special Presentation," *Journal of Personality and Social Psychology*, 1968, 10, pp. 354-62.

Archibald, W. Peter and Ronald Cohen, "Self-Presentation, Embarrassment, and Facework as a Function of Self-Evaluation, Conditions of Self-Presentation, and

Feedback from Others," *Journal of Personality and Social Psychology,* 1971, 20, pp. 287-97.

Ardrey, Robert, *The Territorial Imperative.* New York: Atheneum, 1966.

Aronson, Elliot and James M. Carlsmith, "Performance Expectancy as a Determinant of Actual Performance," *Journal of Abnormal and Social Psychology,* 1962, 65, pp. 178-82.

Aronson, Elliot and Darwyn E. Linder, "Gain and Loss of Esteem as Determinants of Interpersonal Attractiveness," *Journal of Experimental Social Psychology,* 1965, 1, pp. 156-72.

Arrowood, A. John and Ronald Friend, "Other Factors Determining the Choice of a Comparison Other," *Journal of Experimental Social Psychology,* 1969, 5, pp. 233-39.

Astin, Alexander W., "Effects of Different College Environments on the Vocational Choices of High Aptitude Students," *Journal of Counseling Psychology,* 1965, 12, pp. 28-34.

Averill, James R., "Grief: Its Nature and Significance," *Psychological Bulletin,* 1968, 70, pp. 721-48.

Bachman, Jerald G., *Youth in Transition,* Vol. 2. *The Impact of Family Background and Intelligence on Tenth-Grade Boys.* Ann Arbor, Michigan: Institute For Social Research, University of Michigan, 1970.

Backman, Carl W. and Paul F. Secord, "The Effect of Perceived Liking on Interpersonal Attraction," *Human Relations,* 1959, 12, pp. 379-84.

———, "The Self and Role Selection," pp. 289-96 in Chad Gordon and Kenneth J. Gergen (eds.), *The Self in Social Interaction.* New York: John Wiley and Sons, 1968.

Backman, Carl W., P. F. Secord and J. Peirce, "Resistance to Change in Self-Concept as a Function of Consensus Among Significant Others," *Sociometry,* 1963, 26, pp. 102-11.

Bales, Robert F., *Interaction Process Analysis.* Cambridge, Massachusetts: Addison-Wesley, 1950.

Bandura, Albert, "Influences of the Models' Reinforcement Contingencies on the Acquisition of Imitative Responses," *Journal of Personality and Social Psychology,* 1965, 1, pp. 589-95.

———, "Social Learning Theory of Identificatory Processes," pp. 213-62 in David A. Goslin (ed.), *Handbook of Socialization Theory and Research.* Chicago: Rand McNally & Company, 1969a.

———, *Principles of Behavior Modification.* New York: Holt, Rinehart and Winston, 1969b.

——, *Social Learning Theory*. Morristown, New Jersey: General Learning Press, 1971.

——, *Social Learning Theory*. Englewood Cliffs, New Jersey: Prentice-Hall, Inc., 1977.

Bandura, Albert, D. Ross and S. A. Ross, "Transmission of Aggression Through Imitation of Aggressive Models," *Journal of Abnormal and Social Psychology*, 1961, 63, pp. 575-82.

——, "A Comparative Test of the Status Envy, Social Power, and Secondary Reinforcement Theories of Identificatory Learning," *Journal of Abnormal and Social Psychology*, 1963a, 67, pp. 527-34.

——, "Vicarious Reinforcement and Imitative Learning," *Journal of Abnormal and Social Psychology*, 1963b, 67, pp. 601-07.

——, "Imitation of Film-Mediated Aggressive Models," *Journal of Abnormal and Social Psychology*, 1963c, 66, pp. 3-11.

Banton, Michael P., *Roles, An Introduction to the Study of Social Relations*. London: Tavistock, 1965.

Baron, Penny H., "Self-Esteem, Ingratiation, and Evaluation of Unknown Others," *Journal of Personality and Social Psychology*, 1974, 30, pp. 104-09.

Baron, Robert A., *Human Aggression*. New York: Plenum Press, 1977.

Bass, Bernard M., "Effects on the Subsequent Performance of Negotiators of Studying Issues or Planning Strategies Alone or in Groups," *Psychological Monographs*, 1966, 80, whole no. 614.

Baughman, E. Earl, *Black Americans*. New York: Academic Press, 1971.

Becker, Howard S., B. Geer, E. C. Hughes and A. Strauss, *Boys in White: Student Culture in Medical School*. Chicago: University of Chicago Press, 1961.

Benedict, Ruth, "Continuities and Discontinuities in Cultural Conditioning," *Psychiatry*, 1938, 1, pp. 161-67.

Benton, Alan A., H. H. Kelley and B. Liebling, "Effects of Extremity of Offers and Concession Rate on the Outcomes of Bargaining," *Journal of Personality and Social Psychology*, 1972, 24, pp. 73-83.

Bergin, Allen E., "The Effect of Dissonant Persuasive Communications upon Changes in Self-Referring Attitudes," *Journal of Personality*, 1962, 30, pp. 423-38.

Berkowitz, Leonard, "The Frustration-Aggression Hypothesis Revisited," pp. 1-28 in Leonard Berkowitz (ed.), *Roots of Aggression*. New York: Atherton Press, 1969.

——, "Social Norms, Feelings, and Other Factors Affecting Helping and Altruism," pp. 63-108 in Leonard Berkowitz (ed.), *Advances in Experimental Social Psychology*, Vol. 6. New York: Academic Press, 1972.

Berkowitz, Leonard and Richard M. Lundy, "Personality Characteristics Related to Influence by Peers or Authority Figures," *Journal of Personality,* 1957, 25, pp. 306–16.

Bible, Bond and Coy G. McNabb, "Role Consensus and Administrative Effectiveness," *Rural Sociology,* 1966, 31, pp. 5–14.

Biller, Henry B., *Paternal Determinants of Personality.* Lexington, Massachusetts: D. C. Heath, 1971.

Birmingham, Daniel L., *Situational and Personality Factors in Conformity.* Unpublished Ph.D. thesis, St. Louis University, 1974 (*Dissertation Abstracts International,* 1974, 35, p. 2421b.)

Blake, Robert R., "The Other Person in the Situation," pp. 229–42 in Renato Tagiuri and Luigi Petrullo (eds.), *Person Perception and Interpersonal Behavior.* Stanford, California: Stanford University Press, 1958.

Blake, Robert R. and Jane S. Mouton, "Loyalty of Representatives to Ingroup Positions Under Intergroup Competition," *Sociometry,* 1961, 24, pp. 177–83.

Blau, Zena Smith, "Changes in Status and Age Identification," *American Sociological Review,* 1956, 21, pp. 198–203.

Blumer, Herbert, "Sociological Implications of the Thought of George Herbert Mead," *American Journal of Sociology,* 1966, 71, pp. 535–44. (Reprinted as pp. 61-77 in Herbert Blumer, *Symbolic Interactionism.* Englewood Cliffs, New Jersey: Prentice-Hall, Inc., 1969.)

——, "The Methodological Position of Symbolic Interactionism," (Reprinted as pp. 1-60 in Herbert Blumer, *Symbolic Interactionism.* Englewood Cliffs, New Jersey: Prentice-Hall, Inc., 1969a.)

——, *Symbolic Interactionism.* Englewood Cliffs, New Jersey: Prentice-Hall, Inc., 1969b.

Blumstein, Philip W., "Audience, Machiavellianism, and Tactics of Identity Bargaining," *Sociometry,* 1973, 36, pp. 346–65.

——, "Identity Bargaining and Self-Conception," *Social Forces,* 1974–75, 53, pp. 476–85.

Blumstein, Philip W., et al., "The Honoring of Accounts," *American Sociological Review,* 1974, 39, pp. 551–66.

Bonoma, Thomas V., J. T. Tedeschi and S. Lindskold, "A Note Regarding an Expected Value Model for Social Power," *Behavioral Science,* 1972, 17, pp. 221–28.

Bonoma, Thomas V. and James T. Tedeschi, "Some Effects of Source Behavior on Target's Compliance to Threats," *Behavioral Science,* 1973, 18, pp. 34–41.

Bordua, David J., "Educational Aspirations and Parental Stress on College," *Social Forces,* 1963, 38, pp. 262-69.

Borislow, Bernard, "Self-Evaluation and Academic Achievement," *Journal of Counseling Psychology,* 1962, 9, pp. 246-54.

Boudreau, Frances A., *Selves and Significant Others: A Study of Women Who Drop Back In.* Unpublished Ph.D. thesis, University of Connecticut, 1980.

Boykin, E., *This Way Please.* New York: Macmillan, 1958. (Cited in Sherri Cavan, "The Etiquette of Youth," pp. 554-65 in Gregory P. Stone and Harvey Farberman (eds.), *Social Psychology Through Symbolic Interaction.* Waltham, Massachusetts: Ginn-Blaisdell, 1970.)

Brehm, Jack W. and Arthur R. Cohen, *Explorations in Cognitive Dissonance.* New York: John Wiley and Sons, Inc., 1962.

Brickman, Philip, J. A. Linsenmeier and A. G. McCareins, "Performance Enhancement by Relevant Success and Irrelevant Failure," *Journal of Personality and Social Psychology,* 1972, 33, pp. 149-60.

Brim, Orville G., Jr., "Family Structure and Sex Role Learning by Children: A Further Analysis of Helen Koch's Data," *Sociometry,* 1958, 21, pp. 1-16.

——, "Personality Development as Role Learning," pp. 127-59 in Ira Iscoe and Harold W. Stevenson (eds.), *Personality Development in Children.* Austin: University of Texas Press, 1960.

Brissett, Dennis and Charles Edgley, *Life as Theater.* Chicago: Aldine, 1975.

Brittain, Clay V., "Adolescent Choices and Parent-Peer Cross-Pressures," *American Sociological Review,* 1963, 28, pp. 385-91.

Brock, T., S. Edelman, D. C. Edwards and J. R. Schuck, "Seven Studies of Performance Expectancy as a Determinant of Actual Performance," *Journal of Experimental Social Psychology,* 1965, 1, pp. 295-310.

Bronfenbrenner, Urie, J. S. Harding and M. O. Gallwey, *The Measurement of Skill in Interpersonal Perception.* Princeton, New Jersey: Van Nostrand, 1958.

Brookover, Wilbur B., J. M. Le Pere, E. L. Erikson and S. Thomas, "Definitions of Others, Self-Concept and Academic Achievement: A Longitudinal Study," paper presented at the annual meeting of the American Sociological Association, Chicago, 1965. (Cited in Carl W. Backman and Paul F. Secord, *A Social Psychological View of Education.* New York: Harcourt, Brace Jovanovich, Inc., 1968.)

Brookover, Wilbur B., S. Thomas and A. Paterson, "Self-Concept of Ability and School Achievement," *Sociology of Education,* 1963-64, 37, pp. 271-78.

Brown, Bert R., "The Effects of Need to Maintain Face on Interpersonal Bargaining," *Journal of Experimental and Social Psychology,* 1968, 4, pp. 107-22.

——, "Face Saving Following Experimentally Induced Embarrassment," *Journal of Experimental Social Psychology,* 1970, 6, pp. 255-71.

——, "Face Saving and Face Restoration in Negotiation," pp. 275-99 in Daniel Druckman (ed.), *Negotiations—Social Psychological Perspectives.* Beverly Hills, California: Sage Publications, 1977.

Brown, Bert R. and Howard Garland, "The Effects of Incompetency, Audience Acquaintanceship, and Anticipated Evaluative Feedback on Face Saving Behavior," *Journal of Experimental Social Psychology,* 1971, 7, pp. 490-502.

Brown, Roger, *Social Psychology.* New York: The Free Press, 1965.

Brown, Roger and Richard J. Herrnstein, *Psychology.* Boston: Little, Brown and Company, 1975.

Bruner, Jerome S., D. Shapiro and R. Tagiuri, "The Meaning of Traits in Isolation and in Combination," pp. 277-88 in Renato Tagiuri and Luigi Petrullo (eds.), *Person Perception and Interpersonal Behavior.* Stanford, California: Stanford University Press, 1958.

Bryan, James H., "Apprentices in Prostitution," *Social Problems,* 1965, 12, pp. 287-97.

Bryan, James H. and Mary Ann Test, "Models and Helping: Naturalistic Studies in Aiding Behavior," *Journal of Personality and Social Psychology,* 1967, 6, pp. 400-07, 1967.

Bryant, B., *Miss Behavior.* Indianapolis, Indiana: Bobbs-Merrill, 1960. (Cited in Sherri Cavan, "The Etiquette of Youth," pp. 554-65 in Gregory P. Stone and Harvey A Farberman (eds.), *Social Psychology Through Symbolic Interaction.* Waltham, Massachusetts: Ginn-Blaisdell, 1970.)

Burchard, Waldo W., "Role Conflicts of Military Chaplains," *American Sociological Review,* 1954, 19, pp. 528-35.

Burnstein, Eugene, E. Stotland and A. Zander, "Similarity to a Model and Self-Evaluation," *Journal of Abnormal and Social Psychology,* 1961, 62, pp. 257-64.

Burton, Roger and John W. M. Whiting, "The Absent Father and Cross-Sex Identity," *Merrill-Palmer Quarterly,* 1961, 7, pp. 85-96.

Busch, John C. and Lawrence M. De Ridder, "Conformity in Preschool Disadvantaged Children as Related to Field Dependence, Sex, and Verbal Reinforcement," *Psychological Reports,* 1973, 32, pp. 667-73.

Byrne, Donn, "Parental Antecedents of Authoritarianism," *Journal of Personality and Social Psychology,* 1965, 1, pp. 369-73.

——, "Attitudes and Attraction," pp. 36-89 in Leonard Berkowitz (ed.), *Advances in Experimental Social Psychology.* Vol. 4. New York: Academic Press, 1969.

——, *The Attraction Paradigm*. New York: Academic Press, 1971.

Calonico, James M. and Darwin Thomas, "Role-Taking as a Function of Value Similarity and Affect in the Nuclear Family," *Journal of Marriage and the Family*, 1973, 35, pp. 655–65.

Carlisle, E. Fred, *The Uncertain Self: Whitman's Drama of Identity*. East Lansing: Michigan State University Press, 1973.

Carlsmith, J. Merrill and Alan E. Gross, "Some Effects of Guilt on Compliance," *Journal of Personality and Social Psychology*, 1969, 11, pp. 232–39.

Cheney, John, T. Harford and L. Solomon, "The Effects of Communicating Threats and Promises Upon the Bargaining Process," *Journal of Conflict Resolution*, 1972, 16, pp. 99–107.

Chertkoff, Jerome M. and James K. Esser, "A Review of Experiments in Explicit Bargaining," *Journal of Experimental Social Psychology*, 1976, 12, pp. 464–86.

Cline, Victor B., "Ability to Judge Personality Assessed with Stress Interview and Sound-Film Technique," *Journal of Abnormal and Social Psychology*, 1955, 50, pp. 193–97.

——, "Interpersonal Perception," pp. 221–84 in B. A. Maher (ed.), *Progress in Experimental Personality Research*. Vol. 1. New York: Academic Press, 1964.

Cohen, Albert K., *Delinquent Boys: The Culture of the Gang*. Glencoe, Illinois: The Free Press, 1955.

Cohen, Arthur R., "Some Implications of Self-Esteem for Social Influence," pp. 102–20 in Irving L. Janis, et al., *Personality and Persuasibility*. New Haven, Connecticut: Yale University Press, 1959.

Cohen, Richard M., "A Model of the Effect of Status Change on Self Attitudes," paper presented at the annual meeting of the American Sociological Association. Chicago, 1977.

Cooley, Charles Horton, *Human Nature and the Social Order*. New York: Schocken Books, 1964. (Originally published by Charles Scribner's Sons, 1902.)

Coombs, Robert H., "Social Participation, Self-Concept, and Interpersonal Valuation," *Sociometry*, 1969, 32, pp. 273–86.

Coombs, Robert H. and Vernon Davies, "Self-Conception and the Relationship Between High School and College Scholastic Achievement," *Sociology and Social Research*, 1966, 50, pp. 460–71.

Coopersmith, Stanley, *The Antecedents of Self-Esteem*. San Francisco: W. H. Freeman and Co., 1967.

Costner, Herbert and Robert L. Leik, "Deductions from Axiomatic Theory," *American Sociological Review*, 1964, 29, pp. 819–35.

Couch, Carl J., "The Use of the Concept 'Role' and Its Derivatives in a Study of Marriage," *Marriage and Family Living,* 1958, 20, pp. 353-57.

Cox, Donald F. and Raymond A. Bauer, "Self-Confidence and Persuasibility in Women," *Public Opinion Quarterly,* 1964, 28, pp. 453-66.

Cronbach, Lee J., "Processes Affecting Scores on 'Understanding of Others' and 'Assumed Similarity'," *Psychological Bulletin,* May 1955, 52, pp. 177-93.

——, "Proposals Leading to the Analytic Treatment of Social Perception Scores," pp. 353-80 in Renato Tagiuri and Luigi Petrullo (eds.), *Person Perception and Interpersonal Behavior.* Stanford, California: Stanford University Press, 1958.

Crow, W. J., "The Effect of Training upon Accuracy and Variability in Interpersonal Perception," *Journal of Abnormal and Social Psychology,* 1957, 55, pp. 355-59.

Curtiss, Susan, *Genie–A Psycholinguistic Study of a Modern-Day "Wild Child."* New York: Academic Press, 1977.

Davidson, Helen H. and Gerhard Lang, "Children's Perceptions of Their Teacher's Feelings Toward Them Related to Self-Perception, School Achievement and Behavior," *Journal of Experimental Education,* 1960, 29, pp. 107-18.

Davis, Kingsley, "Final Notes on a Case of Extreme Isolation," *American Journal of Sociology,* 1947, 52, pp. 432-37.

Dentler, Robert A. and J. Glenn Hutchinson, "Socioeconomic Versus Family Membership Status as Sources of Family Attitude Consensus," *Child Development,* 1961, 32, pp. 249-54.

Deutsch, Morton and Robert M. Krauss, "Studies of Interpersonal Bargaining," *Journal of Conflict Resolution,* 1962, 6, pp. 52-76.

Deutsch, Morton and Leonard Solomon, "Reactions to Evaluations by Others as Influenced by Self-Evaluations," *Sociometry,* 1959, 22, pp. 93-112.

Diggory, James C., *Self-Evaluation: Concepts and Studies.* New York: John Wiley and Sons, 1966.

Diggory, James C., S. J. Klein and N. M. Cohen, "Muscle Action Potentials and Estimated Probability of Success," *Journal of Experimental Psychology,* 1964, 68, pp. 449-55.

Dittes, James E., "Attractiveness of Group as a Function of Self-Esteem and Acceptance by Group," *Journal of Abnormal and Social Psychology,* 1959, 59, pp. 77-82.

DiVesta, Frances J., "Effects of Confidence and Motivation on Susceptibility to Informational Social Influence," *Journal of Abnormal and Social Psychology,* 1959, 59, pp. 204-09.

Druckman, Daniel, "Dogmatism, Pre-negotiation Experience, and Simulated Group

Representation as Determinants of Dyadic Behavior in a Bargaining Situation," *Journal of Personality and Social Psychology,* 1967, 6, pp. 279-90.

——, "Pre-negotiation Experience and Dyadic Conflict Resolution in a Bargaining Situation," *Journal of Experimental Social Psychology,* 1968, 4, pp. 367-83.

——, (ed.), *Negotiations: Social Psychological Perspectives.* Beverly Hills, California: Sage Publications, 1977.

Druckman, Daniel, R. Rozelle and K. Zechmeister, "Conflict of Interest and Value Dissensus: Two Perspectives," pp. 105-31 in Daniel Druckman (ed.), *Negotiations: Social Psychological Perspectives.* Beverly Hills, California: Sage Publications, 1977.

Elliott, Rogers, "Interrelationships Among Measures of Field Dependence, Ability and Personality Traits," *Journal of Abnormal and Social Psychology,* 1961, 63, pp. 27-36.

Ellis, Robert A. and W. Clayton Lane, "Structural Supports for Upward Mobility," *American Sociological Review,* 1963, 28, pp. 743-56.

Elms, Alan C., ed., *Role Playing, Reward, and Attitude Change.* New York: Van Nostrand Reinhold Company, 1969.

Esser, James K. and S. S. Komorita, "Reciprocity and Concession-Making in Bargaining," *Journal of Personality and Social Psychology,* 1975, 31, pp. 864-72.

Faley, T. and James T. Tedeschi, "Status and Reaction to Threats," *Journal of Personality and Social Psychology,* 1971, 17, pp. 192-99.

Feather, Norman T., "The Effects of Differential Failure on Expectation of Success, Reported Anxiety, and Response Uncertainty," *Journal of Personality,* 1963, 31, pp. 289-312.

——, "Effects of Prior Success and Failure on Expectations of Success and Subsequent Performance," *Journal of Personality and Social Psychology,* 1966, 3, pp. 287-98.

——, "Change in Confidence Following Success or Failure as a Predictor of Subsequent Performance," *Journal of Personality and Social Psychology,* 1968, 9, pp. 38-46.

Feather, Norman T. and Margaret R. Saville, "Effects of Amount of Prior Success and Failure on Expectations of Success and Subsequent Task Performance," *Journal of Personality and Social Psychology,* 1967, 5, pp. 226-32.

Feldman, Kenneth and Theodore M. Newcomb, *The Impact of College on Students.* Vol. 1. San Francisco: Jossey-Bass Publishers, 1969.

Ferreira, Antonio and William D. Winter, "Family Interaction and Decision Making," *Archives of General Psychiatry,* 1965, 13, pp. 214-23.

———, "On the Nature of Marital Relationships: Measurable Differences in Spontaneous Agreement," *Family Process,* 1974, 13, pp. 355-69.

Festinger, Leon, "A Theory of Social Comparison Processes," *Human Relations,* 1954, 7, pp. 117-40.

———, *A Theory of Cognitive Dissonance.* Stanford, California: Stanford University Press, 1957.

Festinger, Leon, H. W. Riecken and S. Schachter, *When Prophecy Fails.* Minneapolis: University of Minnesota Press, 1956.

Festinger, Leon, J. Torrey and B. Willerman, "Self-Evaluation as a Function of Attraction to the Group," *Human Relations,* 1954, 7, pp. 161-74.

Fitts, William H., et al., *The Self-Concept and Self-Actualization.* Nashville, Tennessee: The Dede Wallace Center, 1971.

Fleming, Joyce Dudney, "Field Report: The State of the Apes," *Psychology Today,* January 1974, 7, pp. 31-37, 43-46.

Foote, Nelson N. and Leonard S. Cottrell, Jr., *Identity and Interpersonal Competence.* Chicago: University of Chicago Press, 1955.

Franks, David D. and Joseph Marolla, "Efficacious Action and Self-Approval as Interacting Dimensions of Self-Esteem: A Tentative Formulation Through Construct Validity," *Sociometry,* 1976, 39, pp. 324-41.

Freed, Alvyn M., P. J. Chandler, J. S. Mouton and R. R. Blake, "Stimulus and Background Factors in Sign Violation," *Journal of Personality,* 1955, 23, p. 499.

French, John R. P., Jr. and Robert D. Caplan, "Organizational Stress and Individual Strain," pp. 30-66 in A. Marrow (ed.), *The Failure of Success.* New York: AMACOM, 1972. (Cited in Stephen R. Marks, "Multiple Roles and Role Strain: Some Notes on Human Energy, Time and Commitment," *American Sociological Review,* 1977, 42, pp. 921-36.)

French, John R. P., Jr., J. J. Sherwood and D. L. Bradford, "Change in Self-Identity in a Management Training Conference," *Journal of Applied Behavioral Science,* 1966, 2, pp. 210-18.

Friedman, Jonathan L., S. A. Wallington and E. Bless, "Compliance without Pressure," *Journal of Personality and Social Psychology,* 1967, 7, pp. 117-24.

Friend, Ronald M. and Joel Gilbert, "Threat and Fear of Negative Evaluation as Determinants of Locus of Social Comparison," *Journal of Personality,* 1973, 41, pp. 328-40.

von Frisch, Karl, *Bees—Their Vision, Chemical Senses, and Language,* revised edition. Ithaca, New York: Cornell University Press, 1971.

Fromm, Erich, "Selfishness and Self-Love." *Psychiatry,* 1939, 2, pp. 507-23.

——, *The Art of Loving.* New York: Harper and Row, 1956.

Fry, P. S., "Affect and Resistance to Temptation," *Developmental Psychology,* 1975, 11, pp. 466-72.

Gage, Nathan L. and Lee J. Cronbach, "Conceptual and Methodological Problems in Interpersonal Perception," *Psychological Review,* 1955, 62, pp. 411-23.

Gallup, Gordon G., "Self Awareness in Primates," *The American Scientist,* 1979, 67, pp. 417-21.

Gecas, Viktor, "Parental Behavior and Dimensions of Adolescent Self-Evaluation," *Sociometry,* 1971, 34, pp. 466-82.

——, "Parental Behavior and Contextual Variations in Adolescent Self-Esteem," *Sociometry,* 1972, 35, pp. 466-82.

Gecas, Viktor, D. Thomas and A. Weigert, "Perceived Parent-Child Interaction and Boys' Self-Esteem in Two Cultural Contexts," *International Journal of Comparative Sociology,* 1970, 11, pp. 317-32.

Gelfand, Donna M., "The Influence of Self-Esteem on the Rate of Verbal Conditioning and Social Matching Behavior," *Journal of Abnormal and Social Psychology,* 1962, 65, pp. 259-65.

Gerard, Harold B., "Some Determinants of Self-Evaluation," *Journal of Abnormal and Social Psychology,* 1961, 62, pp. 288-93.

Gergen, Kenneth J., "The Effects of Interaction Goals and Personalistic Feedback on the Presentation of Self," *Journal of Personality and Social Psychology,* 1965, 1, pp. 413-23.

——, "Personal Consistency and the Presentation of Self," pp. 299-308 in Kenneth J. Gergen and Chad Gordon (eds.), *The Self in Social Interaction.* New York: John Wiley and Sons, Inc., 1968.

——, *The Concept of Self.* New York: Holt, Rinehart and Winston, 1971.

——, "The Social Construction of Self-Knowledge," pp. 139-69 in Theodore Mischel (ed.), *The Self: Psychological and Philosophical Issues.* Totowa, New Jersey: Rowman and Littlefield, 1977.

Gergen, Kenneth J. and Raymond A. Bauer, "Interactive Effects of Self-Esteem and Task Difficulty on Social Conformity," *Journal of Personality and Social Psychology,* 1967, 6, pp. 16-22.

Gergen, Kenneth J. and Margaret S. Gibbs, "Role-Playing and Modifying the Self-Concept," paper presented at the annual meeting of the Eastern Psychological Association, 1966. (Cited in Kenneth J. Gergen, "The Social Construction of

Self-Knowledge," pp. 139–69 in Theodore Mischel (ed.), *The Self: Psychological and Philosophical Issues.* Totowa, New Jersey: Rowman and Littlefield, 1977.)

Gergen, Kenneth J. and M. G. Taylor, "Role-Playing and Modifying the Self-Concept," paper presented at the annual meetings of the Eastern Psychological Association, 1966. (Cited in Kenneth J. Gergen, *The Concept of Self.* New York: Holt, Rinehart and Winston, 1971.)

——, "Social Expectancy and Self-Presentation in a Status Hierarchy," *Journal of Experimental Social Psychology,* 1969, 5, pp. 79-92.

Gergen, Kenneth J. and Barbara Wishnov, "Others' Self-Evaluations and Interaction Anticipation as Determinants of Self-Presentation," *Journal of Personality and Social Psychology,* 1965, 2, pp. 348-58.

Gerwirtz, Jacob L., "Mechanisms of Social Learning. Some Roles of Stimulation and Behavior in Early Human Development," pp. 57-2212 in David A. Goslin (ed.), *Handbook of Socialization Theory and Research.* Chicago: Rand McNally & Company, 1969.

Goffman, Erving, "Embarrassment and Social Organization," *American Journal of Sociology,* 1956, 62, pp. 264-71.

——, *The Presentation of Self in Everyday Life.* Garden City, New York: Doubleday & Company, Inc., 1959.

——, *Stigma: Notes on the Management of Spoiled Identity.* Englewood Cliffs, New Jersey: Prentice-Hall, Inc., 1963.

Gollob, Harry F. and James E. Dittes, "Effects of Manipulated Self-Esteem on Persuasibility Depending on Threat and Complexity of Communication," *Journal of Personality and Social Psychology,* 1965, 2, pp. 195-201.

Goode, William J., "A Theory of Role Strain," *American Sociological Review,* 1960a, 25, pp. 483-96.

——, "Norm Commitment and Conformity to Role-Status Obligations," *American Journal of Sociology,* 1960b, 66, pp. 246-58.

Goranson, Richard E., "Media Violence and Aggressive Behavior: A Review of Experimental Research," pp. 2-31 in Leonard Berkowitz (ed.), *Advances in Experimental Social Psychology.* Vol. 5. New York: Academic Press, 1970.

Gordon, Chad, "Self-Conceptions: Configurations of Context," pp. 115-36 in Chad Gordon and Kenneth J. Gergen (eds.), *The Self in Social Interaction.* Vol. 1. New York: John Wiley and Sons, Inc., 1968.

——, *Looking Ahead.* Washington, D.C.: American Sociological Association, n.d.

Goslin, David A., "Accuracy of Self-Perception and Social Acceptance," *Sociometry,* 1962, 25, pp. 283-96.

Gould, Robert, P. J. Brounstein and H. Sigall, "Attributing Ability to an Opponent: Public Aggrandizement and Private Denigration," *Sociometry,* 1977, 40, pp. 254-61.

Graf, Richard G., "Induced Self-Esteem As a Determinant of Behavior," *Journal of Social Psychology,* 1971, 85, pp. 213-17.

Greene, Les R., "Effects of Field Independence, Physical Proximity, and Evaluative Feedback on Affective Reactions and Compliance in a Dyadic Interaction," unpublished Ph.D. thesis, Yale University, 1973. (*Dissertation Abstracts International,* 1973, 34, pp. 2284B-85B.)

Gross, Edward and Gregory P. Stone, "Embarrassment and the Analysis of Role Requirements," *American Journal of Sociology,* 1964, 70, pp. 1-15.

Gross, Neal, W. S. Mason and A. W. McEachern, *Explorations in Role Analysis.* New York: John Wiley and Sons, 1958.

Grotevant, Harold D., "Family Similarities in Interests and Orientations," *Merrill-Palmer Quarterly,* 1976, 22, pp. 61-72.

Gruder, Charles L., "Determinants of Social Comparison Choices," *Journal of Experimental Social Psychology,* 1971, 7, pp. 473-89.

——, "Choice of Comparison Persons in Evaluating Oneself," pp. 21-42 in Jerry M. Suls and Richard L. Miller (eds.), *Social Comparison Processes.* Washington, D.C.: Hemisphere Publishing Company, 1977.

Haas, Harold I. and Martin L. Maehr, "Two Experiments on the Concept of Self and the Reaction of Others," *Journal of Personality and Social Psychology,* 1965, 1, pp. 100-05.

Haas, J. Eugene, *Role Conception and Group Consensus. A Study of Disharmony in Hospital Work Groups.* Columbus, Ohio: Bureau of Business Research, The Ohio State University, 1964.

Haiman, Franklyn S., "An Experimental Study of the Effects of Ethos in Public Speaking," *Speech Monographs,* 1949, 16, pp. 190-202.

Hakmiller, Karl L., "Need for Self-Evaluation, Perceived Similarity, and Comparison Choice," *Journal of Experimental Social Psychology,* 1966, 1, pp. 49-54.

Hamachek, Don E., *Encounters with the Self.* New York: Holt, Rinehart and Winston, 1971.

Hannerz, Ulf, *Soulside.* New York: Columbia University Press, 1969.

Hartnett, Donald L., L. L. Cummings and W. C. Hammer, "Personality, Bargaining Style and Payoff in Bilateral Monopoly Bargaining Among European Managers," *Sociometry,* 1973, 36, pp. 325-45.

Harvey, O. J., "Personality Factors in the Resolution of Conceptual Incongruities," *Sociometry,* 1962, 25, pp. 336-52.

Harvey, O. J. and William F. Clapp. "Hope, Expectancy, and Reactions to the Unexpected," *Journal of Personality and Social Psychology,* 1965, 2, pp. 45-52.

Harvey, O. J., H. H. Kelley and M. M. Shapiro, "Reactions to Unfavorable Evaluations of the Self Made by Other Persons," *Journal of Personality,* 1956-57, 25, pp. 393-411.

Hastorf, Albert H., "The Creation of Group Leaders," pp. 105-20 in Kenneth J. Gergen and David Marlowe (eds.), *Personality and Social Behavior.* Reading, Mass.: Addison-Wesley, 1970.

Hastorf, Albert H. and I. E. Bender, "A Caution Respecting the Measurement of Empathic Ability," *Journal of Abnormal and Social Psychology,* 1952, 47, pp. 574-76.

Hastorf, Albert H., I. E. Bender and D. J. Weintaub, "The Influence of Response Patterns on the 'Refined Empathy Score'," *Journal of Abnormal and Social Psychology,* 1956, 51, pp. 341-43.

Heider, Fritz, *The Psychology of Interpersonal Relations.* New York: John Wiley and Sons, Inc., 1948.

Heilman, Madeline E., "Threats and Promises: Reputational Consequences and Transfer of Credibility," *Journal of Experimental Social Psychology,* 1974, 10, pp. 310-24.

Heise, David R., *Understanding Events.* Cambridge: Cambridge University Press, 1979.

Heiss, Jerold, "Social Roles," in Morris Rosenberg and Ralph H. Turner (eds.), *Sociological Perspectives on Social Psychology.* New York: Basic Books, Inc., forthcoming.

Heiss, Jerold and Susan Owens, "The Self-Evaluations of Blacks and Whites," *American Journal of Sociology,* 1972, 78, pp. 360-70.

Hetherington, E. Mavis and Gary Frankie, "Effects of Parental Dominance, Warmth and Conflict on Imitation in Children," *Journal of Personality and Social Psychology,* 1967, 6, pp. 119-25.

Hewitt, John P., *Self and Society.* Boston: Allyn and Bacon, Inc., 1976.

——, *Self and Society.* Revised Edition. Boston: Allyn and Bacon, Inc., 1979.

Hewitt, John P. and Randall Stokes, "Disclaimers," *American Sociological Review,* 1975, 40, pp. 1-11.

Hill, Reuben, J. M. Stycos and K. W. Back, *The Family and Population Control.* Chapel Hill: University of North Carolina Press, 1959.

Hobart, Charles W., "Disagreement and Non-Empathy During Courtship: A Re-study," *Marriage and Family Living,* 1956, 18, pp. 317-22.

Hobart, Charles W. and William J. Klausner, "Some Social Interactional Correlates of Marital Role Disagreement and Marital Adjustment," *Marriage and Family Living,* 1959, 21, pp. 256-63.

Hochbaum, Godfrey M., "The Relations Between Group Members' Self-Confidence and Their Reaction to Group Pressures to Uniformity," *American Sociological Review,* 1954, 19, pp. 678-87.

Hochschild, Arlie Russell, "The Sociology of Feeling and Emotion," pp. 280-307 in Marcia Millman and Rosabeth Moss Kanter (eds.), *Another Voice.* Garden City, New York: Anchor Books, 1975.

——, "Emotion Work, Feeling Rules, and Social Structure," *American Journal of Sociology,* 1979, 85, pp. 551-75.

Hockett, Charles D., "The Origin of Speech," *Scientific American,* September, 1960, 203, pp. 88-96.

Holmstrom, Lynda Lytle, *The Two-Career Family.* Cambridge, Massachusetts: Schenkman Publishing Company, 1972.

Homans, George C., *The Human Group.* New York: Harcourt Brace Jovanovich, 1950.

——, *Social Behavior: Its Elementary Forms.* New York: Harcourt Brace Jovanovich, 1961.

——, "Bringing Men Back In," *American Sociological Review,* 1964, 29, pp. 809-18.

Hopmann, P. Terrence and Charles Walcott, "The Impact of External Stresses and Tensions on Negotiations," pp. 301-23 in Daniel Druckman (ed.), *Negotiations— Social Psychological Perspectives.* Beverly Hills, California: Sage Publications, 1977.

Hornstein, Harvey A., "The Effects of Different Magnitudes of Threat Upon Interpersonal Bargaining," *Journal of Experimental Social Psychology,* 1965, 1, pp. 282-93.

Horowitz, Esther, "Reported Embarrassment Memories of Elementary School, High School and College Students," *Journal of Social Psychology,* 1962, 56, pp. 317-25.

Hovland, Carl I. and Walter Weiss, "The Influence of Source Credibility on Communication Effectiveness," *Public Opinion Quarterly,* 1952, 15, pp. 635-50.

Howard, Robert C. and Leonard Berkowitz, "Reactions to the Evaluators of One's Performance," *Journal of Personality,* 1958, 26, pp. 494-507.

Huntington, Mary Jean, "The Development of a Professional Self-Image," pp. 179-87 in Robert K. Merton, G. G. Reader and P. L. Kendall (eds.), *The Student Physician*. Cambridge: Harvard University Press, 1957.

Hyman, Herbert H., "The Psychology of Status," *Archives of Psychology,* 1942, 38, no. 269, pp. 1-94.

Hyman, Herbert and E. Singer, (eds.), *Readings in Reference Group Theory.* New York: Free Press, 1968.

Insko, Chester A., *Theories of Attitude Change.* New York: Appleton-Century-Crofts, 1976.

Israel, Joachim, *Self-Evaluation and Rejection in Groups.* Stockholm: Almquist and Wiksell, 1956. (Quoted in Murray Webster, Jr. and Barbara Sobieszek, *Sources of Self-Evaluation.* New York: John Wiley and Sons, Inc., 1974.)

Izard, Carroll E., *Human Emotions.* New York: Plenum Press, 1977.

Jaco, Daniel and Jon M. Shepard, "Demographic Homogeneity and Spousal Consensus: A Methodological Perspective," *Journal of Marriage and the Family,* 1975, 37, pp. 161-69.

Jacques, Jeffrey M. and Karen J. Chason, "Self-Esteem and Low Status Groups: A Changing Scene," *Sociological Quarterly,* 1977, 18, pp. 399-412.

James, William, *Principles of Psychology.* Chicago: Encyclopaedia Britannica, 1952. (Originally published in 1890 by Henry Holt and Company.)

Janis, Irving L., "Personality Correlates of Susceptibility to Persuasion," *Journal of Personality,* 1953-54, 22, pp. 504-18.

——, "Attitude Change Via Role Playing," pp. 810-18 in Robert P. Abelson et al. (eds.), *Theories of Cognitive Consistency: A Sourcebook.* Chicago: Rand McNally & Company, 1968.

Janis, Irving L. and Peter B. Field, "Sex Differences and Personality Factors Related to Persuasibility," pp. 55-68 in Irving L. Janis et al., *Personality and Persuasibility.* New Haven, Connecticut: Yale University Press, 1959.

Janis, Irving L. and Donald Rife, "Persuasibility and Emotional Disorder," pp. 121-37 in Irving L. Janis et al., *Personality and Persuasibility.* New Haven, Connecticut: Yale University Press, 1959.

Jenkins, James J., "The Acquisition of Language," pp. 661-86 in David A. Goslin, (eds.), *Handbook of Socialization Theory and Research.* Chicago: Rand McNally & Company, 1969.

Jennings, M. Kent and Richard G. Niemi, "The Transmission of Political Values from Parent to Child," *American Political Science Review,* 1968, 62, pp. 169-84.

Johnson, David W., *The Social Psychology of Education.* New York: Holt, Rinehart and Winston, Inc., 1970.

Johnson, Thomas J., R. Feigenbaum and M. Werby, "Some Determinants and Consequences of the Teacher's Perception of Causality," *Journal of Educational Psychology,* 1964, 55, pp. 237–46.

Jones, Edward E., K. E. Davis and K. J. Gergen, "Role-Playing Variations and Their Value for Person Perception," *Journal of Abnormal and Social Psychology,* 1961, 63, pp. 302–10.

Jones, Edward E., K. J. Gergen and K. Davis, "Some Reactions to Being Approved or Disapproved As a Person," *Psychological Monographs,* 1962, 76, no. 521.

Jones, Edward E., K. J. Gergen and R. G. Jones, "Tactics of Ingratiation Among Leaders and Subordinates in a Status Hierarchy," *Psychological Monographs,* 1963, 77, no. 566.

Jones, Edward E. and George R. Goethals, "Order Effects in Impression Formation Attribution Context and the Nature of the Entity," pp. 27–46 in Edward E. Jones et al., (eds.), *Attribution: Perceiving the Causes of Behavior.* Morristown, New Jersey: General Learning Press, 1972.

Jones, Edward E., S. L. Hester, A. Farina and K. E. Davis, "Reactions to Unfavorable Personal Evaluations as a Function of the Evaluator's Perceived Adjustment," *Journal of Abnormal and Social Psychology,* 1959, 59, 363–70.

Jones, Edward E. and John W. Thibaut, "Interaction Goals as Bases of Inference in Interpersonal Perception," pp. 151–78 in Renato Tagiuri and Luigi Petrullo, (eds.), *Person Perception and Interpersonal Behavior.* Stanford, California: Stanford University Press, 1958.

Jones, Frank E., "Structural Determinants of Consensus and Cohesion in Complex Organizations," *Canadian Journal of Sociology and Anthropology,* 1968, 5, pp. 219–40.

Jones, Robert G., L. Rock, K. G. Shaver, G. R. Goethals and L. M. Ward, "Pattern of Performance and Ability Attribution, An Unexpected Primacy Effect," *Journal of Personality and Social Psychology,* 1968, 10, pp. 317–40.

Jones, Robert G. and James B. Welsh, "Ability Attribution and Impression Formation in a Strategic Game: A Limiting Case of the Primacy Effect," *Journal of Personality and Social Psychology,* 1971, 20, pp. 166–75.

Jones, Stephen C., "Some Determinants of Interpersonal Evaluating Behavior," *Journal of Personality and Social Psychology,* 1966, 3, pp. 397–403.

——, "Some Effects of Interpersonal Evaluations on Group Process and Social Perception," *Sociometry,* 1968, 31, pp. 150–61.

Jones, Stephen C. and Harvey A. Pines, "Self-Revealing Events and Interpersonal Evaluations," *Journal of Personality and Social Psychology,* 1968, 8, pp. 277–81.

Jourard, Sidney M., *The Transparent Self.* Revised Edition. New York: Van Nostrand Reinhold Company, 1971.

Jourard, Sidney M. and R. M. Remy, "Perceived Parental Attitudes, the Self, and Security," *Journal of Abnormal and Social Psychology,* 1955, 56, pp. 91-98.

Justice, Marcus T., "Field Dependency, Intimacy of Topic and Interperson Distance," Unpublished Ph.D. thesis, University of Florida, 1969. (*Dissertation Abstracts International,* 1970, 31, pp. 395B-96B.)

Kadushin, Charles, "The Professional Self-Concept of Music Students," *American Journal of Sociology,* 1969, 75, pp. 389-403.

Kagan, Jerome, "Acquisition and Significance of Sex Typing and Sex Role Identity," pp. 139-67 in Martin L. and Lois W. Hoffman, (eds.), *Review of Child Development Research.* Vol. 1. New York: Russell Sage Foundation, 1964.

Kahl, Joseph, "Educational and Occupational Aspirations of 'Common-Man' Boys," *Harvard Educational Review,* 1953, 23, pp. 186-203.

Kahn, Arnold S. and John W. Kohls, "Determinants of Toughness in Dyadic Bargaining," *Sociometry,* 1972, 35, pp. 305-15.

Kanareff, Vera and John T. Lanzetta, "The Acquisition of Imitative and Opposition Responses Under Two Conditions of Instruction-Induced Set," *Journal of Experimental Psychology,* 1958, 56, pp. 516-28.

——, "Effects of Task Definition and Probability of Reinforcement Upon the Acquisition and Extinction of Imitative Responses," *Journal of Experimental Psychology,* 1960, 60, pp. 340-48.

Keerdoja, Eileen and Richard Manning, "Son of Washoe Learns to Talk," *Newsweek,* May 28, 1979, p. 17.

Kelley, Harold H., "Two Functions of Reference Groups," pp. 410-14 in Guy F. Swanson, T. M. Newcomb and E. L. Hartley, (eds.), *Readings in Social Psychology.* Revised Edition. New York: Henry Holt, 1952.

Kelley, Harold H., et al., "A Comparative Experimental Study of Negotiation Behavior," *Journal of Personality and Social Psychology,* 1970, 16, pp. 411-38.

Kelman, Herbert C. and Carl I. Hovland, "'Reinstatement' of the Communicator in Delayed Measurement of Opinion Change," *Journal of Abnormal and Social Psychology,* 1953, 48, pp. 327-35.

Kemper, Theodore D., "Reference Groups, Socialization and Achievement," *American Sociological Review,* 1968, 33, pp. 31-45.

——, *A Social Interactional Theory of Emotions.* New York: John Wiley and Sons, 1978.

Kerckhoff, Alan C., "Early Antecedents of Role-Taking and Role-Playing Ability," *Merrill-Palmer Quarterly,* 1969, 15, pp. 229-47.

Kinch, John W., "Experiments on Factors Related to Self-Concept Change," *Journal of Social Psychology,* 1968, 74, pp. 251-58.

Kirkpatrick, Clifford and Charles Hobart, "Disagreement, Disagreement Estimate, and Non-Empathic Imputations for Intimacy Groups Varying from Favorite Date to Married," *American Sociological Review,* 1954, 19, pp. 10-20.

Kogan, Nathan, H. Lamm and G. Trommsdorff, "Negotiation Constraints in the Risk-Taking Domain," *Journal of Personality and Social Psychology,* 1972, 23, pp. 143-56.

Komorita, S. S. and Marc Barnes, "Effects of Pressures to Reach Agreement in Bargaining," *Journal of Personality and Social Psychology,* 1969, 13, pp. 245-52.

Konecni, Vladimir J. and Anthony N. Doob, "Catharsis through Displacement of Aggression," *Journal of Personality and Social Psychology,* 1972, 23, pp. 379-87.

Konstadt, Norma and Elaine Forman, "Field Dependence and External Directedness," *Journal of Personality and Social Psychology,* 1965, 1, pp. 490-93.

Kuhn, Manford H., "The Reference Group Reconsidered," *Sociological Quarterly,* 1964a, 5, pp. 5-24.

——, "Major Trends in Symbolic Interaction Theory in the Past Twenty-Five Years," *Sociological Quarterly,* 1964b, 5, pp. 61-84.

Kuhn, Manford H. and Thomas S. McPartland, "An Empirical Investigation of Self-Attitudes," *American Sociological Review,* 1954, 19, pp. 68-76.

Ladner, Joyce A., *Tomorrow's Tomorrow.* New York: Doubleday, 1971.

Lana, Robert E., "Interest, Media, and Order Effects in Persuasive Communications," *Journal of Psychology,* 1963, 56, pp. 9-13.

Landers, O. R., *Modern Etiquette for Young People.* New York: Greenberg, 1936. (Cited in Sherri Cavan, "The Etiquette of Youth," pp. 554-65 in Gregory P. Stone and Harvey A. Farberman, (eds.), *Social Psychology Through Symbolic Interaction.* Waltham, Massachusetts: Ginn-Blaisdell, 1970.)

Lanzetta, John T. and Vera T. Kanareff, "The Effects of a Monetary Reward on the Acquisition of An Imitative Response," *Journal of Abnormal and Social Psychology,* 1959, 59, pp. 120-27.

Latané, Bibb, (ed.), "Studies in Social Comparison," *Journal of Experimental Social Psychology,* 1966, Supplement 1.

Lauer, Robert H. and Warren H. Handel, *Social Psychology: The Theory and Application of Symbolic Interactionism.* Boston: Houghton-Mifflin Company, 1977.

Lawick-Goodall, Baronness Jane van, *In the Shadow of Man.* Boston: Houghton-Mifflin Company, 1971.

League, Betty Jo and Douglas N. Jackson, "Conformity, Veridicality, and Self-Esteem," *Journal of Abnormal and Social Psychology,* 1964, 68, pp. 113-15.

Lefkowitz, Monroe, R. R. Blake and J. S. Mouton, "Status Factors in Pedestrian Violation of Traffic Signals," *Journal of Abnormal and Social Psychology,* 1955, 51, pp. 704-06.

Leichty, Mary M., "The Effects of Father-Absence During Early Childhood Upon the Oedipal Situation as Reflected in Young Adults," *Merrill-Palmer Quarterly,* 1960, 6, pp. 212-17.

Lesser, Gerald S. and Robert P. Abelson, "Personality Correlates of Persuasibility in Children," pp. 187-206 in I. L. Janis et al., (eds.), *Personality and Persuasibility.* New Haven, Connecticut: Yale University Press, 1959.

Leventhal, Gerald S., "Sex of Sibling as a Predictor of Personality Characteristics," Paper presented at the annual meeting of the Southeastern Psychological Association. (Cited in Gerald S. Leventhal, "Influence of Brothers and Sisters on Sex-Role Behavior," *Journal of Personality and Social Psychology,* 1970, 16, pp. 452-65.)

———, "Influence of Brothers and Sisters on Sex-Role Behavior," *Journal of Personality and Social Psychology,* 1970, 16, pp. 452-65.

Leventhal, Howard and Sidney I. Perloe, "A Relationship Between Self-Esteem and Persuasibility," *Journal of Abnormal and Social Psychology,* 1962, 64, pp. 385-88.

Levy, Robert I., *Tahitians.* Chicago: University of Chicago Press, 1973.

Lewicki, Roy J. and Jeffrey Z. Rubin, "Effects of Variations in the Informational Clarity of Threats and Promises Upon Interpersonal Bargaining," Proceedings, 81st Annual Convention, American Psychological Association, 1973, 8, pp. 137-38.

Lewis, R. W. B., *Trials of the World.* New Haven, Connecticut: Yale University Press, 1965.

Lewis, Robert A., "Empathy in the Dating Dyad: A Retesting of Earlier Theory," Paper delivered at the annual meeting of the National Council on Family Relations, San Francisco, California, 1967. (Cited in Robert A. Lewis, "A Developmental Framework for the Analysis of Premarital Dyadic Formation," *Family Process,* 1972, 11, pp. 17-48.)

———, "A Developmental Framework for the Analysis of Premarital Dyadic Formation," *Family Process,* 1972, 11, pp. 17-48.

Lieberman, Seymour, "The Effects of Changes in Roles on the Attitudes of Role Occupants," *Human Relations,* 1950, 9, pp. 385-403.

Liebow, Elliot, *Tally's Corner.* Boston: Little, Brown and Company, 1967.

Lindauer, Martin, *Communication Among Social Bees.* Cambridge, Massachusetts: Harvard University Press, 1971.

Lindesmith, Alfred R., A. L. Strauss and N. K. Denzin, *Social Psychology.* 5th edition. New York: Holt, Rinehart and Winston, 1977.

Lippitt, Ronald, "The Psychodrama in Leadership Training," *Sociometry,* 1943, 6, pp. 286-92.

Loveless, Eugene J., "Cognitive Styles, Orienting Responses and Self-Report Measures of Personality," *Journal of Personality Assessment,* 1972, 36, pp. 273-81.

Lown, Aaron and Gilda Frankel Epstein, "Does Expectancy Determine Performance?" *Journal of Experimental Social Psychology,* 1965, 1, pp. 248-55.

Luchins, Abraham S., "Primacy-Recency in Impression Formation," pp. 33-61 in Carl Hovland et al., *The Order of Presentation in Persuasion.* New Haven, Connecticut: Yale University Press, 1957a.

——, "Experimental Attempts to Minimize the Impact of First Impressions," pp. 62-75 in Carl Hovland et al., *The Order of Presentation in Persuasion.* New Haven, Connecticut: Yale University Press, 1957b.

Ludwig, David J. and Martin L. Maehr, "Changes in Self-Concept and Stated Behavioral Preferences," *Child Development,* 1967, 38, pp. 453-67.

Luria, A. R., *Human Brain and Psychological Processes.* New York: Harper and Row, Publishers, Inc., 1966.

McCall, George J. and Jerry L. Simmons, *Identities and Interactions.* Revised Edition. New York: The Free Press, 1978.

McCandless, Boyd R., *Children and Development.* New York: Holt, Rinehart and Winston, 1967.

Maccoby, Eleanor E., *The Development of Sex Differences.* Stanford, California: Stanford University Press, 1966.

Maccoby, Eleanor Emmons and Carol Nagy Jacklin, *The Psychology of Sex Differences.* Stanford, California: Stanford University Press, 1974.

McGrath, Joseph E., "A Social Psychological Approach to the Study of Negotiation," pp. 101-34 in Raymond V. Bowers, (ed.), *Studies on Behavior in Organizations.* Athens: University of Georgia Press, 1966.

McGuire, William J., "The Nature of Attitudes and Attitude Change," pp. 136-314 in Gardner Lindzey and Elliot Aronson, (eds.), *The Handbook of Social Psychology.* Second Edition. Vol. 3. Reading, Massachusetts: Addison-Wesley, 1969.

MacKinnon, Neil J. and Gene F. Summers, "Homogeneity and Role Consensus: A Multivariate Exploration in Role Analysis," *Canadian Journal of Sociology*, 1976, 1, pp. 439-62.

Maehr, Martin L., J. Mensing and S. Nafzger, "Concept of Self and the Reaction of Others," *Sociometry*, 1962, 25, pp. 353-57.

Malec, Michael A., J. B. Williams and E. Z. Dager, "Family Integration, Achievement Values, Academic Self-Concept and Dropping Out of High School," paper presented at the annual meeting of the Eastern Sociological Society, New York, 1969.

Malewski, A., "Some Limitations of the Theory of Cognitive Dissonance," *Polish Sociological Bulletin*, 1962, 3-4, pp. 39-49. (Cited in J. Sidney Shrauger, "Responses to Evaluations as a Function of Initial Self-Perceptions," *Psychological Bulletin*, 1975, 82, pp. 581-96.)

Manis, Jerome G. and Bernard N. Meltzer, "Conclusion," pp. 437-40 in J. G. Manis and B. N. Meltzer, (eds.), *Symbolic Interaction*, Third Edition. Boston: Allyn and Bacon, 1978.

——, *Symbolic Interaction*, Third Edition. Boston: Allyn and Bacon, 1978.

Manis, Melvin, "Social Interaction and the Self-Concept," *Journal of Abnormal and Social Psychology*, 1955, 51, pp. 362-70.

Mann, John H., "Experimental Evaluations of Role Playing," *Psychological Bulletin*, 1956, 53, pp. 227-34.

Mann, John H. and Carola H. Mann, "The Effect of Role-Playing Experience on Role-Playing Ability," *Sociometry*, 1959, 22, pp. 64-74.

Mann, Leon and Irving L. Janis, "A Follow-Up Study on the Long-Term Effects of Emotional Role Playing," *Journal of Personality and Social Psychology*, 1968, 8, pp. 339-42.

Marks, Stephen R., "Multiple Roles and Role Strain: Some Notes on Human Energy, Time and Commitment," *American Sociological Review*, 1977, 42, pp. 921-36.

Marlowe, David and Kenneth J. Gergen, "Personality and Social Behavior," pp. 590-665 in Gardner Lindzey and Elliot Aronson, (eds.), *The Handbook of Social Psychology*. 2nd edition. Vol. 3. Reading, Massachusetts: Addison-Wesley, 1969.

Mausner, Bernard, "The Effects of One Partner's Success in a Relevant Task on the Interaction of Observer Pairs," *Journal of Abnormal and Social Psychology*, 1954, 49, pp. 557-60.

Mead, George H., *Mind, Self, and Society*. Charles W. Morris, ed., Chicago: The University of Chicago Press, 1934.

Meddin, Jay, "Chimpanzees, Symbols, and the Reflective Self," *Social Psychology Quarterly*, 1979, 42, pp. 99-109.

Medinnus, Gene R., "Adolescents' Self-Acceptance and Perceptions of their Parents," *Journal of Consulting Psychology*, 1965, 29, pp. 150-54.

Meltzer, Bernard N., J. W. Petras and L. T. Reynolds, *Symbolic Interactionism: Genesis, Varieties and Criticism*, London: Routledge and Kegan Paul, 1975.

——, "Varieties of Symbolic Interactionism," pp. 41-57 in Jerome G. Manis and Bernard N. Meltzer, (eds.), *Symbolic Interaction*. Third Edition. Boston: Allyn and Bacon, 1978.

Meltzer, Bernard N. and John W. Petras, "The Chicago and Iowa Schools of Symbolic Interactionism," pp. 3-17 in Tamotsu Shibutani, (ed.), *Human Nature and Collective Behavior*, Englewood Cliffs, New Jersey: Prentice-Hall, Inc., 1970.

Merton, Robert K., "The Role-Set: Problems in Sociological Theory," *British Journal of Sociology*, 1957, 8, pp. 106-20.

——, "Structural Analysis in Sociology," pp. 21-52 in Peter H. Blau, (ed.), *Approaches to the Study of Social Structure*. New York: The Free Press, 1975.

——, *Sociological Ambivalence and Other Essays*. New York: The Free Press, 1976.

Merton, Robert K. and Alice S. Kitt, "Contributions to the Theory of Reference Group Behavior," pp. 40-105 in Robert K. Merton and Paul F. Lazarsfeld, (eds.), *Continuities in Social Research—Studies in the Scope and Method of "The American Soldier."* Glencoe, Illinois: The Free Press, 1950.

Messinger, Sheldon E., H. Sampson and R. D. Towne, "Life As Theater: Some Notes on the Dramaturgic Approach to Social Reality," *Sociometry*, 1962, 25, pp. 98-110.

Mettee, David R. and Gregory Smith, "Social Comparison and Interpersonal Attraction," pp. 69-101 in Jerry M. Suls and Richard L. Miller, (eds.), *Social Comparison Processes*. Washington, D.C.: Hemisphere Publishing Corp., 1977.

Miller, Kent S. and Philip Worchel, "The Effects of Need—Achievement and Self-Ideal Discrepancy on Performance under Stress," *Journal of Personality*, 1956-57, 25, pp. 176-90.

Mischel, Walter, "A Social-Learning View of Sex Differences in Behavior," pp. 56-58 in Eleanor E. Maccoby, (ed.), *The Development of Sex Differences*. Stanford, California: Stanford University Press, 1966.

Miyamoto, S. Frank and Sanford M. Dornbusch, "A Test of Interactionist Hypotheses of Self-Conception," *American Journal of Sociology*, 1956, 61, pp. 399-403.

Modigliani, Andre, "Embarrassment and Embarrassability," *Sociometry*, 1968, 31, pp. 313-26.

Moore, Bert S., B. Underwood and D. Rosenhan, "Affect and Altruism," *Developmental Psychology*, 1973, 8, pp. 99-104.

Moore, J. C., "A Further Test of Interactionist Hypotheses of Self-Conception," Technical Report No. 6, Laboratory for Social Research, Stanford University, Stanford, California, 1964. (Cited in Murray Webster, Jr. and Barbara Sobieszek, *Sources of Self-Evaluation.* New York: John Wiley and Sons, Inc., 1974.)

Morris, Jan, *Conundrum.* New York: New American Library, 1975.

Morse, Stan and Kenneth J. Gergen, "Social Comparison, Self-Consistency and the Concept of Self," *Journal of Personality and Social Psychology,* 1970, 16, pp. 148-56.

Mulford, Harold and Wilfield Salisbury II, "Self-Conceptions in a General Population," *Sociological Quarterly,* 1964, 5, pp. 35-46.

Mussen, Paul H., "Early Sex-Role Development," pp. 707-31 in David A. Goslin, (ed.), *Handbook of Socialization Theory and Research.* Chicago: Rand McNally and Company, 1969.

Mussen, Paul and Luther Distler, "Masculinity, Identification, and Father-Son Relationships," *Journal of Abnormal and Social Psychology,* 1959, 59, pp. 350-56.

Mussen, Paul and Eldred Rutherford, "Parent-Child Relations and Parental Personality in Relation to Young Child's Sex Role Preference," *Child Development,* 1963, 34, pp. 589-607.

Nevill, Dorothy, "Experimental Manipulation of Dependency Motivation and its Effects on Eye Contact and Measures of Field Dependency," *Journal of Personality and Social Psychology,* 1974, 29, pp. 72-79.

Newcomb, Theodore M., "Attitude Development as a Function of Reference Groups: The Bennington Study," pp. 265-75 in Eleanor E. Maccoby, T. M. Newcomb, L. Hartley, (eds.), *Readings in Social Psychology.* Third Edition. New York: Henry Holt and Company, 1958.

Newcomb, Theodore M., K. E. Koenig, R. Flacks and D. P. Warwick, *Persistence and Change: Bennington College and its Students After Twenty-Five Years.* New York: John Wiley and Sons, Inc., 1967.

Nietzsche, Friedrich, *On the Genealogy of Morals and Ecce Homo.* Walter Kaufmann, (ed.), New York: Vintage Books, 1969.

Nisbett, Richard E. and Andrew Gordon, "Self-Esteem and Susceptibility to Social Influence," *Journal of Personality and Social Psychology,* 1967, 5, pp. 268-76.

Nutting, Anthony, *Lawrence of Arabia.* New York: Clarkson N. Potter, 1961.

Olesen, Virginia and Elvi Whittaker, *The Silent Dialogue: A Study in the Social Psychology of Professional Socialization,* San Francisco: Jossey-Bass, 1968.

Otto, Luther B., "Girl Friends as Significant Others: Their Influence on Young Men's Career Aspirations and Achievements," *Sociometry,* 1977, 40, pp. 287-93.

Paeth, Charles A., "A Likert Scaling of Student Value Statements, Field Independence-Field Dependence, and Experimentally Induced Change," Unpublished Ph.D. thesis, Oregon State University, 1973. (*Dissertation Abstracts International,* 1973, 34, pp. 2288B-89B.)

Parton, David, "Learning to Imitate in Infancy," *Child Development,* 1976, 47, pp. 14-31.

Patchen, Martin, "A Conceptual Framework and Some Empirical Data Regarding Comparisons of Social Rewards," *Sociometry,* 1961, 24, pp. 136-50.

Payne, Donald and Paul H. Mussen, "Parent-Child Relations and Father Identification Among Adolescent Boys," *Journal of Abnormal and Social Psychology,* 1956, 52, pp. 358-62.

Pepitone, Albert, *Attraction and Hostility.* New York: Atherton Press, 1964.

Perry, Stewart E. and Lyman C. Wynne, "Role Conflict, Role Redefinition and Social Change in a Clinical Research Organization," *Social Forces,* 1959, 38, pp. 62-65.

Peter, Laurence J. and R. Hull, *The Peter Principle.* New York: Morrow, 1969.

Phillips, Bernard S., "A Role Theory Approach to Adjustment in Old Age," *American Sociological Review,* 1957, 22, pp. 212-17.

Piaget, Jean, *The Moral Judgment of the Child.* Glencoe, Illinois: The Free Press, 1948.

Pilisuk, Marc, "Cognitive Balance and Self-Relevant Attitudes," *Journal of Abnormal and Social Psychology,* 1962, 65, pp. 95-103.

Plutchik, Robert, *The Emotions.* New York: Random House, 1962.

——, "Cognitions in the Service of Emotions," in Douglas K. Candland, J. P. Fell, E. Keen, A. I. Leshner, R. M. Tarpy, R. Plutchik, *Emotion.* Monterey, Ca.: Brooks/Cole Publishing Company, 1977.

——, "A Language for the Emotions," *Psychology Today,* February, 1980, pp. 68-78.

Podhoretz, Norman, *Making It.* New York: Bantam Books, 1969.

Preiss, Jack J., "Self and Role in Medical Education," pp. 207-18 in Chad Gordon and Kenneth J. Gergen, (eds.), *The Self in Social Interaction.* New York: John Wiley and Sons, Inc., 1968.

Presthus, Robert, *Men at the Top.* New York: Oxford University Press, 1964.

Pruitt, Dean G. and Douglas F. Johnson, "Mediation As an Aid to Face-Saving in Negotiation," *Journal of Personality and Social Psychology,* 1970, 14, pp. 239-46.

Quarantelli, Enrico L. and Joseph Cooper, "Self-Conceptions and Others: A Further Test of Meadian Hypotheses," *Sociological Quarterly,* 1966, 7, pp. 281-97.

Rapoport, Rhona and Robert Rapoport, *Dual-Career Families Re-Examined*. New York: Harper and Row, 1976.

Rawlings, Edna I., "Reactive Guilt and Anticipatory Guilt in Altruistic Behavior," pp. 163-78 in Jacqueline Macaulay and Leonard Berkowitz, *Altruism and Helping Behavior*. New York: Academic Press, 1970.

Reeder, Leo G., A. Donohue and A. Biblarz, "Conceptions of Self and Others," *American Journal of Sociology*, 1960, 66, 153-59.

Remmers, H. H. and D. H. Radler, *The American Teenager*. Indianapolis, Indiana: Bobbs-Merrill, 1957.

Rheingold, Harriet, "The Social and Socializing Infant," pp. 779-90 in David Goslin, (ed.), *Handbook of Socialization Theory and Research*. Chicago: Rand McNally and Company, 1969.

Riesman, David, *The Lonely Crowd*. New Haven, Connecticut: Yale University Press, 1950.

——, "On Autonomy," pp. 445-61 in Chad Gordon and Kenneth J. Gergen, (eds.), *The Self in Social Interaction*. New York: John Wiley and Sons, Inc., 1968.

Rogers, Carl, *Client-Centered Therapy*. Boston: Houghton-Mifflin Company, 1951.

——, *On Becoming a Person*. Boston: Houghton-Mifflin Company, 1961.

Rosenbaum, Milton E. and Irving F. Tucker, "The Competence of the Model and the Learning of Imitation and Non-Imitation," *Journal of Experimental Psychology*, 1962, 63, pp. 183-90.

Rosenberg, B. G. and Brian Sutton-Smith, "Ordinal Position and Sex-Role Identification," *Genetic Psychology Monographs*, 1964, 70, pp. 297-328.

Rosenberg, Morris, *Society and the Adolescent Self-Image*. Princeton, New Jersey: Princeton University Press, 1965.

——, "Psychological Selectivity in Self-Esteem Formation," pp. 339-46 in Chad Gordon and Kenneth J. Gergen, (eds.), *The Self in Social Interaction*. New York: John Wiley and Sons, Inc., 1968.

——, "Which Significant Others?," *American Behavioral Scientist*, 1973, 16, pp. 829-60.

——, *Conceiving the Self*. New York: Basic Books, Inc., 1979.

Rosenberg, Morris and Roberta Simmons, *Black and White Self-Esteem: The Urban School Child*. Washington, D.C.: American Sociological Association, n.d.

Rosenblatt, Paul C., "Uses of Ethnography in Understanding Grief and Mourning," pp. 41-49 in Bernard Schoenberg, I. Gerber, A. Wienir, H. Kutscher, D. Peretz and

C. Carr, (eds.), *Bereavement—Its Psychosocial Aspects.* New York: Columbia University Press, 1975.

Rosenblatt, Paul C., R. P. Walsh and D. A. Jackson, *Grief and Mourning in Cross-Cultural Perspective.* Human Relations Area Files Press, 1976.

Rotter, Julian B., "Generalized Expectancies for Internal versus External Control of Reinforcement," *Psychological Monographs,* 1966, 80, no. 1, whole no. 609.

Rubin, Jeffrey and Bert R. Brown, *The Social Psychology of Bargaining and Negotiation.* New York: Academic Press, 1975.

Rubin, Jeffrey R. and Roy J. Lewicki, "A Three Factor Experimental Analysis of Promises and Threats," *Journal of Applied Social Psychology,* 1973, 3, pp. 240-57.

Rubin, Jeffrey R., R. J. Lewicki and L. Dunn, "Perception of Promisers and Threateners," Proceedings of the 81st annual convention of the American Psychological Association, 1973, 8, pp. 141-42.

Ruble, Diane N. and Charles Y. Nakamura, "Task Orientation versus Social Orientation in Young Children and their Attention to Relevant Social Cues," *Child Development,* 1972, 43, pp. 471-80.

Ryckman, Richard M. and William C. Rodda, "Confidence Maintenance and Performance as a Function of Chronic Self-Esteem and Initial Task Experiences," *The Psychological Record,* 1972, 22, pp. 241-47.

Samuel, William, "On Clarifying Some Interpretations of Social Comparison Theory," *Journal of Experimental and Social Psychology,* 1973, 9, pp. 450 65.

Sansom, William, *A Contest of Ladies.* London: Hogarth, 1965. (Quoted in Erving Goffman, *The Presentation of Self in Everyday Life.* Garden City, N.Y.: Doubleday Anchor, 1959.)

Savage-Rumbaugh, E. Sue, D. M. Rumbaugh and S. Baysen, "Symbolic Communication Between Two Chimpanzees (*Pan troglodytes*)," *Science,* 1978, 201, pp. 641-44.

Schachter, Stanley, *Psychology of Affiliation.* Stanford, California: Stanford University Press, 1959.

Schalon, Charles L., "Effects of Self-Esteem Upon Performance Following Failure Stress," *Journal of Consulting and Clinical Psychology,* 1968, 32, p. 497.

Scheff, Thomas J. "Toward a Sociological Model of Consensus," *American Sociological Review,* 1967, 32, pp. 32-46.

——, "Negotiating Reality: Notes on Power in the Assessment of Responsibility," *Social Problems,* 1968, 16, pp. 3-17.

Schlenker, Barry R., T. V. Bonoma, J. T. Tedeschi and W. P. Pivnick, "Compliance to Threats as a Function of the Wording of the Threat and the Exploitativeness of the Threatener," *Sociometry*, 1970, 33, pp. 394-408.

Schmitt, Raymond L., *The Reference Other Orientation.* Carbondale, Illinois: Southern Illinois University Press, 1972.

Scott, Marvin and Stanford Lyman, "Accounts," *American Sociological Review,* 1968, 33, pp. 46-62.

Secord, Paul F. and Carl W. Backman, *Social Psychology.* New York: McGraw-Hill Book Company, 1964.

Shaara, Michael, *The Killer Angels.* New York: Ballantine Books, 1975.

Shein, Edgar H., "The Effects of Reward on Adult Imitative Behavior," *Journal of Abnormal and Social Psychology,* 1954, 49, pp. 389-95.

Sherohman, James, "Conceptual and Methodological Issues in the Study of Role-Taking Accuracy," *Symbolic Interaction,* 1977, 1, pp. 121-31.

Sherwood, John J., "Self-Identity and Referent Others," *Sociometry,* 1965, 28, pp. 66-81.

——, "Increased Self-Evaluation as a Function of Ambiguous Evaluations by Referent Others," *Sociometry,* 1967, 30, pp. 404-09.

Shibutani, Tamotsu, "Reference Groups as Perspectives," *American Journal of Sociology,* 1955, 60, pp. 562-69.

——, *Society and Personality.* Englewood Cliffs, N.J.: Prentice-Hall, Inc., 1961.

Shoobs, Nahum E., "Psychodrama in the Schools," *Sociometry,* 1944, 7, pp. 152-68.

Shott, Susan, "Emotion and Social Life: A Symbolic Interactionist Analysis," *American Journal of Sociology,* 1979, 84, pp. 1317-34.

Shrauger, J. Sidney, "Self-Esteem and Reaction to Being Observed by Others," *Journal of Personality and Social Psychology,* 1972, 23, pp. 192-200.

——, "Responses to Evaluations as a Function of Initial Self-Perceptions," *Psychological Bulletin,* 1975, 82, pp. 581-96.

Shrauger, J. Sidney and Stephen C. Jones, "Social Validation and Interpersonal Evaluations," *Journal of Experimental Psychology,* 1968, 4, pp. 315-23.

Shrauger, J. Sidney and Saul E. Rosenberg, "Self-Esteem and the Effects of Success and Failure Feedback on Performance," *Journal of Personality,* 1970, 38, pp. 404-17.

Shrauger, J. Sidney and Peter B. Sorman, "Self-Evaluations, Initial Success and Failure, and Improvement as Determinants of Persistence," *Journal of Consulting and Clinical Psychology,* 1977, 45, pp. 784-95.

Sieber, Sam D., "Toward a Theory of Role Accumulation," *American Sociological Review,* 1974, 39, pp. 467-78.

Sigall, Harold and Robert Gould, "The Effects of Self-Esteem and Evaluator Demandingness on Effort Expenditure," *Journal of Personality and Social Psychology,* 1977, 35, pp. 12-20.

Silverberg, William V., *Childhood Experience and Personal Destiny.* New York: Springer, 1952.

Silverman, Irwin, H. Ford, Jr. and J. Morganti, "Inter-related Effects of Social Desirability, Sex, Self-Esteem and Complexity of Argument on Persuasibility," *Journal of Personality,* 1966, 34, pp. 555-68.

Simpson, Richard L., "Parental Influence, Anticipatory Socialization and Social Mobility," *American Sociological Review,* 1962, 27, pp. 517-27.

——, *Theories of Social Exchange.* Morristown, New Jersey: General Learning Press, 1972.

Sobel, Dava, "Researchers Challenge Conclusion that Apes can Learn Language," *New York Times,* November 21, 1979, pp. 1, 57.

Sobieszek, Barbara and Murray Webster, Jr., "Conflicting Sources of Evaluation," *Sociometry,* 1973, 36, pp. 550-60.

Solley, Charles M. and Ross Stagner, "Effects of Magnitude of Temporal Barriers, Type of Goal, and Perception of Self," *Journal of Experimental Psychology,* 1956, 51, pp. 62-70.

Sousa-Poza, Joaquin F. and Robert Rohrberg, "Communicational and Interactional Aspects of Self-Disclosure in Psychotherapy: Differences Related to Cognitive Style," *Psychiatry,* 1976, 39, pp. 81-91.

Speight, John F., "Community Homogeneity and Consensus on Leadership," *Sociological Quarterly,* 1968, 9, pp. 387-96.

Spitzer, Stephen, C. Couch and J. Stratton, *The Assessment of Self.* Iowa City: Escort-Sernoll, n.d.

Stebbins, Robert A., "Studying the Definition of the Situation: Theory and Field Research Strategies," *Canadian Review of Sociology and Anthropology,* 1972, 6, pp. 193-211.

Steiner, Ivan D., "Reactions to Adverse and Favorable Evaluations of One's Self," *Journal of Personality,* 1968, 36, pp. 553-63.

Stone, Gregory P., "Appearance and the Self," pp. 86-118 in Arnold Rose, (ed.), *Human Behavior and Social Processes.* Boston: Houghton-Mifflin Company, 1962.

——, "Sex and Age as Universes of Appearance," pp. 221–36 in Gregory P. Stone and Harvey A. Farberman, (eds.), *Social Psychology Through Symbolic Interaction*. Waltham, Massachusetts: Ginn-Blaisdell, 1970.

Stotland, Ezra, S. Thorley, E. Thomas, A. R. Cohen and Alvin Zander. "The Effect of Group Evaluations and Self-Esteem upon Self-Evaluations," *Journal of Abnormal and Social Psychology*, 1957, 54, pp. 55–63.

Stouffer, Samuel A., E. A. Suchman, L. C. Devinney, S. A. Star and R. M. Williams, Jr., *The American Soldier*. Vol. I: *Adjustment During Army Life*. Princeton, New Jersey: Princeton University Press, 1949.

Strauss, Anselm, *Mirrors and Masks*. Glencoe, Illinois: The Free Press, 1958.

——, *Negotiations: Varieties, Contexts, Processes, and Social Order*. San Francisco: Jossey-Bass Publishers, 1978.

Streufert, Siegfried and Susan C. Streufert, "Effects of Conceptual Structure, Failure, and Success on Attribution of Causality and Interpersonal Attitudes," *Journal of Personality and Social Psychology*, 1969, 11, pp. 137–47.

Stryker, Sheldon, "Relationship of Married Offspring and Parents: A Test of Mead's Theory," *American Journal of Sociology*, 1956, 62, pp. 308–19.

——, "Role-Taking Accuracy and Adjustment," *Sociometry*, 1957, 20, pp. 286–96.

——, "Symbolic Interaction as an Approach to Family Research," *Marriage and Family Living*, 1959, 21, pp. 111–19.

——, "Identity Salience and Role Performance: The Relevance of Symbolic Interaction Theory for Family Research," *Journal of Marriage and the Family*, 1968, 30, pp. 558–64.

——, *Symbolic Interaction: A Social Structural Version*. Menlo Park, California: Benjamin/Cummings, 1980.

Suls, Jerry M. and Richard L. Miller, *Social Comparison Processes*. Washington, D.C.: Hemisphere Publishing Corp., 1977.

Sutton-Smith, Brian and B. G. Rosenberg, "Age Changes in the Effects of Ordinal Position on Sex-Role Identification," *Journal of Genetic Psychology*, 1965, 107, pp. 61–73.

Taft, Ronald, "The Ability to Judge People," *Psychological Bulletin*, 1955, 52, pp. 1–23.

Tagiuri, Renato, "Person Perception," pp. 395–449 in Gardner Lindzey and Elliot Aronson, (eds.), *The Handbook of Social Psychology*. Second Edition. Vol. 3. Reading, Massachusetts: Addison-Wesley, 1969.

Tedeschi, James T., B. R. Schlenker and T. V. Bonoma, "Compliance to Threats as a

Function of Source Attractiveness and Esteem," *Sociometry,* 1975, 38, pp. 81-98.

Tedeschi, James T. and Thomas V. Bonoma, "Measures of Last Resort: Coercion and Aggression in Bargaining," pp. 213-41 in Daniel Druckman, (ed.), *Negotiations: Social Psychological Perspectives.* Beverly Hills, California: Sage Publications, 1977.

Tedeschi, James T., T. V. Bonoma and R. C. Brown, "A Paradigm for the Study of Coercive Power," *Journal of Conflict Resolution,* 1971, 15, pp. 197-223.

Tedeschi, James T., T. V. Bonoma and H. Novinson, "Behavior of a Threatener: Retaliation versus Fixed Opportunity Costs," *Journal of Conflict Resolution,* 1970, 14, pp. 69-76.

Teevan, James J., Jr., "Reference Groups and Premarital Sexual Behavior," *Journal of Marriage and the Family,* 1972, 34, pp. 283-91.

Thibaut, John W., "The Development of Contractual Norms in Bargaining: Replications and Variations," *Journal of Conflict Resolution,* 1968, 12, pp. 102-12.

Thibaut, John W. and Claude Faucheux, "The Development of Contractual Norms in a Bargaining Situation Under Two Types of Stress," *Journal of Experimental Social Psychology,* 1965, 1, pp. 89-102.

Thibaut, John W. and Charles L. Gruder, "The Formation of Agreement Between Parties of Unequal Power," *Journal of Personality and Social Psychology,* 1969, 11, pp. 59-65.

Thibaut, John W. and Harold H. Kelley, *The Social Psychology of Groups.* New York: John Wiley and Sons, 1959.

Thistlethwaite, Donald L., "Effects of College Upon Student Aspirations," U.S. Department of Health, Education and Welfare. Cooperative Research Project No. D-098. Nashville, Tennessee, 1965. (Cited in Kenneth A. Feldman and Theodore M. Newcomb, *The Impact of College on Students.* Vol. I. San Francisco: Jossey-Bass Publishers, 1965.)

Thistlethwaite, Donald L. and Norman Wheeler, "Effects of Teacher and Peers' Sub-Cultures upon Student Aspirations," *Journal of Educational Psychology,* 1966, 57, pp. 35-47.

Thomas, Darwin, J. M. Calonico and D. D. Franks, "Role-Taking and Power in Social Psychology," *American Sociological Review,* 1972, 37, pp. 605-14.

Thomas, Sharon, "Perceived Parental Acceptance and Children's Self-Concept," unpublished Master's Thesis, Brigham Young University, 1967. (Cited in William H. Fitts et al., *The Self-Concept and Self-Actualization.* Nashville, Tennessee: The Dede Wallace Center, 1971.)

Thompson, Warren, *Correlates of the Self Concept.* Nashville, Tennessee: The Dede Wallace Center, 1972.

Tippett, Jean S. and Earle Silber, "Autonomy of Self-Esteem: An Experimental Approach," *Archives of General Psychiatry,* 1966, 14, pp. 372-83.

Travisano, Richard V., "Attitudes as Promises: A Symbolic Interactionist Approach to the Unconscious," pp. 272-80 in Carl J. Couch and Robert A. Hintz, Jr., (eds.), *Constructing Social Life: Readings in Behavioral Sociology from the Iowa School,* Champaign, Illinois: Stipes Publishing Company, 1975.

Tucker, Charles W., "Some Methodological Problems of Kuhn's Self Theory," *Sociological Quarterly,* 1966, 7, pp. 345-58.

Turner, Ralph H., "Role-Taking, Role Standpoint and Reference Group Behavior," *American Journal of Sociology,* 1956, 61, pp. 316-28.

——, "Role-Taking: Process versus Conformity," pp. 20-40 in Arnold M. Rose, (ed.), *Human Behavior and Social Process: An Interactionist Approach,* Boston: Houghton-Mifflin Company, 1962.

——, "The Real Self: From Institution to Impulse," *American Journal of Sociology,* 1976, 81, pp. 989-1016.

——, "The Role and the Person," *American Journal of Sociology,* 1978, 84, pp. 1-23.

Udry, J. Richard, H. A. Nelson and R. Nelson, "An Empirical Investigation of Some Widely Held Beliefs about Marriage Interaction," *Marriage and Family Living,* 1961, 23, pp. 388-50.

Van Es, J. C. and P. M. Shingi, "Response Consistency of Husband and Wife for Selected Attitudinal Items," *Journal of Marriage and the Family,* 1972, 34, pp. 741-49.

Van Ostrand, D., "Reactions to Positive and Negative Information About the Self as a Function of Certain Personality Characteristics of the Recipient," Unpublished Master's Thesis, University of Colorado, 1960. (Cited in O. J. Harvey and William Clapp, "Hope, Expectancy, and Reaction to the Unexpected," *Journal of Personality and Social Psychology,* 1965, 2, pp. 45-52.)

Vaughan, Ted R. and Larry T. Reynolds, "The Sociology of Symbolic Interactionism," *American Sociologist,* 1968, 3, pp. 208-14.

Vernon, Glenn M. and Robert L. Stewart, "Empathy as a Process in the Dating Relationship," *American Sociological Review,* 1957, 22, pp. 48-52.

Videbeck, Richard, "Self-Conceptions and the Reactions of Others," *Sociometry,* 1960, 23, pp. 351-59.

Wallace Walter L., "Institutional and Life-Cycle Socialization of College Freshmen," *American Journal of Sociology,* 1964, 70, pp. 303-18.

—, *Student Culture: Social Structure and Continuity in a Liberal Arts College.* Chicago: Aldine Publishing Company, 1966.

Waller, Willard, "The Rating and Dating Complex," *American Sociological Review,* 1937, 2, pp. 727-34.

—, *The Sociology of Teaching.* New York: John Wiley and Sons, Inc., 1932.

Waller, Willard and Reuben Hill. *The Family, A Dynamic Interpretation.* Revised Edition. New York: Dryden Press, 1951.

Walters, Robert H., R. D. Parke and V. A. Cane, "Timing of Punishment and the Observation of Consequences to Others as Determinants of Response Inhibition," *Journal of Experimental Child Psychology,* 1965, 2, pp. 10-30.

Warshay, Leon, "The Current State of Sociological Theory: Diversity, Polarity, Empiricism and Small Theories," *Sociological Quarterly,* 1971, 12, pp. 23-45.

Webster, Murray, Jr. and Barbara Sobieszek, *Sources of Self-Evaluation.* New York: John Wiley and Sons, Inc., 1974.

Weinstein, Eugene A. and Judith M. Tanur, "Meanings, Purposes, and Structural Resources in Social Interaction," pp. 138-46 in Jerome G. Manis and Bernard N. Meltzer, (eds.), *Symbolic Interaction.* Boston: Allyn and Bacon, 1978. (Originally published in the *Cornell Journal of Social Relations,* 1976, 11, pp. 105-10.)

Wheeler, Ladd, K. G. Schauer, R. A. Jones, G. R. Goethals, J. Cooper, J. E. Robinson, C. L. Gruder and K. W. Butzine, "Factors Determining Choice of a Comparison Other," *Journal of Experimental Social Psychology,* 1969, 5, pp. 219-32.

White, Robert W., "Ego and Reality in Psychoanalytic Theory," *Psychological Issues,* 1963, 3, no. 3. New York: International Universities Press.

—, "The Experience of Efficacy in Schizophrenia," *Psychiatry,* 1965, 28, pp. 199-211.

Whitman, Walt, *The Poetry and Prose of Walt Whitman.* Louis Untermeyer, ed., New York: Simon and Schuster, 1949.

Williams, Margaret A., "Reference Groups: A Review and Commentary," *Sociological Quarterly,* 1970, 11, pp. 545-54.

Wilson, Stephen R. and Larry A. Benner, "The Effects of Self-Esteem and Situation upon Comparison Choices During Ability Evaluation," *Sociometry,* 1971, 34, pp. 381-97.

Wilson, Warren R., "The Incentive Value of a Promised Social Standard of Comparison," *Journal of Social Psychology,* 1963, 59, pp. 169-74.

Witkin, Herman A., "A Cognitive Style Approach to Cross-Cultural Research," *International Journal of Psychology,* 1967, 2, pp. 233-50.

——, *Personality Through Perception.* New York: Harper and Row Publishers, 1972.

Witkin, Herman A., R. B. Dyle, H. F. Faterson, D. R. Goodenough and S. A. Karp, *Psychological Differentiation, Studies of Development.* New York: John Wiley and Sons, Inc., 1962.

Wylie, Ruth, *The Self-Concept.* Second Edition. Vol. I. Lincoln: The University of Nebraska Press, 1974.

Zajonc, Robert B., "Social Facilitation," *Science,* July 16, 1965, 149, pp. 269-74.

Zander, Alvin and Ronald Lippitt, "Reality Practice as Education Method," *Sociometry,* 1944, 7, pp. 129-51.

Zanna, Mark P., G. R. Goethals and J. E. Hill, "Evaluating a Sex-Related Ability: Social Comparison with Similar Others and Standard Setters," *Journal of Experimental Social Psychology,* 1971, 11, pp. 86-93.

Zimbardo, Philip and Robert Formica, "Emotional Comparison and Self-Esteem as Determinants of Affiliation," *Journal of Personality,* 1963, 31, pp. 141-62.

NAME INDEX

SUBJECT INDEX